INTERPRETATIONS
OF
PIERS PLOWMAN

VASTA, Edward, ed. **Interpretations of <u>Piers Plowman</u>. Notre Dame,** 1968. 378p tab bibl 68-12296. 9.95
A collection of 14 previously printed articles and parts of books concerning the texts, structure, and meaning of *Piers Plowman*. The pieces collected are mostly well known and easily reached in their original form; bringing them together as a book is therefore little justified, except as a 10-dollar convenience, and we must hope that the idea of putting together *original* essays, as in Rowland's *Companion to Chaucer Studies* (CHOICE, Dec. 1968), will catch on. The editor's introduction well and briefly summarizes the half-century of *Piers* criticism here represented, and a selected bibliography at the end lists some 200 additional critical books and articles.

CHOICE NOV. '69
Language & Literature
English & American

in process

INTERPRETATIONS
OF
PIERS PLOWMAN

EDITED BY

Edward Vasta

UNIVERSITY OF NOTRE DAME PRESS

Notre Dame   London

Library of Congress Catalog Card Number: 68-12296

Manufactured in the United States of America

To Mortimer J. Donovan

CONTENTS

INTRODUCTION

AFTER THE PUBLICATION of Skeat's parallel text edition in 1886, interpretive scholarship on *Piers Plowman* developed through three discernible stages and accumulated in the proportions of something like a cornucopia. During the first forty-odd years, while the problems of text, date and authorship generated a prolific yield, the harvest of interpretive criticism was sparse. It included several books and articles by a handful of scholars— notably Jusserand, Hanscom, Dorothy Owen, H. S. V. Jones and R. W. Chambers[1]—and portions, ranging from a paragraph to a chapter, of histories of English literature or of other works of similarly large scope. During this period there was general unanimity among scholars concerning the meaning and structure of *Piers Plowman*.

Then in 1929, Henry W. Wells, in his article "The Construction of *Piers Plowman*," offered a number of seminal ideas that were taken up by a steady series of studies over approximately the next twenty years. These studies, culminating in 1951 with the publication of *Piers Plowman and Scriptural Tradition* by D. W. Robertson, Jr. and Bernard F. Huppé, expanded the application of Wells' principal ideas and explored their doctrinal and literary backgrounds. In addition, they uncovered many new problems in the poem and offered solutions that went

---

[1] In order to avoid burdening this introduction with footnotes, I must ask the reader to consult the bibliography at the end of this anthology for the works of the scholars mentioned above and hereafter.

far beyond Wells. Thus the term "complexity" rather than "unanimity" better characterizes the community of understanding brought about during this second stage.

It had already become clear by this time that understanding the meaning and structure of *Piers Plowman* presented an enormous, rewarding and therefore attractive scholarly challenge. In addition, having agreed on the necessity of new editions of the poem's three versions, scholars had begun to postpone further labors in the historical, textual and authorial fields. In medieval studies generally, the critical atmosphere had changed to one that nourished greater interest than previously in matters of form and idea. All of these circumstances helped to bring the attention of still larger numbers of *Piers Plowman* scholars to matters of interpretation and thus led to the third period which began in the early 1950's and is still in progress today. During the past fifteen years or so, the outpouring of interpretive studies has become abundant. But interpretations have also diverged. Under the scrutiny of such scholars as R. W. Frank, Jr. and S. S. Hussey, fundamental ideas of the previous period have been reexamined and some have been rejected. New interpretations, such as those offered by David Fowler, John Lawlor, Elizabeth Salter and Donald Howard, for example, as well as by Frank and Bloomfield, have taken independent directions. After unanimity and complexity, therefore, has come diversity. Today our horn-of-plenty, to bring this analogy to an end, not only overflows but also provides a somewhat bewildering variety.

Such a brief historical sketch of *Piers Plowman* criticism is necessarily simplified. It does not pretend to embrace all contributions; the history of scholarship on any subject is never so neat. But it does account, I trust, for the general lines of development, and the essays included in the present anthology should throw these lines into relief. The burden of this introduction is to tie these essays together by placing them in the pattern of development sketched above.

The first period of criticism is represented by G. R. Owst, who was interested in *Piers Plowman* as a work of social satire concerned with the reform of contemporary abuses. In the course of demonstrating that medieval sermons contributed formatively to Langland's fundamental thinking, Owst defines much of the doctrine that constitutes the poet's social thought. Man is a social animal. Society is properly made up of the three offices of priesthood, knighthood and the laboring class, and each office has a special social function which its members are morally obligated to perform. Social ranks are necessarily immutable. Their members should work together in harmony and love because the peace of the community, and their own salvations, depend on it. Sin has not only an individual but also a social and national significance. The existence of the poor, furthermore, is both justified and necessary, and the sanctity of labor and the virtues of poverty demand reverence for the laboring poor. These ideas lie behind much of the social satire in *Piers Plowman* and illuminate the character of Piers Plowman himself. Owst's interest in them is characteristic of the criticism prevalent in the first forty years.[2] Thus in *A Manual of the Writings in Middle English: 1050–1400,* published in 1926, *Piers Plowman* is included in the chapter entitled "Works Dealing with Contemporary Conditions" and placed under the subcategory of Satire and Complaint. In its summary of scholarship, the *Manual*[3] reports: "Almost every critic of the poem has styled the poet a reformer. . . . The work reflects at all points the general current realization of the monstrous abuses in Church and in State and in common social and industrial conditions" (p. 266).

[2] Although *Literature and Pulpit in Medieval England,* from which "A Literary Echo of the Social Gospel" is taken, appeared four years after the article by Wells, it made available research begun by Owst long before.

[3] By John Edwin Wells, whom I do not name above in order to avoid confusion with Henry W. Wells.

In bringing about a new and more complicated view of *Piers Plowman,* Henry W. Wells by no means rejected the previous study of the poem's social satire. Nor has this aspect ever ceased to be important or come to be ignored. He did reject, however, the accompanying view that Langland's poem was unified by its pervasive social concern but by no artistic design. The structure of the poem is described by the *Manual* as "a great series of portraits, of scenes from life" (p. 265).

> Its achievements are not through conscious selection or skilful management toward a clearly preconceived design, but through sheer native aspiration and power. Indeed, it knows little of formal art. Swept along by the impulse of the moment, it forgets that it has a reader, it breaks up its pictures, it confuses its aims. (p. 264)

The "Social Vignette" theory, as it has since come to be called, necessarily prevailed when interpretive scholarship limited the poem to the genre of social satire. Thus in opposing this theory by uncovering elements of design in the work, Wells also revealed *Piers Plowman* to be much more than a social document.

Through the appeal of his ideas as well as direct argument, Wells also freed criticism from the so-called *"Piers Plowman* Question"—does *Piers Plowman* have one author or several. This question is inevitably asked of a poem that seems almost completely disunified and exists in three distinct versions. It was raised by a break in the continuity of the poem, a break which suggested to J. M. Manly the loss of a leaf in an early manuscript of the A text. Manly published his first report in 1906 and after subsequent study posited five authors: three for the A text, one for the B and one for the C. The issue he raised generated a quantity of scholarship that is massive in comparison to the quantity of interpretive criticism produced during the same period. But the important point is that from the beginning the question of unity was centrally involved in the authorial question, and it was Wells who first dissociated the two issues. In the opening paragraphs of "The Construction of *Piers Plow-*

man," he argues that the study of the poem's design can take place unhampered by the problems of authorship.

Wells, finally, introduced a set of concepts and accompanying terminology that became the basis of future criticism. He argued that *Piers Plowman* as a whole dramatizes the quest for individual perfection and has a doctrinal unity. Giving short titles, which have since become standard usage, to the two parts of the poem, he pointed out that the *Visio* concerns problems confronting the unlearned layman while the *Vita* concerns the more advanced problems of the learned clergy. The *Visio* deals with life in this world, but the *Vita* deals with the higher life of the spirit. The *Visio* embraces only the active life while the *Vita* extends over the entire range of spiritual states required first for the active life of the spirit, then the contemplative life and culminating in the life that combines both, or as it came to be called in future criticism, the mixed life. Wells further argued that the meaning of Dowel, Dobet and Dobest, the respective subjects of the three parts of the *Vita,* are cumulative. Dobet presupposes all that is involved in Dowel, and Dobest includes the lives of Dowel and Dobet. These names are Langland's terms, according to Wells, for three successive stages in the spiritual life which carry the individual through three ascending degrees of holiness. Wells also pointed out that the three Persons of the Trinity constitute a principle of design in the *Vita:* God the Father governs the Life of Dowel; the Son, the life of Dobet; and the Holy Spirit, Dobest.

Inspired by Wells' ideas, particularly the triad of active, contemplative and mixed lives, Nevill Coghill built directly on Wells' article. He explored in detail the virtues discussed in the B version in connection with the three lives and emphasized the objective status of the persons who lived them (layman, priest and bishop) as distinct from the subjective spiritual conditions they were obligated to achieve. Coghill also gave further specification to the structure of the poem. The *Visio, Dobet* and *Dobest* present each of the three lives allegorically, he pointed out, but *Dowel* covers all three and is a kind of abstract exposition rather than allegory. *Dowel,* therefore, supplies the moral argument for the work as a whole. The principal objective of Coghill's article is to explore the character of Piers Plowman in terms of the triadic lives. He concluded that Piers embodies each of them in turn through three stages of his growth.

T. P. Dunning added further insights to the growing awareness of the poem's complexities and more than any previous critic based his interpretation on the teaching of the Fathers of the Church. He confined his study to the A text, which Wells had said was doctrinally whole but artistically incomplete. For Wells, the A-*Vita* stops at the point where problems concerning the learned clergy would have to be taken up. For Dunning, however, the *Visio* and *Vita* of the A version, excluding the passage at the end appended by a John But, are two intimately related but distinct and complete poems. Each has its own unifying theme. Like Wells, Dunning saw the *Visio* as concerned with worldly life as it relates to man's salvation; but unlike Wells, he interpreted the *Visio* as dealing with this problem from a particular point of view: the right use of temporal goods. Similarly, Dunning saw the *Vita* as dealing with the spiritual life but making the single and unifying point that every man can Dowel, Dobet and Dobest if he obeys his own conscience "a cordynge with holy churche." In the course of tracing this theme in the *Vita,* Dunning found that the three lives are discussed in terms of both objective status and subjective condition. The primacy of the latter, he concluded, constitutes the A-*Vita's* final message concerning the three lives. He also suggested that Dowel, Dobet and Dobest are substantially the purgative, illuminative and unitive stages or ways of perfection as defined by mystical theologians.

At this point Wells returned to print in order to offer new observations and to react to the studies of Coghill and Dunning. He observed in the poem a pattern of historical allegory, similar to the historiography developed by Joachim of Flora in the twelfth century, in which Dowel deals with the pre-Christian world, Dobet with the time of Jesus and Dobest with the reign of the Holy Spirit since the Ascension. He also expressed his conviction that Dowel, Dobet and Dobest stand for subjective rather than objective states and agreed that they are similar to the purgative, illuminative, unitive stages in the mystic's way of perfection.

The three remaining critics represented in the present anthology and falling within what I have termed the second stage of interpretive scholarship assimilated many of the ideas thus far developed and added their own qualifications and insights. E. Talbot Donaldson, arguing for single authorship in *Piers Plowman: The C-Text and Its Poet,* moved toward a synoptic interpretation, one that could account for the meaning and structure of all three versions. He focused more definitely on the inward perfection of the individual as the controlling theme of the *Vita* and stressed the importance of the purgative-illuminative-unitive triad for Dowel, Dobet and Dobest. In the portion of his book excerpted for this anthology, Donaldson shows how major revisions in the C version, which he takes to be Langland's last and most accurate statement, work consistently toward clarifying the virtues involved in the mystical triad. D. W. Robertson, Jr. and Bernard F. Huppé together applied in great detail the fourfold method of allegorical exegesis, already urged by Coghill and approved by Wells, and thereby developed the most elaborate interpretation yet offered. Practically all of the themes and triads come into play in their view of the poem, and they added new ideas as well. The essay included in the present collection is made up of only the first and last chapters of their book, but it explains their method fully and gives sufficient indication of the rich patterns of meaning they saw in the poem. In simple summary of their view: the literal level depicts the misguided Dreamer's development toward humility and charity, the tropological level dramatizes the stages of moral and spiritual perfection, the allegorical level deals with the structure of authority in the Church and the abuses of this authority by the friars and the anagogical level opposes Babylon, the present world of spiritual decay, to the Heavenly perfection of The New Jerusalem.

Thus by the early 1950's a broad complex of ideas about the meaning and structure of *Piers Plowman* had been built on the framework offered by Wells. But despite the common ground they shared, these studies so qualified each other that the poem's unifying principles seemed to most scholars to have been as much obscured as clarified. At this point a reaction began to materialize, precipitated in large part by the interpretation offered by Robertson and Huppé. They had previously argued for universal application of the fourfold method to medieval literature generally, and their interpretation of *Piers Plowman* had been awaited as a kind of test case for the validity of their argument. A large number of scholars remained unconvinced, and *Piers Plowman* was caught up in the reaction to the wider issue. In "The Art of Reading Medieval Personification-Allegory," Frank argued that personification allegory, of which *Piers Plowman* is an example, should for all practical purposes be read literally. The personifications themselves, he noted, are never allegorical. Their situations and actions may be, but often not even these have allegorical significance. He rejected outright the possibility of reading personification-allegory according to the fourfold method. In 1956, Morton W. Bloomfield also published an influential article, not included in this anthology, opposing the general application of the fourfold method,[4] and later developed an interpretation of *Piers Plowman* based on the literal content of the poem. In 1960, the controversy having reached a fever pitch, Robert E. Kaske defended the exegetical approach. Working with a number of passages from Chaucer and Langland, he showed ways in which the tradition of biblical exegesis can illuminate images and allusions. He also suggested that judgment of the fourfold method be postponed until it has been more widely and painstakingly tried.

---

[4] "Symbolism in Medieval Literature," *MP*, LVI (1956), 73–81.

A reaction also developed against the triadic notions in terms of which Dowel, Dobet and Dobest had been defined. Dunning returned to print in order to sketch out the structure of the B text and did so along the lines of previous scholarship. He reasserted the importance of the three lives and the stages of perfection and defined them more clearly than previous scholars had done. But in an article written simultaneously and published a few months before, S. S. Hussey examined the medieval sources that had been offered for these notions, principally Walter Hilton, and concluded that neither the active, contemplative and mixed lives nor the purgative, illuminative and unitive stages, at least as Hilton had defined them, could be identified with Dowel, Dobet and Dobest. In 1957, these triads were rejected entirely by Frank in *Piers Plowman and the Scheme of Salvation.* Frank reexamined crucial passages linking the *Visio* and *Vita,* as well as the triads themselves in the light of medieval doctrine, and concluded that neither the three lives nor the three stages function as structural principles in the poem. He also rejected the view that the character of Piers Plowman embodied the three lives.

As these reactions developed, interpretations took new directions. In the year following the articles by Hussey and Dunning (1957), John Lawlor reminded critics that preoccupation with doctrine overlooks, and fails to appreciate, the achievement of *Piers Plowman* as a work of imaginative literature. Without rejecting previous scholarship, Lawlor set out to discover the imaginative unity of the poem and offered as the basis of this unity the idea that truth must be lived as well as known. Frank not only rejected previous interpretations but also developed his own. He saw *Piers Plowman* as concerned with both the possibility of and the requirements for man's salvation. The *Visio* dramatizes the evil to be avoided and the good to be pursued; the *Vita* explores in detail the life of good work and the possibility of man's living it. For Frank, the Divine Trinity and the stages of history under the successive guidance of the

Father, Son and Holy Spirit, which Wells observed as factors in the unity of the poem, constitute its central unifying principles. Man is saved by living the life of love, and the gifts of the three Persons of the Trinity make this life possible. Bloomfield, on the other hand, interpreted the poem as concerned with the perfection of Christian society rather than the individual. He saw *Piers Plowman* as basically apocalyptic rather than mystical. Like Robertson and Huppé, he felt that Langland aims his message at the friars on whose reform the reform of society depends, but like Frank he interpreted the poem literally. Criticism since Bloomfield has generally continued along these lines: points of agreement and disagreement but clear divergence concerning the poem's governing ideas. Although the present anthology could not include selections from the half dozen books and numerous articles published since 1961, the examples of Lawlor, Frank and Bloomfield suggest the trend in *Piers Plowman* scholarship today.

In this anthology, I have sought to include items that assist in the study of the poem as a whole, that were written by major participants in the conversations of the past eighty years and that stand well together side by side. Some of these come from a chapter, or several chapters, of books. In these cases I have excised passages and emended cross-references in order to make the selections readable as self-contained essays. No alterations were made, at least knowingly, that in any way obscured or modified the views of the writers. Since every order but the chronological seemed to cause difficulties, I have arranged the selections according to the date of first publication.

Every anthology suffers from inconsistency. In order to give this one some semblance of continuity, all quotations from *Piers Plowman* have been checked against and normalized to Skeat's parallel text edition published by Oxford in 1886.[5] A consist-

[5] *The Vision of William Concerning Piers the Plowman in Three Parallel Texts Together with Richard the Redeless,* ed. Rev. Walter W. Skeat, 2 vols. (Oxford: Clarendon Press, 1886). By permission of the Clarendon Press.

ent spelling of proper names has been adopted; matters of mechanics and spelling have been made consistent with American practice and all selections have been made consistent in these respects with each other. Here and there stylistic preferences have been introduced, but sparingly and only when it seemed advantageous. Two passages have been translated: a tercet of Dante's Italian quoted by Dunning (p. 94) and a familiar biblical passage which provides the scriptural basis for Donaldson's interpretation (p. 134). Footnotes have been made consistent with MLA style.

It remains to thank those who helped me bring out this anthology. First thanks go to the contributors and their publishers for permission to reprint these essays and to the Oxford University Press for permission to quote from Skeat's edition. I must also thank Anne Kozak, a free-lance editor for the University of Notre Dame Press who was assigned to this anthology. I offer my best thanks to Mortimer Donovan, with whom I consulted as this book took shape and who gave this introduction a critical reading. But he has read most things I have subsequently managed to publish, and I have relied on his knowledge and judgement, as well as friendship, for some ten years. I happily acknowledge my debt to Mortimer Donovan, and with equal happiness I dedicate this book to him.

E.V.

University of Notre Dame
February 4, 1968

THE CONSTRUCTION OF *PIERS PLOWMAN**

Henry W. Wells

MANY STRIKINGLY DIVERGENT views have been advanced as to the structural integrity or looseness of *Piers Plowman*. Its early critics, to be sure, had little to say upon the subject but there seemed to be general agreement in the view that the work is loosely put together. The long summaries by Morley and others, for example, give small evidence that the critics had detected any strong organizing elements in the design. With the strenuous attack by Professor Manly, a new epoch in the criticism of the work began. Scholars who favored multiple authorship naturally agreed that the poem lacks a well-defined plan, and even advanced the view that we have in fact not only from two to five authors but from two to five poems, all upon themes in important respects dissimilar and more or less loosely constructed. While Manly tore Piers' seamless coat asunder, the advocates of a single authorship—somewhat less emphatically, to be sure— found relative coherence in the poem as a whole and discounted the view that the style is excessively digressive. Throughout the controversy the critics dealt largely with textual problems, only occasionally turning to consider the primary subject matter of the work. The articles of Mensendieck furnished the most important contributions to an interpretation of an underlying plan,

* Reprinted, by permission of the Modern Language Association, from *PMLA*, XLIV (1929), 123–140.

especially in regard to the most difficult section, the *Vita de Dowel*. His chief concern, however, was with a few theses relating to special passages, so that his studies hardly deal with the larger problem of the enveloping thoughts of the poem, if indeed such thoughts exist. Thus far investigation has resulted in many contradictory views but in no detailed statement upon the cardinal problem in the interpretation of *Piers Plowman*.

The problem of the authorship of the poem actually bears only indirectly on that of the poem's organization. It should not be forgotten that some of the most loosely constructed of Elizabethan plays, as *Old Fortunatus,* are apparently the work of one poet, while some of the best unified, as *The Maid's Tragedy* and *Eastward Ho!,* are known to have been written by two or more poets. I cannot regard the assumption of divided authorship as decisive one way or another in determining the philosophical or aesthetic coherence of the medieval poem. Certain of the conclusions reached in the present investigation seem favorable to divided authorship, while rather more of them favor single authorship. But I do not wish the present article to be viewed as a contribution to the controversy in any but a distinctly secondary degree.

Undoubtedly the author or authors enjoyed the effect of violent transitions and surprises and definitely sought this effect in the poem. This is merely to recognize it as a dream poem, composed in the same spirit that dominates gothic architecture. The poem undoubtedly has a rough surface. To read it is like riding over a bad road; we are jerked and bounced and tossed. But so we may be at the hands of the most rigorous logician. That the poem has a rough surface should by no means prejudice us as to its fundamental coherence or incoherence. Thus, although Dean Swift's sermons are as smooth as polished marble and Donne's as rough as a thistle, the latter are quite as likely to be fundamentally coherent as those by the Dean of Saint Patrick's. That a poem is of the gothic spirit really tells us nothing of its essential organization or disorganization. The latter qualities cannot be felt by mere surface touch, such as we employ for style. An alligator's skin may be rougher than the surface of a pile of sand, but one covers an exquisite organism and the other is merely a confused heap. We cannot "sense" the answer to our problem; we must analyze the poem.

In this discussion I shall distinguish the two chief parts of the poem by the names generally employed in the colophons themselves. The first part of the work, which concludes with the story of Piers' pardon and the poet's reflections thereon, I shall call the *Visio,* and the remainder of the poem, the *Vita,* which is itself divided into three parts, the *Vita de Dowel, Dobet* and *Dobest.* I shall examine first the *Visio* and the *Vita,* secondly the relations to each other of the subsections of the *Visio* and finally the relations of the subsections in the *Vita.*

I.

The relation of the *Visio* and the *Vita* has never been carefully stated and often has been, at least from my own point of view, ill understood. The *Visio* is a study of the life of the laity both as it is and as it should be. We have in this part of the poem that which the common communicant ought to know, and nothing more. We have no abstruse theological or philosophical problems, no allegory of learning, no account of the saintly life and no thorough and detailed analysis of the functioning of the Church as the coordinating principle in society. On the other hand, we have such social satire and such an account of man's religious duties as the humblest medieval reader might be expected to understand. If he follows the road here traced by the poet, he is considered to be sure of salvation. With the *Vita* the theme is changed. We have an account of the world as seen by the thinker who has passed through the medieval disciplines of learning, asceticism and priestly responsibility. He has known the intellectual life, the mystic and the active life, and so fulfilled the more arduous duties which heaven imposes upon its specially chosen warriors. In this part of the poem the satire falls

3

not upon delinquencies in secular duties, but upon faults peculiar to persons dedicated to the life of scholarship and religious
practice: upon those who, like the gluttonous Doctor, the feign-
ing Hermit and the over-indulgent Confessor, betray learning,
devotion and the institution of the Church. This part of the
poem deals with ideals superfluous to and improper in a layman,
but to which God's select soldiers must conform if they are to
remain loyal and in turn win their salvation.

To a certain point the two lives agree. This is why the author
of the so-called A text continued his poem beyond the *Visio*.
The *Vita* begins humbly. It gives an account of the life of man
from his birth to his intellectual and spiritual maturity. It contains passages dealing successively with the creation of the world,
the birth and care of children, marriage and the preliminary
disciplines of study. The chief figures encountered in the allegory are Will, the name symbolically given to the Christian Pilgrim at birth; Thought, who meets him in his earliest years; Wit,
his first teacher; and Study, who gives him elementary training
and who introduces him to Scripture and to Clergye, who is with
Scripture. But in the A text the pilgrim learns little from Scripture and nothing from Clergye, who will have nothing to do
with him. The word Clergye the poet here uses, of course, as
virtually synonymous with learning. In short, the A text breaks
off just where the education of the more enterprising layman
would be expected to conclude. Born with will, early endowed
with thought and wit, acquainted with elementary learning, he
represents the foundation upon which, after all, even the greatest seer and the deepest thinker of the Church must build.

We may now see why the A text was circulated so widely. It
contained what the common man needed to know and no more.
If the A text had ended with the *Visio,* it would have instructed
the layman in all his primary duties to God and man, but it
would not have shown him concretely his place in society and
his relation to the Clergye and the Religious. Thus the section
of the *Vita* included in the A text formed a part of that manu-

script version as circulated among the people. I have no opinion as to whether the author soon after writing the A text died, or continued his poem and encouraged reproductions of the A text even after the B text had been finished. I observe, however, that the A text ends at a point which, if unsatisfactory from an aesthetic standpoint, is entirely satisfactory from a doctrinal standpoint. The *Vita* repeats certain elements of the *Visio*. The man of religion must be born, possess will, thought and wit, and know his ABC's just as a common communicant. His salvation comes from the same source. Piers the Plowman saves one no less than the other. Each must to some degree Do Well. Each must know and seriously consider the Creed and Paternoster and follow the road of the ten commandments. Each requires the same sacraments. Thus in each section we have allusions to baptism and burial and elaborate passages dealing with penance and the Mass. These repetitions may or may not, I take it, be viewed as inartistic, but are clearly necessary to the subject in hand. The poem in its design may be thought of as one of those great canvasses which Veronese and Tintoretto delighted to paint in which a pillar divides the picture into two finely balanced scenes of approximately equal magnitude, although one is slightly more significant than the other.

My view is confirmed by colophons in the B text Manuscripts which describe the part of the poem that the *Vita de Dowel* and

The *Visio*	The *Vita* (A Text)	Remaining Section of the *Vita*
The life of the common communicant: the demands of nature; plowmen, artisans, knights, ladies, merchants and lawyers: *Conscience;* the ten commandments; the elements of the faith; sacramental needs	Common attributes of laity and clergy: the demands of nature; *Anima, Inwit, Will, Thought,* (*elementary*) *Study; Conscience;* the ten commandments; the elements of the faith; sacramental needs	The higher order of perfection required of the Priesthood, or *Clergye*

5

the A text have in common as both a part of the *Visio* and of the *Vita*. The foregoing conclusions may be expressed in tabular form.

While the *Vita* is clearly stated to be divided into three parts, it is commonly observed that the *Visio* is also divided into three parts. Closely following upon the first vision of the Field of Folk and of Holy Church, which is clearly introductory, we have the Story of Lady Mede, the Confession and Absolution of the Sins at Church, and the two concluding Passus dealing with Piers and his servants and concluding with the story of the pardon. I shall later examine the character of the transitions in greater detail. For the present, however, I am concerned only with observing those parallels which I believe to be deliberate between the three parts of the *Visio* and the three parts of the *Vita*. A tabular scheme may here prove useful:

	Visio	*Vita*
	Story of Lady Mede	*Vita de Dowel*
Part I	Problems of economic and secular government; temporal welfare; *Reasoun;* the active life	Problems of theology and Church government; eternal salvation; *Reasoun;* the active life (Part I): *Activa Vita*
	The Sins	*Vita de Dobet*
Part II	Inner life of the ordinary Christian; preparation for the Mass	The contemplative or religious life: solitude and faithful hermits; preparation for the Mass
	The Plowman's Pardon	*Vita de Dobest*
Part III	The plow of the honest laborer; hope for salvation of the individual; satire on indulgences; the active life	The mystic plow with which Christ cultivates souls; despair for the spiritual welfare of Christian Society (*Unitas*); satire on indulgences; the active life (Part II): Christ as Preacher; the cure of souls

The first main part of the *Visio,* namely the Story of Lady Mede, deals with the problem of secular government and nearly at its conclusion introduces us to a figure named Reasoun, who decides for the king the quarrel between Mede and Conscience. Reasoun thus becomes the central figure in this section of the poem. The first part of the *Vita,* or the *Vita de Dowel,* deals with problems of theology. Again Reasoun proves the culminating figure, since all the preceding allegorical types in the *Vita de Dowel* lead up to it, and after its appearance we enter the long transition to the *Vita de Dobet.* The chief problem in the Story of Lady Mede is man's well-being in this world. The chief problem debated in the *Vita de Dowel* is man's eternal well-being. One section deals with the active life of secular affairs, the other, with the active life of industrious theological study. The Story of the Confession and Absolution of the Sins deals obviously with the more personal, intimate and inner life. It concludes with an allegory of the Mass, the sacrament which restores man to the grace of his Creator. The *Vita de Dobet* deals with the life of solitude and contemplation (of this I shall have more to say later), and concludes with the bells that ring in Easter and which summon the Dreamer to the sacrament. The Story of Piers in the *Visio* deals with the theme of honest work and its reward, which is pardon and salvation. Here for the first time we meet the image of the plow, in this case simply the plow of the farmer. In outward appearance at least even Piers himself is no more than an overseer or even a participant in these physical labors. He exacts honest labor and receives no easy indulgences in his pardon. In the *Vita de Dobest* we have an allegory of the entire community envisaged as Unitas laboring at its myriad tasks under the guidance of the Church. Here Piers and his plow once more appear, but Piers is now indubitably Christ, his plow the word of God, man the harvest and the barn the heaven of divine rest. This imagery has, to be sure, been hinted in the *Vita de Dobet,* but here is first objectified. Piers' wicked servants, the unscrupulous priests and friars, grant easy indulgences. In the *Visio* we have seen the promise of salvation for the honest worker. The individual may be saved. In the *Vita* we have the picture of society retrogressing rather than progressing. Individuals, as notably an honest priest, may still be saved. But the community goes from bad to worse. We should, I think, regard as deliberate both these comparisons and these contrasts between the six major sections of the poem. In each case the lines seem to me to have been too sharply drawn to be accidental. I believe that the author or authors deliberately repeated the major elements in the design.

II.

The *Vita* is obviously the more complex part of the poem, as it is also the longer part. It has, however, been the less discussed. I shall glance comparatively briefly at the outstanding features in the construction of the *Visio*. I consider that they show a point of view by no means haphazard or confused. For each of the major images presented there can, I think, be given convincing reasons as to why it is pertinent to the theme of the poem as a whole and as to why it occupies the position which it actually holds in the work.

We are introduced to the Field of Folk because the poet begins his teaching not with revelation nor with religion but with nature. So he begins later in his *Vita de Dowel* and at the conclusion of that section of the poem assures us that even Saracens in substance know the first Person of the Trinity. Moreover *Piers Plowman,* unlike the poems by Dante and Milton, contains no scene in heaven. Once only and for the space of but three hundred lines the scene sinks to the deep dungeon and dark from which Christ rescues our forefathers in darkness. With the exception of the Harrowing of Hell the poet avoids all scenes that belong to another life than that of this world. In short, the scene of *Piers Plowman* is precisely the opposite of that of Dante's poem. The Italian poet deals only with life beyond the grave, the English poet only with life upon this side

8

of the grave. The whole poem deals in this sense with the Field of Folk. Its author or authors contrived most vividly and forcefully to state an initial proposition. The work remains in this respect at least remarkably true to its premises. Even from an aesthetic standpoint it holds faithful to this field and to this earth. Its varied imagery always breathes earth-odors.

Holy Church, the figure who next appears, begins her instructions with homely and materialistic observations. She too acknowledges first of all the animal nature of man. Three things she tells the Dreamer are necessary, food, drink and clothing. From this characteristic teaching she elevates her discussion until at the last she states the doctrine of the Redemption and its moral of charity. But she always fulfills the function of a Prologue. She never tells the Dreamer more than any child might be expected to know. She reads him, as it were, his catechism, stating simply those ideas upon which the whole of the Christian System rests: the doctrine of free will, of the depravity of the body, of obedience to God, of charity and of grace.

In her last words Holy Church warns the pilgrim of evil and bids him be wary of distributing blame. She disappears, after serving not only as a Prologue but as a link to the first part of the story proper, the allegory of Lady Mede. The Greek mind would of course have left the problem of the state to the last, as the highest and most important of all problems. The medieval poet, however, true to premises already contained in his poem, regards religion and the Church as the supreme guide in life, and hence treats the state as an initial problem to be faced before proceeding to far graver problems. Thus the political life vividly introduces us to sin. Man's error lies not in false political theory but in his personal weakness. Sin becomes the vital issue. Thus we are logically led to the second chief division of the *Visio,* The Story of the Confession and Absolution of the Sins.

If it should be urged against my view of the distinct functions of the *Visio* and *Vita* that of the six or seven characters representing the sins (for the number differs in the different texts)

9

one of the characters is a priest, I should reply that in embodying sloth in human form the poet followed a well-tried tradition in making Sloth a priest. It should be noted that the faults ascribed to this idler include many omissions and commissions not in the least peculiar to his profession. He is the eternal truant from duty. His truancy, not his duty, concerns the poet here. Sloth cannot be said to represent the shortcomings of the Clergye as such. A further objection might be raised in that the C text of the *Visio,* and this only, contains a passage of some length on the sins of monks and friars. The lines occur in the sermon of Reasoun, which introduces the Story of the Sins and links it with the preceding Story of Lady Mede, wherein Reasoun is also a character. Reasoun's sermon is obviously intended to enumerate the outstanding sins of all orders of society. That in two texts the clergy and the religious receive slight notice and in the third no more than a moderate proportion of attention seems to me on the whole to support rather than to damage my position. The clergy appear almost forgotten in many long passages. In the lines dealing with Hunger we hear of the friars only as laborers in the common fields, driven by famine to desert their normal course of life. We should of course remember that the *Visio* reflects life as the layman sees it, not merely as he lives it. Although not a participant in their peculiar problems, he both observes the clergy and the learned and recognizes the great influence which they exercise upon him.

The confession of the Sinners is followed by their absolution and by the quest of society for a better life. This leads us to the third section of the *Visio.* The extremely popular appeal of the *Visio* as a whole is powerfully enhanced by the allegory in the Passus dealing with Famine. Although in this section of the poem the activities of the higher orders of society are noted, as that of knights and ladies, we hear most of the common laborers and especially of their unwillingness to do honest work in the plowfields. The opening of the last Passus of the *Visio* gives a list of all classes, in which the clergy are but hastily mentioned, while detailed attention is accorded to merchants, lawyers and, once more, to laborers. Laymen pretending to be priests are condemned.

We should observe caution in our interpretation of Piers' pardon. It states that all who do well shall be saved and that all who do evil shall be damned. Later the author gives his own view as somewhat more moderate, for he grants that the Pope and the prayers of the Church have some power to save souls, although to trust in such aids is not so safe as to do well. Piers' pardon is simply Do Well as applied in particular to the laity. The clergy and the religious must also Do Well, and in a more exacting degree. By "doing" and by "working" medieval authors do not of course mean merely temporal actions. Thus Hilton's treatise *On Daily Work* deals in large part with prayer and meditation. Piers never of course fancied that a Christian could forsake faith, devotion and the sacraments and by mere bodily works go to heaven. He meant that a man must be saved primarily upon his own merits and by God's grace, and not by the aid of indulgences. It is not from the nature of this pardon but from the character of the *Visio* as a whole that we may safely regard the *Visio* as addressed primarily to the laity. Piers' pardon, even in the *Visio,* applies to all mankind. That a priest scorns it, however, helps us to perceive its applicability to the people. The *Visio* ends with the pardon because with the need for a pardon it begins. Man is shown in a transient state. He may, on dying, go either to the deep dungeon or to the fair tower. The first prayer which the pilgrim passionately addresses to Holy Church consists in the one vital question for every devout medieval man. The question is simply, how may I save my soul? We may conclude then that so far as the larger contours of form are concerned the *Visio* is a well-arranged poem. Like the typical dream allegory, it appears even wildly discordant upon the surface. But when the meanings of the symbols are considered, we become aware of the presence of no inconsiderable design.

III.

The *Visio* introduces us not only to the name of Dowel but to the need for the *Vita* as a whole. In his last speeches Piers in the *Visio* states that he will change his course of life: instead of being so busy about his physical welfare, he will do as the apostles did and turn chiefly to the cultivation of his soul. This forewarns us of the change which we are about to encounter in the second part of the poem. And here we are faced with our gravest problems, to which, however, answers may be given I think with even more assurance than in the case of the *Visio*. Again I shall venture to clarify my views by the use of a tabular scheme:

Dowel	*Dobet*	*Dobest*
The active life of intellectual s t u d i e s and priestly duties; *Activa Vita;*	The contemplative life; discussion of faithful hermits;	The active life expressed in the corporate Church, or Unitas; especially the rule of the Bishop;
self-rule; the ten commandments a n d the seven sins; allegorical figures and contemporary allusions;	self-obliteration; t h e three contemplative or Christian virtues; many scriptural figures;	the cure of souls; the four active or moral virtues; allegorical figures and contemporary allusions again;
the protection of the Father	the protection of the Son	the protection of the Holy Spirit

Let us review a few of the outstanding features of the *Vita de Dowel, Dobet* and *Dobest*. This part of the poem represents the search of an imaginary pilgrim for three "lives" or "virtues" or, as we should be more likely to say in the language of present-day psychology, three states. The pilgrim meets many characters, the chief of whom are in the order in which he meets them, Thought, Wit, Study, Scripture, Clergye, Nature, Patience, Haukyn the Active Man and Piers Plowman. From most of these characters, the pilgrim inquires who are Dowel, Dobet and Dobest, and from no two of them does he receive quite the same answer. Had they agreed, he might possibly have given up the quest. Wit tells him that Dowel is to labor honestly, while Clergye tells him that Dowel is principally to be loyal to the Faith. Clearly each character has something to contribute to the pilgrim's growing knowledge of his life's journey. Each represents a progressive stage in his education. The different answers show not that the poet himself is confused (the poet knew, I think, his answer from the beginning) but that his pilgrim is groping his way, as do all men toward a solution of life's difficulties. He quarrels with all his teachers, makes mistakes, falls by the way, because of his peculiar temperament profits more from some teachers than from others and ultimately reaches the knowledge which he desires, only to find that in forgetting himself and taking upon himself the burden of society he has borne Christ's cross. For the individual Christian may be saved, but society as a whole is not destined to achieve harmony on earth. The kingdom of Piers the Plowman is not of this world.

The three stages of life are always described as three grades of holiness. About the last grade we have from the first the greatest agreement. Again and again it is allegorized in the image of the bishop who guards his flock. To rule others is to Do Best. To rule one's self is to Do Well. Dobet is described as an advanced state of charity and humility. But the states are clearly and consistently presented in themselves, that is, in the three several parts of the poem; and we need not be overly puzzled by what the first persons whom the pilgrim meets say about them. We may I think say confidently on the basis of the entire character of the Passus dealing with Dowel that this state is one of self-culture through knowledge. All the chief figures whom the pilgrim meets until very near the end of this section of the poem are evidently stages in his scholastic training. If he lapses for a time to follow Desire of the Eyes and

Lust of the Flesh, he in time returns. Even his detour with Nature is at least a part of his academic life. The Life of Dobet begins with a long passage in praise of faithful hermits and in behalf of a true priesthood, introducing us to the three Christian or contemplative virtues—faith, hope and charity, here named Abraham, Spes and Piers Plowman. This part of the poem is centered in the biblical narrative. Its chief images are not, as elsewhere, of the poet's own invention, but are drawn from the synoptic Gospels and from the Apocrypha. The *Vita de Dobest* narrates the history of the Church from its beginning in the Resurrection, through the period of its primitive purity to its present state of degeneration. The story is told primarily not from the individual but from the social point of view. It is the story of Unitas, of Piers' family. It deals in particular with the government, or misgovernment, of this family, and hence with the responsibility of those who rule the Church, the confessors and prelates. It tells of the Christian society that, although protected by the Holy Spirit and sustained by the bread of the sacrament, is subject to ceaseless incursions from its enemies, led by Satan. The four active or cardinal virtues, justice, prudence, fortitude and temperance, are discussed at considerable length. Allusions of a clearly secondary importance, however, are still made to the pilgrim, who is now old and hoar but has not as yet attained true happiness on earth. The Field of Folk cannot give such happiness. Salvation is not of this world. Here the poem ends.

Once in the course of his journey the Pilgrim expresses surprise to learn that there are three states of life instead of two. He had always supposed that the two stages were the active life and the contemplative life. But he finds himself unmistakably in a world ordered in patterns of three. His teacher at this point gives just such an ambiguous answer as a good teacher always gives when he knows that it is best for his pupil to find the answer in his own experience. Yet the doctrine upon which the triple division of the poem has been made was really a familiar one in medieval thought. Saint Thomas expresses it as follows:

> Vita contemplativa simpliciter est melior quam activa quae occupatur circa corporales actus: sed vita activa, secundum quam aliquis praedicando et docendo contemplata aliis tradit, est perfectior quam vita quae solum est contemplativa: quia talis vita praesupponit abundantiam contemplationis. Et ideo Christus talem vitam elegit (*S.T.*, III, XL, 1).

A summary of Bernard's view may be found in a work very popular in England in the fourteenth century, the *Meditationes Vitae Christi*. As the reader will at once observe, this passage agrees with the poem in some interesting points of detail.

> Est igitur vita actiua, quae designatur per Martham. Sed actiuae vitae, sicut ex dictis Bernardi colligere possum, duae sunt partes. Prima pars, qua quis se exercet ad suam principaliter vtilitatem corrigendo se, emendando a vitiis, & informando virtutibus. Et idem secundario sit ad vtilitatem etiam proximi per opera iustitiae, & obsequia pietatis, & charitatis. Secunda pars eius est, quo modo quis principaliter suum exercitium confert in vtilitatem proximi, quamvis ad suum etiam maius meritum, vt alios regendo, docendo, & adiuuando in animarum salutem, vt faciunt Praelati, & Praedicatores, & huiusmodi. & inter has duas partes vitae actiuae, est vita contemplatiua, vt iste sit ordo, quod primo quis se exerceat, & laboret in oratione, & sacrarum studio literarum, & aliis operibus bonis, & obsequiis in conuersatione, quasi corrigendo se a vitiis, & acquirendo virtutes. Secundo quiescat in contemplatione, solitudinem mentis quaerens, & soli Deo vacans toto posse. Tertio per praedicta duo exercitia, virtutibus, & vera sapientia imbutus & illuminatus, & feruidus effectus, ad aliorum salutem intendat. Primo, igitur, vt tetigi, oportet, quod in prima actiua parte, mens expurgetur, depuretur, & roboretur per exercitia virtutum: deinde in contemplatiua informetur, illuminetur, & instruatur: postea confidenter potest ad aliorum profectus exire, vt eos possit adiuuare.

Here we have the chief elements comprising the three "lives" in *Piers Plowman*. Walter Hilton in the fourteenth and Thomas Peacock in the fifteenth century also evince the popular interest in the problem of the three states. The *Meditationes,* which was commonly ascribed to St. Bonaventura, was translated into English during the latter century by Nicholas Love.

There is still a further organizing factor to be noted in the instance of the poem. St. Augustine had advanced what has come to be known as the "psychological trinity." *Piers Plowman* does not follow Augustine's thought but presents a somewhat similar conception. The poet several times quotes the familiar text which declares man to be fashioned in God's image. He evidently considered that, since God is a Trinity, man must in some sense also be a trinity. Each of the three Parts of the *Vita* begins with allusions to the interrelation of the three parts of the Trinity and each is clearly dedicated to a special Person of the Trinity. At the conclusion of the *Vita de Dowel* we are told that even the Saracens believe in God the Father. It is this Person of the Trinity who clearly presides over the Life of Dowel. Christ as Piers the Plowman is the central theme of the *Vita de Dobet.* In this part of the poem the life of Christ, his crucifixion and the harrowing of hell supply the chief narrative elements. The *Vita de Dobest* is no less clearly dedicated to the Holy Spirit, since it narrates at considerable length the descent of the Spirit at Pentecost, the Gifts of the Spirit and the rule of the Spirit within the Church, protecting it from even greater inroads than have as yet been made by the armies of Antichrist. Such is the spiritual trinity of man according to *Piers Plowman,* a thought of no considerable importance in the organization of the work.

It would be manifestly impossible in the brief space of this paper to discuss any large number of details in the *Vita* which indicate the organizing genius of its author or authors. I should prefer to allow my statements relative to the major plan of the poem to stand out for the time being conspicuously, rather than to run the risk of smothering these primary outlines under a mass of detail, however interesting that detail might be to careful students of the poem. A few observations of lesser importance may however detain us.

In the first place it will not of course be assumed that because the Life of Dobest is dedicated to God the Holy Spirit and the Life of Dowel to God the Father that the poet had fallen into the heresy of holding the Third greater than the First Person of the Trinity. The poem and the states are of course cumulative. The poet learns early in his career that the Life of Dobest for example presumes that of Dobet. And it not only presumes this preceding life, but includes it. This the imagery of the poem makes clear. Piers the Plowman is still active in the Life of Dobest. But to know Piers the Plowman it becomes necessary to meet him in the Life of Dobet. Man never loses his need for learning or contemplation. He does not outgrow these powers but by them and by their constant use attains a third power, namely, the ability and the right to rule other men. It is better to know two persons of the Trinity than to know one, and better to know three Persons than to know two. Indeed none can truly be known without a knowledge of all.

The first third of the *Vita de Dowel,* that is, the part contained in the A text, is naturally the easiest and most straightforward. We should never here be seriously in doubt of the reasonable sequence of the thought. As first episode we have the meeting of the pilgrim with the two friars. The friars give him no satisfactory answer to his questions. The poet probably means to satirize the friars, who in reply to a serious question give merely an entertaining story. In any event, the incident teaches the pilgrim the need of searching for Truth deeply and the vanity of relying upon persons. He learns at once that no glib phrases can solve his problem. He must labor himself. He cannot, as the illiterate poor, merely believe what he hears without long pondering upon it. He must use his own wit and go through the arduous disciplines of thought, study, learning, reason, humility and contemplation.

Having brushed specious explanations aside, the pilgrim is

prepared to begin his quest in earnest and to consider man from the cradle to beyond the grave. He first hears from Wit, who is of course Mother Wit or the primitive natural reason, of the creation of the world and of the soul, of the vital principle, or *anima,* and of the rational nature of man, or Inwit. This Inwit, we are told, is the greatest of gifts after the grace of God. By an exercise of Inwit the pilgrim is of course to advance on the road to knowledge. But Inwit does not exist in drunkards, imbeciles and children. Therefore men should avoid excessive drink and care for helpless children and imbeciles. The theme of child care leads naturally to the subject of marriage. The pilgrim has now reached a stage in his progress when a new teacher is required. He goes therefore to Dame Study, who begins with a long satirical address against the abuse of study and learning by the unfit. Study says that she has taught Scripture the rudiments of learning, and in due time turns over the youthful adventurer to his new master. He has now passed through trivium and quadrivium and may commence his theological studies. These studies however begin badly. The pilgrim is recalcitrant and quotes Augustine to the effect that many a poor man enters the palace of heaven with no other help than good works and a paternoster. Naturally Scripture and Clergye (learning) will have nothing to do with such a perverse pupil. Here the A text ends.

The B and C texts relate how the pilgrim, after trying the joys of a worldly life, returns at length to his old teachers, Scripture and Clergye. But he returns by no means wholly cured of his bad manners, and shortly after some reckless words (in the C text they are assigned to Recklessness, but this is merely a name which the pilgrim assumes during a reckless stage in his career) he goes off with Nature. This teacher however can give him no knowledge which aids the solution of the supreme problem, that of salvation. He now meets one Imaginatyf who recalls to him all the points in the previous debates and carefully sets him right as to the advantage of learning, the necessity of a priesthood, the danger of overemphasizing the virtues of poverty and the vanity of merely natural reason. Much rectified in heart, he now enters the house of Theological Reason, accompanied by Patience and by Conscience. Conscience is of course also a character in the *Visio*.

Here occurs some fine satire on false Doctors of Divinity with their gross habits and really superficial learning. The pilgrim sees however that the best learning has its limitations. Learning is not enough. It is necessary also to lead the life of penance, devotion and contemplation. The figure of Activa Vita appears and confesses himself unworthy and a sinner. He must purge himself by meditation. The poet passes therefore to an account of the contemplative life which begins in the despising of earthly goods and in the love of meekness and poverty. His new teacher informs him both wherein the true life of devotion consists and how basely the clergy and the religious have in the fourteenth century betrayed their duty toward that life. Thus we are introduced to the *Vita de Dobet*.

The Life of Dowel is in fact the only part of the second half of the poem difficult to follow. This difficulty is present because throughout his Life the pilgrim engages in many arguments with his teachers, showing all the restlessness of a disputatious nature. We easily infer from it how lively and contentious medieval schools of philosophy and theology as a rule became. The scholar's obstinacy accounts for the vitality of this section of the poem and totally precludes the insipidity into which an allegory of the life of learning is only too likely to fall. The relatively straightforward arguments of the *Vita de Dobet,* depicting the Christian or Contemplative Virtues, and of the *Vita de Dobest,* depicting the reception which the four active or moral virtues meet with at the hands of the Christian world, scarcely need further comment than that which they have already received in preceding paragraphs.

IV.

I have now stated as briefly as possible what I consider to be the chief organizing elements in the thought of *Piers Plowman*. But I do not wish to have it appear that I consider the poet or poets incapable at times of virtual irrelevancies, of digressions and repetitions. Certain of the repetitions, as already pointed out, arise from reduplications necessitated by the twofold division of the poem. The author evidently realized his embarrassment, for he, or his collaborators, not infrequently shifted passages about, especially in the C text, where many passages formerly in the *Vita* have been brought forward to the *Visio*. This, however, is much more confusing to the eye of the reader of Skeat's edition than to the content of the poem. It is not by these transpositions that the essential organization is bettered or defaced. The poet, however, shows throughout a fondness for certain topics that push themselves unceremoniously to the fore and break the flow of the argument. First of all we have the author's singular affection for the theme of poverty. In the *Visio* he again and again digresses from what seems his main line of argument to urge patient, honest work. In the *Vita* he may at any moment break out into the praise of poverty. This thought clearly belongs to the Prologue of the *Vita de Dobet,* which is the life of contemplation. It is not so clear that it becomes other parts of the work. In both *Vita* and *Visio* he may at any time incite his reader to pity the sufferings of the poor. Two long passages added in the C text, one in the *Vita* and one in the *Visio,* deal with this theme. The very pervasiveness of these digressions make them, to be sure, in a sense less digressive. Like a recurrent theme in music, they give a unity of tone to the work as a whole. Yet, to repeat, they do interfere with the argument of the poem and must in that respect be considered a defect.

Another characteristic of the poet is his fondness for satire, especially against the clergy. Most of this satire occurs in the *Vita*, where it has the better right to be. Yet it does not always seem logically introduced. We feel it often as an artistic fault. The poet of B.XI pleasantly confesses at least one of his sins as follows:

> This lokynge on lewed prestes hath don me lepe fram
> pouerte,
> The whiche I preyse there pacyence is more parfyt than
> richesse.

(309–310)

Another prejudice which the poet reveals in his somewhat irascible poem is disgust at lawyers. A more orderly author would presumably have found one Passus in which the law might properly have been discussed, said therein all that he had to say on the subject, and from thenceforth held his peace. Not so, however, the author or authors of *Piers Plowman*. This is something more than a merely stylistic feature. With problems of style I am, of course, not concerned in the present paper. Insofar as the intrusion of passages on poverty, ecclesiastical satire and satire upon the lawyers breaks the argument of the poem as a whole, we might conceivably deduce evidence in favor of divided authorship. Such intrusions are often artistic faults. On the other hand, the pervasive nature of these intrusions, noticeable not only in the C text, and by no means in one section of the poem more than in another, suggests a single authorship, and certainly gives unity of tone to the work when viewed in its entirety.

I have attempted in this paper to show the poem to be a really finely built structure, the nave for the people, the choir for the clergy, yet, like many a church in the Middle Ages, so crowded with tombs, rood-screens, chantries and side altars, that the total effect is a most curious blending of order and confusion. On the whole I am chiefly impressed by the order of the work, and this has I feel certain been the aspect of the poem the more slighted by its critics. However, I should not wish to deny that *Piers Plowman* is rough in certain elements of construction as well as in language. Nor do I regard the departures from logical precision to be invariably artistic defects.

2

A LITERARY ECHO OF THE
SOCIAL GOSPEL*

G. R. Owst

IN HIS LAST sketch of English Medieval Literature, the late
Professor W. P. Ker put forward what apparently he considered to be an important argument for single authorship of the
Vision of Piers Plowman and its three well-known versions. Of
"the tone of thought in the poem," he remarks:

> it is hard to believe that there were two authors in the same reign
> who had the same strong and weak points, the same inconsisten-
> cies, wavering between lively imagination and formal allegory,
> the same indignation and the same tolerance. *Piers Plowman* is
> one of the most impartial of all reformers. He makes heavy
> charges against many ranks and orders of men, but he always re-
> members the good that is to be said for them. His remedy for the
> evils of the world would be to bring the different estates—knights,
> clergy, labourers and all—to understand their proper duty. His
> political ideal is the commonwealth as it exists, only with each
> part working as it was meant to do; the king making the peace,
> with the knights to help him, the clergy studying and praying, the

* Reprinted, by permission, from G. R. Owst, *Literature and Pulpit in
Medieval England* (New York: Barnes & Noble, Inc., 1966), pp. 548–575.
The first edition of Professor Owst's book was published by the Cam-
bridge University Press in 1933; the second revised edition, reprinted by
Barnes & Noble, was published by Basil Blackwell in 1961.

commons working honestly, and the higher estates also giving work and getting wages.[1]

Now, in the course of our study of Sermon Satire and Complaint against the ruling class we had occasion to note, strangely enough, another and a kindred suggestion of uncommon impartiality of view in social matters attributed to John Wyclif by G. M. Trevelyan.[2] That view, it will be recalled, proved, when we examined it in the light of the sermons, to be false in its limited application to the Reformer, but thoroughly true and typical if applied to medieval homilists *as a whole*. The present case is precisely analogous. So far from being in any way unique, this "tone of thought" in *Piers Plowman* appears, on investigation, to be in perfect accord with that of the most commonplace orthodox preaching of the times—indeed a perfect echo in every respect of the Church's message to the world. If in his final phrase here Ker means nothing more than "getting wages" in the figurative sense of the Gospel Parable of the Husbandmen,[3] we may accept his summary forthwith as an accurate statement of Langland's constructive social gospel and proceed at once to hear what our preachers have to say upon the subject. The task should make a fitting conclusion to our studies not only of the sermons but also of the great poem itself. For we have already been led to discover in the former the sources of its "formal allegories," its "lively imagination" along with many of its characters, and more recently still of its "indignation" and its "heavy charges against many ranks and orders of men" delivered with an impressive "impartiality."[4] Varieties of

[1] *Medieval English Literature* (London, 1912), p. 200. Cf. also on this subject, E. G. W. J. Courthope, *A History of English Poetry* (London, 1895–1910), I, 227–233, 236.

[2] Cf. *Literature and Pulpit in Medieval England*, p. 289.

[3] See below, pp. 26 and 37–38.

[4] Cf. Ker above; this may also apply to the poets' "discursiveness, see *Lit. and Pulpit*," p. 89.

interpretation still continue to pour forth unabated[5] and many problems remain. But with the due establishment of this further point of indebtedness, we may surely claim that the medieval pulpit helped to fashion much of the poet's fundamental thinking. Finally, for its own sake, the social message of the pulpits deserves our closest attention. For here we exchange the more rarified yet more familiar atmosphere of the Schools, the inner chambers of eminent scholar and learned jurist, for that of the platform and the street-corner, for a political propaganda—if such it may be called—planned and broadcast for the ears of common folk.[6]

A favorite *figure* used by the preachers to set forth their political or social ideal is that of the vineyard with its three orders of husbandmen.[7] Let us listen to Master Thomas Wimbledon haranguing at Paul's Cross, the recognized national platform for public discussion of all such questions of the day,[8] in language that probably owes much to St Anselm, and certainly beyond him not a little in the first instance to the *Republic* of Plato.[9]

> For, right as ye see that in tilling of the materiall vine there ben divers labours—for some kutten awey the void branches, some maken forkis and railis to beren up the vine, and some diggen away the old earth fro the rote, and leyn there fatter; and all this offices ben so necessary to the vine that, if any of them faile, it shal harme greatly other destroy the vine; for but if the vine be kutte, she shall waxe wilde, but if she be rayled, she shall be ourgo with netles and wedis, and but if the rote be fatted with dong,

[5] Cf., for example, recent studies by T. P. Dunning, G. Hort and R. W. Frank as well as numerous articles and books listed in J. E. Wells, *Manual of Writings in Middle English* (New Haven, 1916), supplements 6–9.

[6] Those unfamiliar with the broad outlines of this doctrine in its academic (Thomist, etc.) form should consult chap. 2, Ernst Troeltsch, *Die Soziallehren der christlichen Kirchen und Gruppen* (*The Social Teachings of the Christian Church*), trans. O. Wyon (London, 1931).

[7] See, e.g., Matt. 20:1–16.

[8] Cf. *Lit. and Pulpit,* p. 586.

[9] Cf. esp. bk. ii, ff.

she for feblenes shuld wax baraine—right so in the church beth
nedeful these three offices, priesthood, knythode, and laborers. To
priesthood it falleth to kut away the void braunches of sinnes
with the swerd of her tong. To knighthode it falleth to letten
wrongs and thefftes to ben done, and to maintaine Goddis law
and them that ben techers thereof, and also to kepe the londe
from enemies of other londes. And to labourers it falleth to
travail bodelich and with their sore swete geten out of the earth
bodilech lifelode for hem and other partes. And these states beth
also nedefull to the church, that none may well ben without other.
For if priesthood lacked, the people for default of knowing of
Goddis lawe, should waxe wilde in vices, and deyen gostely: and
if the knithod laked, and men to rulin the puple by law and hardi-
nesse, theeves and enemies shulden so encres, that no man shuld
live in peace: and if the laborers were nought, both knightes and
priestes must become acre men and herdis, and els they shuld for
defaut of bodily sustenance deye. And therefore, saith clerke
Avicenne,[10] that every unreasonable best, if he have that that
kind hath ordeined for him, as kind hath ordeined it he has
suffisance to live by himselfe without any help of other of the
same kind. And if there were but one horse, other one shepe in
the world, yet if he had grasse and corne as kind hath ordeined
for such beasts, he shuld live well enow. But if there ne were
but o man in the world, though he had all that good that is
therein, yet for defaut he shuld deie, or his life shuld be wors than
if he were naught: and the cause is this, for that thing that kind
ordeineth for a mans sustenance without other arraieing than it
hath of kind accordeth nought to him. As though a man have
corne as it commeth from the earth, yet it is no meate according
to him, unto it be by mans craft chaunged into bread; and though
he have flesh other fish, yet while it is rawe as kind ordeined it,
till it be by mans travaile sodden, rosted, or baken, it corded not
to mans lifelode. And, right so, wolle that the sheepe beareth mot
by mannis divers craftis and travailes be chaunged, or it be able
to cloth any man; and certis, o man by himselfe shuld never doo
all these labours. And therefore, saith this clerke, it is neede that
some be acre men, some bakers, some makers of cloth, and some

---

[10] Avicenna is, of course, the famous Arab philosopher and physician
Ibn Sīnā (fl. 988–1037), a transmitter of the ancient Greek wisdom to
the Medieval West, notably that of Aristotle.

marchaunts to fetch that that one londe fetteth from an other, as there it is plentie.

And certis, this shuld be a cause why every state should love other; and men of o craft shuld not despise ne hate men of none other craft, sith they be so nedefull everich to other; and oft thelke crafts that ben most unhonest might worst ben forbore. And o thing I dare well say, that he that is neither travailing in this world on studieng, on praiers, on preaching for helpe of the people—as it falleth to priests, neither ruling the people, mainteining ne defending fro enemies—as it falleth to knights, neither traveling on earth in diverse craftes—as it falleth to labourers, whan the day of reckening commeth, that is, the end of this life, right as he lived here withouten travaile, so he shall there lack the reward of "the penie", that is, the endles ioie of heaven. And as he was here living after none state ne order, so he shall be put than in that place that no order is in, but everlasting horror and sorrow, that is, in hell. Herfore everich man see to what state God hath cleped him, and dwell he therein by travile according to his degree.[11] Thou that art a laborer or a crafty man, do this truelly. If thou art a servant or a bondman, be suget and lowe,
· in drede of displeasing of thy Lord. If thou art a marchaunt, disceive nought thy brother in chaffering. If thou art a knight or a lord, defend the poore man and needy fro hands that will harme them. If thou art a iustice or a iudge, go not on the right hand by favour, neither on the left hand to punish any man for hate. If thou art a priest, undernime,[12] praye, and reprove, in all maner patience and doctrine. Undernime thilke that ben negligent, pray for thilke that bene obedient, reprove tho that ben unobedient to God. So every man travaile in his degree. For whan the even his come, that is, the end of this worlde, than everye man shall take reward, good or evill, after that he hath travailed here.[13]

[11] Cf. I Cor. 7:20.
[12] = rebuke (not "instruct," as in ed. 1563: cf. 2 Tim. 4:2).
[13] Sermon at St. Paul's Cross, 1388 in *Church History of England,* Vol. *III, Pt. 1: Acts and Mons,* ed. Jos. Foxe, pp. 293–294. MS. Linc. Cath. Libr. A. 6. 2, fols. 67b–68b is another example, where the above theme of Wimbledon has been incorporated practically verbatim in a late fifteenth-century sermon of Septuagesima Sunday (*"Voca operarios et redde illis mercedem suam"*—Matt. 20:8). Cf. further, MS. Add. 41321, fol. 65 ("Upon this gospel a man miʒte touche that, riʒt as in a bodili vineʒard ben thre maner of werk-folk with diverse occupacions, so in this gosteli vineʒerd beth also the same . . ."; John Bromyard, *Summa*

Such, then, in brief is the whole Law and the Prophets in the Church's positive teaching upon the social question. The actual *figure* chosen to express it may change from the vineyard to the body and its members,[14] to the edifice of the Church with its component architectural parts,[15] or even to the animals of the farm:[16] the doctrine itself remains rigidly constant. Within the strict limits of each divinely appointed order a further elaboration of reasons and duties often follows. Thus Master Rypon in his sermon identifies the origins of knighthood and the derivation of the title, in typical fictitious manner, with the work of King Romulus at Rome: "De institutione militie dicitur in principio quarto Historie Romanorum quod, condita civitate a Romulo, quam ex nomine Roman vocavit, mille pugnatores de populo elegit, quos a numero appellavit 'milites'. Dicitur, enim, 'miles', i.e. unus ex mille; et sicut 'miles' est nomen laboris, ita est nomen honoris. . . ." After explaining, from the *Policraticus* of John of Salisbury[17] and the *De Re Militari* of Vegetius, the significance of the knightly oath and the special purport of their "election," he goes on to describe the necessary steps by which "Knights may ascend to heaven." First, there is the virtue of fortitude to be exhibited in bold and strenuous defence of Church and State. Secondly, there is justice: "that they fight

---

Predicantium (Venice, 1586), s.v. "Compassio," etc.: Robert Rypon, MS. Harl. 4894, fols. 187–188, John Myre, *Festival,* EETS, p. 65; MS. Roy. 18. B. xxiii, fol. 129.

[14] Cf. Bromyard, for example, s. v. "Caritas"; Brunton as quoted in *Lit. and Pulpit,* p. 587; Rypon in MS. Harl. 4894, fol. 189; *Pricke of Conscience,* ed. Philological Society, pp. 160–161; Michel of Northgate, *Ayenbite of Inwyt,* EETS, O.S., no. 23 (London, 1866), e.g., pp. 102, 146–149, (A.D. 1340). Cf. here the political poem "The Descryvyng of Mannes Membres" in *Twenty-six Political and other Poems,* ed. D. J. Kail, EETS, O.S. no. 124, pp. 64–66 (and Gratian's *Decretum*).

[15] Cf. Rypon, MS. Harl. 4894, fol. 188. An early example (The Three Props of the Throne) is given from the tenth-century MS. Cotton Nero A. i, fol. 72, in T. Wright, *Political Songs,* Camden Society, p. 365. See further *Lit. and Pulpit,* p. 72 (the Ship and its parts).

[16] Cf. Nicole Bozon, *Metaphysica, chap. xviii* (quoting St. Basil?).

[17] Lib. vi., chap. v, as quoted by Rypon.

in a just cause, and do no injury or insult to any man"; thirdly, prudence in action; fourthly, moderation: "not only in food, indeed, but also in a rational appetite for wealth," "that they be 'content with their wages',[18] and not plunderers and destroyers of their neighbours' goods." In honoring Holy Church, let them follow in the steps of Julius Caesar and Alexander the Great, who prohibited the spoliation of temples and spared the church.[19] Likewise the agricultural laborers, in their turn, are bidden by the same speaker to recognize their ancestry in both Adam, "the first husbandman,"[20] and his sons; their special task is "to sustain the body of the Church, by preparing and yielding up the necessities of life. Therefore their office is to labor faithfully, bravely and usefully."[21] "These moun be understonde," explains a quaint vernacularist:

> bi the lowist estaat of holi chirche, that is the comyne peple, whos ocupacions stondeth in grobbyng aboute the erthe, as in erynge and dungynge and sowynge and harwynge and other ocupacions that longeth to the erthe. And this schulde be do iustli and for a good ende, withoute feyntise or falshede or grucchynge of hire estaat. . . . ffor this was the first degree that longeth to alle men: and thus with hire tr[e]we labour thei schul bere up and susteyne the othere tweie parties of the chirche, that is knyȝtes and clerkis.[22]

The unknown author of the English version of the *Gesta Romanorum* calls them "the lewde men" that "most holde up the laame men" of Holy Church, that "have not of hire owne to lyve with."[23] There is a tendency on the part of some preach-

[18] See Luke, 3:14.

[19] MS. Harl. 4894, fols. 188b–189.

[20] Cf. MS. Glouc. Cath. Libr. Homilies as below, p. 29, n. 5: "for labour was the testament of Adam that he left to all his successorys."

[21] MS. Harl. 4894, fol. 189, et seq. (He adds: "Iste triplex modus laborandi pertinet tam ad cives quam ad agricultores.")

[22] MS. Add. 41321, fol. 65b. Cf. esp. *Piers Plowman,* B. VI., for example.

[23] EETS ed., pp. 16–17. Cf. Bromyard's defense, s.v. "Civitas," of the position that clergy should not do *manual* labor, with arguments from

ers to recognize none but the three historic orders, that have been mentioned, as the divinely instituted pillars of society. In one or other of the three categories all men must find their place, their fundamental avocation, responsibilities, privileges and general outlook. God had no room or reason for more. Thus a sermon *exemplum* of earlier date, preserved in an English manuscript of the fourteenth century along with the *Alphabetum Narrationum,* remarks significantly of the rising middle-class that God made the clergy, knights and laborers, but the Devil made the burghers and usurers.[24] Not even a conservative pulpit, however, could for long refuse a special place of honor in its discourses for those upon whose new wealth and enterprise the future greatness of kingdoms was to be built. Brunton, preaching in the heart of London amid evidences of such successful industry on every side, declares unreservedly that "merchants and faithful mechanics are the left hand" of the body politic, and "citizens and burgesses, placed as it were in the middle, are its heart."[25] So, the vernacular preacher in his turn, who has been discussing the three great traditional orders of society, finds, with Plato, a fundamental need and justification for the "merchauntes": "for to sett in one londe that is not in a-nother londe, and so for to make plenty of all maner thing in tyme of nede."[26]

Bound up with this doctrine of the body politic, it will be seen, are certain important corollaries which receive their due emphasis in the social gospel of the times. First, there is the doctrine of work for all. The preachers' ideal state provides no

Greek and Roman authors (". . . Ista sunt contra illos qui improperant religiosis viris et ecclesiasticis, quod non prosunt reipublicae, quia non laborant manualiter. Sed illi tamen, si boni sunt, plus prosunt consulendo, docendo, orando. Unde Seneca").

[24] MS. Harl. 268, fol. 29. The same idea is expressed in a vernacular poem, *Von Wuocher,* by the early thirteenth-century German didactic poet Freidank (see *Deutsche Nat.-Litteratur,* Bd. ix [Didaktik], p. 275).

[25] As quoted in *Lit. and Pulpit,* p. 587.

[26] MS. Linc. Cath. Libr. A., 6. 2, fol. 69. Similarly, Wimbledon, as above, p. 28.

place for the indolent. Says our representative Dominican upon this point:

> God has ordained three classes of men, namely, labourers such as husbandmen and craftsmen to support the whole body of the Church after the manner of feet, knights to defend it in the fashion of hands, clergy to rule and lead it after the manner of eyes. And all the aforesaid who maintain their own status are of the family of God. The Devil, however, finds a certain class, namely, the slothful, who belong to no Order. They neither labour with the rustics, nor travel about with the merchants, nor fight with the knights, nor pray and chant with the clergy. Therefore they shall go with their own Abbot, of whose Order they are, namely, the Devil, where no Order exists but horror eternal.[27]

Again, reference is made to the learned Avicenna on this point. For he argues that the man who has no laudable status in the community and obeys no master is useless to it, forfeits his birthright therein and should be expelled from it for his sloth and idleness. "If Saracens have made such ordinances in their States," exclaims the Dominican, "how much more should Christians do the same!"[28] Pulpit use of the word *labor* is apt to be ambiguous: sometimes it clearly refers to *manual* labor alone.[29] But English homilists alike of the twelfth and the fifteenth centuries leave us in no doubt that Adam's curse lies heavy upon us all: *"In sudore valtus tui vesceris pane tuo."*[30] "So did he first, and we all do so after. Every man in his way uses such labour as he is tied to: the cleric after his mode, the knight in his way, the husbandman in his, and such practice of

---

[27] S.v. "Accidia." Similarly Wimbledon, as quoted above, p. 26, and cf. further John of Mirfield, *Florarium Bartholomei,* s.v. "De Labore Manuum," MS. Camb. Univ. Libr. Mm. ii. 10, fol. 99b (". . . Et ita omnes clerici ad operandum validi artificiosa et literas discant . . .").

[28] S.v. "Civitas."

[29] Cf. below, p. 46.

[30] Gen. 3:19 (as quoted here: cf. also *Piers Plowman,* e.g., A. VII, 219–220.

each craft as he is tied to."[31] "For this ye may understonde that hit ys the wylle of Gode that every man and woman schuld labour besyly. For yf Adam and Eve had ben occupyed wyth labour, the serpent had not overcum them: for ydulnesse ys the devylles dyssyr. Wherfor ye may know well yt ys the wylle of Gode that we schuld labour and put our body to penaunce for to fle synne. Thus dyd Adam and Eve, to example of all tho that schuld come after them."[32] But human toil, though so unpleasant in its origins, might yet prove a blessing in disguise for the sons of Adam. In the preachers' eyes it had a salutary value in itself, even apart from the immediate spiritual condition of the toiler. "Per viam laboris pervenit ad mercedem consolationis."[33] For the reprobate, indeed, it might be considered the first step on the road to spiritual reclamation. "But natheles, thouӡ werkes doon in dedli synne profiteth noӡt to encrecyng of blisse, ӡeet thei profiten to thre thynges: oon is that the worldli goodes of suche men schul encrece the more; another is that thei schullen the sunnere have grace to arise ouӡt of here synne; another is, if thei schul be dampned, hire peyne schal be the lesse. And therfore it is good evere to wirche wel."[34] "For nothing in this life," says Bozon, "is worth so much for body and soul as well-ordered work. As to which Holy Scripture describes work in this fashion: 'Work is the life of man and keeper of health. Work drives away occasion for sin, and makes a man rest himself, is the relief of languor, a stay to illness, safety of the people, sharpener of all the senses, step-

[31] *Old English Homilies of the Twelfth Century* 2nd Ser., EETS, O.S., no. 53, p. 181. Cf. *Speculum Laicorum* (13th cent.), chap. xlvii, ed. Welter, p. 69. "Laborant homines tripliciter: quidam vero laborant circa spiritualia . . . , quidam laborant circa temporalia ut habeant quibus se et suos sustineant, sicut boni activi . . . , quidam laborant circa delenda vicia, ut peddata puniant . . ."; Bromyard, for example, s.v. "Labor" (14th cent.).

[32] MS. Glouc. Cath. Libr. *Sermo de doctrina in Septuag.* (15th cent.).

[33] Bromyard, s.v. "Beatitudo." Cf. further, *Ayenb. of Inwyt,* p. 206.

[34] MS. Add. 41321, fols. 10b–11.

mother to idleness, duty to the young and merit to the old.'
Hence he who would give up the joy of everlasting life takes
care, says Scripture, that he does not work at all in this life.
Wherefore it is better to be an ass than a pig" (as in the following fable).[35] Finally, when the ordinary day's work is over, there
is no need or right for any to be idle, for there are yet "mery-
tory werkes" to be done, "and thu wilte be perfite in the
feyȝth."[36] While the rich man sets about his various deeds of
mercy, even laborers are expected by Rypon—in the words
of "Wallensis"[37]—"to pay their tithes and offerings to the
Church, and do alms so far as they can."[38] When, in his turn,
the Lollard preacher, driven to denounce the supposed merits
of pilgrimaging, reminds his hearers of "the trewe labour that
thei shulden do at home in help of hemsilf and hore neȝeboris"
in place of all such idle tasks,[39] we ourselves are reminded of
the honored place which work has continued to hold in Protestant faith and practice. Its subsequent achievements, alike in
science and industry, art and philanthropy, when "meritory
works" were finally discountenanced, prove once again our
kinship with the past. The gulf of the Reformation is thus
bridged once more,[40] and the spiritual continuity of our history
maintained in the face of all such inevitable changes. Mean-

[35] Bozon, *Metaphs.*, chap. cxxi. The references to Scripture are erroneous.

[36] MS. Roy. 18, B. xxiii, fol. 97b ("good werkes"). Cf. *Gesta Romanorum* Engl. version, pp. 249, 305; Bromyard, s.v. "Caritas." The typical
list—clothing the naked, feeding the hungry, visiting the sick and im-
prisoned, harboring the stranger, burying the dead—appears, e.g., in
MS. Harl. 2398, fols. 24–26, including in addition "makynge of churches
and of brigges and causyes and amendment of perilous weyes in savyng
of mennes lyves and eke of bestes."

[37] I.e. John Walleys, or Wallis, S.T.D. Franciscan (fl. 1260).

[38] MS. Harl. 4894, fol. 189. It is interesting to observe that s.v. "Intentio," Bromyard reckons manual labor as "sometimes" worthy of a
place among Good Works meritory of Eternal Life.

[39] MS. Add. 24202, fol. 27b (cf. further, fol. 28b).

[40] See my *Preaching in Medieval England* (Cambridge, Eng., 1926), p.
280.

while, students familiar with the poem of *Piers Plowman* will not fail to recognize the profound influence of this medieval doctrine upon the poet's Vision.[41]

> Treuthe herde telle her-of · and to Peres he sent
> To taken his teme · and tulyen the erthe,
> And purchaced hym a pardoun · *a pena et a culpa*
> For hym and for his heires · for euermore after.
> And bad hym holde hym at home · and eryen his leyes;
> And alle that halpe hym to erie · to sette or to sowe
> Or any other myster · that miȝte Pieres availle,
> Pardoun with Pieres plowman · treuthe hath ygraunted.
>
> (B. VII. 1–8)

.   .   .   .   .   .

> For-thi I conseille alle Cristene · to crye God mercy,
> And Marie his moder · be owre mene bitwene,
> That God gyve s grace here · ar we gone hennes,
> Suche werkes to werche · while we ben here,
> That after owre deth-day · Dowel reherce,
> At the day of dome · we dede as he hiȝte.
>
> (B. VII. 195–200)

From the doctrine which we have just considered it follows naturally that each man's first duty—be he knight or priest, workman or merchant—is to learn and labor truly in the things of his own particular calling, resting content therewith[42] and not aspiring to meddle with the tasks and mysteries of others. The social ranks and their respective duties, ordained by God for humanity, were intended to remain fixed and immutable. Like the limbs of the Body they cannot properly exchange either their place or function. "Some folk are good for one function, others for others."[43] We have, indeed, seen already how Master Wimbledon bases upon the command of St Paul:—"Let each man abide in the same calling wherein he was called"—a doc-

---

[41] Cf. esp. A. VII and VIII and the equivalent in the other versions.
[42] Cf. *Lit. and Pulpit,* e.g., pp. 314, 353, 370.
[43] Bozon, chap. xviii.

trine of social distinctions and barriers of this kind.[44] In the *Summa Predicantium* a pleasing *figure* is used to emphasize the same argument. Here Bromyard compares society to a delicately-stringed harp.

> The order of these various ranks in the community ought to be like the position of the strings upon the harp. Here it is essential for the purpose of good melody that each string should keep to its own place, the shorter in their appropriate place, those of medium length in the middle, and the taller in their own part of the instrument. So, in any community each man ought to keep to his own station—the lower in working and obeying, those who are called "ministers", the lawyers and the churchmen, in consulting, praying and speaking, the rulers in ruling and protecting, whose office is like to that of the harpist.

As long as the proper position and touch of the strings is observed, so long will the community give forth a sweet melody. As soon as the strings are disarranged, the melody jars, and the State or community and its internal peace are rudely confounded. Such is the case "when he who is unworthy in respect of manners, knowledge and wisdom is set in high position through favour, bribery or inordinate love. Behold the string out of its place which destroys the whole melody! Likewise, conversely, when he who for the merit of good life and learning should be set in high position is thrust down. . . ."[45] The prime task of every individual in the State is well set forth for us in the warnings of a vernacular sermon:

> And so it were ryght fittyng that every man hold hym content to common maters of ys faculte, polocy and governaunce. So that

---

[44] See I Cor. 7:20 and above, p. 26. Cf. here the recent interesting correspondence in *The Times* by Mr. H. A. L. Fisher and others over the statement in the Prayer-Book *Catechism* concerning "that state of life unto which it shall please God to call me." The present author suggested in the course of it, in the same columns (Aug. 11, 1928), that here the influence of this pre-Reformation social doctrine is still clearly traceable, in the sense in which Mr. Fisher interprets the above phrase.

[45] S.v. "Civitas."

kynthes and other gentils with hem shuld sett her besines abowte the good governaunce in the temporalltee in the tyme of pees, and also abowte duds [and] poyntes of armes in the tyme of werre, as the lawe and the cronicle techeth hem. For ther beth many sotell questions and conclusions in mater of warre and armes, as the phylo[so]fre declareth, *de Re Militari.* . . .[46] Prestes shuld principally entermet[47] to lerne the lawe of Criste and lawfully to teche itt; and lower men shuld hold hem contente with here own occupacions, and not entremet farther than reson and lawe rewels to hem.[48]

Speaking of the social order beyond the grave, in terms of the Chessmen "when thei be put up in the poket" at the end of the game, our English *Gesta Romanorum* remarks consolingly: "Therefor let us not change of oure estatis," for "then hit is no charge who be above or who be byneth!"[49]

Class duties and class distinctions, however, do not exhaust between them all the important consequences which flow from this doctrine of the medieval pulpits. If the work and status of rulers and ruled, students and toilers, learned and "lewd" could never be confused or intermingled without harm to the Body Politic, at the same time it is equally true that all were designed for a common purpose. The members were differentiated, as we have already seen, the better to supply the needs of the one body of which they formed part: "And if we had no laborers, then prestes and knyȝtes muste nedes labor themselffe [i.e., of course, *manualiter*]; and thei can not. And if that thei dyd labor, thei scholde peressche in a lityll tyme for defawte of sustynaunce."[50] The various types of husbandmen were all busy about the same vineyard. That is, each, by doing

[46] I.e. Vegetius. The preacher here may have in mind the case of Sir John Oldcastle, as in Hoccleve's *Poem* addressed to the Lollard knight, advocating similarly the reading of "Vegece, of the aart of Chivalrie" (*Minor Poems,* EETS, Extr. S., no. 61, p. 14, st. 25).

[47] = meddle, interpose.

[48] MS. Roy. 18, B. xxiii, fol. 129.

[49] EETS, p. 71. Cf. Bromyard, s.v. "mundus."

[50] MS. Linc. Cath. Libr. A. 6. 2, fol. 68b.

his own work faithfully was serving a supreme common good. Hence it follows that, although no single individual was to take upon himself the special work and concerns that belonged to another station, yet each and all were to be ever conscious of their relations to the whole and to one another in unity of spirit and disinterested service. Society, therefore, must be continually made to realize its corporate nature. "For," as Master Rypon observes, "the unity of the State exists not merely in its houses or its streets, but, as all the philosophers testify, in the agreement of its minds. Even among infidels it is so; therefore so much the more should it be among the faithful."[51] To convey this vital truth to the popular mind in an arresting way, the preachers make use of very varying imagery. Thus Bozon, for example, points to the habits of stags when seeking pasture across a stretch of sea. "Each of them puts his head on the other's rump," he says, "with the strong in front. When the leader weakened by toil withdraws, another puts himself in front; and so each is aided by the other. So ought it to be with us who are passing this perilous sea. . . . Each ought to aid and support the other, as the apostle Paul teaches us, 'forbearing one another in love.' "[52] Bromyard, for his part, points to the mail hauberk, "in which all the rings are linked together and give mutual support. . . . With the snapping of a single ring, danger threatens the whole of the body, when its wearer is attacked. . . . Wherefore, as mutual concatenation is essential for the protection of the outward man, so mutual support and fellowship are essential in universal human society."[53] It is this same fundamental idea which comes to the rescue, when our preachers have to wrestle with the age-long problem of riches and poverty. "The rich and the poor", argues Bishop Brunton, drawing upon a homily of Augustine:

[51] MS. Harl. 4894, fol. 182.
[52] *Metaphs.*, chap. xxxviii (Isidore).
[53] S.v. "Justitia." Cf. further, s.v. "Compassio"; and *Spec. Laic.* Chap. xiv (sheep; stars; cranes).

although they may appear contrary, are nevertheless very necessary to each other. For, if all men were poor, there would be none to support the other. If all were rich, then no one would work; and so the world would at once decay. Therefore the rich man has been created for the benefit of the poor, and the poor man for the benefit of the rich. . . . Catholic doctors are in agreement upon that saying of the Gospel—"the poor ye have always with you",[54] etc., where they set forth the reasons why God has allowed the poor to remain amongst us, when nevertheless he is able to provide sufficient for all. First, because, just as a mother provides enough for her child when she gives sufficient to the nurse whence she can nourish both herself and the infant, so the Lord provides enough for the poor while so much is bestowed on the rich whence they can supply food and drink to themselves and the poor also. . . . Secondly, the poor are allowed to exist in order that God may test the love of the rich. . . . Therefore He has willed that the poor should be in want, so that by this means He might prove what rich men are His friends and what His enemies. Thirdly, to increase the merit of the poor. . . .[55]

If we turn now to the sermons of Master Ralph of Acton, we find precisely the same argument employed upon a wider scale:

When God could have made all men strong, wise and rich, He was unwilling to do so. He wished instead that these men should be strong, those weak; these wise, those foolish; these rich and those poor. For if all were strong, wise and wealthy, one would not be in need of the other. Again, if all were feeble, foolish and poor, one would not be able to help the other. Therefore He willed these men to be strong and healthy, wise or rich, that they might save their own souls by helping others through love of them: those others He willed to be weak or foolish or in want, that they might save their own souls by enduring hardship in patience.[56] Hence God says—"The poor ye have always with you". . . .[57]

While Brunton points out, as the natural sequel to his argu-

---

[54] E.g., Matt. 26:11.

[55] MS. Harl. 3760, fol. 111b et seq.

[56] See further *Lit. and Pulpit*, pp. 296–297.

[57] MS. John Rylands Library, Manchester, Lat. 367, fol. 4.

ment, that "the rich man's duty is to dispense,[58] the poor man's
to pray, inasmuch as he is obliged to pray for the rich as soon
as he has received alms from him," so Bromyard, in his turn,
declares that the rich have been deputed by God to be the pro-
tectors of the poor, as the tutor is for the pupil, because they
live from the labors of the poor. For this guardianship they
receive payment from God in the shape of townships, estates
and rents. Thus, their subjects are bound to toil and serve them
faithfully, while they themselves bestow honest government and
payment for these services.[59] The rich, the wise and the strong
are to aid the poor, the foolish and the weak, the first with his
gifts, the second with his information, the third with his protection.[60] Once again, the parallel with Langland's doctrine in the
Vision is manifest and illuminating.[61] Says the author of the
Pricke of Conscience in the same strain:

> Ful many men lyfes here of tha
> That er halden for to do swa:
> Als he that gret and myghty es
> Es halden to defende tham that er les;
> And the ryche that mykel rychesces has,
> To gyf tham that here in povert gas;
> And men of laghe alswa to travayle
> And to counsaile tham that askes counsayle;
> And leches alswa, if thai wyse ware,
> To hele tham that er seke and sare;

[58] The reader who desires to make acquaintance with the patristic and
later sources of this typical teaching may here be directed to an essay by
A. J. Carlyle, on "The Theory of Property in Med. Theology," in *Property, its Duties and Rights* (New York, 1913), pp. 119–132, with important references, in connection with the above, to the works of
Ambrose, Augustine and Aquinas, and the *Opusculum* of Peter Damian.
Cf. further in our English homiletic literature, e.g., *Gesta Rom.*, Engl.
version, EETS, p. 353 ("What is than for to do riche men? . . . Forsothe,
that thei divide her temporall goodes to poore men, as it is written—
'yeve almesse' . . .").
[59] Bromyard, s.v. "Furtum."
[60] S.v. "Justitia." Cf. for example, *Ayenb. of Inwyt*, pp. 145–149.
[61] I.e., notably, A. VII and VIII.

38

And maysters of thair science to ken
Namly, tham that er unlered men;
And precheours Goddes worde to preche
And the way of lyfe other to teche.
Thus es ilk man halden with gude intent
To help other of that God has tham lent
Frely for goddes luf, and for noght elles.[62]

From such an ideal, then, implanted by the medieval pulpit, however naive and unsatisfying, have sprung in subsequent centuries the finest traditions of English manorial life, now alas! wellnigh perished from the countryside. The preachers' vision of the ideal Christian commonwealth is that of a battleline "constipata et compensata," in which no gap appears but all stand shoulder to shoulder in a common love to God and to their fellows. For such was to be the bond between class and class. "And sothely this is the cawse that every man schold love other, for none of hem may be sparyd from other. And that crafte peraventure that semyth moste dishoneste[63] may the worste be sparyd."[64] As members of the one body, or as rays proceeding from the one sun, so each one benefits by his neighbor's good, "just as in a merchants' company, where, when one makes profit, all profit, and when one loses, all lose." "If," on the other hand, "love be wanting through the evil of discord, a gap yawns in the ranks."[65] Here the actual world facing our homilist compared all too ill with his ideal. "A division of parties and of hearts" had brought back the ancient curse of the builders of Babel[66]—ruin and infidelity. In the first place, local feeling and a growing spirit of national self-consciousness drove those whom Bromyard calls "citizens of the Devil's State" to "divide others from them on the score of country, race or language, provoking them in an attitude of wrath and tumult,

[62] Philological Society edition, pp. 160–161.
[63] I.e., least respectable.
[64] MS. Linc. Cath. Libr. A. 6. 2, fol. 69. Similarly, above, p. 26.
[65] Bromyard, s.v. "Civitas," as before.
[66] See Gen 11:1–9.

saying—'You are a Northerner', 'You are a Southerner', or 'you are of such and such a nation', after the manner of that cursed maid of the guest-house who cried out at Peter, saying— "Thou are a Galilean, for thy speech agreeth thereto.' "[67] Thus do they rend the Body of Christ limb from limb, contrary to that saying of Scripture: "There is no difference between Jew and Greek."[68] Secondly, as we have seen, of the several classes within the nation "ich on now-a-daies is besy to accuse other in exscusyng of hemselfe."[69] Amongst these citizens of the modern Babylon, "the dividing-up of tongues" spelt a dividing-up of affections, and that in its turn "is cause of all ruin and impoverishment, in that one man does not help the other, as the members in the body. . . . Thus in that Devil's State this division is the beginning of wars and distresses. . . ."[70]

> ffor we bid and preye iche day in holy churche—all maner of prestes and other men also—for to have pees. But the more harme is, we have evermore strives and debates, iche man wel nye with other, that there is no pees in herte. For no man loveth other. And outwardly we may knowe all that we ben in warre aʒeyns many londes on iche syde, and thei aʒeyns us.[71]

Everywhere, indeed, the world seemed torn by the hatred and envy which Master Rypon, like his fellows, declares to be the chief destruction of States.[72] The harp-strings were disordered;

---

[67] Mark 14:69–70.

[68] Rom. 10:12 (Bromyard here, s.v. "Civitas," also emphasizes the hostility between townsmen and rustics. The former love to deceive the latter in their simplicities with false oaths, weights, measures and the like, when they come to market.) With the above, contrast the nationalistic type of preaching, as indicated in *Lit. and Pulpit,* pp. 225 ff.

[69] MS. Roy. 18. B. xxiii, fol. 167. See further *Lit. and Pulpit,* p. 272.

[70] S.P. "Civitas," as before. Cf. further here: "Vice . . . contradictionem cordium, quia nullus alium diligit; vel linguarum, scil., inter advocatos et legistas; et inter nationes diversarum plagarum vel operum, quia quilibet nititur alium deprimere, et specialiter adventantes et pauperes qui vellent inter eos vivere."

[71] MS. Roy. 18. B. xxiii, fol. 65.

[72] MS. Harl. 4894, fol. 182. Cf. further *Lit. and Pulpit,* pp. 452–460.

the harpists would not play correctly according to the rules of their art:[73] all was disharmony.

Unable to read aright many of the deeper signs of the times, the preachers strove nevertheless, not without real spiritual discernment within their limited sphere, to probe this evil to its roots and to rescue the community from imminent peril of disintegration. The social system itself was sound enough. No other was conceivable to them. Why, then, did its component parts refuse to function properly: why this current lack of charity, this disunity, this conflict? The answer must lie in the state of unregenerate human nature. Deadly sin, sins in the individuals who composed, like so many cells, the various limbs of the body, engendered of worldliness, was the true explanation. Hence the volume of pulpit satire and rebuke that has engaged so much of our attention. In a sermon on the very theme— *"Quomodo stabit regnum?,"*[74] one of our homilists insists, with profound truthfulness, that all sin has a social and national as well as a merely individual significance. Says he: "Each sinner in the realm is making for the destruction of that realm in part or in whole." Take the gluttons for example. They work not only for their own undoing, but for that of the needy also,

[73] In illustration of this (cf. above, p. 34), Bromyard says:: "sicut patet quando illa [chorda] quae debet tangi non tangitur, et alia ultra vires tangitur. Ita quaecumque communitas modo confunditur ex hoc— quod malefactores non 'tanguntur' nec puniuntur. . . . [In the State] Latrones, homicidae et hujus modi propter sanguinis nobilitatem vel propter munera a suspendio liberantur. Duodecim enim latrones [i.e. jurors] liberant coram judice tredecimum. Ecce, chorda quae deberet tangi non tangitur, et hoc propter munerum perceptores! Et haec est causa quare tot sunt latrones et homicidae; quia in terra, ubi non est justicia, multiplicabuntur latrones et homicidae." Likewise in the Church, the "robbers of God" escape, lechers, adulterers, etc.—"quia citharedi ecclesiastici eos non tangunt sicut deberent, sed accipiunt munera, vel vident lupum et timent." Finally—"iterum pax in ista cythara impeditur ex hoc —quod una chorda plus stringitur et durius tangitur quam deberet," i.e. the poor ("chorda parva"): "Unus pauper modicum delinquens in curia mundi graviter et ultra justiciam amerciabitur . . ."; etc.

[74] Matt. 12:26.

for whom they ought to provide sustenance. "The proud, too, in our midst, threaten destruction to our realm, because he who is proud desires to have no superior or equal, and so, as far as in him lies, destroys all his superiors and equals."[75] Most patent of all is the insatiable avarice of the age. Upon this current selfishness John Bromyard remarks significantly that, unlike the old Roman days, the rule of life now is each one for himself: "Sed moderno tempore circa honorem et commodum proprium quasi tota utatur intentio."[76] For the rest, he sees the evil influence of the vicious spreading rapidly, where men are always prone to copy the worst in others. The World, the Flesh and the Devil had the mastery over them. Thus, our body and its limbs are torn asunder; and the ideal society fashioned by God himself, according to His good will and purpose, is about to perish through human wickedness. Such, then, is the message not of our sermons alone, but also of the "faire felde ful of folke" less fair than their surroundings, to which Langland introduces us at the outset of his famous Dream. It is the same company again, so we read, that faces Reasoun, when he goes arrayed "alle the reume to preche," bidding them turn from their evil ways to that particular work and service for the community which Heaven had ordained for them (A. v. 9–42). In no other direction might men arrive at the Truth—in things political or personal.

But finally, there is one further question to settle. Can we find in this sermon-literature any traces whatever of Piers Plowman himself? In an important chapter of his learned work on *The Medieval Village,* G. G. Coulton, discussing "Church Estimates of the Peasant" on the European scale, has delivered a verdict which will seem at the outset to discourage any answer in the affirmative. On the other hand, our own researches in the English section of this field have already proved beyond doubt that there is still very much to be said for the opposing

[75] MS. Camb. Univ. Libr. II. iii. 8, fol. 149b. Cf. *Ayenb. of Inwyt,* p. 102; and *Lit. and Pulpit,* in chaps. vi and vii, passim.
[76] S.v. "Civitas," as before.

view of Guérard and Delisle that the voice of the preachers "was a continual appeal to the emancipation of the people,"[77] so far, at all events, as medieval England is concerned. The passionate sympathy of John Bromyard, for example, some of whose language Coulton himself has recognized as an inheritance from Jacques de Vitry,[78] needs always to be set alongside the somewhat severer strictures of other friars like Berthold of Regensburg and Alvarus Pelagius. Similarly, we have seen that "the theoretical Socialism" of Gower is no poet's fancy, but a regular part of the social message of the pulpit:[79] likewise, again, its praise for the virtues of honest toil, of which more will be said later.[80] No one who has any real knowledge of the subject matter will be inclined to question either the validity of Coulton's actual sources or his own unrivalled mastery in the European field. But there is a further important question of the kind of conclusions which we are entitled to draw from such evidence as he produces, of where, in the midst of so much apparently conflicting sentiment, the final emphasis should be laid. Here there is certainly room for some difference of opinion. On the strength of it, the present writer is compelled at this point to put forward two criticisms in the light of what has gone before. First, we may ask—is Coulton really justified in making so radical a contrast between what he appears to consider the lip service of "egalitarian rhetoric" and the innate "class-snobbery" or aristocratic prejudices of these same clergy? We think not. Once again our learned author, as in a previous case which we discussed of clerical relations to art,[81] seems to have discovered a definite confusion of mind as well as an insincerity of speech in the Church's attitude, where none really

---

[77] See here G. G. Coulton, *Medieval Village* (New York, 1960,) pp. 231, 238, and cf. *Lit. and Pulpit,* pp. 287–307.

[78] Cf. ibid., p. 20.

[79] See *Lit. and Pulpit*, p. 292.

[80] See above, pp. 29–33 and below, pp. 45–47 (and cf. Coulton, pp. 233 ff.

[81] See *Lit. and Pulpit,* p. 49, n. 5.

exists. A backward glance at the arguments of the present chapter should be sufficient to show that, however fundamentally gratuitous you please, there is nothing contradictory or illogical about her belief, stated again and again in expository literature, that, while in origins and at death all men are equal, during their career on earth God has chosen to ordain for them a graded "class"-system with varying privileges and duties.[82] Secondly, it is of the greatest importance to observe that most of the strictures and rebukes which Coulton has quoted come from that part of a literature which is devoted exclusively to the task of moral *correction*. The same fact, of course, has a vital bearing on the censure of clerical vices. It is not merely a part of the business, it is the whole business of these moralists here to expose the various follies of the community, to criticize those whose moral welfare is thus at stake. They are not at the moment concerned with the distribution of praise. Thus, we ourselves have had occasion to note how the English peasant and laborer receive in their due turn that homiletic chastisement which falls without fear or favor upon every rank of society throughout Christendom.[83] None escapes that fate. "Omnes enim peccaverunt, et egent gloria Dei." So far, then, the peasant is in no way different from anybody else. We do gain from these indictments, it is true, much valuable information concerning the specific sins of the various classes. But it is unreasonable to expect to derive therefrom any direct comparative moral estimate of the classes as a whole, even where fervid oratory has cooled and solidified upon the manuscript page. These catalogues of vices, after all, are not carefully balanced statistical tables from which we can reckon up, as it were, in modern currency, from the respective amounts of accusation allotted to each group in the literature concerned, the debit or credit balance of a spiritual account.[84] Where, however, in the

[82] Cf. *Lit. and Pulpit,* e.g., pp. 292 ff., 528.

[83] Cf. *Lit. and Pulpit,* p. 361.

[84] Although I uttered this warning in my first volume (cf. p. 190), some of my reviewers appeared to be unaware of it.

present writer's judgment, it is possible to get a more accurate knowledge of the Church's current estimate is in the preacher's less conventional remarks, the frank comments and confessions scattered here and there in the body of his narrative, some casual observation made in the course of an independent argument, or, better still, on that yet rarer occasion when the speaker himself ventures on a comparative class-estimate of his own.[85] Above all, we may learn much from any favorable comments which he may be willing to pass. Does our preacher ever bestow, we ask, some rare word of praise upon clergy or knights, merchants or laborers, and what is the comparative extent of his appreciations? Here, indeed, as we shall see, is a most significant test for "Church estimates of the peasant" in medieval England.

With the way thus cleared for fresh consideration of our problem, let us first return for a moment to the doctrine of work in the sermons. "England," says the Dutch historian Huizinga of Leyden "gave towards the end of the fourteenth century, the first expression to the sentiment of the sanctity of productive labour in that strangely fantastic and touching poem *The Vision of William concerning Piers Plowman*."[86] S. Huizinga's lack of acquaintance here with medieval homiletic literature is no more extraordinary than that of the other scholars whom it has been our task modestly to combat, for the honor of the pulpit. But in this case his error is the less pardonable in that, more than forty years ago, that learned French *savant* Paul Meyer took the trouble to draw our attention to "the Canonization of Hard Work" in the sermon-stories of Nicole Bozon.[87] More recently, a fellow-countryman, Emile Mâle, in connection with his study of the illustrative calendars of the Middle Ages, has pointed to the thirteenth-century *Speculum Doctrinale* of Vincent of Beauvais[88] as an important source of the same idea, for art as well

[85] Cf. *Preaching in Med. Engl.* p. 130, n. 3; and *Lit. and Pulpit*, pp. 259–260, 268.
[86] *The Waning of the Middle Ages*, trans. (London, 1924), p. 162.
[87] *Les Contes Moral, de N. B.*, p. xxvii.
[88] Pars I, Chap. IX.

as for letters.[89] This "Beatification of Manual Labour," as Mâle styles it, though not so clearly expressed, is none the less in keeping with the place of honor accorded to the *"boni activi"*— between the Contemplatives and the Destroyers of Vices—in our English *Speculum Laicorum*.[90] The *Summa Predicantium* accords a similar place of honor to the "craftsman, whoever he be, who ceases not to labour in lawful pursuits."[91] Other homilists, like Master Ralph of Acton, again leave us in no doubt as to the kind of humble labor which is thus worthy to be "canonized": "Labour of the hands confers four benefits. It destroys vices, it nourishes virtues, it provides necessaries, it gives alms."[92] There seems to be no place in our sermons for the sneers of a William of Auvergne at *servilia opera*.[93] Clearly, then, the doctrine of Langland in this respect is no innovation, but a re-emphasis of the doctrines of the pulpit. But what now of the honest toiling poor themselves? The very phrases of the preachers already quoted spring at once to the mind, eloquent of much: "simple working folk, . . . the righteous poor,"[94] "patientes pauperes,"[95] "fideles simplices,"[96] "the trewe pore peple,"[97] "goddes knyghtes," proved by "angres, tribulaciouns and woo."[98] In a manuscript of

[89] *Religious Art in France in the Thirteenth Century* (London, 1913), pp. 64–65.

[90] See above, p. 31, n. 31.

[91] S.v. "Labor." Here, at the end of a list of those who labor well, with merit and subsequent reward (see § 4, etc.).

[92] MS. Jo. Rylands Libr. Manch. Lat. 367, fol. 190b. Cf. further, e.g., Jo. of Mirfield, *Flor. Barthol,* s.v. "De Labore Manuum," MS. Camb. Univ. Libr. Mm. ii. 10, fol. 98b, et seq. (Manual labor shields men from temptation, from sloth, and from vain and idle thoughts, etc.)

[93] See Coulton, pp. 233–234.

[94] Bozon, *Metaphs.* Chap. xxiv (as in *Lit. and Pulpit,* p. 299).

[95] Brunton, MS. Harl. 3760, fol. 111b (as in *Lit. and Pulpit,* p. 296).

[96] Bromyard, s.v. "Ministratio" (as in *Lit. and Pulpit,* p. 206); s.v. "Passio Christi" (as below, p. 50); etc.

[97] MS. Roy. 18. B. xxiii, fol. 142 (as in *Lit and Pulpit,* p. 69).

[98] MS. Harl. 45, fol. 80 ("for a worldliche knyght may never be proved, til he have be assayed by bataile and werre").

the fifteenth century in the *Bibliothèque Nationale*,[99] there is a miniature—assuredly the very negation of what we find in Coulton's *Medieval Village*—setting forth for us pictorially and in retrospect, as it were, in the most vivid fashion, one influence at work in the history of our pulpit which helped materially to determine the preachers' attitude to the humble toiler. On one side of the picture, there stands a feudal castle upon a hill, on the other a cottage with gaping roof. A path leads down from the former to the latter. In the foreground we behold four kneeling figures on the greensward: two are those of a peasant and his wife, presumably from the cottage adjoining. Both are clad in ragged garments: the woman, carrying a distaff, suckles an infant at her breast, while at her husband's side lies his own instrument of toil, the spade. Facing the peasant is a Franciscan friar, his book on the ground before him, emblem of his faithful spiritual labors. Beside him is a fellow Dominican. The eyes of the Greyfriar and the peasants are raised to heaven, where, in a parting of the clouds, the figure of God the Father appears, clothed with the symbols of that Majesty which will one day ensure that justice is done upon His righteous poor. The woman's hands are busy with her child, but the hands of the other two are raised in prayer and supplication. Meanwhile, the Friar Preacher, himself in a tunic full of holes, directs the attention of two ill-clad beggars to the same heavenly vision. It is a picture of the perfect union of Holy Poverty and Beatified Labor, Secular and Religious together, Active and Contemplative, peasant and preacher. Now our miniature may well be a full century later than Langland's own masterpiece while, in the latter, already the corrupted and avaricious Mendicants and the faithful ploughman are many leagues asunder. Nevertheless, the fact remains that in the earlier days of Mendicant zeal, the poverty and sufferings which such

[99] MS. franç. 9608, fol. 11b: reproduced in E. Mâle, *L'Art. relig. de la fin du moyen âge en France*, (Paris, 1908) p. 308. Mâle's accompanying description does not quite bring out the full significance of the scene, as will be recognized by the account following above.

layfolk endured in a spirit of patience and meekness did link them with those, whom Bozon calls "the folk that have put themselves into poor Religion for God," in bonds of sympathy and a common hope which no mere stern necessity of rebuking sin would weaken. Even when, at length, the Orders themselves to a large extent had degenerated, and in losing touch with the poorer masses now incurred the rebuke of their own faithful preachers,[100] we still hear expressed, as on the lips of Bozon and Bromyard, not merely that same sympathy with the righteous laborer's lot, but also a very definite belief that of such is the Kingdom of Heaven.

With the French miniature still in mind, then, we turn to the pulpit orators of England. Once again let it be emphasized that, in keeping with the special character of their task, the actual references in their sermons to the virtues of the laboring poor are as few in number as their denunciations of the oppressors are many. Albeit, the references are there. Of the virtues of other classes we hear hardly a word. If we begin, early in the thirteenth century, with the Cistercian Odo of Cheriton, for example, we find that important link between the religious and the secular poor man to which allusion has just been made. In a sermon on the theme of Dives and Lazarus,[101] attacking the vices of the rich, Odo quotes a significant passage from St Ambrose: "The poor man in his hut, wealthy in conscience, sleeps safer upon earth than the rich man in his gold and purple." "Wherefore," the preacher continues, "when a certain hermit was asked why he dwelt in so tiny a hovel, he replied well in saying—'One can leap to heaven more quickly from a little hut than from the lofty palace of kings.' "[102] The unknown author of *Speculum Laicorum,* later in the same century, echoes similar sentiments from the *Speculum Historiale* of Vincent of Beauvais: "Poverty, as saith the philosopher Secundus, is a

[100] See here in my *Preaching in Med. Engl.* pp. 90–91, etc.
[101] Luke 16:19.
[102] MS. Arund. 231. ii. fol. 47b.

hateful good, the mother of liberty, a remover of cares, felicity without solicitude, faculty without difficulty." It should be embraced upon the threefold example of Christ, the Apostles and the Philosophers.[103] This is as near as ever we get in sermon-literature to that "classic praise of rustic life" which, as Coulton observes, is so conspicuously lacking from the medieval moralist's pages. To the latter, indeed, all existence in the natural world proceeded under a cloud.[104] What, however, in respect of mere poverty, held good for the Religious, held good equally for the rustic layman. For, be that state voluntary or involuntary, the purpose of God was, as we have seen, precisely the same in both cases.[105] Coming to friar Bozon in the early years of the fourteenth century, we still find this association—to use the friar's own phrase—of "society in the world and in religion," where the merits of "poor folk who are the children of God" are being discussed.[106] Here, too, Holy Scripture[107] lends the full weight of its testimony in support of "the simple folk who know not covetousness, nor trickery, nor wish to learn it, to save their conscience," still the constant prey of injustice and oppression in the high places. Such, then, is he who, in the words of Isaiah, "departeth from evil" only to be spoiled thus;[108] "the poor innocents" of Jeremiah, whose blood is to be found upon the wings of cruel lords,[109] the poor man of the Book of Proverbs, "better . . . in his uprightness than he that is perverse

[103] Chap. lxiv (ed. Welter, p. 87). The reasons given are—(1) "quia viatorem exonerat," (2) "quia a laqueis diaboli liberat," (3) "quia celestis regni divicias impetrat." Cf., for example, *Piers Pl.* B. xiv 275.

[104] Coulton, however (p. 234), is hardly justified in omitting this observation. Cf. Bromyard's typical plaint, s.v. "Mundus"—"Tempore moderno nec terra vel arbores vel aquae tantae sunt fertilitatis sicut esse solebant"—with *Piers Pl.* C. xviii. 88–89.

[105] Cf. *Lit. and Pulpit,* pp. 297 and 561, and below, pp. 51–52. Again, Coulton appears to have missed the point, p. 241.

[106] Cf. chaps. xi and cxxi.

[107] Cf. similarly, *Lit. and Pulpit,* pp. 297–298.

[108] Chap. iii (Isa. 59:15).

[109] Chap. vi (Jer. 2:34).

in his ways, though he be rich";[110] even the very Lord of Heaven
Himself "in the person of the poor man,"[111] crying out against
the spoilers in the passionate language of the prophet Micah
—"I am as the grape gleanings of the vintage!"[112] It is in the
Summa Predicantium, however, that vast storehouse of sermon-
lore, that we catch the clearest glimpses of the *fideles simplices*
of lay society, now no longer confused with their brethren in
"poor Religion." We see them here still unspoiled by evil example or outrageous hardship in a world of avarice, pride, sloth
and self-indulgence, living "content with their lowly and honest
status," in spite of the sneers of their superiors.[113] "Now the
honest and simple folk, desiring to honour Christ, go to church,
to mass, to sermons, to learn how they ought to honour Him;
while the greater, richer and falser men, whom the Apostle
[Paul] calls 'enemies of the cross of Christ' " (Phil. iii), indulge
in those things which are contrary to Christ, in taverns, assizes,
traffickings and falsities, 'crucifying afresh the Son of God'
(Hebr. vi)."[114] "So He is received in the souls of the poor
rather than of the rich. . . . For the rich and noble offend Him
with false oaths and vows at almost every word."[115] "The rich
commonly are worse sinners than the poor and do less pen-

---

[110] Chap. xi (Prov. 28:6).

[111] It is clearly this favorite transfiguration in the sermons that is the
secret of the famous scene of Dobet in *Piers Plowman* (cf. C. XXI), in
which Piers becomes Christ himself wearing the Ploughman's "coat-
armour." For another example of this association in our homilies, cf.
Lit. and Pulpit (Bromyard), p. 262. The whole conception clearly springs
from the medieval system of interpreting Scripture, as described in *Lit.
and Pulpit,* p. 60, in this case from the imagery of Matt. 25:35–40.

[112] Chap. xii (Micah vii, i).

[113] Bromyard, s.v. "Ministratio."

[114] S.v. "Passio Christi" (Bromyard goes on to tell how these *in-
feriores* may be corrupted by their superiors). Cf. similarly the later
vernacularist, MS. Roy. 18. B. xxiii, fol. 125: "thus itt farethe be many
men in this world, whils that thei are poure they are meke and wor-
shippeth God; but when that thei are riche, anone thei forӡete God." Cf.
here *Piers Pl.,* B. XIV. 207–220.

[115] S.v. "Adventus."

ance."[116] We see them again, "the simple folk," who, "as frequently happens, receive beggars into their barns and the other confined little hovels where they live more willingly than the rich in their great palaces. (So Elias was granted hospitality by the widow rather than by the king—iii Reg. xvii)."[117] Again, be it noted, "in the art of the Soul," Bromyard declares that "clerics of the highest rank who are negligent about the soul's salvation are plunged into hell, where poor diligent lay-folk are saved."[118] "Moreover, to the humble He preached who says —'He sent me to preach the Gospel to the poor' "; and such humble folk "He chose to be His poor disciples."[119] Following a typical discussion upon the ethics of riches and poverty, the same homilist observes that "for certain we have great evidence from what we daily hear and read" that sinners and those abounding in this world's goods may well fear that they are no friends of God. For God allowed His own Mother and His Apostles, whom He called His friends, to be poor in this world, when He could have made them rich, if He had liked, thus to enrich them with spiritual goods. So those who are born to a poor man's lot will one day thank their Creator for thus having rescued them from the flames of hell—like the poor man at Chartres who lacked even the necessary halfpenny to get a night's lodging, only to learn later that that very night the lodging-house had been burnt to the ground.[120] It may be true that the peasant class furnishes few saints to the Calendar.[121] None the less it is equally clear that there will be many of their number among the obscurer souls of the Redeemed in Paradise: "Nonne Deus elegit pauperes in hoc mundo divites in fide

[116] S.v. "Eleemosyna."

[117] S.v. "Adventus." For further references to the "simple, honest folk," see, e.g., s.v. "Acquisitio Mala," "Advocatus," "Falsitas," etc.

[118] S.v. "Accidia." Cf. further Rypon, quoting Jo. Walleys, MS. Harl. 4894, fol. 189.

[119] S.v. "Humilitas" (see Luke 4:18).

[120] S.v. "Bonitas." Cf. *Jacob's Well*, p. 80 ("smale folk").

[121] Cf. Coulton, pp. 241 and 526–527.

et heredes regni?"[122] In the *Summa* we behold these faithful
sons of toil as the Pawn among the world's Chessmen. He, it
is, "who moves only one square at a time. He is the simple or
poor man, who in this world seeks the maintenance of life
alone. Such an one always 'goes straight', save when he 'takes';
for, while he dwells in simplicity and truth, he lives in straightforward fashion and safety (Prov. 10)."[123] For, to the poor is
vouchsafed the supreme hope and consolation of a happy conscience,[124] mitigating all their labors and hardships. The *Summa
Predicantium,* like many another homily-book of its scope and
learning, may well strike the reader as a queer assortment of
ill-digested matter and shifting sentiment. Nevertheless, by now
he will be able to recognize, emerging from its pages here and
there, very dimly, very tentatively, the familiar features of a
literary hero.[125] It is none other than our immortal PIERES THE
PLOWMAN, he who by a stroke of poetic genius was one day
himself to become the chosen prophet of the Gospel of Truth
and Reconciliation.

Such, then, is the kind of sources from which Langland drew
the first great message of his *Vision,* its "heavy charges," its
"remedy for the evils of the world," and its "political ideal."
The messages of preacher and poet are fundamentally the same.
Langland's "common-sense," as Jusserand styles it, his cham-
pionship of justice for the oppressed, his sane admixture of
respect for institutions with his rebuke for those who defile
them, his gospel of mutual sympathy and work as contrasted
with revolution, his stress upon good deeds and moral reform
without theological subtlety—all these and more were being

[122] James 2:5. Cf. here, *Ayenb. of Inwyt,* pp. 138, 150, 188, etc.

[123] S.v. "Mundus." Sim. *Gesta Rom.* EETS., pp. 460–461. Cf. also
Ayenb. of Inwyt, p. 139, and *Lit. and Pulpit,* p. 296.

[124] S.v. "Conscientia" (cf. also "Discordia," "Ministratio," etc.). With
this and the numerous other references to the virtue elsewhere in sermon-literature, cf. the part played by Conscience in *Piers Plowman.*

[125] Cf. also the virtuous *Plowman* of Chaucer's *Cant. Tales,* Prol. ll.
530–541 (as discussed in *Lit. and Pulpit,* p. 370).

proclaimed unceasingly from the pulpits of the land. We hear them in the simpler accents of the *Ayenbite of Inwyt,* the *Metaphors* of Brother Bozon, the *Pricke of Conscience,* the expanded versions of Rolle's Psalter,[126] the *Myrour for Lewde Men,* the Book of *Catoun* and the many vernacular homilies "compiled for the mass of the people, rather than for the exalted ones."[127] We hear them again in John Bromyard's *Summa Predicantium* and Bishop Brunton's sermons with all that they represent of many noted preachers of the day at Paul's Cross or St Mary Spital, with their wider interests and more learned appeal, talking of leaders and public affairs in Church and State amid the bustling scenes of city life.

[126] It is difficult to understand R. W. Chambers' apparent surprise at Langland's "appeal to the Psalter, with a constancy which we cannot match elsewhere in great literature, save in Thomas à Kempis" (see *Essays and Studies by Members of the Engl. Assoc.* vol. ix, p. 51). "Great literature" and Thomas à Kempis have really nothing to do with the matter. Langland is simply following here the general practice of the English homilists, writing and preaching under "the prevailing influence of Hampole." (See, e.g., my *Preaching in Med. Engl.* p. 291, etc.)

[127] (J. J. Jusserand, *"Piers Plowman": A Contribution to the History of English Mysticism,* trans. [London, 1894], p. 173.)

3

THE CHARACTER OF PIERS PLOWMAN CONSIDERED FROM THE B TEXT*

Nevill K. Coghill

I.

THE PURPOSE OF this essay is to show reason for believing that the character of Piers Plowman was intended as an emblem or personification of Dowel, Dobet and Dobest successively.

It was formerly believed that Langland's poem lacked a preconceived logical form, that the visions merged as it were fortuitously, one into the next, without a plan to determine their sequence or goal, so also the meaning of Piers, the central character, remained imprecise—a puzzle with variations each of which was more deeply mysterious than what went before. But of late the main architectural lines of the poem have been rediscovered,[1] and so it becomes possible to show that Piers himself is functionally related to that architecture, a triple caryatid supporting the whole. This is no very surprising conclusion, for Langland was not an idle allegorist seeking to beautify his verses by the dark introduction of an enigma; he created Piers to clarify his thought, not to obscure it, but because his way of thinking passed out of fashion, Piers, who was designed to embody it, became a mystery. Yet a right understanding of the

---

* Reprinted, by permission, from *Medium Aevum,* II (1933), 108–135.
[1] H. W. Wells "The Construction of *Piers Plowman,*" above, pp. 1–21.

person of Piers Plowman must be requisite to a right understanding of the poem named after him.

The analysis offered by Skeat showed Piers to have three
significances: first "the type of ideal honest man," secondly the
Incarnate Jesus and lastly ". . . Saint Peter the Apostle . . . and
this Piers was again succeeded by the Popes of Rome . . . the
ambiguity is surely not very great."[2] It is true the ambiguity is
not great, but there seems something inconsequential in these
epiphanies: the three steps do not belong to the same stairway.

Jusserand maintained what is substantially the same view; he
described Piers as "a variable emblem . . . now the honest man
of the people, now the Pope, now Christ."[3]

Wells does not explicitly repudiate this by-now-traditional
view, but he associates Piers far more significantly with the
structure of the poem than did its earlier critics. He writes:

> Here for the first time we meet the image of the plow, in this
> case simply the plow of the farmer. In outward appearance at
> least even Piers himself is no more than an overseer or even a
> participant in these physical labors. . . . In the *Vita de Dobest* . . .
> Piers and his plow once more appear, but Piers is now indubitably
> Christ, his plow the word of God, man the harvest and the barn
> the heaven of divine rest.[4]

H. W. Troyer, in a still more recent explanation of Piers,[5]
derived from a study of St. Thomas Aquinas, advances the interesting theory that Piers is to be understood allegorically, morally
and anagogically; his exposition of the critical results that follow from this theory is illuminating; I venture to think that Piers
is not so "multifold" a symbol as he would maintain, but wel-

[2] *The Vision of William concerning Piers the Plowman, in three
parallel texts, etc., by William-Langland,* ed. W. W. Skeat (Oxford,
1896), II, pp. xxvi–vii.
[3] J. J. Jusserand in *Piers Plowman, A Contribution to the History of
English Mysticism* (London, 1894), pp. 29, 155.
[4] P. 7 above.
[5] Howard William Troyer "Who is Piers Plowman?" *PMLA,* XLVII
(1932), 368–384.

come the method of triple interpretation, the application of which is immediately fruitful. The character of Piers can be simplified beyond what Troyer offers without sacrificing the allegorical, moral and anagogical readings of his character and without omitting anything stated of Piers in the B text. I have confined my own observations to that text; for the development of the character of Piers the incompleted A text is insufficient, and the C text offers some complications of rearrangement which might cloud the immediate issue. It is therefore reasonable to adopt the B text as the surest basis for comment at present.[6]

Troyer's argument, for all its fascination, leads him toward thoughts which I cannot but believe are twentieth- rather than fourteenth-century thoughts; some of his conclusions, indeed, would have been condemned as heretical in Langland's day and punished at the stake a few years later. Piers Plowman, as a poem, is almost passionately orthodox, and is, I think, impossible to reconcile with quasiheretical interpretation.

For instance Troyer writes:

> And the plowman tearing his pardon was perhaps to be symbolic of how utterly futile the author felt men had made the atonement by their own lives, a view certainly not out of harmony with the note of despair on which the poem itself ends later on. Whether or not such an extreme interpretation is justified, it is apparent that the episode, as those preceding it, is one of multifold aspect. (378)

Now such an interpretation is more than extreme; it is impossible, at least to a Catholic such as Langland was. No human action, whether that of an individual or of "man the race" (to use Troyer's phrase), could possibly make the Atonement "utterly futile." The Atonement was not made by man and could not be marred by man. Again, in summing up, Troyer writes:

> Piers is a multifold symbol. He is allegorically man the race. He is sometimes an individual man, who is in his integrity a pic-

[6] All references throughout are to the B text.

ture of moral perfection in the functions of society which the race
has developed. And he is also the great God-man, the highest
achievement of the race in the figure of its own redeemer. (384)

Now, setting aside the question whether Humanitarianism
and Perfectibility are rather nineteenth- or twentieth-century
than fourteenth-century ideas, there remains what is in essence
this same heresy. It may be that Troyer did not intend his
words so to be understood, but they suggest once more the
notion that the Incarnation and the Atonement were somehow
man-made (or man-marred); if we excuse the phrase "great
God-man" for smacking somewhat of anthropological research,
we still have to reckon with the idea that the Redemption was
a *racial achievement,* something only different *in degree* from
the Great Pyramid, that Jesus was a man upon whose birth
the race might congratulate itself. But in Catholic theology the
birth of the Savior differs not merely in degree, but *in kind* from
all other births; it was the deliberate and only Incarnation of the
Son of God and was irrespective of the efforts or deservings of
mankind; it was an Act of Grace.

Any account of Piers which involves notions that Langland
would have repudiated cannot be wholly acceptable to us, but
the triple method of interpretation (allegorical, moral and anagogical), which I take to be Troyer's principal contribution, can
be applied without heresy and is of great value in the understanding of Piers.

II.

The allegory of Piers, I have asserted, is simply this, that he
successively embodies the ideas of Dowel, Dobet and Dobest.
These are the three stages recognized by Skeat and Jusserand
but interpreted in accordance with the design of the poem. Piers
is therefore *not a man at all,* neither an individual nor an aggre-
gate; he is the allegorical symbol for *three cumulative ways of
life.* These three ways of life are exhibited in him, made incarnate; and since it is open to all human beings to live any one of

them, it need not surprise us that he appears to be "a labourer, an overseer, a king, the pope, Adam, St. Peter, and Christ, sometimes individually, sometimes compositely" (to quote again from Troyer's article [373]). For to be Piers is to do well or to do better or to do best, as this essay hopes to show; once this is recognized and applied to the visions as a whole, the poem becomes harmonious and consistent, declaring itself logically, as well as psychologically, a unity.

Two lines of argument will be followed in support of this interpretation.

    1. To consider, in their order, each personal entry of Piers into the poem, together with the changes that seem to occur in his nature at those entries and to show not only that the timing of his entries corresponds with the divisions of the poem (*Visio de Petro Plowman, Vita de Dowel, Vita de Dobet, Vita de Dobest*), but that the changes in his nature are equally relevant to those divisions.

    2. To consider the three groups of abstract virtues which Langland laid down as appropriate to the three types of life respectively and to show their exact correspondence to the moral qualities that are stressed in the nature of Piers step by step as it unfolds.

It these arguments can be substantiated they will be seen to lead from different premises to the same conclusion, namely that Langland intended the character of Piers to be the organ of his three abstractions, the good life, the better and the best; for such a correspondence could not happen accidentally inasmuch as Langland, as Wells has demonstrated, had special genius in the disposing of the larger architectural lines of his work; a man capable of such gigantic and comprehensive planning could not without absurdity be supposed ignorant of the movements of his own hero, of their dovetailing with the main divisions of his poem and of his hero's specific possession of the abstract virtues about which he had chosen to write.

Since the contentions here advanced unite the character of Piers with the structure of the poem as a whole, some account

of that structure must first be given; many of the ideas advanced
here will be recognized as identical with those put forward by
Wells in his invaluable article referred to above. I would avoid
this recapitulation of what is already known were it possible
to conduct my argument without it, but the Piers-Idea is so
manifestly built into the whole edifice of Langland's thought
that I am obliged to repeat some of the conclusions of Wells;
and this I shall do without further acknowledgment or restitu-
tion by footnote. I can but hope he will not echo the words
of Repentance to Covetyse:

> 'That was no restitucioun,' quod Repentance · 'but a robberes
> thefte;
> Thow haddest be better worthy · be hanged therfore
> Than for al that · that thow hast here shewed.'

III.

The poem is divided into four major sections usually designated as the *Visio de Petro Plowman* (Prol. to VII inclusive),
Vita de Dowel (VIII to XV inclusive), the *Vita de Dobet* (XVI
to XVIII inclusive) and the *Vita de Dobest* (XIX to the end). Of
these sections the least obviously picturesque, and therefore the
most generally neglected, is the second, the *Vita de Dowel*. Yet
this *Dowel* expounds the basic doctrines of all Langland's
thought, and for an understanding enjoyment of his poem it is
the critical section, as will be presently shown.

The first section (the *Visio de Petro Plowman*) is a study
of human life in the active world as it existed before Langland's
eyes; it concerns itself particularly with the following problems:

(1) What, in this business of honest and dishonest moneymak-
ing that seems to keep the Field of Folk on the move, is to
be rendered to Cæsar, and what to God? (Prol., I)

(2) How is a corrupt administration to be set to rights? (II, III,
IV)

(3) How is society in general to purify itself? (V)

(4) The problem of labor versus famine and the twin problems
of the shirkers and the impotent. (VI)

> (5) Whether the solutions offered to these problems as they arise are pleasing to God, and if so, what is the meaning of pardon, and what disciplines or virtues underlie these solutions? (VII) *This subsection may be regarded as the hinge upon which the poem turns toward an abstract consideration of Dowel, Dobet and Dobest.*

All these problems are considered *sub specie æternitatis,* and are riders to the principal problem—the grand subject of the poem—namely, how is man to work out his salvation? Thus far the first major section, which concerns the existing order of the active life in the world as lived by all men, but particularly as lived by the laity.

The second section, the *Vita de Dowel,* immediately following, holds the keys to all the others. This section, under the guise of a vague allegorical autobiography of the poet,[7] considers (1) what abstract virtues should underlie the active life, and whether they can win salvation (and in the answers which this study suggests lie the full understanding of what has gone before in the *Visio*); (2) the virtues that should underlie the contemplative or clerkly life, i.e. the *Vita de Dobet*; and (3) the virtues that should underlie the pontifical life or life of spiritual authority, which is the Life of Dobest.

The whole of his great section (*Dowel*), and all these disquisitions are seasoned with both Langland's mental autobiography and with a running commentary on the existing state of affairs (with particular reference to the Clergy and their shortcomings), as well as with problems germane to the central argument, such as the possibility of salvation for pre-Christian "clerks" like Aristotle, or "worthies" like Trajan, and the general unreasonableness of man in the indulging of his instincts, contrasted with the notorious decency and sweet moderation of the lower creatures.

This section, then, expounds the true principles upon which

---

[7] See Mensendieck, "The Authorship of Piers Plowman," *JEGP,* IX (1910), 404–420.

to base human conduct if salvation to to be attained, whether by living the "lewed" life of Dowel, the "clerkly" life of Dobet or the "episcopal" life of Dobest; thus it supplies the *moral argument* upon which the whole fabric of vision and allegory is based. Unless that argument is grasped, it is almost impossible to understand what the poem as a whole is driving at; and because it has been neglected, Langland has no general fame other than as the author of discontented and disconnected satires, somewhat lively in their presentation but defaced by a dreary intermingling of prolonged theologizings—matter enough for social historians and philologists but no great matter for those who ask of a poet some largely imagined and harmonious unit of vision. And yet, in this precise respect, *Troilus and Criseyde* itself is not greater than *Piers Plowman.*

The third section (*Dobet*) is simply the embodiment of Langland's foregoing theories of the clerkly virtues, shown allegorically in a narrative, and the fourth section (*Dobest*) allegorically embodies the life of authority and the need for it in a world beset by corruption from within the human heart and menaced by the assault of Antichrist from without.

Of these four sections, as has been said, the second is a kind of abstract of the other three, or, if that is too inaccurate an expression, it has a more-than-narrative relationship to them; it is their exposition. Of the other three, the first is concerned with, or as if dedicated to, God the Father; the next (*Dobet*) with God the Son, and the last with God the Holy Ghost, proceeding from Them just as *Dobest* proceeds from *Dowel* and *Dobet:* as if God in creating the world was Active, in redeeming the world was Contemplative and in sustaining the spiritual life of Christendom was Authoritative. This last is the anagogical aspect of the poem.

IV.

Into this structure, at certain premeditated points, irrupts the figure of Piers Plowman. Perhaps in no other work of equal scope does the hero appear so seldom in person, but every appearance in this poem has a calculated significance.

Piers first "put forth his hed" (v. 544) when the secular world of action had confessed its sins and was attempting satisfaction for them (the third part of a valid penance) by seeking St. Truth. This would seem a late entry for the hero. But if he is accepted as an emblem of Dowel, of the active unlettered life as it should be, there is no earlier point at which he could have made his appearance. For a glance at the analysis of the first section above shows that the first three subsections are quite general and deal with all the world, not omitting the governing class, and as such are not amenable to the simple solution of "Dowel" but ask the higher wisdom of Holy Church who offers advanced reflections on the purposes of human life under the hand of God. Her teaching is quite beyond the province of Piers as Dowel, just as is the advice later given to the King. Up to this point, therefore, there is no mention of either Dowel or Piers. The Confession of the Seven Sins is again quite general; it is not even confined to the Laity (Wrath was a Regular), and it is prompted by the sermon of Reasoun, who proves that the pestilences were in consequence of sin (v. 15) and for no other reason. Here again it would not have been becoming to the trend of the allegory for simple unlettered Dowel to usurp the position and authority of Reasoun in preaching repentance to the world. And therefore the figure of Piers is still withheld. Indeed he remains hidden until the more exalted and theoretic advice has failed. In their efforts to seek the Shrine of Truth the worldlings "blustreden forth as bestes" (v. 521), not knowing which way to turn. They had had *spiritual* advice from their confessor and were trying to follow it; what they lacked was *practical* advice, and this, as might be expected, the finical Palmer, all decked out and arrayed with the trophies of his pilgrimages, could not supply. For practical advice a practical man is needed and therefore, modestly, but with the assurance of one who speaks from fifty years' experience, Piers emerges as a leader, "the type of ideal honest man," in short *Dowel*.

At first he offers them spiritual advice in practical form, a sort of map of the common road to Truth (i.e. to Honesty, Evenhandedness), a Mosaic *Carte du Tendre* (v. 568 ff.), and in this there is nothing which the ordinary unlettered Christian was not supposed to know—the ten commandments, the obligations of penance and amendment and charity, etc. But even this is too abstruse for the for-wandered world:

> 'This were a wikked way · but who-so hadde a gyde'
> (VI. 1)

So with a still more practical insight Piers sets them all to *work*. That had been his own solution to the problem of seeking Truth, that had been his own life,

> I dyke and I delue · I do that treuthe hoteth
> (v. 552)

that, in fact, was as much as, in his simplicity, he knew, or needed to know, in the active life of Dowel.

It should be noted that the problems of famine and unemployment, which in essence are no less general than those of public administration or social purification, were shelved by Langland until after the emergence of Piers. Langland believed that famine and unemployment could be avoided if only the secular world would lead the simple, honest, hard-working Life of Dowel, each according to his station, whereas those other problems of the purposes of human endeavor in general and the right practice of statecraft were above the powers and pretensions of a simple farmer. They therefore come under the arbitration, not of Piers, but of Conscience or Reasoun or Holy Church.

The last and most vexed matter in this first epiphany of Dowel under the form of Piers is that of the pardon sent by Truth to his servant.

> Treuthe herde telle her-of · and to Peres he sent,
> To taken his teme · and tulyen the erthe,

> And purchaced hym a pardoun · *a pena et a culpa*
> For hym, and for his heires · for euermore after.
> (VII. 1–4)

The "purchace" is of course the purchase on Calvary when "god bouȝte vs alle" (VI. 210) and is our Redemption. Now, that Redemption is believed, and has always been believed, *conditional;* it is for the Christian to avail himself of it by faith and works. It will be seen presently that the essence of Dowel, theoretically speaking, includes faith and works with no little emphasis. And this should be borne in mind in considering the enigmatic text of the pardon sent by Truth.[8]

The condition in the pardon is thus expressed:

> Al in two lynes it lay · and nouȝt a leef more,
> And was writen riȝt thus · in witnesse of treuthe;
> > *Et qui bona egerunt, ibunt in vitam eternam;*
> > *Qui vero mala, in ignem eternum.*
> (VII. 110–113)

This pardon lay in the hand of Piers the unlettered ploughman, simplest embodiment of Dowel, or *Bonum Agere;* there is an irony in that he could not even read it, did not know that it referred precisely and exclusively to himself. He had accepted it without examination upon pure faith; he had not so much as unfolded it.

> 'Pieres,' quod a prest tho · 'thi pardoun most I rede,
> For I wil construe eche a clause · and kenne it the on
> > Engliche.'
> And Pieres at his preyere · the pardoun vnfoldeth.
> (VII. 106–108)

This trustful illiteracy of Piers, because it is entirely in character with the Life of Dowel, is the first of two important points that emerge from this episode of Truth's pardon. The

---

[8] This pardon, it may be noted, links up with that other pardon that is conditional upon *redde quod debes* in XIX. 388; virtually they are the same in promise and condition.

second is the "pure teen" (VII. 116) for which Piers tore up the pardon when the priest, who could not recognize *Bonum Agere* in Piers any more than Piers did himself, explained to him that it was no pardon at all but the simple statement of an exactly proportionate requital—such a pardon as might be conceded by Mrs. Be-done-by-as-you-did.

Perhaps all readers have found this "teen" obscure. Vexation or petulance seem scarcely appropriate impulses in a character such as that of Piers, whatever that character embodies; yet the action of pardon-tearing is somehow satisfactory to the reader psychologically; it is almost as if Piers had torn the priest up and revenged us upon his sophistries. But I think a better explanation would be to think of "teen" as disappointed mortification. *Piers believed the priest* (Dowel is humble and obedient to the Church); their later jangle does not concern the pardon but arises from his resentment of the gratuitous and insulting mockery flung at him by the priest. Piers believed that the pardon, like so many others in the fourteenth century, was worthless, and so, in his disappointment, committed himself to the pure assurance of his faith rather than to a piece of parchment, for as he tears it he repeats:

> *Si ambulavero in medio umbre mortis, non timebo mala;*
> *quoniam tu mecum es.*

But there is mortification as well as disappointment, as if he thought that perhaps after all the simple life of action was of insufficient merit, in spite of his fifty years of following Truth. More could be demanded of him.

> 'I shal cessen of my sowyng,' quod Pieres · 'and swynk nouȝt so
>   harde,
> Ne about my bely-ioye · so bisi be namore!
> Of preyers and of penaunce · my plow shal ben herafter,
> And wepen whan I shulde slepe · though whete-bred me faille.'
>
> (VII. 117–120)

These are the words immediately following in which Piers

announces his conversion to the clerkly Life of Dobet, and for this reason *he does not return in person into the narrative* until Passus XVI, *"primus de Dobet."*

It may well be asked: "If Piers embodies Dowel, why does he drop out of the poem through all those long Passus that purport to deal with Dowel?" (VIII–XV). I suggest in answer that in the first place the *Visio de Petro Plowman* (Prol.–VII) exhibits Dowel allegorically, whereas the *Vita de Dowel* exhibits it morally; in the case of Dowel alone the practice is discussed before the moral theory (whereas in the case of Dobet and Dobest the theory is fully discussed in the preceding *Vita de Dowel,* and the practice of those Higher Lives is not shown until the sections that bear their name). Thus, since Piers has demonstrated how to handle the active world, there is no need for him to reappear until he is wanted to demonstrate the handling of the contemplative world. He makes three grand appearances, one for each kind of life, and it would have confused the symmetry of the allegory to have brought him in redundantly as Dowel. Secondly the *Vita de Dowel,* as has been said, is really far wider in scope than the mere good active life, inasmuch as it includes disquisitions on the other lives, and on other matters. It is, in so far as it concerns the lives of Piers, purely theoretical or moral, whereas the hero is *always* flesh and blood, a figure of the actual world, whether active, contemplative or authoritarian. Compare with the robustness of Piers those shadowy phantoms, Thought, Clergye, Imaginatyf or even Haukyn; Piers is not a theory but a life and for so long as he represents Dowel, the perfection of unletteredness, it would be inappropriate to introduce him into a realm of disputation such as is the section called the *Vita de Dowel.*

Piers, then, bursts into the poem at precisely the point where the practice and example of a simple honest man (Dowel) can benefit the active world and disappears, uttering a prophecy of his transformation into Dobet (VII. 117–120), just at the moment when Langland retires into a realm of speculation, where Piers as Dowel cannot follow him and where the path of Dobet has not yet sufficiently been marked out for Piers as Dobet to be intelligible. Without that long hiatus in the narrative allegory of the poem, where Dowel, Dobet and Dobest are theoretically evaluated, the changes in the meaning of Piers would indeed have been confusing, for imagine Passus VIII to XV omitted; what key would then remain to the triple gates of Langland's thought?

The correspondence that has been traced between Piers and the structural disposition of Dowel, exists also, and more obviously, in Dobet. No sooner does *Passus xvj et primus de Dobet* begin than Piers returns into the poem in person, and he returns a changed being. Here is no more the simple, unlettered and incorruptible farmer, but a teacher who can expound the allegory of the Tree of Charity, with its Triune props (XVI. 21–72), and, later, the Holy Trinity Itself (XVII. 138–256); a healer and tender of the sick and afflicted (in the person of the Good Samaritan, XVII. 48 ff.; identified with Piers in XVIII. 10); and a Jouster in whose armour Christ is to ride to His Passion (XVIII. 21–25). The full importance of these roles will be seen when the theoretical essences of Dowel, Dobet and Dobest have been considered; what is here emphasized is that a strong change takes place in the character of Piers and that *this change coincides with the Dobet division of the poem;* this correspondence, too, cannot be accidental.

From XVIII. 25, there is no more mention of Piers until XIX. 6. In these 412 lines are described the Passion of Christ and the Harrowing of Hell. Let us for the moment be cautious of any hasty identification of Christ with Piers. That they are in an important sense identified cannot be denied, but it would be truer to say of them that Jesus *lives* Piers (for Piers is a way of Life), than that Jesus *is* Piers or that Piers *is* Jesus. Indeed the plain truth is best stated by Langland himself when he says:

> This Iesus of his gentrice · wole Iuste in Piers armes,
> In his helme and in his haberioun · *humana natura;*

That Cryst be nouȝt biknowe here · for *consummatus deus,*
In Piers paltok the Plowman · this priker shal ryde;

(XVIII. 22–25)

The reason for our caution is that Piers is primarily of *this* world as, humanly speaking, are the active, contemplative and pontifical lives. This explains why there is no mention of Piers in the long and splendid Harrowing of Hell; Christ had for a while borrowed the human garments of Piers, but yielded them up again (it may be understood) at death, at the line:

'*Consummatum est,*' quod Cryst · and comsed forto swowe.

(XVIII. 57)

Thereafter Christ clearly is recognized as Divine (though some still deny and scoff); Lucifer and Goblin know with Whom they have to deal.

Some seyde that he was goddes sone · that so faire deyde,
 Vere filius dei erat iste, etc.
And somme saide he was a wicche. . . .

(XVIII. 68–69)

Piers does not return to the poem until after Hell has been harrowed: he returns in the opening lines of XIX, which is headed *"Passus xix^{us}; et explicit Dobet; et incipit Dobest."*

I do not know what importance to attach to this heading; it contains the suggestion that we are to expect a little Dobet, which will be concluded, and that the rest will begin Dobest. If this suggestion is accepted, it will be found to support the theory here advanced. What is most noticeable about this re-entry of Piers is its likeness to his re-entry at the beginning of the previous Passus. *No apparent change has taken place in the character of Piers.* If the passage already quoted (XVIII. 22–25) be compared with the lines

'thise aren Pieres armes,
His coloures and his cote-armure · ac he that cometh so blody
Is Cryst with his crosse · conqueroure of Crystene'

(XIX. 12–14)

the similarity is obvious.

If this similarity is taken in conjunction with the hint given by the Passus-heading, it is not difficult to believe that we still have here to take Piers as *Dobet,* and this interpretation of the allegory fits with the return of Christ to Galilee after His descent into Hell and *before* the sending forth of the Disciples with loosing and binding power, which, for Langland, is one of the turning points in Christian history. For Christ was still *humanly embodied,* as the episode of Doubting Thomas proves (XIX. 161–176), and it was in the body of Piers, who had not yet become Dobest. *"Explicit Dobet"* might then properly be written after line 176 of XIX (the story of Doubting Thomas), which is immediately succeeded by these lines:

> And whan this dede was done · Dobest he tauȝte,
> And ȝaf Pieres power · and pardoun he graunted
> To alle manere men · mercy and forȝyfnes,
> Hym myȝte men to assoille · of alle manere synnes,
> In couenant that thei come · and knowleche to paye,
> To Pieres pardon the Plowman · *redde quod debes.*
> (XIX. 177–182)

Whether or not this explanation puts too much weight on the mere heading of a Passus, the final change in the significance of Piers does not come until this point. He is no longer identifiable in any sense with Christ but is one to whom Christ *delegates power.* The power was won by Christ (as Langland explains in the mouth of Conscience, XIX. 26–55) when he descended into and harrowed Hell, an action in which Piers, as we have seen, had no part. Christ, therefore, *as God,* has won a Victory, the fruits of which are entrusted to the New Piers. And in this way the New Piers becomes Dobest, the embodiment of the life of authority. This authority is confirmed and upheld by the Holy Ghost at Pentecost (XIX. 196), and is the sanction by which Piers is to build the House of Unitas, "holicherche on Englisshe" (XIX. 325).

The argument here offered has so far shown a correspondence between each change in the significance of Piers and the several transitions from Dowel to Dobet and Dobet to Dobest.

It may be objected as follows: "Why, if Piers is Dobest, the life of authority that should sustain the Church, does he appear to desert his trust, or at least to leave it in the hands of Conscience?" It is true that after XIX. 331 Piers ceases to dominate the poem and Conscience assumes the role of hero. Indeed Piers once more is lost; we are not told when or how he vanishes from the Barn of Holy Church which he has been at such pains to build; when he is most needed, (at the onslaughts of the Deadly Sins under Pride, XIX. 331 and of the Host of Antichrist, XX. 52, he is nowhere to be found, and the poem ends with the quest for its hero:

'Bi Cryste,' quod Conscience tho · 'I wil bicome a pilgryme,...
...To seke Piers the Plowman · that Pryde may destruye...
.............now Kynde me auenge,
And sende me happe and hele til I haue Piers the Plowman!'
And sitthe he gradde after grace · til I gan awake.

(XX. 378 to end)

I think this was intended as a melancholy comment on the world—an intimation that in Langland's opinion the proper exercise of authority had vanished from the earth, and it is in keeping with his expressed estimate of Bishops and Cardinals (cf. XIX. 411–415, Prol. 78, 79, VII. 13, XI. 303–310, etc.). It may be noted that the difficulty of Piers' vanishing at this point is not overcome by supposing him to be the Pope or Man the Race. Neither of these had disappeared; indeed there were shortly to be two Popes at once; on the other hand the Babylonish Captivity at Avignon had been in full swing, at the time of the writing of the B text, for nearly seventy years. Possibly Langland had this declension of the life of authority in mind. There are other possibilities also that suggest themselves glibly enough: such as that perhaps Langland had in mind a more general collapse of the Order of Christendom than that figured forth in the Papal Captivity, which he might have regarded as a symptom of his declining era rather than as its disease; or possibly Langland wished to stress the necessity of a renewed personal effort in all men and therefore chose to portray them as fighting through the Dark Night of the Soul under Conscience only; or, like earlier prophets he may have had no wish to speak smooth things to an unruly people. Conjectures of this kind are always easy and often worthless; readers of Langland are more likely to experience surprise at the absence of topical allusion that can now be understood than the reverse. The matter of dating the texts illustrates this paucity of topical comment, this reserve of allusion that should caution us against rash assignment of historical interpretations and inner readings of Langland's unexpressed sentiments about contemporary personages and events.[9]

A correspondence between the personal entries of Piers and the architectural divisions, Dowel, Dobet and Dobest, has been indicated, and a second line of argument remains, namely the discovery and tabulation of the Virtues assigned by Langland to those ways of life, and the fitting of them to Piers in the three stages of his growth.

Before this new phase in the argument is attempted, a consideration of the supposed identity of Piers and Christ may be offered. What is here contended is that Piers and Christ are parallel exemplars of the same sets of ideas. That Christ lived Dowel, Dobet and Dobest successively, Langland explicitly tells us (XIX. 104–189); that Piers is a parallel embodiment of those lives is the thesis of this paper. I use the word parallel designedly, for by a curious but not unlawful play of ideas, the metaphor from geometry fits the thesis with a pleasing exactness, for we are told that parallel straight lines meet at infinity and that is precisely where the characters of Piers and Jesus meet and

[9] Notwithstanding the position sketched by Mr. Cargill in "Date of A Text of *Piers Plowman*," *PMLA*, XLVII (1932), 354–362, which appears to me untenable and inaccurate.

are one. They meet in the Infinity of Christ's Nature and in that
of Dowel and Dobet:

> ' . . . Dowel and Dobet · aren two infinites,
> Whiche infinites, with a feith · fynden oute Dobest,
> Which shal saue mannes soule . thus seith Piers the
>   Ploughman·'

> (XIII. 127–129)

These three ways of life, lived allegorically by Piers and historically by Christ, are inexhaustible. An infinite goodness in
simplicity and even-handed action, an infinite goodness in compassionate care for the ignorant and the sick and a readiness
to suffer for others, learnt in contemplation, and an infinite
goodness in command—each of these roads leads to salvation.
Each way of life is to be understood *allegorically,* as bodied in
Piers and as touching the proper relations between man and
man; each is in the same way to be understood *morally,* as having in the abstract certain basic essential or characteristic virtues,
and each way is to be understood as touching everlasting things,
analogically that is, namely the fulfilling of God's purposes in
creating, redeeming and giving grace to man.

I do not say that Langland was meticulously precise in his
use of the Piers symbol; it would, for instance, be impossible,
perhaps, to go through the poem substituting for every mention of Piers the words Dowel, Dobet or Dobest; in the last-cited
passage, for instance, it is not very clear in which capacity Piers
is being quoted. We are told immediately before that "one Pieres
the Ploughman" has "sette alle sciences at a soppe saue loue
one," and this suggests Dowel, the first Piers. But to overwork
the interpretation of an allegory that has so large and general a
scope is the treason of pedantry. There is, however, one passage
in the poem which seems to undo much of the argument so far
advanced by this paper. It occurs in Passus XV, in the allocu-
tion of that strangely tongueless and toothless being Anima who
is defining Charity to the Dreamer in a passage of extraordinary

72

poetic force. The passus in question is headed *"Passus xv^{us}: finit Dowel; et incipit Dobet,"* and if this can be accepted as evidence, we are justified in supposing that somewhere within this passus is the turning point away from the matter of Dowel and toward the matter of Dobet. I suggest that the turning point comes at xv. 144, for it is at this line that the nature of Charity comes up for discussion. Now Faith, Hope and Charity, under the forms of Abraham, Moses and the Good Samaritan, are the subjects of Passus xvi and xvii, so that this turning-point passage can be considered as a *moral* explanation of or introduction to the Good Samaritan, who is an *allegorical* emblem of Charity; and this figure turns out later (xviii. 10 ff.) to be indistinguishable from Piers and Jesus, so that it is raised, and with it the whole discussion, to the *anagogical* plane of heavenly Truth.

If these three shadowings of meaning be allowed to drift like veils over the discourse of Anima, an understanding of it will arise that is not inconsistent with the interpretation of Piers as Dowel, Dobet and Dobest; the passage in question is as follows: Langland is moved to exclaim at the lyrical account of the person of Charity given by Anima:

> 'By Cryst, I wolde that I knewe hym,' quod I · 'no creature
>   leuere!'
> 'With-outen helpe of Piers Plowman,' quod he · 'his persone
>   seestow neuere.'
> 'Where clerkes knowen hym,' quod I · 'that kepen holykirke?'
>   'Clerkes haue no knowyng,' quod he · 'but by werkes and
>   bi wordes.
> Ac Piers the Plowman · parceyueth more depper
> What is the wille and wherfore . that many wyȝte suffreth,
>   *Et vidit deus cogitaciones eorum.*
> . . . For there ar beggeres and bidderes · bedemen as it were,
> Loketh as lambren · and semen lyf-holy,
> Ac it is more to haue her mete · with such an esy manere,
> Than for penaunce and parfitnesse · the pouerte that such
>   taketh.
> There-fore by coloure ne by clergye · knowe shaltow hym
>   neuere,

Noyther thorw wordes ne werkes · but thorw wille one.
And that knoweth no clerke · ne creature in erthe,
But Piers the Plowman · *Petrus, id est, Christus.*'

(xv. 189–206)

It would seem clear from Langland's instant association of the name Piers the Plowman with Clerkes (for the force of the question in the third line of the above seems to be "Then do the Clergy recognize true Charity in the hearts of men?"), that Piers as Dobet, allegory of the clerkly life, was intended (this would corroborate the *incipit Dobet* suggestion made above); and indeed I think it is for Dobet that Piers is here standing. But it is a Piers-Dobet on the anagogical plane, for Anima associates Piers not with "clerkes" as the Dreamer does but with God and Christ. What then is to be understood by this passage? The virtues of Dobet as will presently be shown, are to teach, to heal and to suffer. These, on the heavenly or anagogical plane, as attributes of God would be just such as Christ manifested on earth in his contemplative character when he "did bet"; but the contemplations of God penetrate into the human heart and can see if Charity exists there or not. Since, however, Christ was God uniquely incarnate, that knowledge of the inner human motive was also, for the first and last time, known upon earth, by Jesus during his ministry of Dobet when he was living the second life of Piers. No Piers-life, *of itself,* can teach men to see into the true motives of their fellows, but the Piers-life raised to the Heavenly plane, as it was by Jesus, could bring that knowledge to earth in virtue of the Incarnation. This gives a new and I believe a true value to the phrase *"Petrus, id est Christus"* and saves the allegory from obscurity and even from wreck. Another analogy from Euclid may clarify my contention: a chord cuts a circle at two points; if the chord be moved to a tangential position, there are still two points at which it cuts, but they are coincident. The chord of Dobet cuts the circle of life in Heaven and on Earth, and in Christ Heaven and Earth were united. The symbol Piers is filled by the reality Christ: symbol and reality coincide.

V.

As has been said, the theoretic explanation of Dowel, Dobet and Dobest is largely contained in the second section of the poem, that which is called Dowel. This explanation is of snow-ball growth, but I have gathered together the principal pronouncements offered during the course of Passus VIII to XIX. All but one occur within the *Vita de Dowel,* as will be seen.

DOWEL	DOBET	DOBEST

VIII. 78 ff. Thought speaking:

DOWEL	DOBET	DOBEST
Three fair virtues that are not far to find.		
True of tongue and hand; wins livelihood by labor or land; trusty of his tally; takes but his own; is not drunken or disdainful.	Is the same, but does right more; low as a lamb; loving of speech; helps all according to their needs; has broken the purses of the avaricious; "And is ronne i n t o Religioun, and hath rendred the bible," preaching "Suffer fools gladly" and doing them good with glad will.	Is above both; a Bishop's Cross he bears to hale men from Hell and bash down the wicked. Must protect Dowel. If Dowel or Dobet go contrary to Dobest, the King they have set up above them (i.e. God) will cast them in irons unless Dobest pleads for them.

IX. 1 ff. Witte speaking:

DOWEL	DOBET	DOBEST
Lives in the Castle of the four Elements, is set there to guard Anima for Kynde. Dowel is Lord of the Marches against "a proud pricker of F r a n c e, Princeps hujis mundi."	Dobet is handmaid to Anima and daughter to Dowel.	Dobest is above both, a Bishop's peer. What he bids must be done. Anima is led by his teaching.

IX. 107 ff. (Still Witte):

Dowel is true wedded life; works and wins to sustain the world. To beget bastards is to do ill. (Piers is married at his first entry: see VI. 80.) But of course no more is heard of his wife when he becomes Dobet.

DOWEL	DOBET	DOBEST

IX. 199. Witte still speaking:

DOWEL	DOBET	DOBEST
To do as the Law teaches. To dread God. Wicked will drives away Dowel.	To love friend and foe. To suffer.	To give and guard both young and old, to heal and help. Dobest comes of Dowel and Dobet. He brings down the proud for the protection of Dowel.

X. 129. Dame Studye speaking:

May he grow deaf who blinds men's wits with fine distinctions between Dowel and Dobet. Unless a man lives the life Dowel he need not hope for Dobet, though Dobest "drawe on hym" day after day.

X. 187. Dame Studye still speaking:

DOWEL	DOBET	DOBEST
See that you love loyally if you have a fancy to Dowel.	Dobet and Dobest are of Love's kin (also, by implication, pray for enemies, return g o o d for evil).	

X. 230 ff. Clergye speaking:

DOWEL	DOBET	DOBEST
A common life; to believe in the Church, and all the articles of the Faith that are necessary to know, i.e. in One God without beginning. His true Son who saved Man from Death and the Devil, t h r o u g h the Holy Ghost that is of Both, but all Three are One. The Lewed that wish to Do well must so believe.	Dobet is to suffer for the good of your soul all that the Book, by the Church's teaching, bids, viz. Practice what you preach. Be what you seem.	Dobest is bold to blame the Guilty, being clean within himself.

X. 330. Langland speaking:

Dowel and Dobet are Dominus and Knighthood? (cf. A text: Knighthood, Kingship and Cæsardom are Dowel, Dobet and Dobest?) Scripture replies that neither Kinghood nor Knighthood help to Heaven.

DOWEL	DOBET	DOBEST

XI. 402. Langland suggests that Dowel is to see much and suffer more, but is rebuked by Imaginatyf, who retorts *Philosophus esses, si tacuisses.*

XII. 30. Imaginatyf speaking:

Faith, Hope and Charity are Dowel, as St. Paul says. Dowel does as loyalty teaches; if married, love your mate. If you are Religious (i.e. Dobet?), keep your rule and do not run to Rome.

XIII. 103. The Drunken Doctor speaking:

Do no evil to fellow Christians. And Dowel is to do what Clergy teach (l. 115).	Dobet is he that labors to teach others.	Dobest practices what he preaches.

XIII. 127. Clergye speaking, quoting Piers Plowman:

Clergye denies all knowledge of his own, for Piers Plowman has set all science at a sop, save Love only (i.e. Piers Plowman, in the role of Dowel, has asserted that salvation is gained by love, not learning). Piers says (Clergye continues) that Dowel and Dobet are two infinities, which, with a faith, find out Dobest. And that shall save man's soul.

Ibid. 136. Patience speaking:

"Disce, doce et dilige inimicos."

Disce is Dowel.	Doce is Dobet.	Dilige is Dobest.

(Patience claims she learnt this from Love (line 139), but cf. the remarks of the Drunken Doctor.)

XIV. 16–21. Conscience speaking to Haukyn:

Dowel, Dobet and Dobest are the three parts of Valid Penance, i.e.

Contrition	Confession	Satisfaction

(This doctrine is expanded in XIV. 87–96. It is not so much a doctrine as an analogy.)

XIX. 104 ff. Conscience speaking:

Christ, turning the water to wine began Dowel, as Wine is like Law and the Holy Life and thus Christ taught us to love our enemies. He was then known as the Son of Mary.	Later in His Ministry He made the lame to leap and comforted the sad, was crucified, rose again and earned the title of Son of David. Then He was Dobet.	He taught Dobest when He gave Piers authority to bind and unbind sin on condition of *"redde quod debes."*

Langland was a poet who liked to be seen feeling for his ideas; he tries out successive notions and noses his way among opinions before the reader's eyes. Never, perhaps, a learned man, as Chaucer was, he gives the effect of one who listened gladly to disputation, contributing now and then his native opinion to a discussion that was, philosophically, somewhat above his head; much as an undergraduate, reading for Honors in History, and having friends reading Greats, might pick up from conversation as much of philosophy as he could clumsily understand and despise the rest as quibbling subtlety. [10]

Langland's definitions, then, unlike the successive definitions of Justice in the *Republic* (where every successive definition is allowed to cancel its forerunner), are *cumulative*. He has not the dialectic technique so much as the ruminative technique; he has a set of ideas at the back of his head, and, being a better poet than logician, he *feels* for them, rather than *thinks* them. With this ruminant poet, then, each restatement may be taken as a new slant of thought upon the same idea, a succession of facets cut upon the same stone.

It is therefore justifiable to gather together into three lots all that is offered to us as Dowel, Dobet and Dobest respectively, and to presume that each lot, as a whole, and taken with the general context of the poem, sums up all that Langland ever thought about the lives. It will be quickly noticed that the virtues of Dowel encroach upon those of Dobet and Dobest, as though at first Langland had not completely disentangled the virtues proper to it from those proper to the other two. Nor is this apparent confusion surprising, for he is emphatic that whoever would Dobet, must first Dowel; so also with Dobest. Thus, much of what belongs to Dobet and Dobest also belongs to Dowel, and all that belongs to Dowel, belongs also to Dobet and Dobest. For the lives are infinites, can be lived inexhaustibly without contradiction among themselves.

[10] Cf. G. R. Owst, *Literature and Pulpit in Medieval England* (New York, 1966).

First to collect the material into three lots:

Dowel is a manual life lived in honesty of word and deed; reliable, sober, humble-hearted; protects the soul against Satan; exists in matrimony (i.e. celibacy is not a condition to salvation); it does the world's work, is obedient to law, and fears God; is the prerequisite of Dobet; is loyal in love (i.e. charitable and trusty); is a common life to be lived in the Articles of the Faith, as taught by the Church, and particularly in the Holy Trinity; is to live in faith, hope, and charity; to hurt no fellow Christian; to obey the Clergy; is an "infinite," that by Faith, finds out Dobest; is *"Disce"* (book-learning cannot be meant here; I take *"disce"* to mean willing attention to the teaching of the Church); is (analogous to) contrition (the first part of a valid penance); is obedience to the great commandments of Christ, the wine-like law of love, even of your enemies.

Dobet is all this, and in addition: *low as a lamb;*[11] *loving of speech; helps all according to their needs;* has broken the purses of the avaricious; has entered Holy Orders and expounded the Bible; is handmaid to the Soul; *loves friend and foe;* suffers; is based upon Dowel; *is of Love's kin;* is to suffer what the Bible, by the Church's teaching, enjoins. Is to practice what you preach and be what you seem; is to keep your rule and not to run to Rome (?); is to labor to teach others; is an "infinite"; is *"Doce";* is (analogous to) confession (second part of a valid penance); is to heal the sick, comfort the afflicted and suffer (martyrdom, if necessary).

Dobest is above Dowel and Dobet; bears a Bishop's crook to hale men from Hell and bash down the wicked; protects Dowel; intercedes with God for those who have offended against Dobest; has authority over Anima; *succours* and guards young and old, *heals and helps;* issues from Dowel and Dobet; draws on Dowel to Dobet (i.e. encourages and ordains candidates for Holy Orders?); *is of Love's kin; must practice what he preaches;*

---

[11] I have put in italics those virtues in Dobet and Dobest upon which Dowel seems to encroach, or to have included before.

is found out by Dowel and Dobet "with a feith"; and saves man's soul (so also do the other lives, of course, but here, I think, is meant that it has the authority to ordain the other two lives in such a way as to make them worthy of salvation); *is Dilige;* is (analogous to) satisfaction (third part of valid penance); has authority to bind and unbind on condition of *Redde quod Debes.* (It would seem at first that this was a virtue of Dobet, the priestly life, inasmuch as priests have power of communicating absolution; but they do not have this power in virtue of their contemplative lives, but in virtue of the *Episcopal Authority* that ordained them.)

To condense these scattered sayings about the three lives:

The life of Dowel is inexhaustible in itself and is sufficient for salvation; it is a life of faith and work, the life of the manual worker and layman, to live which he must be humble, temperate, obedient to the Church, honest, compassionate, fearing God and loving men with a warm neighborly love. He must know and believe in the simple elements of the Christian faith. In the character of this life it is not difficult to recognize the spiritual lineaments of Piers Plowman as they are portrayed in the *Visio;* the following quotations will authenticate this recognition:

> I haue ben his folwar . al this fifty wyntre;
> . . . I dyke and I delue . I do that treuthe hoteth;
> Some tyme I sowe · and some tyme I thresche,
> In tailoures crafte and tynkares crafte · what Treuthe can deuyse,
> I weue an I wynde · and do what Treuthe hoteth. . . .
>
> (v. 549–555)

> . . . ȝe mote go thourgh Mekenesse · both men and wyues,
> Tyl ȝe come in-to Conscience · that Cryst wite the sothe,
> That ȝe louen owre lorde god · leuest of alle thinges,
> And thanne ȝowre neighbores nexte.
>
> (v. 570–573)

> I parfourned the penaunce · the preest me enioyned,
> And am ful sori for my synnes   and so I shal euere. . . .
>
> (v. 607–608)

late Mercy be taxoure,
And Mekenesse thi mayster · maugre Medes chekes. . . .

(vi. 40, 41)

And that thow be trewe of thi tonge · and tales that thow hatie.

(Ibid. 52)

In dei nomine, amen · I make it my-seluen.
He shal haue my soule · that best hath yserued it,
And fro the fende it defende · for so I bileue,
Til I come to his acountes · as my *credo* me telleth,
To haue a relees and a remissioun · on that rental I leue.
The kirke shal haue my caroigne · and kepe my bones;
For of my corne and catel · he craued the tythe,
I payed it hym prestly · for peril of my soule,
For-thy is he holden, I hope · to haue me in his masse,
And mengen in his memorye · amonge alle Crystene.
My wyf shal haue of that I wan · with treuthe, and nomore,
And dele amonge my douȝtres · and my dere children.
For thowghe I deye to-daye · my dettes are quitte,
I bare home that I borwed · ar I to bedde ȝede.
And with the residue and the remenaunte · bi the rode of
    Lukes!
I wil worschip ther-with · Treuthe bi my lyue,
And ben his pilgryme atte plow · for pore mennes sake.

(vi. 88–104)

In exclaiming at the beauty and depth of these lines, it is easy to forget that perhaps those very qualities of beauty and depth arise from the disregarded meditations of the *Vita de Dowel* and that in this love-attracting character of Piers are no more than the simple virtues of Dowel, exactly as they have been discovered by our analysis, but rounded forth with a consummate allegorical imagination.

It would be tedious to particularize every instance in which Piers at his first entry fulfills emblematically the moral obligations of the active life. So simple is the allegory, and so well-framed to illustrate Dowel in practice, that further comment is perhaps superfluous, but there is one episode of special poignancy to show the implications of that true neighborly love,

which is to include even the enemies of Dowel; it is the episode
of the Britoner who

> . . . a-bosted Pieres als,
> And bad hym go pissen with his plow · for-pyned schrewe!
>
> (VI. 156–157)

When the too-courteous Knight failed to bring the wretch to
reason, Piers felt obliged to send for Hunger, who took the
offender, buffeted him about the cheeks so that he looked like
a lantern all his life after and beat him so as almost to burst his
guts. But the sight of the Britoner's misery touched Piers' heart.

> Thanne hadde Peres pite · and preyed Hunger to wende
>   Home . . .
> 'Ac I preye the, ar thow passe' · quod Pieres to Hunger,
> 'Of beggeres and bidderes · what best be to done?
> For I wote wel, be thow went · thei wil worche ful ille;
> For myschief it maketh · thei beth so meke nouthe,
> And for defaute of her fode · this folke is at my wille.
> They are my blody bretheren,' quod Pieres·'for god bouȝte
>   vs alle;
> Treute tauȝte me ones · to louye hem vchone,
> And to helpen hem of alle thinge · ay as hem nedeth.'
>
> (VI. 202–212)

Material evils, for Langland, could best be combatted by
spiritual good; at the same time even God used violence to
"bring folke to his wille"—as may be seen from the sermon of
Reason (V. 13), and the behavior of Kynde (XX. 79), who is
assisting Conscience by sending fevers, fluxes, coughs, cardiacles,
cramps and toothaches; for sickness reminds men of death, and
therefore of Judgment, and therefore brings repentance—so it
is not out of character in Piers to "houp after Hunger" (VI. 174);
Treuthe would have done the same. And yet the loving-kindness
of Piers, which is so pre-eminently a quality of Dowel, moves
him to ask Hunger if there is not a kindlier way of handling
wasters justly.

To condense the sayings that concern Dobet, it is easier to

omit those which are included in Dowel, for they are included *ex hypothesi* and need not be repeated. Dobet, then, adds nothing to Dowel except the following: he is a contemplative or clerk who teaches, heals and suffers and who lives in accordance with what he professes.

It is true that in his entry in XVI Piers is not described as a priest, but all the other conditions of Dobet are fulfilled in him; he teaches Langland at great length the nature of the Tree of Charity and how it is supported by the Holy Trinity (XVI. 25–89). The particular praise accorded to Virginity by Piers (ibid. 67–72) is what might be expected of a contemplative, or cleric, and is therefore in character with Piers as Dobet. Further there are the twin disquisitions on the Trinity (XVII. 138–249), in both of which Piers fulfills the role of teacher. As healer and succorer of the afflicted, he becomes the Good Samaritan (XVII. 48–79), though the actual identification of Piers with him is kept back by Langland for the more affecting surprise of the later line:

> One semblable to the Samaritan · and some-del to Piers the Plowman.
>
> (XVIII. 10)

And as Sufferer, Piers is united to the sufferings of Christ between Palm Sunday and Good Friday:

> 'Is Piers in this place?' quod I · and he preynte on me,
> 'This Iesus of his gentrice · wole iuste in Piers armes
> 'In his helme and in his haberioun · *humana natura. . . .*'
> (XVIII. 21–23)

Two things equal to the same thing are equal to one another, and this maxim is of clearer service in the matter of Piers and Dobet than it is in the matters of Dowel and Dobest. But even in Dobest the correspondence between that life and Piers is evident enough, although, as has been admitted, the disappearance of the Plowman from his barn *Unitas* when it is in its last jeopardy, is strange; one looks for him to hold his ground. But this difficulty is inherent in the fable, and not in the interpretation that is put upon the character of Piers.

The virtues of Dobest over and above those of Dowel and Dobet are simply these: to exercise episcopal authority for the protection of the simple, the abashing of the wicked and the maintaining of the sacramental life of the Church (particularly are mentioned the sacraments of Penance and of the Altar; cf. XIX. 178–182, and ibid. 384–386). The Life of Dobest is in fact that which cares for the salvation of men through the right administration of the instituted Christian Church.

It is to Piers, therefore, in his final significance, that grace gives the four oxen of the Evangelists, the grain of the four cardinal virtues, the Cross of Christ and the Crown of Thorns for the timbering of the Church (XIX. 257–321); for it is in receiving these gifts and in putting them to the use of Christendom together with the sacraments committed to his charge, that Piers Does-best. Piers is the embodiment of God's Authority on earth, and Dobest is a way of life in which that Authority is embodied.

The sowing of the four seeds of prudence, fortitude, temperance and justice (XIX. 271–308), and the ploughing and harrowing with the Four Evangelists and the Four Fathers of the Church (XIX. 257–269), is reminiscent of the Life of Dobet in that these are allegorical Acts of Teaching; and the Mortar of Mercy, made of the Blood and Baptism of Christ (XIX. 320–321), recalls, at a distance, the loving-kindness of Dowel in handling his blood-brother, the Britoner, on whose misery he had pity (VI. 210). But, as can be seen from the table of abstract qualities of the three lives, which I offered above, this inclusion of Dowel- and Dobet-elements in Dobest is essential to Langland's thought. Nothing is more certain in his mind than that you cannot Do better unless you have first Done well, and still Do well, nor can you Do best unless you continue to Do well and to Do better also.

How could this central idea be better expressed than by em-

84

bodying it in a single man, in a Piers? We cannot forget the first Piers, though we pass on to the second or to the third; the cumulative quality in the lives is thus not only stated as a theorem, but demonstrated in a growing and inclusive personal symbol in Piers. The progress of Piers is not as that of caterpillar to chrysalis to butterfly, but as that of blade-ear-grain, where one identity becomes successively more and more fruitful while remaining visibly the same. It is this *organic* quality in Piers which, for me at least, is the masterstroke of Langland's myth-creating power; without this understanding of its hero the reader loses sight of the fine contours and frontiers, and the poem becomes a mapless jungle of visions and discourses.

Allegory, once believed to be the life of poetry, is now commonly thought the death of it. This may have come about from the general changes in English ways of thinking, but I suggest it comes more particularly from the contempt in which the allegorical aspects of later works such as *The Faerie Queene* are commonly held. Hazlitt has voiced his contempt once and for all. The difference between the allegory of Spenser and that of Langland is the difference between a pleasing formal artifice and a natural growth; there is a topiary effect in *The Faerie Queene;* the allegory is the carpentered work of an unmatched artist-craftsman, but in *Piers Plowman* the allegory is organic, the bone in the body. His allegory we now have to understand by an intellectual process not unlike deliberate translation, for we are unaccustomed to reading in allegory. Just as the reader of a French book is not *reading French* as long as he mentally translates it into his own tongue while reading, so in Langland we are not reading allegory as long as we are analyzing and making an argued interpretation. The real reader of a foreign tongue thinks immediately in that tongue; the language of allegory asks the same unselfconscious comprehension.

It remains to be noticed that the allegorical scheme here deduced from the B text is strongly hinted in the A text, where Piers is clearly the simple embodiment of the active life of

Dowel and where the rough suggestions of the moral natures proper to Dobet and Dobest respectively are in complete harmony with their later elaboration in the B text. The extension of the embodiment of Piers as Dowel to his embodiment (in the B text) as Dobet and Dobest is the very signature of the author of A. It seems to me impossible that a B mind could have caught on to and developed this allegory and also the moral natures of the higher lives from the A fragment, and have done so exactly in the manner of A, unless the B mind *was* the A mind: in other words, I believe that Langland wrote both A and B.

4

PIERS PLOWMAN:
AN INTERPRETATION OF THE A TEXT*

T. P. Dunning

I. THE THEME OF THE *VISIO*

IN TREATING OF human activity in terms of man's final end, Langland made use of the positive dogmatic system promulgated by the Church and accepted by the consciences of the faithful. For the medievals, this system constituted a complete interpretation of human life and destiny. "Christianity was presented through the Church," as Powicke observes, "as an interpretation of the Universe"; the Church's "secret was not merely part of life, it gave meaning to life, and was the spring of that knowledge of the Universe of which the Church was the vehicle."[1] Langland, therefore, was confined within very well-defined limits; as far as the moral side of things was concerned, the theologians left very little room for doubt on any point. St. Thomas, for instance, discusses such questions as: "Is there any sin in being too little disposed to sport and play?" "Can there be virtue or vice in matters of toilet?"[2] The poet, then, was limited in regard to his subject matter, but this limitation

* Reprinted, by permission, from *Piers Plowman: An Interpretation of the A-Text* (London: Longmans, Green and Co., 1937), pp. 16–23, 167, 169–186.
[1] *The Christian Life in the Middle Ages* (Oxford, 1935), pp. 21, 13.
[2] ST, II-II, 99. clxviii. -xix., a.a. 4 and 1.

brought freedom of another sort. Since his matter was known —that is, the moral system of the Church, which everyone had to know, at least in outline, under pain of sin—he could unify his material under a particular aspect without fear of being misunderstood. And this is what Langland does in the *Visio*. While setting out ostensibly to treat of human life and destiny in general, he makes *the right use of temporal goods* his theme, knowing that he can rely on his readers to remember that it is not wholly or mainly by this that man's final end is to be attained.

In the Prologue, the poet looks on the world and finds it wanting, and the vice he sees everywhere is cupidity, the inordinate love of temporal goods. In Passus I, the question to be discussed between Holy Church and the Dreamer—and, seemingly, that which *is* discussed—is clearly man's purpose in life, how he is to reach the Tower and avoid the Dungeon, that is, to reach Heaven and avoid Hell.

Yet the Lady practically confines her summary of Christian doctrine to the general principles regulating man's relations with the goods of this world. The remainder of the poem develops naturally from Passus I and is concerned with the allegorical exposition of these same principles.[3] The subject, then, may be said to be *Temporalia—sub specie aeternitatis*. The point to be stressed, however, is that the poet by no means wishes to imply that the proper use of the *bona temporalia* is all that is needed to attain man's final end; indeed, the whole conduct of the poem, and in particular its magnificent climax, is expressly designed to prove the contrary. For, as Langland well knew, the right use of the *bona spiritualia*—Mass, the Sacraments, Prayer—is, in the mind of the Church, of infinitely more importance to man in attaining the Tower and avoiding the Dungeon than the mere fulfilling of his duties with regard to the temporalia.

[3] R. W. Chambers, "The Authorship of *Piers Plowman*," *MLR,* v (1910), 12, 13.

No doubt, the reason Langland chose to concentrate on cupidity was that actually it was the chief evil of his time:

> In the later Middle Ages the conditions of power had been changed by the increased circulation of money, and an illimitable field opened up to whosoever was desirous of satisfying his ambitions by heaping up wealth. To this epoch, cupidity became the predominant sin. . . .[4]

Trade and commerce had begun to flourish, the old feudal system of land tenure (i.e. nonliquid property) and payment in service or kind was everywhere breaking down.[5] In 1372, the Commons of England saluted Edward III as "King of the Sea";[6] and, as Jusserand observes, "avec le commerce viennent le luxe, le confort et le goût des arts." The distinguishing characteristic of the latter half of the fourteenth century is, according to him, "le culte du luxe": "On songe au confort et à l'élégance de la table"; "le luxe des vêtements est poussé à l'extrême."[7]

Moreover, questions concerning the use of temporal goods, the lawfulness of private property and so on, were in the air all through the Middle Ages, but more especially in the fourteenth century. First, there were the Manicheans, Albigensians and Vaudois, for whom all material creation was a thing of evil. The published records of the Inquisition refer incessantly to preachers who denied the right of private property and asserted that no rich man could get to Heaven.[8] St. Thomas

[4] J. Huizinga, trans., *The Waning of the Middle Ages* (London, 1924), p. 18.

[5] J. J. Jusserand, *Histoire litteraire du peuple anglais* (Paris, 1895),I, 256–267; L. F. Salzmann, *English Industries of the Middle Ages* (Oxford, 1913), pp. 203 ff. The Black Death did much to hasten the return of trade and commerce to the West.

[6] *46 Ed III. Rotuli Parliamentorum,* 6 vols. (London, 1767–1777), II, 311.

[7] Pp. 260, 264, 266.

[8] Bede Jarrett, O.P., *Medieval Socialism* (London, 1913), p. 30. See Chapter III also.

Aquinas expressly mentions a sect of communists calling themselves the *Apostolici,* who clung to the system in vogue among the first Christians. Then there were the *Fraticelli* or Spiritual Franciscans, who denied private property altogether, and were condemned by the Pope in 1322. Ockham, the brilliant Oxford Franciscan, has some strange views on property and man's right to temporal goods. Closely allied to the *Fraticelli* in spirit were the curious medieval bodies of the *Beguins* and *Beghards,* who considered the communistic form of life an essential religious duty. In England, Wyclif threw over private property as a general institution and upheld the principle that only the just could possess property, and inordinate attachment to temporal goods was the principal fault the Lollards found with the Church of the fourteenth century:

> Ʒwan the Chirche of Yngeland began to dote in temporalte after her stepmother, the grete Chirche of Rome, . . . feyth, hope, and Charite begunne for to fle out of oure Chirche. . . .[9]

And John Ball, the leader of the English Peasant Revolt of 1381, was an ardent exponent of communistic principles.[10]

As a result, discussions on the right use of temporal goods and the lawfulness of property abound in the writings of the Middle Ages.[11] The schoolmen were at pains to draw up a systematic and detailed exposition of the Church's doctrine on the matter, based on the teaching of the Fathers; and St. Thomas's elaborate statement of the case (ST, II–II, lxvi) "was

[9] Quoted from the first of the twelve "conclusions" urged in Parliament "about the 18th year of Richard II," by the Lollards. J. Gairdner, *Lollardy and the Reformation* (London, 1908), I, 44.

[10] See a typical sermon of Ball's (thought most probably exaggerated) quoted by Froissart, *Chronicle* (London, 1848), book ii., chap. 73, pp. 652–653.

[11] Cf. A. J. Carlyle, *A History of Medieval Political Theory in the West* (London, 1915), II, Part i, pp. 136–142; Part ii, pp. 41–49. Also the second part of the *Roman de la Rose,* especially lines 5876–11443 (Ed. Michel [Paris, 1894] I.).

widely accepted through all the Middle Ages."[12] The rights of private ownership and the use of temporal goods in general were also treated of in detail by the lawyers, both civil and canonical. Bracton and his school in England, Pierre du Bois (*De Recuperatione Terre Sancte*), Ockham and the group of pamphleteers who defended Louis of Bavaria against Pope John XXII (first half of the fourteenth century), Nicole Oresme, Bishop of Lisieux and the first man to translate Aristotle's *Politics* into French, Phillip de Meziers, Pope Innocent IV, Antonio Roselli and many others wrote and argued on these questions.

Even more important still . . . are the writings of Richard Fitzralph, Archbishop of Armagh and Chancellor of Oxford against the Mendicant Friars. In particular, one must note his *De Pauperie Salvatoris,* begun in 1350 and completed in 1356, which contains an elaborate discussion of dominion and property and from which Wyclif largely borrowed.[13] The famous sermons against the Mendicants which involved Fitzralph in a serious quarrel with the Friars lasting until his death in 1360 were preached in English at St. Paul's Cross in the winter of 1356–1357. The *Defensorium Curatorum*—the most widely read of Fitzralph's sermons—was preached at Avignon before Innocent VI in full consistory on November 8, 1357. These sermons likewise contain discussions on the right to property and its use, and all—even after Fitzralph's death—were read and copied frequently; Trevisa, for instance, made a translation of the *Defensorium Curatorum* toward the end of the century. Furthermore, if Father Aubrey Gwynn is right in thinking that line 62 of the Prologue,

---

[12] Jarrett, p. 49.
[13] See R. Lane Poole's preface to the edition of Books I-IV, which he edited as an appendix to Wyclif's *De Dominio Divino* (Wyclif Soc., 1890).

Mony ferlyes han bi-falle · in a fewe ȝeres,

refers to the serious trouble just mentioned between Fitzralph and the Friars, as it surely seems to do, there is further reason for believing that Langland was familiar with the Archbishop's preaching.[14]

In thus combining satire on contemporary evils with the enunciation and allegorical exposition of the moral principles applicable to them, Langland was quite in line with the ordinary practice of the vision-allegorists of the period. In Rutebeuf's *Voie de Paradis,* for instance, the depraved condition of the world is evidently the poet's motive in describing for his contemporaries the way men should live if they wish to attain to Paradise. Again, De Guileville's obvious intention in the *Pèlerinage de Vie Humaine*—perhaps the most famous of these moral allegories, composed c. 1330–1331—is to teach the various classes of the Society of his day the duties they were so badly neglecting; Avarice, for instance, in the middle of a long didactic exposition (she is expounding the spectacle of the Chessmen) breaks out into fierce satire of Kings, Nobles and Bishops, and the allegory for the time being is completely forgotten.[15] Miss Owen notes this point with regard to the French allegories, but not interpreting *Piers Plowman* as I do, she fails to note the connected didactic exposition the latter contains.

A comparison with the *Divina Commedia* will postulate the correctness of my theory with regard to the theme of the *Visio.* This is a comparison which immediately suggests itself and has already been made at some length by both Courthope and Stanley B. James.[16]

[14] See Aubrey, Gwynn, S.J., "Richard Fitzralph, Archbishop of Armagh," *Studies,* March, 1937, which gives a full account of these closing years of Fitzralph's life.

[15] First recension, ed. J. J. Stürzinger, II, 282–317.

[16] Chap. VI, "Back to Langland" in *History of English Poetry,* I (London, 1935); Mr. James, however, is concerned with *Piers Plowman* insofar as it preaches a doctrine suited to present-day needs: his com-

Dante, like Langland, looked on the world of his times and found it wanting. He, too, conceived the idea of writing a poem which would be at the same time a work of art and a work of moral instruction:

> Now the kind of philosophy under which we proceed in the whole . . . is moral philosophy or ethics; because the whole was undertaken not for speculation but for practice. For, although in some place or passage it may be handled in the manner of speculative philosophy, this is not for the sake of speculative philosophy, but for the sake of practical needs.[17]

His matter is the same as that of Langland:

> As far as his ethical system is concerned, I am unable to find, either in the *Convivio* or in the *Commedia,* any originality worth mentioning. Dominant throughout is the Catholic doctrine of the seven virtues and the seven sins.[18]

Indeed, to both Dante and Langland, there could be only one remedy for any and every possible evil, namely, the moral teaching of the Church. Moreover, it would seem that the same vice which so impressed Langland was considered also by Dante to be the source of all the evils of his day. He says in the *Convito:*

> What but this new heaping-up of goods daily endangers, nay destroys cities, countries, individuals? This first purpose of both laws, civil and ecclesiastical, is to prevent this covetousness.
>
> (IV. 12)

parison with Dante is not literary. Christopher Dawson also makes this comparison in *Medieval Religion* (New York, 1934) p. 170, but shortly, on general lines and on the basis of the C text.

[17] *Epistle to Can Grande della Scala*, Latham's trans. (London, 1891), p. 199. Herr Vossler remarks: "Dante assures us in the dedicatory letter . . . that the dominant philosophic bias of the poem is towards ethics. Even if this testimony be not genuine, it still remains accurate." (*Medieval Culture,* I, p. 84.)

[18] Vossler, I., 346.

And in the *De Monarchia,* speaking of the perfect monarchy of Caesar Augustus, he exclaims:

> But in what fashion the world has been moved from that time to this, so that the seamless vesture has been torn by the nails of avarice, we have read, and God grant that we could be beyond reach of seeing!

Evidences from the *Commedia* could be multiplied. Avarice, or cupidity, is represented by the she-wolf, who with the panther (Lust) and the lion (Pride), strive to impede Dante from ascending the Delectable Mountain:[19] but the she-wolf has more prey than all the other beasts—

> Accursed be thou ancient she-wolf,
> Who more than all other beasts hast prey,
> For your hunger endlessly deep.[20]

Until the wolf is put to flight by "him who is to come" misery will hold sway on earth (*Purg.* xx. 13–15).

Yet, in order "to remove those living in this life from their state of misery and lead them to the state of felicity" (the end of the *Commedia* according to the *Epistle to Can Grande*), Dante chose to treat of man's purpose in life and his final destiny, as interpreted by the Church, in its entire connotation. For, in choosing as the unifying principle of his work the freedom of man's will—"the subject is man, liable to the reward or punishment of Justice, according as through the freedom of the will he is deserving or undeserving"[21]—Dante virtually took on himself to expound the whole range of moral theology. He knew quite well, as did Langland, that it did not matter what sin was the most prevalent in the world: the entire moral law

[19] "The earliest view of these three beasts remains the most probable, according to which they symbolise Luxury in its medieval sense, Pride, Avarice or Cupidity in its widest meaning." (E. G. Gardner, *Dante* [London, 1905], p. 90).

[20] *Purg.* xx. ll. 10–12. Cf. also: *Purg.* xix. 115 ff.; *Par.* xxvii. ll. 121 ff., etc.

[21] *Ep. to Can Grande,* p. 194.

had to be observed in all its detail before man could pass "from the state of misery to the state of felicity."[22] Langland, on the other hand, chose exactly the same subject, namely, man's purpose in life, and presupposing a knowledge of much of what Dante painstakingly treats of in detail, confined his attention to one aspect of the moral law, making it quite clear at the same time that he was not losing his proper perspective on Eternity. His poem says quite simply: *haec autem oportuit facere, et illa non omittere (Luc.* xi. 42).[23] That is how the *Visio* specifically differs from the *Commedia:* the *genus* in both cases is the same.

There are three points, then . . . :

(1) that Langland concentrates on one particular aspect in the general scheme of man's destiny and by so doing introduces unity, in the artistic sense, into his material;

(2) that at the same time he makes it clear that he understands the necessity of fulfilling the whole moral law;

(3) that the poem is a carefully and accurately planned work, not the formless outpouring of a man whose confusion of mind was only exceeded by the confusion of his art.

II. THE *VITA DE DOWEL, DOBET ET DOBEST*

The *Vita* in the A Text is a distinct poem from the *Visio:* "in all the best A MSS.," as Chambers notes, "it is carefully dis-

[22] Cf. Jac. II. 10: "Quicumque autem totam legem servaverit, offendat autem in uno, factus est omnium reus."

[23] James has already noted this point although he misses altogether (since he is studying the C text) its significance with regard to the A text: "The work is Dantesque in conception. . . . It is in execution that Langland's hand falters. The ground is strewn with nobel fragments suggestive of some vast scheme of things, which yet never takes shape as a co-ordinated whole. So long as you possess the key, that is, if you are familiar with the medieval Creed, philosophy and social order, you can fill in the gaps; otherwise you must be content to admire isolated portions" (p. 31). But it must be remembered that Langland was writing for people who *did* all know the Medieval Creed, philosophy, social order, etc.—they lived it.

tinguished from the 'Vision' proper."[24] There is, however, a connection between the two poems, which the frequent mention of Dowel in the concluding lines of the *Visio* (five times between lines 156 and 187) indicates. Details in the MSS. suggest that the *Vita* is the corollary, as it were, of the *Visio*. Chambers has characterized it as "the sequel . . . a very short and unimportant fragment,"[25] and it is, in fact, as a sequel that I consider it—not, however, as a fragment, but as a finished poem. . . .

From its form or structure alone, the *Vita* in A seems to me to be simply one of those *débats* which were a common feature of medieval literature and which is exemplified in the debate between Mede and Conscience in the second section of the *Visio*. Courthope observes that:

> Throughout the thirteenth century, numerous poems were produced, imitating the form of a scholastic debate, in which two opposing reasoners advanced arguments on each side of a question, and contended till the dispute was determined by a logical conclusion.[26]

In the *Vita,* a poem of the following century, we have a development of this form. Instead of having the same two people present all the time, as in the *Disputacijoun de la Sinagogue et de la Sainte Eglise,* or even two separate pairs, as in the numerous debates on the subject of the Heavenly Virtues (occasioned by Ps. 84:11, 12), the Dreamer in the *Vita* meets with a number of different characters in turn, some of whom he hears in silence, and others with whom he contends. But the essential *débat*-form is maintained throughout: the allegory is of the thinnest—there is no action whatever, and the entire object of the poem, as in the case of the *débats,* is to give infor-

[24] "The Original Form of the A-text of *Piers Plowman*," *MLR*, VI (1911), 306.
[25] Preface to *New Light on "Piers Plowman,"* A. H. Bright, (Oxford, 1928), p. 16.
[26] *History of English Poetry* (London, 1919), I, 66.

mation on a particular subject, in direct fashion, but weighed carefully and considered from many angles; again, the Dreamer, when countering an argument, employs the exact formula used in the debates of the Schools; and finally, there is the summing-up by the Dreamer of the results of his wanderings—that is to say, his judgment on what he has heard (Passus II. [XI. in Skeat], 250 to the end), which constitute, as Skeat observed, a most excellent conclusion, "wrought with peculiar care" with a view to making clear "the result which . . . the author wished to bring out strongly."

For this reason I cannot regard the development of the poem as marking a definite progression toward the knowledge of *Dowel,* in the sense that each definition of Dowel, Dobet and Dobest rules out and is superior to the one preceding it: the development of the poem can be considered progressive only in so far as each new speaker provides further material for the Dreamer's consideration, and for comparison with what he has already heard. It is the judgment of the Dreamer, concluding the debate, that must finally decide what conclusions we are to carry away with us from the poem.

In the course of his wanderings in search of Dowel, the Dreamer meets with two friars, Thought, Wit, Study, Clergye and Scripture, each of whom he questions concerning the whereabouts of Dowel. The friars give him some information concerning Dowel alone, and from Thought, Wit and Clergye he obtains definitions of Dowel, Dobet and Dobest. The structure of the poem is as follows:

> *Prologue* (118 lines): Dreamer talks with the friars about Dowel —8–52.
> Thought defines Dowel, Dobet and Dobest—61–100.
>
> Passus I. (213 lines): the entire passus taken up with Wit's explanation of Dowel, Dobet and Dobest.
>
> Passus II. (303 lines): Study speaks—1–91; 103–162. Clergye defines Dowel, Dobet and Dobest—179–215. Dreamer

and Scripture argue—216–249. Dreamer sums up—
250–303.

Passus III. (117 lines in full): Epilogue.

Now it is at once evident from this outline that Wit's definition of Dowel, Dobet and Dobest occupies most space in the
poem, and forms as it were the "body" of the work. Furthermore, it must be pointed out that the colophon which as Chambers points out,[27] with unessential variants, is common to all
the A MSS., and is, moreover, *peculiar to the A MSS.,* speaks
of the "Vita de Dowel, Dobet et Dobest *secundum wyt et
resoun."* There is surely some connection between the fact that
a whole passus of 213 lines is given up to Wit's explanation of
Dowel, Dobet and Dobest and the fact that the poem itself
is said to be the "Vita de Dowel," . . . *secundum wyt et resoun.*
It seems to me that "wyt" and "resoun" must be taken together
as signifying one and the same thing, as "resoun and kuynde
wit" do in the *Visio;* for "wit," when not used as one of the
five senses, signifies the reason or understanding (see *NED*).
"Wyt et resoun" may, I think, be taken as another instance of
the pairing of virtually synonymous terms to denote one object
of thought, of which there are many examples in Middle English
—compare, for example, *The Lay-Folks Catechism:* "withouten travaile or trey," "to knowe and to kun" (p. 4); "com-
andes and biddes" (p. 20). . . . In Passus I. of the *Vita,* Inwit
is used to denote the practical reason—being said to keep *Caro
et Anima* "In rule and in reson" (line 51), and being synonymous with "wys vnderstandinge" (line 71). I have no doubt
that the Wit who is speaking in Passus I. is to be identified with
the Inwit he is speaking of and that when it is said that this
poem is the "Vita de Dowel, . . . secundum wyt et resoun," the
reference is precisely to this exposition of Wit in Passus I. For
the line of thought in the *Vita* seems to point quite definitely to
Wit's explanation of Dowel, Dobet and Dobest as that most
acceptable to the Dreamer.

[27] " . . . Form of the A-text," 306–313.

PROLOGUE

The Dreamer sets out to seek Dowel, which in the *Visio* has been defined in general as loving God and avoiding mortal sin. The first information he gets concerning Dowel comes from two friars, "men of grete wittes." It is to be noted that they implicitly understand Dowel as defined in the *Visio*—the avoidance of deadly sin. Moreover, they not only show the Dreamer how Dowel may be said to dwell with them, but also how he may dwell with every man. By means of the example of the man in the boat, they distinguish between sins of frailty and deliberate or deadly sins. No sin is deadly, according to the theologians, unless performed with the full consent of the will: hence the friars conclude that doing well, or avoiding deadly sin, is in the power of every man—"for thi-self hast the maistrie." Everything, then, depends on the will. The Dreamer thanks them, but declares that he has "no kynde knowynge . . . to conceyue thi wordes,"[28] so he will continue his quest. But it must be noted that he does not contradict the friars: he merely implies that their explanation needs further elaboration before it becomes intelligible, and his parting with them is most courteous on both sides (50–52). These friars are the only real persons the Dreamer meets with in the poem, for he now lies down, falls asleep and dreams: all the other characters are met in the vision, and all are personified abstractions. This point is worth noting, I think.

Thought next comes to the Dreamer in vision, and the inevitable question is put to him. Thought, answering, defines Dowel, Dobet and Dobest in terms of the active, contemplative and "mixed" life, as Wells and Coghill have pointed out.[29] It must be noted that the three "lives" mentioned by Thought as Dowel, Dobet and Dobest are not subjective but objective

[28] A. I. [IX] 9, 47, 48. Cf. *Visio,* A. I. 127–128.

[29] I do not think, however, that the "King" here is God as Coghill says (p. 75 above), for the functions of the King as laid down here will be seen to correspond exactly to the medieval conception of kingship as defined by Carlyle.

states of perfection or well-doing: religious and prelates, as St. Thomas points out, are objectively in a state of perfection inasmuch as their mode of life is more perfect than any other; but individual religious and prelates may not be in a greater subjective state of perfection than persons living in other states of life.[30] Now it must be noted that the Dreamer definitely does not like Thought's explanation (line 102), and craves "more kuynde knowynge." Thought and he dispute on Dowel until they meet Wit. It is noteworthy that when they meet Wit, the Dreamer —who up to this has been only too anxious to ask everybody he meets with concerning the whereabouts of Dowel—now will not ask Wit, but begs Thought "to beo mene bi-twene,"

> To putte forth sum purpos · to preuen his wittes.
> ([ix]. 115)

I think this incident is intended to express the functions of Thought and Wit: according to the Scholastics, the reason needs concepts, or thoughts, for its operations. The Prologue ends with Thought's petition to Wit to know Dowel, Dobet and Dobest.

In the next two passus we have another evidence of the parallelism already noticed in the *Visio;* as in the case of the *Visio* the entire poem is contained in germ in Passus I, so here it is contained in the Prologue. For Passus I of the *Vita,* containing Wit's exposition of Dowel, Dobet and Dobest, is simply the elaboration looked for by the Dreamer, of the principle given to him by the friars, which he accepts but does not fully understand; and Passus II corresponds exactly to Thought's definition of Dowel, Dobet and Dobest which in the Prologue does not please the Dreamer and which in Passus II he definitely rejects.

PASSUS I

Wit immediately defines Dowel, Dobet and Dobest as subjective states of perfection or well-doing: they are the guard-

[30] S.T., II-II., clxxxiv.

ians of the soul. He then gives an accurate and well-constructed description of man's soul and stresses exactly the same point as did the friars, namely, that by his reason or understanding, man

> Is cheef souereyn of himself · his soule for to ʒeme.
> ([x]. 72)

In the Prologue, the friars have shown that Dowel is to avoid deliberate sin—in other words, to obey God's law, or conscience; here it is shown that conscience or reason must direct the will. Dowel is to fear God, Dobet to suffer and be chastised, and from both these arises Dobest. Substantially, these are the well-known purgative, illuminative and unitive states or ways of perfection (well-doing) which have been commonplaces in mystical theology since the time of the Pseudo-Dionysius.[31] The Fathers and spiritual writers are unanimous in stating that religion, or turning to God ("conversion") begins with fear of God's judgment.[32] The effect of this fear is that man begins fighting against his passions and practicing virtue—this entails mortification:

> Well then, he has begun to fear the day of judgment: by fearing let him correct himself, let him watch against his enemies, i.e. his sins; let him begin to come to life inwardly and to mortify his members which are upon the earth. . . . Now in proportion as this man who has begun to fear the day of judgment, mortifies his members which are upon the earth, in that proportion the heavenly members rise up and are strengthened. . . .[33]

Moreover, God enters into this purifying process, and by means of suffering endeavors to help the soul to withdraw itself from attachment to the world and cleave to Him. Hence Wit says:

> Virga tua et baculus tuus, ipsa me consolata sunt.

---

[31] v. S.T., II-II., clxxxii. 4.

[32] Cf. Aug., *Tractat. ix. in* I *Joann.* Ox. trans., p. 1206; Greg., *Moralia,* lib. v., cap. xvi. Ox. trans., i., p. 266.

[33] Ibid.

On this verse (Ps. 22:5), St. Thomas says:

> Et hoc potest dupliciter intelligi, Uno modo ut per virgam intelligamus directionem viae . . . Alio modo, ut exponatur hoc pertinere ad correctionem, quia virga fit correctio. Prov. 13. "Qui parcit virgae odit filium suum." *Et baculus tuus,* scilicet sanioris disciplinae; quasi dicat: Mitis et dura correctio tua dedit mihi consolationem.[34]

Rolle combines the two senses distinguished by St. Thomas:

> Sothly i sall dred nan ill: for thi wand that is thi light discyplyne that chasties me as thi sun, and thi stafe, that is thi stalworth help . . . thai haf conforted me. . . .[35]

Fear of God and suffering (whether self-inflicted or sent by God) are ordained toward only one end, namely, the overcoming of self-will by reason. . . . A will, ruled by right reason, cleaves inevitably to God, according to the ascetical writers, and union with God through love is Dobest:

> And so cometh Dobest aboute · and bringeth a-down
> modi [i.e. the stubborn one],
> And that is wikkede Wil · that mony werke schendeth.
> ([x]. 212–213)

And:

> So Dobest out of Dowel · and Dobet doth springe.
> ([x]. 123)

Secondly, Wit teaches that perfection does not depend on one's state of life; hence a man must remain in his own state and not seek to remove to another. Dowel consists in doing as God's word teaches and obeying Conscience in all things. The doctrine is that of St. Paul and the Fathers (cf. 1 Cor. 7), and is the foundation on which the medieval hierarchic conception of Society, or the Church . . . was built. Each man had his own proper vocation in life, to which God called him—that is, each

---

[34] *Commentarium in Psalmos LI,* p. 298.
[35] *English Psalter,* ed. Branley (Oxford, 1884), p. 84.

man had his proper and peculiar place in the structure of the Church:

> The variety of states and offices in the Church points in the first place to the perfection of the Church. . . . Secondly, it is a matter of necessity for the necessary work of the Church. . . . Thirdly, this is part of the dignity and beauty of the Church. . . .[36]

Compare Rolle with Passus I, 88 ff.:

> Tumbyl noght fra þe state þat þou hase tane þe tille;
> It ledes til þe Kynges ȝhate, þare þou may layke
>   þi fille.[37]

> For I will not þat þou wene þat all er hali þat hase þe abet of halynes, and er noght ocupyed with þe worlde; ne þat all er ill þat melles þam with erthly bysines. Bot þai er anly hali, what state or degre þai be in, þe whilk despises all erthly thyng, þat es at say, lufs it noght, and byrnes in þe luf of Jhesu Criste . . . and hates all synn and ceses noght of gode werkys. . . .[38]

Every man, therefore, as the friars pointed out, can Do well according to the grace that is given him; and if he be meek and kind and humble, God will give him grace to Do bet and Do best. Everything consists in obeying the "counseil of conscience · a cordynge with holy churche" (line 89). This is exactly the doctrine of St. Thomas, who teaches that:

   (1) Every man is bound to tend to perfection;

   (2) perfection does not consist in the evangelical counsels of poverty, chastity, etc.—these are merely helps to the perfect life—but in the observance of the commandments, which are summed-up in the love of God and neighbor;

   (3) conscience, or the judgment of the practical reason "a-cordynge with holy churche" is the sole subjective, intrinsic norm of morality man has.[39]

---

[36] S.T., II-II, clxxxiii, 2.

[37] *Exhortations, English Writings of R. R.,* ed. H. Allen (Oxford, 1931), p. 39, ll. 3–4.

[38] *Form of Living,* chap. 3, ll. 5–13.

[39] Cf. S.T., II-II, clxxxiv. aa. 1, 2, 3; Ibid. liv. I; I-II, xix. aa. 5, 6; etc. Also, Dom Butler, *Ways of Christian Life,* chapter on Dominican Spirituality.

Since the first necessary state in the scheme of things is that of wedlock, Wit turns his attention to the question of marriages. "Folk that . . . libbeth as heore lawe wole" are the "rote of Dowel," for of such marriages come Confessors, Virgins, Martyrs, Monks and Knights and men to fill all the different offices and states in the Church, or society. Wit then goes on to show that bad marriages—those entered into with a wrong intention (through covetousness, for instance—line 177), and in which the two parties do not keep God's law—are the cause of much evil, and breed a cursed race that

> . . . wandren as wolues · and wasten ȝif thei mouwen.
> A-ȝeyn Dowel thei don vuele · and the deuel plesen. . . .
> ([x]. 207–208)

He then sums up what has been his teaching on the subject of Dowel, Dobet and Dobest—emphasizing their functions as regards the will.

PASSUS II

This, as I have noted, falls into four parts: Study's speech, the journey to Clergye and Scripture and Clergye's exposition of Dowel, Dobet and Dobest, the argument between Scripture and the Dreamer, and finally, the Dreamer's summing-up of the poem.

Wit's wife, Study, immediately begins to upbraid her husband for giving such wisdom to the Dreamer; he is casting pearls before swine, she says, since now men have no thought of anything but land and lordship, riches, rents and ease; wisdom and wit are counted unworthy of attention except insofar as they further the interests of covetousness. He that has Holy Writ "euer in his mouthe" is little loved; both clerics and laymen discuss and argue on points of faith and dogma in light and disrespectful fashion: "atte mete in heor murthe · whom munstrals beoth stille," while the poor and needy clamor, unheeded, at the gate outside. There are two lines here which are reminiscent of the saying of Peter Cantor quoted before:

> Clerkes and kete men · carpen of god ofte,
> And han him muche in heore mouth · bote mene men
>   in herte.
>
> ([xi]. 56–57)

Men ask reasons and seek to discover human explanations for points of supernatural faith: for apparently, knowledge and learning "hath puffed them up" (St. Paul).

> But Austin the olde · for alle suche precheth . . .
> *Non plus sapere quam oportet sapere.*
>
> ([xi]. 72–73).

Therefore, says Study, instead of arguing and looking for reasons, you should believe in what Holy Church teaches.

> And preye him [God] of pardoun · and penaunce in
>   thi lyve.
>
> ([xi]. 77)

And now, she says, here comes a stupid fellow, "and wolde cacchen of my wittes, What is Dowel from Dobet"; he must be daft, she says, since unless

> . . . he liue in the leste degre · that longeth to Dowel,
> I dar ben his borw · that Dobet nul he neuere,
> Thau3 Dobest drawe on him · day aftur othur.
>
> ([xi]. 89–91)

Now this is exactly what Wit has just shown, since he has pointed out that Dowel, Dobet and Dobest are three states of soul; this is in complete opposition to Thought's teaching, who defined Dowel, Dobet and Dobest as three states of life. But Dowel, Dobet and Dobest are essentially subjective states of soul, for regardless in what state of life a man is, be he a follower of the active, contemplative or mixed life, unless he follows also the advice given by Wit in Passus I, he neither does well, nor makes any progess in well-doing. As St. Thomas says (and by "State of perfection" he means objective state, that of religious and prelates):

> And therefore there may be some perfect people who are not in a state of perfection; and some in a state of perfection who yet are not perfect.[40]

Study then sends the Dreamer to Clergye and Scripture. The Dreamer puts his question, and Clergye defines Dowel, Dobet and Dobest just as Thought had done, that is, in terms of the active, contemplative and "mixed" lives, with some comments on the conduct of the religious of his times. Just as Thought's definition did not please the Dreamer, so now he is not satisfied with this either, and answers that he had thought Knighthood and Kinghood, Kaisers and Earls to be Dowel, Dobet and Dobest of all. Scripture argues with him and shows that neither lordship nor wealth can help toward heaven; man must gain heaven by observing God's law—

> *Dilige deum, etc., et proximum tuum . . .*
> ([xi]. 236)

Especially must he fulfill his obligations of fraternal charity: which is exactly the teaching at the end of the *Visio*.

The Dreamer now sums up. That it is a summing-up is, I think, indicated by the first lines,[41] and more particularly, as Skeat noticed, by the ending. Moreover, it is not an answer to Scripture, since in Passus III it is Clergye who first speaks. The Dreamer now brings forward what seems at first sight an insuperable difficulty to the solving of this problem of Dowel— that is, the matter of predestination. Solomon and Aristotle are in hell, the Penitent Thief, Mary Magdalen and St. Paul are in

---

[40] S.T., II-II, clxxxiv. 4.
[41] "ȝet am I neuere the ner · for nouȝt I have walkid
To wyte what is Do-wel · witterly in herte;
For how I werche in this world · wrong other ellis,
I was markid withoute mercy . . ."
([XI]. 250–253)

heaven: yet the former, to all appearances, lived virtuously, the latter—at least for a time—wickedly. Now I think we must connect these lines on predestination with what Study said after Wit had concluded his explanation to the Dreamer. Then it will be seen that this is merely an example of what Study so strongly denounced, namely, the endeavor "to wite the weyes of god almihti," into which one is led through a too great desire for knowledge or "Clergye." For the Dreamer now obviously remembers this, and remembers that, according to Wit's teaching, learning is not necessarily a condition of Dowel:

> And ȝet I forget ferthere · of fyue wyttis techinge,
> That clergie of Cristis mouth · comendit was euer.
> ([xɪ]. 285–286)

And the "douȝtiest doctor, Austyn the olde," says that:

> "Arn none rathere yrauisshid · fro the riȝte beleue
> Thanne arn thise grete clerkis · that conne many bokis;
> Ne none sonnere ysauid · ne saddere of conscience,
> Thanne pore peple as plouȝmen · and pastours of bestis.
> ([xɪ]. 297–300)

These lines are paralleled by many in Study's first speech—cf. lines 53–55, 56–57—and I think are clearly meant to recall them, in particular the other quotation given there from "Austyn the olde," which sums up the Dreamer's judgment on what Clergye has just told him:

> *Non plus sapere quam oportet sapere;*

and forms an admirable comment on these lines here.

So the Dreamer must not imitate the "clerkes and kete men" that "carpen of god ofte" and indulge in profitless discussions, but rather the "mene men" who have God "in herte" (56–57). This, then, is his solution of the problem: he virtually rejects Clergye's definition as inadequate by his repudiation of the value of Learning; and judges that Dowel, Dobet and Dobest are chiefly to be found amongst the "pore peple as plouӡmen". . .

> Souteris and seweris · such lewide Iottis
> Percen with a *pater-noster* · the paleis of heuene,
> Withoute penaunce, at here partynge · in-to heiӡe
> blisse.[42]

([XI]. 301–303)

This is exactly the ideal that has been set up in the *Visio* in the person of Piers Plowman, but there considered under a different aspect. It is very interesting to note, too, that the end of the *Visio* prepares us for the problems of the *Vita* and their solution not only by the frequent mention of Dowel, but also, as has been noted, by the jangle between Piers and the priest, when the latter sneers at Piers' lack of learning.

Everything in the *Vita* has led up to this conclusion of the Dreamer. The full philosophical explanation of this teaching, and the fundamental basis on which it rests, are provided in the example given by the friars as expanded and developed by Wit. To do well and do better and do best is in the power of every man, in every state of life; essentially, it is an affair of the will, for nothing can separate man from God but a deliberate violation of His law. To do well and do better, then, consist in fearing God, bearing sufferings patiently, obeying Conscience "a-cordying with holy Churche," and acting toward the neighbor with meekness and kindness: all this begets and presupposes humility, for love of which "louhnesse," God gives the grace to do best (cf. I 122–126). Now all these conditions are fulfilled in Piers Plowman, as may be seen from his description of his relations with Truth (A. VI. 28–45), and from his treatment of his neighbor in Passus VII. Today learning is rather a hindrance than a help to well-doing, as Study points out; at one and the same time she endorses the explanation just given by Wit and shows the inadequacy of that already given by Thought

---

[42] Cf. Ecclus 35:21: *Oratio humiliantis se nubes penetrabit.*

(and about to be repeated by Clergye, or Learning, cf. 86–91); finally, she more than implies that Dowel, Dobet and Dobest is to be found amongst "mene men." Clergye's definition is inadequate, and the Dreamer later rejects it: for man can Dowel, Dobet and Dobest in any state of life. His argument with Scripture brings out the point that high station and wealth have nothing to do with Dowel, Dobet and Dobest. Then he himself brings forward the last difficulty which can only be solved by means of the advice already given by Study: by abstaining from reasoning out the ways of God, and by believing "on that lore · that lereth holichirche" (74 ff.). Finally the Dreamer passes judgment on all that has been said, in lines which, as Skeat pointed out, constitute a carefully constructed conclusion. And this conclusion has been already clearly hinted at by Study earlier in the Passus (52–57).

The poem is now complete: it has developed logically from the Prologue, the first passus giving the Dreamer the further explanation of the friars' teaching which he needed, the second confirming his dislike of Thought's solution. Thought might be regarded as expressing the Dreamer's preconceived idea of Dowel, Dobet and Dobest, for perfection is easily associated with the state destined toward perfection, and the suggestion of the active, contemplative and mixed lives would be the first to present itself. Wit's explanation, on the other hand, is more fundamental and requires deeper consideration before it can be perceived, since it introduces the distinction between an objective and subjective state of perfection.

PASSUS III

Passus III, then, is hardly needed: in point of fact, it does little more than to reiterate the conclusions arrived at in the end of Passus II. It bears every appearance of being, as Chambers has suggested, an afterthought on the part of the poet—if, indeed, it be genuine at all. But it by no means implies a continuation of the poem: on the contrary, it emphasizes the fact that the poem is at an end, as I shall explain. Its object, I think, is to bring out the place of Clergye—by which is meant theological learning—in the spiritual life. Clergye first says that he has done all he can to teach the Dreamer what is Dowel, Dobet and Dobest, but this can only mean all he can do in view of the Dreamer's present dispositions—which he identifies with those described by Study in her denunciation of the times (II. 1–91). If he knew truly that the Dreamer's desire for this knowledge was accompanied by a firm resolve to shape his conduct according to it, then:

> Al that thou askest · a-soylen I wolde.

He thereby admits the inadequacy of the explanation he has already given. Moreover, these lines confirm what I have said about the Dreamer's difficulty concerning predestination—to which Clergye evidently refers in lines 5–9—being an example of the conduct reprobated by Study. Scripture bids Clergye not to give the Dreamer any further information until he be shriven

> Of the kynde cardinal wit · and cristned in a font
>
> ([XII]. 15)

In other words, until he be baptized—in the state of grace—and live according to Kind Wit's teaching, as contained in Passus I. For, by Baptism man first receives sanctifying grace and is made a child of God; all that he has to do now is to obey his Conscience—i.e. the Practical Reason, Kind Wit—in order to reach Heaven. And it is only to a man in the state of grace and directed by Conscience that learning becomes of any use: such a man will make use of learning to guide his conduct, not to pander to his pride, as people now use learning according to Study. The poet's attack on Learning at the end of the *Vita* is here corrected: Learning may have a place in the life of the spirit. But the poet's conclusion is in no way altered; all through Passus III. he insists on the fact that man must be directed by Kind Wit and be Scripture's servant (l. 39)—in other words, that he must lead a virtuous life according to the dictates of Conscience and keep God's law: the fact emphasized by Wit, Study, Scripture and the Dreamer in the *Vita*.

When the Dreamer declares he will be Scripture's servant, she declares she will direct him to Kind Wit whose lodgings are with Life—for it is the purpose of the moral faculty to direct man through life; she calls a cleric called *Omnia probate* to lead Will to the Town *quod-bonum-est-tenete,* where Kind Wit is. The cleric and the town are named from a verse of St. Paul concerning prophecies or instructions: "Despise not prophecies," he says, "but prove all things: hold fast that which is good" (1 Thess. 5:20–21). On this verse St. John Chrysostom comments as follows:

> Seest thou that this is what he means by, *Prove all things?* Because he had said, *'Despise not prophesyings,'* lest they should think that he opened the pulpit to all, he says, *Prove all things,* that is, such as are really prophecies. . . . That you may by proof distinguish both true things and false, and abstain from the latter and hold fast the former. . . .[43]

This is exactly what the Dreamer has done: he has heard many instructions on the subject of Dowel, Dobet and Dobest, and he has formed his own judgment.

The remaining lines might be taken as expressing the miseries of life in "this vale of tears here below"; it is noteworthy that Fever's advice to the Dreamer closely recalls that of Wit in Passus I.

Langland's poem ends, I think, with lines 97–98 where there is an obvious break in the sense; these lines, indeed, form an excellent ending: they furnish a close parallel to the ending of the *Visio,* they sum up Wit's teaching in Passus I, they are a perfect echo of Scripture's lines (ii. 235–249), and inculcate

---

[43] *Homily XI on 1 Thess.,* Oxford trans., pp. 453–454.

a line of conduct in direct contrast to that denounced by Study. . . .

There is a clear connection between the subject matter of the *Vita* and that of the *Visio*. The ideal the poet sets up for emulation is in both cases the same: that expressed in the life of the ploughman, or poor man, who lives in simplicity and truth, obeying God's law in humility. But whereas in the *Visio* this ideal is set up in contradistinction to the love of the good things of this world—the abuse of temporal goods, here the lowly God-fearing ploughmen and shepherds and "suche lewede Iottis" are placed in opposition to those who, in their pride and arrogance, endeavor "to wite the ways of god almihti" —the abuse of Study and Learning. The sins denounced in the *Visio* are sins of the flesh; those here reprobated are sins of the spirit. In both poems there is the same insistence on the necessity of morally good works—"profitable works"—to attain salvation: the moral law, summed-up in *Dilige Deum tuum . . . et proximum . . .* is insisted on strongly in both, and obedience to a Conscience instructed in this law shown to be man's whole business in life.

These resemblances regard the subject matter: but it is quite clear from the treatment of the subject matter in each, that they are two completely distinct poems. There is no mention whatever in the *Vita* of the field full of folk: it has its own Prologue and its own setting; the field of folk has been finished and done with in the *Visio*. Again, the entire conduct of the action is different in the *Vita,* for the material action is practically nil and the allegory a mere vehicle for long discussions and sermonizing. Furthermore, although the conclusions arrived at in both poems are essentially the same, and the ideal held up in both is Piers Plowman, yet Piers is not mentioned at all in the *Vita;* he is completely a character of the *Visio* and is evidently but merely referred to in the *Vita* when the poet speaks of "mene men," "pore peple as poluȝmen · and pastours of bestis."

Just as in the denunciation of Cupidity in the *Visio,* so also in the denunciation of the abuses of Learning in the *Vita* is it possible to perceive the influence of the time-spirit. In the fourteenth century, decadence had set in strongly in the Schools: learning was pursued as an end in itself, and:

> the heaping of subtlety on subtlety and the interminable controversies of the advocates of Thomism and Scotism bewildered and disgusted the serious seeker after spiritual light and drove him eventually to abandon all intellectual philosophy in favour of a life of contemplation and prayer. Many believed with the author of the *Imitation of Christ* that it is better to feel contrition than to know its definition, and that he is very learned indeed who does the will of God and renounces his own will.[44]

The natural result of this was the revival of the principles of mysticism and the foundation of the mystic school of philosophy. Rolle and his followers in England in the first half of the fourteenth century, and Dame Julian of Norwich and Walter Hilton in the second half, are representative of the general European movement. In the *Incendium Amoris,* Rolle "over and over again deprecates the theology of book-learning";[45] moreover, in the prologue Rolle addresses the work

> non philosophis, non mundi sapientibus, non magnis theologicis infinitis quescionibus implicatis, sed rudibus et indoctis, magis Deum diligere quam multa scire conantibus.

And Miss Allen notes that:

> the mood in which Rolle wrote this work, as expressed in the Prologue . . . must have been a popular one with the public, for that prologue (beginning with the sentence quoted) became attached, in manuscripts at Paris, Munich, and Florence, to the *De Triplici Via* of St. Bonaventura, to which the title was then given of *Incendium Amoris.*[46]

---

[44] W. Turner, *History of Philosophy* (Boston, 1903), p. 411.
[45] H. E. Allen, Writings ascribed to Richard Rolle (New York, 1927), p. 226.
[46] Ibid.

Rolle's mood in the prologue is perfectly duplicated by that of Study in Passus II. 1–91, and the summing-up of the Dreamer at the end of the *Vita*. The *Imìtatio Christi,* at the end of this period, shows the same "mood," and would furnish excellent commentaries on the different parts of the *Vita*:

> Melior est profecto humilis rusticus, qui Deo servit, quam superbus philosophus qui, se neglecto, cursum coeli considerat. . . . Si scirem omnia quae in mundo sunt, et non essem in charitate, quid me juvaret coram Deo, qui me judicaturus est ex facto? . . .[47]
> Beata simplicitas, quae difficiles quaestionum relinquet vias, et plana ac firma pergit semita mandatorum Dei.[48]

[47] Lib. I, chap. ii.
[48] Lib. IV, chap. xviii. All this chapter is illuminating for Langland's point of view in the *Vita,* as expressed principally in Study's speech, Passus II. 1–91.

5

THE PHILOSOPHY OF PIERS PLOWMAN*

Henry W. Wells

INVITING THE READER to exercise his own imagination with the aid of hints and cues rather than putting his meaning in prosaic terms, the meditative author of *Piers Plowman* takes one of the well-known roads of poetical composition. He stands with the poets who find it more to their liking to hint than to assert. On this account their work becomes relatively difficult to interpret. Time further adds to the obstacles implicit in their technique. Hence many of the controversies of scholars and the justification for what may at first glance seem a wasteful commentary. One cannot expect to leap suddenly to an understanding of so subtle and complex an allegory as *Piers Plowman*. Only through honest controversy and repeated effort is marked progress to be made.

The subject is complicated by discrepancies between the versions of the poem as preserved in the manuscripts. The facts in a broad way are so familiar as to call for only the briefest summary. The version commonly called the A text consists of approximately twelve passus. The B text contains considerable rewriting of the A text and nine long additional passus. The C text is marked by further rewriting and occasional expansions or omissions. Presumably the major lines of thought in B

* Reprinted, by permission of the Modern Language Association, from *PMLA*, LIII (1938), 339–349.

and C are much the same. But students of the A text are obviously criticizing a work considerably different from either of the longer versions, the differences being in about equal proportion in style and thought. The B text does not, I think, greatly alter the thought of the earlier so far as the two run parallel, but obviously contributes much that is new in its additional passus.

Since the present study is a commentary on the B and C texts, it is not primarily concerned with A text or its critics. Thus I am more indebted to the article[1] by Coghill than to Father Dunning's recent book on the A text. The latter scholar is chiefly engaged in advancing the view that the entire A text is a thesis on the proper use of material goods with special reference to their misuse through cupidity. My own interpretation of the B text bears the same relation to Father Dunning's view which I understand the B text to bear to the A text. The longer version includes the earlier, slightly alters it, and expands and clarifies certain of its ideas. At first glance Father Dunning's interpretation and my own may seem to clash, but such, I think, is not actually the case, and he himself, if I understand him correctly, recognizes no fundamental inconsistency. While he generally passes over in silence such views as I may have expressed[2] relative to the A text, he differs from me specifically only regarding the figure of Holy Church.[3] My views on the *Vita* of the B text he holds plausible though not fully demonstrated. I may add that I accept his own views concerning the important figure of Piers Plowman and regarding the interpretation of the *Vita* in the A text. I entirely accept his uncommonly thorough statement of the importance of the theme of cupidity in the A text. The same theme, though Father Dunning nowhere discusses the subject, has obviously much importance for the complete

[1] Nevill K. Coghill, "The Character of *Piers Plowman*," pp. 54–86. above.

[2] H. W. Wells, "The Construction of Piers Plowman," pp. 1–21.

[3] T. P. Dunning, *Piers Plowman, An Interpretation of the A. Text* (Dublin, 1937), p. 58.

B text as well. It is clear, indeed, that any discussion of sin itself must be largely a discussion of cupidity, as that sin is so liberally defined by scholastic tradition as quoted fully on the subject by Father Dunning. But if the idea which he finds dominant in the A text is also in some form present throughout the B text, so the elements and ideas which I shall point out as conspicuous in the B text are to some extent present in the A text. The main thesis of Father Dunning's book is not my particular concern here. Neither am I occupied with the unanswered (and, I fear, unanswerable) question as to whether one poet or two or more poets wrote *Piers Plowman.* Langland's poem I am willing to leave in this respect with Homer's. For convenience sake merely I shall refer to the author as Langland. I am for the present chiefly interested in the longer version of the work, seeking in particular to arrive at a more just statement of its guiding ideas than has as yet been given either by Coghill or myself. My present view will, I trust, be found a warranted simplification. At no point is it a rejection of observations either by Coghill or myself. It appears to me that a more comprehensive statement of Langland's ideas than has previously been made is possible and that this revised view should incorporate earlier propositions into larger and ampler ones.

Langland was concerned with ideas which he expressed in the somewhat awkward terminology of the Life of Dowel, Dobet and Dobest. As his poem enters its most critical stage these terms in over a score of places are used and observations made as to their meaning. Numbering the passus as in the B text,[4] the first seven following the original glosses may be called the *Visio,* while the thirteen succeeding sections are described in turn as the Life of Dowel (VIII–XIV), the Life of Dobet (XV–XVIII) and the Life of Dobest (XIX–XX). Thus in the simplest way possible one sees how important in Langland's

---

[4] Unless otherwise stated, the references are to the B text.

eyes these three categories become. The only question is what he meant by them.

There are several ways of attacking the problem. One is to seek in medieval literature for a less cryptic and poetical, a simpler and more prosaic statement of what appears to be the same idea, and so, if possible, to find the sources of Langland's view. Some such sources I believe are found in quotations which I advanced from the popular *Meditationes Vitæ Christi* and from Aquinas. Briefly, the Life of Dowel thus appears as the first or lower stage of the active life, wherein a man by moral and intellectual discipline and simple faith learns to rule himself wisely and to live honestly and humbly in his vocation. He who does well by satisfying these requirements and who essays nothing further will be saved. The Life of Dobet becomes the contemplative life or the life of devotion. This too is a good and safe road for those strong enough to follow it. Finally the Life of Dobest presumes previous discipline in both the preceding lives and consists in authority, as, for example, in episcopal authority. It is the second stage of the active life, based upon the theory that he who has already learned to rule himself will alone know how to rule others. It was sometimes termed the mixed life.

So far as I am aware no one has questioned my evidence that Langland actually held these conventional views expressed in the *Meditationes*. The discussion of scholastic training and intellectual problems, of the active life as such and of the element of Christian morality in VIII–XIV is evidence; so is the long discussion of asceticism in the prologue to the Life of Dobet (XV) and the devotional character of this section of the poem. And the repeated statement that Dobest is the episcopal life and the emphasis in passus XIX–XX upon the active virtues and the government of Unitas, or The Church (with mention also of the State), make Langland's conventional intention abundantly clear. The relation of this tripartite system to the Trinity and a few other matters likewise contribute, as I have already shown (pp. 16–17 above), to the poet's organizing ideas.

But the grave limitation of my previous presentation lies, I believe, in its disposition to make Langland almost wholly conventional. While he remains broadly typical of his age, his thought cannot be rightly understood merely through reference to ulterior sources. He has, in fact, used much more than other men's words. His peculiarly daring, imaginative and penetrating mind turns the ideas of others gently but firmly to his own purposes. It is a most familiar error to overlook a poet's originality through attention to a limited range of source material. While Langland seems never to have been in the least heretical, the originality of his poem lies in the rearrangement of old ideas and images.

Coghill has stressed certain qualifying ideas in his study of the text. He has distinguished sharply between two phases of the life of Dowel: the simple piety and honesty embodied in the figure of Piers as the honest laborer, and the moral and intellectual life in its advanced stages. His comments upon the Life of Dobet have been especially illuminating. While Langland himself seldom if ever directly refers to this state as the life of contemplation, he frequently refers to it in terms that suggest the priestly life, a life of aggressive altruism and sacrifice to one's neighbors. Coghill cannot, of course, say that Dowel is the laity, Dobet the priesthood and Dobest the episcopacy—if for no other reason than that the intellectual life so clearly included under the heading of Dowel hardly corresponds with medieval notions of the life of those out of holy orders. Nevertheless, Coghill points so strongly to the note of active, wholly altruistic service in his conception of Dobet that one almost loses sight of the description of this state as the life of contemplation. He is particularly categorical in his interpretation of Dobest as the episcopal life.

The danger of this method of approach is that unchecked from other sources it becomes overliteral. The question is simply asked: what passages in Langland's poem make specific statements regarding the three terms. Now in the story of the poem a pilgrim is depicted as seeking for these three virtues. But the

poem itself is divided into sections which are themselves designated as the states in question. Most of the specific statements
within the poem regarding the virtues occur in the earlier and
obviously more naive sections of the Life of Dowel. It therefore
becomes natural that very concrete and simple answers are
commonly given. We may easily mistake a symbol for a reality
or a part for the whole. The medieval conception of simplification is always to give the more concrete statement at the ex-
pense of the more abstract, to represent God the Father, for
example, with hands and feet, or in some other way to allegorize an idea by making it visible. Thus a manifestation of an idea
in action is substituted for the more abstract but more direct
and adequate expression. One must be on guard against all
these pedagogical simplifications of poetic language, for, if
pressed no further, they give us only a half truth, or even a
palpable misrepresentation. Dowel, Dobet and Dobest are most
fully expressed by Langland, not in aphorisms, but in the general conduct of the poem itself, and there they must chiefly be
sought by the imaginative reader rather than in these inci-
dental and literal statements of the author or even in parallels
drawn to his literary sources. Useful as the citations and the
sources may be, they can also be overused.

I am still persuaded that Dowel, Dobet and Dobest signify in
Langland the two stages of the active life divided by the contemplative life; I am still persuaded of the force of all that
Coghill has said regarding the moral or intellectual life, the
priestly life and the episcopal life. But Langland's thought here
goes further than anyone has shown.

Let us begin with the leading properties of his poetic mind.
Keenly observant, deeply spiritual, profoundly social—these
three I think characterize him best. No author has a sharper
or more realistic eye for the outward features of the human
scene; none a deeper penetration into the inner springs of the
religious life; and finally, none a more powerful sense of the
Christian commune as a living organism. His bright and child-

like gregariousness plus his spirituality produce his crowning vision of society itself as the body of Christ. This is Langland's threefold vision and its destined culmination. He is in turn a satirist, a dreamer and a social prophet. From this psychological triplicity, all parts and virtues, literary or spiritual, of his work proceed. Seldom has an author measured his accomplishment so perfectly in terms of his genius.

As I have previously noted, his poem falls into two major divisions, the *Visio* and the allegory of the three Lives. These two sections develop along strictly parallel lines. There are no guiding thoughts in the second part which are not to be found in the corresponding sections of the first part. The *Visio* begins with a pragmatic allegory of political and civil corruption (the story of Lady Mede); secondly, it proceeds to an account of the inner life, wherein sins are passionately confessed and absolution accompanies the Mass; and thirdly, the Christian community is depicted as one organism dedicated to one end through all its various pursuits, namely, the quest for Truth, or Well Doing, or the Salvation of Souls. The second and longer part of the poem faithfully preserves the essential outlines of its predecessor. Instead of treating the problems of practical politics and affairs, the first section now deals with the most pressing philosophical, ethical and theological problems; the second section depicts the mysteries of the faith as represented in the Scriptures, implying a devotional attitude, and also concluding with a penitential attitude and the celebration of the Mass; finally, the third section deals primarily with Unitas or the corporate body of the Church, Christendom conceived here as a brotherhood and living society. Many lesser points of comparison which might be adduced would only serve in summary to obscure the profound unity of the design. The best initial guide to a study of Dowel, Dobet and Dobest is thus a study of the *Visio*. The three lives are the moral and intellectual life, the intuitive and devotional life, and the social or communal life. The first life affords the bare necessities for salvation. It includes faith, good works and the hope of heaven. But to it may be added the more inward life of fervent worship and the inwardness that also radiates outward until the individual realizes himself and all men as part of a brotherhood whose root is in God —namely, the vine of Christ.

It is an error to give too narrow an interpretation to any of these three views. Thus especially in his generous interpretation of the life of Dowel, rather, I think, than in his views of Dobet and Dobest, is Coghill to be congratulated. For he has shown very clearly that the flexible conception of Dowel includes both the piety and virtue of the simple Christian, as symbolized in Piers Plowman's first appearance in Passus v, and the more intellectual interpretation obviously intended in Passus x–xiii. The humblest Christian, however, fails to obtain the spiritual stature and complexity requisite to experience either the fullest devotional ardors of Dobet or the complete realization of the fellowship that is Dobest. While his faith is sound, his devotion is only incipient; while he is a good citizen, he has scarcely entered into a full realization of the meaning of the City of God. The humble Christian has indeed made very imperfect progress even in the higher spheres of the Life of Dowel. He has never debated the grave intellectual problems of the Church, and in recompense for this he has never suffered from theological doubts or from the dread of heresy.

Here it becomes necessary to turn to Father Dunning's observations regarding the *Vita* of the A text. He points out that the view of the three "lives" most often held in this passage is that of the purgative, illuminative and unitive states of the soul. "Dowel is to fear God, Dobet to suffer and to be chastised, and from both these arises Dobest."[5] What Father Dunning fails to observe, as being outside the scope of his immediate inquiry, is that these states bear a striking relation to the active, contemplative and mixed states as described by Langland. The knowl-

[5] Dunning's *Piers Plowman,* p. 101 above.

edge and fear of God is described by the poet as a part of the life of Dowel; the Life of Dobet stresses not only contemplation but asceticism and the passion of Christ; while the life of Dobest is clearly the ideal or unitive life. In the B text this general view is stressed in relation to the sacrament of penance. Contrition, confession and satisfaction, for example, in the opening of passus XIV are said to be Do Well, Do Bet and Do Best.

Father Dunning stresses the point that the Dreamer in the A text twice repudiates the explanation of the three lives offered him by his interlocutors as the active, contemplative and mixed states of the soul. But this does not imply that the author of the A text repudiated the theory or cast it aside finally in relation to Dowel, Dobet and Dobest. The Dreamer is always pictured as less enlightened than his spiritual teachers and as frequently fallible. Such is a convention of moral allegory. Similarly Dante objects to Virgil's advice upon their proposed journey through hell and heaven on the ground that he is neither Æneas nor Paul. But the poet of the Divine Comedy clearly intends his pilgrim to be in error here. To his own amazement he is about to be taken in the body to hell and heaven, as were Æneas and Paul before him. In short, Father Dunning's view of the *Vita* in the A text confirms my general view of the B text and by no means clashes with it. Particularly are we in agreement that the *Vita* in the A text merely covers once more the main thesis of the *Visio,* leaving further development to the later section of the poem. But I am rather more sure than Father Dunning that the author of the B text understood the A text. I suspect that he understood it much better than we do. I even suspect he was the same man.

Caution must be observed in describing the Life of Dobet as the priestly life, or that of Dobest as the episcopal life, lest we mistake the language of poetry for that of criticism. The question at once arises what Langland means by his classifications. Does he mean them to be stages in the social order, such as the laity, the clergy and the episcopacy? Does he mean that only one of the lives can be led at a time? Is his poem simply chastisement administered to group after group of the social scale? Because a person has made but slight progress in the more advanced realms of the Christian life, does it follow that he has in no way participated in the Life of Dobet or of Dobest? At times Coghill would seem to answer these questions in the affirmative, whereas I should answer them in the negative.[6] I do not believe that the Life of Dobet is literally the priestly life. Langland does not say categorically that it is. Yet I should not object to its being called the priestly life provided this is understood in a figurative sense. Priests, Langland naturally holds, should be above all superior to their parishioners in contemplation and devotion. Their inner life should be peculiarly astir. By virtue of this superior warmth and charity they will, ideally speaking, be led to a more active life; their prayers, Langland observes, will be of the greater efficacy. But the priesthood is rather a part of Dobet than Dobet of the priesthood. Contemplation, devotion, the life "withinforth" becomes a supreme reality. According to familiar Christian teaching all who are to be saved must in some degree participate in it. It is, as Langland says, a "state"; but not, I think, merely one of the estates of society. In short, it proves a state of the soul through which the Christian will a thousand times pass, however well he knows it or understands it. It is but one of the three districts of the city in which he lives. In the three passus forming the body of the Life of Dobet (XVI–XVIII) little specifically is said of the priesthood. Moreover, I greatly doubt if the life of Christ, which is here depicted, is intended as an allegory of true priesthood. Rather priesthood would be an allegory of Christ. Such symbolism customarily proceeds not from the greater to the less, but from the less to the greater. Christ's life is here ardently presented as the object of devotion, and

[6] Father Dunning in his chapter on the *Vita* holds the view for which I am arguing. Ibid., p. 100 above.

not as an intellectual allegory. Again, to describe Dobet too narrowly even as the life of contemplation would violate Langland's intention. The inward life has many facets, some even pointing outwardly. From the sanctuaries of the contemplatives, according to medieval belief, issue prayers of the sanctified, of the utmost service to the welfare not only of men's souls but of their bodies. Again, devotion leads to saintly acts of more than common charity which are in themselves neither the fruits of Dowel nor of Dobest. Repeatedly Langland describes Dobet as a prodigal giver. He gives many things, first of all being prayers. Then he may preach and exhort men and women. In doing so he does not assume rule, infringe on the episcopal authority, or deal in the academic or merely factual matter pertaining to Dowel. Talking from the fullness of a heart fired with devotion, he speaks as an individual to the individual soul. The secret chambers of the heart produce a voice that is heard also by the private ear, though in the midst of multitudes. When Langland emphasizes the giving properties of Dobet he thinks, I believe, generally of spiritual gifts. Yet more material charities may also in a secondary way be included. Contemplation, needing little, can spare much for his neighbors. Only the heart fired with devotion will experience the zeal for charity, whether to bestow the highest or the lowest things.

Especially one must guard against a too literal view of the phrase common in Langland and in his able critic, Coghill, that Dobest is the episcopal life.[7] The phrase was originally written, I believe, metaphorically. What better symbol is there for the Christian Community as such than the man, or type of man, ultimately responsible for its integrity? "Dobest is a bishop"— but only with this figurative meaning. The entire texture of Langland's poem shows it to be no merely objective statement about society, nor can we think of its conclusion as becoming

[7] In addition to Coghill's article above, see pp. xxi–xxiii of his Introduction to *The Vision of Piers Plowman*, put into modern English by H. W. Wells (London, 1935).

merely objective. Poems of the curious and inner fervor of Langland's are intimately personal. Although Langland has much to say regarding all orders of the clergy and the religious, he has much more to say on the salvation of every man and on his own salvation. There is the rub for him, his poem including but transcending a merely social or political satire. Thus he writes about Dowel, Dobet and Dobest not alone because these are constituent parts of society, but because they are parts of himself and of every man. In any case they are potentially the parts of each man. As Langland says in Passus IV, man is made in the image of the Trinity.[8] The realization that the forces of which he writes are operating within himself is the best explanation for the peculiar poignancy of his style. He introduces himself as an old man (and surely the Dreamer is no bishop) into Passus XX. In short, his three states are psychological rather than sociological. It is chiefly because Coghill fails to make this clear to me that I have written the present paper.

Let us examine the Life of Dobest further. As Coghill very shrewdly states, this section begins not quite with the beginning of a Passus. Or in any case the Prologue to the Life of Dobest consists of Passus XIX, 1–176. The Life proper extends from here to the end of the poem. Now in this section very little is said of bishops, less indeed than in several other parts of the poem. Looking simply at what Langland writes we shall find that the interest actually centers upon Unitas, the symbol for the company of the faithful on earth, the true and loyal Church. All emphasis is throughout upon the idea of the brotherhood of Christendom. The poet, ever gregarious and socially minded, has here plucked the heart of the theme. No longer does he deal merely with the field of folk—the indiscriminate mass of mankind as it appears to the animal eye—but with the fraternity of Christians held together by faith and good works and by the grace and the sacrifice of Christ. The name Unitas

[8] C. IV. 407–409.

proves an inspiration, for it perfectly expresses Langland's thought. He has put into the center of his canvas what deserves to stand there, enlarged on precisely what requires enlargement, leaving other matters for the periphery. Just as the Schools are the center of Dowel, and Christ is of Dobet, so here Unitas proves the keystone of the final arch. In seeking a phrase to express Langland's meaning it would thus be much better to conclude that Dobest is Unitas than the Episcopal Life. If Dobest is ill and distraught, this only means that the Christian Commune has fallen far short of its perfection.

Dobest, we have often been told in earlier sections of the poem, is to command. But such is its most dramatic meaning. Actually to achieve unity in society it becomes equally important that there be both command and obedience to command. Whoever in any capacity acts consciously to aid Unitas, does best, whether it be the Pope himself who issues the command, or the most humble subject who piously obeys it.

A further means of understanding the Life of Dobest is to review the two steps leading up to it. As the poet and his sources repeatedly say, the states are accumulative. Intellectual and moral laws and religious faith are formulated and molded in the state of Dowel. The fires of charity are lighted in the furnaces of Dobet. In these fires the vessels are created that acquire their fullest social significance only in the Life of Dobest. First comes law and reason, then emotion and devotion, and finally the consecration to a communal utility. Langland's poem, beginning with a lively but unregenerate picture of the commune, ends with a profound and spiritual picture of the same world transformed by religion. Because modern readers possess a better eye for picturesque realism than for social and religious visions, the opening lines regarding the field of folk have become much better known than the closing lines regarding Unitas. But this is not even the fault of Langland as an artist. The more serious view of the poem hangs upon the interpretation of its last few pages.

The poet is skillful in social satire and admirable in mysticism, but not wholly effectual along more strictly intellectual lines. Thus the racy realism of much of the *Visio* has rightly attracted many admirers, and at least a few critics have testified as to the profundity of religious emotion expressed, for example, in his passages in the *Visio* on the sins and on the Mass, and in the Lives of Dobet and Dobest. The most disputed, the most perplexing and apparently the least admired section is that on the intellectual and moral life, the section on Dowel. Even Langland himself may have broken down here, for he seems to have settled upon no entirely satisfactory form for his work. He apparently left it a fragment for many years, unable to continue the Life of Dowel to his liking. Dowel *secundum Wyt et Resoun* he finished, but neglected the evidence of his other allegorical figures, Scripture and Clergye. Artistically and in every way he becomes more sure-footed and effective with the lives of Dobet and Dobest. It deserves especially to be noted that while others have surpassed him in theologizing in verse, few have equalled him in powerful presentation of the inner life, and none quite rivalled him in a vivid, visionary realization of the Christian or social commune. It is with this keen awareness that men are members of one Catholic organism that his august poem concludes, and because his communal vision proves at once so darkly veiled in allegory and so darkly magnificent it deserves special study, and once grasped, a tenacious hold. Our conception of his poetic stature depends upon our understanding of these problems.

Finally, Langland's somewhat difficult allegory of the three states is illumined by his own frequent allusions to the Trinity. In my previous article on the subject I pointed out that each of the three divisions of the *Vita* begins with lines on the Trinity, turning special attention to the Person of the Trinity to whom the particular life is, so to speak, dedicated, but presuming the unity as well as the Trinity of God (pp. 16–17 above). Langland frequently states that man is made in the image of the Trinity.[9] And clearly, just as the Persons of the Trinity are according to the doctrine of the Church inseparable, so the states of the soul are ultimately inseparable—each, even Dowel, implying the others. In addition to his anagogical, moral and personal allegories Langland has a historical allegory also intimately associated with theology. The Life of Dowel deals especially with the heathen or pre-Christian world which believes in God but not in the Trinity. The Life of Dobet is associated with the world during the lifetime of Jesus. The Life of Dobest is the subsequent dispensation of the Holy Spirit after the Ascension and both before and after the poet's own lifetime. Here Langland approximates though by no means follows the historical teaching of Joachim of Flora, who, unlike Langland, pressed his mystical views of the three periods of history so far as to impugn the unity of the Trinity and so to become questionable in his orthodoxy. Langland's psychological trinity is intended as a microcosm or an emanation of the divine.

The gist of this article is that Langland's three lives are not vocational callings but mental states, that they rise in a perfectly familiar ascending scale but remain nevertheless a ladder up and down which the true Christian was expected by the poet to pass at will. Some good but simple men would in his view have only a slender acquaintance with the last two "virtues." But they would have some acquaintance; and the fully developed soul on earth, whether bishop or no, would be richly endowed with all three. Such is, I believe, the key to most of the problems in the philosophical interpretation of *Piers Plowman*.

[9] Note especially C. iv. 346–409.

6

PIERS PLOWMAN: THE RELIGIOUS ALLEGORY OF THE C TEXT*

E. Talbot Donaldson

I. INTRODUCTORY: THE THREE WAYS OF LIFE

THE TOPICS THAT are to be discussed here are some of the alterations by the C poet which seem to affect the interpretation of the religious allegory as set forth in the B version; or better, which affect my interpretation of B's allegory. The phrase "the interpretation of the religious allegory" suggests that a widely accepted, all-inclusive interpretation of B is in existence. But this is not true, although, of course, there do exist studies that are of great value in putting one on the road to a satisfactory interpretation. Of these I make considerable use in the following pages; but it is not likely that any of their authors would lay claim to having settled, once and for all, the problem of the religious significance of the B text of *Piers Plowman*. Even the best doctors disagree. Furthermore, none of them has turned his attention to C. As a result, anyone who undertakes a comparative study of B and C is forced, first of all, to choose among several varying interpretations of B, secondly to put his own

* Reprinted, by permission, from E. Talbot Donaldson, *Piers Plowman: The C-Text and Its Poet* (Hamden, Conn.: Archon Books, 1966). Originally published in 1949 by the Yale University Press. The selection reprinted here is Chapter VI, pp. 156–198, under a title appropriate for this anthology and with a few minor excisions.

construction upon the meaning of C, and finally to compare the various aspects of these largely homemade interpretations. . . .

The reader will recall that in all three versions the poem is divided into two main parts: the *Visio de Petro Plowman* proper and the so-called *Vita de Dowel, Dobet et Dobest*. In B and C the second part is subdivided into three sections, one for each member of the triad. The entire poem, in all its versions and in all its sections, concerns, as I believe everyone will agree, a search for the road or roads that lead to salvation. In the *Visio* this search is considered under its social and moral aspects: the seeker is man-in-society, and it is with the problem of social man that the greater part of the material deals. The second part is less easy to characterize and less general agreement as to its meaning exists. Although according to the colophons of B and C the *Vita* purports to take up the three kinds of life one at a time, the lines of demarcation between them as well as the exact shape that any one life assumes, are far from clear. . . . This obscurity, which exists in all three versions, seems to be caused by the fact that the poet is dealing, simultaneously, with at least two, and possibly more, distinct triadic notions. That means that from one point of view—the point of view expressed by some of the personifications the Dreamer encounters—the commonly accepted hypothesis may be quite correct: Dowel equals the active life, Dobet the contemplative and Dobest the mixed. But from another point of view, the subject of the *Visio* is the active life of society, while the *Vita* is concerned with the more subjective and more contemplative life of the individual in his search for perfection: this life itself is divided into three sections, Dowel standing for the initial stage in the journey, Dobet for its medial stage and Dobest for its ultimate stage. These stages may be equated with the purgative, illuminative and unitive conditions of the soul, or, possibly, with other similar triune concepts. For the moment I should like to defer the matter of attaching specific labels in order to emphasize my conviction that the *Vita* handles two basically different concepts at the same time and sometimes in the same terms. The chief difference between the concepts is that the first, as applied to the life of the individual, seems to develop in a sequence from outwardness (the active life) to inwardness (the contemplative life) to inward-outwardness (the mixed life), while the second develops in a sequence of three stages of inwardness, all of which, of course, have also appropriate outward manifestations and all of which are, incidentally, open to men of all vocations. To give a specific example, when Wit explains that

> Trewe wedded libbing folk · in þis worlde is Dowel,
> (B. ix. 107)

he is referring to the active life in ali its externality. But when the Dreamer, blushing with shame at his scolding from Imaginatyf exclaims,

> 'To se moche and suffre more · certes,' . . . 'is Dowel!'
> (B. xi. 402)

the reference is to an inward state, the first stage of a more contemplative life. A similar instance occurs when Conscience, in the B text, defines Dowel as contrition (B. xiv 16–18): the person to whom this definition is made, however, is Haukyn, the type of the active life and hence of one sort of Dowel.

The double purpose, or, if one will, the cross-purpose, is present in all three texts and particularly in the Dowel section of B and C. An important difference between these two later texts is, as I see it, the fact that in the former the larger share of the emphasis seems placed on a definition of Dowel as the external active life, while in the latter the emphasis is so shifted as to effect a definition of Dowel which seems to encompass the spiritual qualities appropriate to the first of the three stages in an inward, contemplative life. How the C poet accomplished this shift, particularly in his revisions of the *Visio* and the section entitled Dowel, will form the basis for a part of the discussion which follows.

If this sort of interpretation seems too complicated, one can only answer, then so is *Piers Plowman*. I think that we err when we try to pin the poet down to any single system of theological thinking. No one has ever made an effective case for his having been a learned man, subjected to the strict discipline of a coherent philosophy;[1] indeed, it seems generally agreed that he was not much more than an avid and indiscriminate reader and an equally avid listener, both to sermons and serious conversation.[2] Therefore it does not seem likely that there can be found for the body and arrangement of his ideas any precise, all-inclusive source or even any very satisfactory analogue. At times one can scarcely refrain from thinking of him as an intellectual catchall. Thus the expert in the philosophy of St. Thomas will notice in *Piers Plowman* much that is Thomistic; students of Christian mysticism will observe many mystical elements; and those who are familiar with the esoteric backwashes of medieval

[1] Miss Hort at one time believed that Langland had some sort of systematic theological training, but she later gave up the idea. See Greta Hjort [Hort], "Theological Schools in Medieval England," *Church Quarterly Review*, cxvi (1933), 201–218, especially p. 201, n. 1; G. G. Coulton, same title, idem, cxviii (1934), 98–101; and Miss Hort's *Piers Plowman and Contemporary Religious Thought* (London, n.d.), pp. 43–59.

[2] See R. W. Chambers, *Man's Unconquerable Mind* (London, 1939), p. 100: ". . . *Piers Plowman* is the work of a well-educated man, not however very learned. . . . Langland's mistakes . . . show that his knowledge of Latin was rather limited. But he has enough Latin to get along, and, it would seem, some French." Idem, p. 104: "Langland, a poor clerk in Fourteenth-Century London, probably had access to few books; we are deceiving ourselves if we suppose that he had read all that an expert in medieval theology has read to-day. His knowledge must have been largely derived from what he heard in sermons, or got from conversation with other men." Miss Hort in her book, pp. 58–59, concludes a study of the poet's theological learning by observing "that Langland at some stage of his life had lived among people who knew much more theology than that contained in the books we know him to have read, and who talked with him and instructed him in theology." See also G. G. Coulton, *Medieval Panorama* (Cambridge, Eng., 1938), pp. 143–145.

thought will perceive odds and ends left over from the most recondite, and least orthodox, of the Fathers. At a time when all religious ideas came, from the analogy of the Trinity, in groups of three, the poet seems now and then to have tried to demonstrate the congruity of quite dissimilar triangles. For his learning and the tendency of his mind were not systematic but eclectic. He exercised the free choice, the *liberum arbitrium,* of an artist who from the vast spectrum of contemporary thought borrows whatever colors will best illumine his own basic ideas. And despite what I have written above, I venture to think that these basic ideas are in themselves relatively simple. It is in the guises and disguises they assume that the difficulty lies. In essence, the C text of *Piers Plowman* is, I conceive, rather like a huge elaboration of an incident in the life of Christ that Matthew recounts in a few verses:

> And behold a certain man came to him and said, "Good Master, what good work shall I do to have eternal life?" He said to him, "Why dost thou ask me about what is good? One there is who is good, and he is God. But if thou wilt enter into life, keep the commandments." He said to him, "Which?" And Jesus said, "Thou shalt not kill, thou shalt not commit adultery, thou shalt not steal, thou shalt not bear false witness, honor thy father and mother, and, thou shalt love thy neighbor as thyself." The young man said to him, "All these I have kept; what is yet wanting to me?" Jesus said to him, "If thou wilt be perfect, go, sell what thou hast, and give to the poor, and thou shalt have treasure in heaven; and come, follow me." But when the young man heard the saying, he went away sad, for he had great possessions.[3]

It is this incident that the poem in its basic structure most resembles, and it is this incident that is acted out in many

---

[3] Matt. 19:16–22. Confraternity Edition. The parable was cited in connection with *Piers Plowman* by Chambers, *Mind,* p. 124, and by Professor Meroney, to whom I owe my use of it, at the beginning of his original paper [delivered before the English I Section of the Modern Language Association of America on December 30, 1946]. The poet alludes to the verses in his discussion of patient poverty, C. XIII. 166 and B. XI. 265.

forms in the great drama in which the Dreamer asks again and again what he must do that he may have eternal life. The two main sections of the poem deal with the first and second of Christ's answers respectively. The *Visio,* with its picture of contemporary society, deals, much of the time by contrast, with the practical and social aspects of the first response: *Keep the commandments.* The *Vita,* a consideration of the degrees of perfection attainable by the individual, is a dramatization of the second response, which begins, *If thou wilt be perfect.* As Chambers has observed, it is "the enormous step from the first to the second" of Christ's precepts that Piers makes when, in the B text, having torn the pardon, "he resolves that he will cease from sowing, that his plough henceforth shall be of prayer and penance, that tears shall be his meat day and night and that he will take no more thought for the morrow than the fowls of the air" (p. 124). Like the young man in Matthew, Piers goes beyond the first answer, but unlike the young man, he is willing to act upon the second. With this transition, the tone of the poem alters. Social well-being, while never in any sense forgotten, tends to become more and more subordinate to the well-being (and better- and best-being) of the spirit of the individual.

II. *THE VISIO: PIERS PLOWMAN AND THE PARDON*

Concerning the nature of the C poet's revision of the *Visio,* I have made some general remarks elsewhere. Most of his alterations either are minute, or take the form of long insertions which, while they may affect the movement of the poem, do not affect the meaning of the allegory. It is only at the very end of the *Visio* in the incident[4] that involves Piers, the Priest and the pardon sent from Truth[5]—the incident by which is accom-

---

[4] A. viii. 90–124, B. vii. 106–137, C. x. 282–291.

[5] Chambers, p. 117, apparently relying on B. viii. 38, C. x. 42, where Piers is said to have purchased the bull, and on the THU-readings *purchace* and *purchasen* in A. viii. 3, says that Truth bade Piers "purchase a

plished the "enormous step" from the first to the second of Christ's precepts—that the C poet makes his first drastic revision, one that seems to change the entire course of the allegory.

Let us look at the incident as it is recorded in the B text. The author having concluded his review of the clauses of Truth's pardon,[6] a priest appears abruptly and asks to see the pardon itself, so that he may construe it to Piers "in English." The Dreamer, standing near, sees that the document consists of just two lines: *Qui bona egerunt, etc.* The Priest, who apparently recognizes the lines as coming from the Athanasian Creed,[7] exclaims that he can find no pardon except the common promise of heaven to the good and hell to the wicked. Piers, acting in "pure teen," tears the pardon asunder, quoting the Twenty-third Psalm: *Si ambulavero in medio umbrae mortis, non timebo mala.* He then resolves to cease from his labors, citing Christ's words to the disciples, *Ne solliciti sitis,*[8] and call-

---

pardon from the Pope," rather than sending him a pardon directly. See Nevill Coghill's discussion of the problem in his Gollancz lecture, *The Pardon of Piers Plowman* (London, 1945), pp. 17–19. It is my belief that, although for purposes of realism the Pope is somehow involved as an agent in the transaction, the poet tended to regard the pardon as coming direct from Truth to Piers. The lines on which the interpretation depends are A. VIII. 1–3, 8, 21, 25; B. VII. 1–3, 8, 19, 23, 38, 104; C. x. 1–3, 8, 23, 27, 42, 59, 184. There seems to be an increasing tendency from text to text to omit the Pope and make the transaction direct.

[6] Though the pardon consists of only two lines, the discussion of its clauses and marginal annotations and of Truth's secret letter to the merchants takes up much of a passus in all texts. In A and B the expositor seems to be the poet himself, but in C Piers is involved in at least part of the exposition. See C. x. 159–160, where Piers is described as saying that lollers are not included in the bull.

[7] The real source of the lines is not given by Skeat. See Konrad Burdach, *Der Dicter des Ackermann aus Böhmen und seine Zeit* (Berlin, 1926–1932), p. 267, n. 1; Chambers, p. 118; Coghill, p. 19, n. 2. The last-named says that the Priest "gives no sign of recognition that the Pardon is nothing but a quotation from the Athanasia Creed." But does not his derogation of the pardon as such spring from an awareness of its source?

[8] Matt. 6:25 and Luke 12:22.

ing upon the Gospel to witness that God will provide for His own. The priest exclaims superciliously at Piers' learning. The two exchange angry remarks and the scene fades out with the Dreamer explaining that as

The prest and perkyn · apposeden eyther other,[9]

their words awoke him and he found himself, at evening, meatless and moneyless on Malvern Hills.

Probably no single incident in the A and B texts of *Piers Plowman* is more puzzling than Piers' angry tearing of the pardon: puzzling, indeed, to the logical mind, but, as J. J. Jusserand pointed out,[10] artistically as effective a scene as the poem provides. The pardon incident is not only the climax of the *Visio* but the point where the transition from the *Visio* to the *Vita* begins, and its importance is emphasized by the vigor with which it is presented. What proves surprising is not Piers' rejection of the life he has been leading[11] (for in this the young man in the Gospel had set a precedent), but the violence of his rejection, exhibited in his tearing of the pardon.[12] For this

[9] B. VII. 138 (A. VIII. 127) C. X. 292 varies.

[10] "*Piers Plowman,* the Work of One or Five," *MP*, VI. (1908), 315: "This is one of the grandest, if not the grandest scene in the poem, the most memorable, even for us to-day, the culminating point of the work."

[11] Despite Piers' assertion that he will not work *so* hard nor be *so* busy about his livelihood, his resolution to reject active life has the effect on the reader of being absolute and unequivocal. See B. VII. 117–129, A. VIII. 102–116.

[12] Piers' anger is explained differently by virtually every critic. See Coghill, pp. 19–20; T. P. Dunning, *Piers Plowman: an Interpretation of the A-Text* (London, 1937), pp. 145–152; Chambers, pp. 118–121. All solutions depend on reading between the lines, since the poet makes no explanation. I am disposed to believe that Piers' anger has a twofold cause. It is aroused by the Priest because he is supercilious and insulting and because, being an ecclesiastical bureaucrat, he refuses to recognize that the promise of the Creed is as effective as any pardon ever granted by the Pope. And Piers' anger is aroused by the pardon itself because Piers is disappointed in it, having apparently expected some larger, less commonplace sanction for his manner of life. Thus Piers finds himself in virtual agreement with his antagonist. In Piers' angry disappointment it is nec-

there seems to be no satisfactory logical explanation in the narrative itself. It is possible that the poet was carried away by the dramatic force of his poem and forgot, for the moment, the remoter ramifications of its allegorical significance. The brilliantly visualized scene brings to fullest realization the humanity of both Piers and the Priest—a simple, honest laborer reacting vigorously to a disappointing explanation given him by a disagreeable, probably sophistical, man of education and authority. Somehow, though we do not understand the reason for it, we are able to sympathize with Piers' tearing of the pardon, as well as with his subsequent, or even concomitant, anger with the Priest. Indeed, the passage is so dramatically apt that only after thinking back does one recall, with a shock, that the pardon Piers has torn was sent to him by Truth and may possibly, if Coghill's surmise is correct, represent the Atonement.[13] Even then, most readers would prefer to keep the scene as it stands and undergo the shock of Piers' seeming ingratitude, rather than have a less vivid presentation. And apparently the B poet, when he came to revise A, felt that the incident was dramatically if not allegorically pertinent, so that he not only retained it but even elaborated the contention between Piers and the Priest.

In his revision the C poet omitted the tearing of the pardon altogether, a change which, while it may have stored up treasure for him in the heaven of the pious, has probably reaped him little praise from the less scrupulous reader. The motive behind

essary to assume a transfer from the poet to Piers of that latent dissatisfaction with Dowel and the active life which becomes explicit when Dowel is found in the honest minstrel Haukyn the Active Man, who is guilty of all the sins in the catalogue, and when the cure for the sins of Dowel is shown to be in the contemplative life of Dobet.

[13] See especially Coghill, pp. 17–20. I am unable to agree that the pardon is the Atonement—that is that the pardon represents the *act* of the Atonement allegorically. Nevertheless, the *fact* of the Atonement is, of course, not far away from the poet's thought, since it is through the Atonement that man receives pardon of any sort, and since the Creed is, in one aspect, an expression of faith in the efficacy of the Atonement. But Piers' pardon seems but to confirm a particular phase of this efficacy and not its whole.

this change was undoubtedly the same that seems to have underlain a number of the C poet's alterations: the desire to rid the poem of elements that might be misconstrued by the ignorant or might give offense to the learned—a desire which in C reflects, perhaps, the belated self-consciousness of a poet who has received recognition from the more or less august for an enterprise directed at the more or less humble. But although he obliterated what could be construed as a serious flaw (would an obedient servant of Truth tear a pardon procured for him by the agency of his master?), the C reviser diminished the artistry of the scene by staling its freshness and blurring its immediacy. And unfortunately the alteration, having achieved an improvement in logic if not in art, did not stop there. Along with the tearing of the pardon the poet in C eliminated the whole quarrel between the Priest and Piers, during which, in the earlier texts, Piers makes his resolution to cease from sowing and to devote himself to a contemplative life. As both Chambers and Burdach, independently of one another, have pointed out,[14] this resolution of Piers' is a vital signpost that directs the reader on the safe way to the *Vita*. It is, indeed, our only indication that from this point on the poem will concern less and less the active life of society and more and more the contemplative life of the individual. Thus it is the connecting link between the two parts of the poem. C takes down the signpost. His Piers neither rejects the one life nor vows to take up the other. The reader is, apparently, left to shift for himself.

In order to explain this omission at all satisfactorily, we must look back over the earlier passus of the poem to a passage which has the same form in the B and C texts. At the conclusion of the confession of the Deadly Sins the Dreamer tells us that

> A thousand of men tho · thrungen togyderes;
> Criede vpward to Cryst · and to his clene moder
> To haue grace to go with hem · Treuthe to seke.[15]

[14] *Mind,* p. 124; *Ackermann,* pp. 269 ff., 309–310.
[15] B. v. 517–519. C. viii. 155–157, A. v. 260–263 vary, C but slightly.

The significance of the pilgrimage which the folk on the field thus abruptly initiate has not, I think, been properly appreciated. All these sinners, these protagonists of the worldly life whose shortcomings have just been fully set forth, spontaneously make a vow which at least suggests a renunciation of their way of living: a single-minded search for God. To the modern reader the pilgrimage may seem no more than an allegorical representation of the sinners' desire to mend their ways, but to the medieval reader it probably meant a good deal more than that. Despite his love for allegory, the medieval reader was able to take the Gospels literally, and the Gospels leave no doubt about the cost that must be defrayed by the soul that would devote itself to seeking God.

> Go and sell that thou hast, and give to the poor, and thou shalt have treasure in heaven: and come and follow me. . . . He that findeth his life shall lose it: and he that loseth his life for my sake shall find it. . . . Take no thought for your life, what ye shall eat, or what ye shall drink; nor yet for your body, what ye shall put on.... Martha, Martha, thou art careful and troubled about many things: But one thing is needful. . . . If any man come to me, and hate not his father, and mother, and wife, and children, and brethren, and sisters, yea, and his own life also, he cannot be my disciple. . . . Whosoever he be of you that forsaketh not all that he hath, he cannot be my disciple. . . .[16]

To undertake a single-minded search for God was to abandon the active life and to take up the contemplative.

The suggestion of the abandonment of the active life is, perhaps, no more than that. None of the biblical texts I have quoted appears in this portion of the poem. Yet surely the "great multitudes" whom Christ warned to count the cost before they should undertake to follow Him[17] must have been in

---

[16] Matt. 19:21, 10:39, 6:25; Luke 10:41–42, 14:26, 33.

[17] Luke 14:28: "For which of you, intending to build a tower, sitteth not down first, and counteth the cost, whether he have sufficient to finish it?"

the poet's mind as he wrote. But on the Field of Folk there is no Messiah—no one who can tell the pilgrims about the path to Truth until Piers Plowman puts forth his head and offers to lead them.[18] Piers declares that he has known and served Truth for many years and that he is well acquainted with the road to his house. The road, as Piers describes it, is little more than the commandments in allegory. It is, indeed, the same road that Christ pointed out to the young man in answer to his first question, the road upon which the representative of the active life may pass to salvation.[19] For the moment the suggestion that the pilgrimage represents a rejection of the active life seems altogether denied. Yet we must bear in mind that the pilgrimage is never actually performed.[20] Before Piers can start out, he must plow and sow his half-acre. The accomplishment of that task is described in the following passus, and at its conclusion Truth procures Piers his pardon and instructs him

> To taken his teme · and tulyen the erthe.[21]

Furthermore, Truth bids Piers

> . . . holde hym at home · and eryen his leyes,
> And alle that halpe hym to erie · to sette or to sowe,

[18] A. vi. 28, B. v. 544, C. viii. 182.

[19] For the moral aspect of Piers' instructions, see Coghill, p. 14; Dunning, p. 121; Chambers, p. 124. Dunning says that "Piers, in describing the way to Truth, first shows that Truth can only be reached by an observance of the entire Christian moral law, as intepreted by the Church." Chambers calls Piers' instructions "a dull and wooden allegory of the Commandments."

[20] F. A. R. Carnegy, *The Relations between the Social and Divine Order in William Langland's "Vision of William concerning Piers the Plowman"* (Breslau, 1934), p. 8, says that the search for Truth "consists in setting the pilgrims to work on the half-acre," and cites in corroboration R. W. Chambers, "The Authorship of 'Piers Plowman,'" *MLR,* v (1910), 13: "Piers' guidance of the pilgrims actually consists in setting them all to work." But while the plowing is, indeed, all the guidance Piers provides, it is not the fulfillment of the search. As Dunning says, p. 128, the "ploughing episode is definitely said to precede the pilgrimage; and the pilgrimage, in point of fact, is never made. . . ."

[21] B. vii. 2 (A. viii. 2, C. x. 2).

> Or any other myster · that myȝte Pieres auaille,
> Pardoun with Pieres plowman · treuthe hath ygraunted.[22]

From these lines the only conclusion I can draw is that Truth has anticipated the pilgrimage and has, in effect, canceled it, so that the pilgrims, led and in a sense typified by Piers, may remain at home and perform the world's work. The pardon, promised them, accords to active life full expectation of salvation. By implication, Truth seems here to recognize what Piers fails to recognize when he so readily explains the way to Truth's dwelling in an allegory of the commandments. The pilgrimage to God, undertaken here on earth, consists in something more than obedience to the tables of the law. It entails a complete rejection of the world's business. And in this instance Truth orders the pilgrims, through Piers, to remain sons of Martha rather than to undertake to imitate their cousins, the sons of Mary. Mary's life may be better, or best, but Martha's is still good and, according to a basic statement of faith, is worthy of salvation. Piers, however, possibly reflecting a spiritual experience of the poet's, seems to have believed that the active life would be accorded some sanction greater than that of the Creed—a comparative or a superlative, instead of a flat positive. It is perhaps his realization of his own error in regard to the value of the virtuous life of Dowel—which he has earlier described to the pilgrims in allegorical terms—that causes the anger in which he tears the pardon.[23] That life is not good enough. Piers suddenly resolves to take an altogether different path to Truth from the one which he has said that he knows so well.

I should be no friend to *Piers Plowman* if I were to point out inconsistencies in one version merely in order to make another seem, by contrast, superior—or less inconsistent. Therefore when I assert that in the A and B texts when Piers resolves to

---

[22] B. VII. 5–8 (C. X. 5–8). A. VIII. 5–8 reads *Pope* for *treuthe* in 8.
[23] See pp. 137–138, n. 12, above.

cease from sowing he acts directly contrary to the instructions that he has received from Truth, who stands for God, I do not do so in order to derogate from the merit of the earlier versions —which is, in any case, sufficiently well-established so that the derogator has to work against great odds. Indeed, I wonder how many readers have noticed this inconsistency, or, if they have, how many have let it affect their pleasure in the poem. But I suggest that, to a poet who had come to esteem his Christian responsibility more highly than his artistic responsibility, a passage which pictured the poem's hero, the old and faithful servant of Truth, as disobedient to him in respect to a quite definite instruction, might seem to require emendation.[24] Granted that the criticism is a quibbling one, since in either way of life Piers is serving God directly, still we are dealing with a period when both poets and their readers could quibble with the best, and readers who read for elevation rather than pleasure might well take offense—probably had taken offense—at the A and B texts. For this reason C's omission of Piers' resolution, as well as of his tearing of the pardon, seems logical.

Yet, as I have said, Piers' resolution provides us with a necessary signpost in our search for the truth of *Piers Plowman*. Did the C poet give us anything in its stead? The answer is, I think, in the affirmative. If we turn back to the conclusion of Piers' speech explaining his conception of the way to Truth, we shall find that in all three texts three persons—an ape-keeper, a pickpocket and a wafer-seller—decide emphatically not to go on the pilgrimage, since they feel that they would not find any relatives at Truth's home.[25] But Piers urges them to persist, saying that a maid named Mercy lives there, who is related to all sinful men. With these remarks A and B close the incident and terminate a passus. But in C, Piers' statement

[24] Perhaps the phrases *so harde* and *so bisi* in Piers' resolution were intended to soften the possible shock of his disobedience upon the reader.

[25] A. VI. 118–126, B. V. 639–651, C. VIII. 283–291. B adds a pardoner and a prostitute, whom C omits.

about Mercy is followed by objections from other persons and these, on first sight, seem a needless continuation of those already made.

> 'ʒe, villam emi,' quath on · 'and now most ich thudere,
> To loke how me lyketh hit' · and tok hus leue at Peers.
> Another a-non ryght · nede seyde he hadde
> To folwen fif ʒokes · 'for-thy me by-houeth
> To gon with a good wil · and greithliche hem dryue;
> For-thy ich praye ʒow, Peers · paraunter, yf ʒe meteth
> Treuthe, telleth to hym · that ich be excused.'
> Thenne was there on heihte Actif · an hosebounde he
>   semed;
> 'Ich haue ywedded a wyf,' quath he · 'wel wantowen of
>   maners;
> Were ich seuenyght fro hure syghte · synnen hue wolde,
> And loure on me and lyghtliche chide · and seye ich loue
>   anothere.
> For-thy, Peers plouhman · ich praye the telle hit Treuthe,
> Ich may nat come for a Kytte · so hue cleueth on me;
>   Vxorem duxi, et ideo non possum uenire.'
>   (C. VIII. 292–304)

But this is more than a continuation of the earlier objections. The lines are, of course, a direct paraphrase from St. Luke's account of the Parable of the Unwilling Guests (Luke 14:18–20), which concerns those who would "eat bread in the kingdom of God." It is in the same chapter of the Gospel that Christ advises the persons in the multitude to count the cost before they decide to become His disciples, warning them that they must first renounce all that they have.[26] Thus the unwilling guests are equated with those who have counted the cost and found it too great—who have determined, in short, to persist in the active life. The C text lines immediately following those quoted read as follows:

> Quath Contemplacion, 'by Crist · thauh ich care suffre,
> Famyn and defaute · folwen ich wolle Peers.'
>   (VIII. 305–306)

[26] See p. 140, n. 17, above.

Only those who are ready to forsake the world and to suffer care, hunger and want will come, after long pilgrimage, to the banquet of the Lord. And, as the C poet makes clear, these are the practitioners of the contemplative life.

These inserted lines, which show that the pilgrimage does indeed entail a renunciation of active life, are also the signpost that the C poet introduced into his version in order to point out to the reader the direction which his poem is, sooner or later, going to take. To claim any great artistry for the inserted signpost would be difficult. It is, in the first place, rather inconspicuous and we come to it some time before we get to the most bewildering crossroads. Then too, it makes the three practical men of business who reject the pilgrimage because it is a renunciation of active life seem possessed of sounder theological learning than Piers, whose description of the highway to Truth has been little more than an outline of the virtuous active life. Furthermore, although three worldly characters withdraw from the pilgrimage, a large number of their fellows continue on it, at least to the extent of performing the preliminary step, the plowing of Piers' half-acre. Nevertheless, when we consider the number of incongruities in all versions of *Piers Plowman,* these do not seem too serious. In C the paraphrase of Luke accomplishes, though less forcefully, the same purpose as Piers' resolution in A and B to cease from his labor, and it does so without making Piers seem disobedient. In all texts Truth affirms the active life. Despite this, in all texts the reader is given to understand that the active life is inadequate—in A and B through Piers' resolution, in C through Contemplation's. It is possible that the C poet was here writing, consciously or unconsciously, as a gloss upon B: the introduction of "one hight Active" would cause the reader familiar with B to recall Haukyn's confession, with its full and unequivocal demonstration of the inadequacy of active life, and this recollection would suggest the proper interpretation to put upon the new lines.

As I have said, no pilgrimage is accomplished in the *Visio,* but the *Vita* is, in a very real sense, nothing but a pilgrimage shared by the Dreamer and Piers Plowman himself. The stages in Piers' advancement on this journey in the *Vita* are not defined in terms of human motivation. He alters from one epiphany to another not by an act of will but by a mystical transition. In the A and B texts his renunciation of the active life is given a sort of dramatic impetus by his anger—no real motivation but something which very nearly replaces it. In C, this is lacking and the transition to his next manifestation is accomplished, like his later transitions, without explanation or intensification of the narrative. Thus Piers is like the young man in Matthew who goes on, apparently without reason, to ask a second question when he might well have been fully satisfied by the answer he received to his first.

III. *DOWEL: RECKLESSNESS, HAUKYN AND PIERS*

We come now to the *Visio de Dowel,* that most elusive of all the sections of the poem. The A text poet apparently conceived it not as a discussion of Dowel alone but as a discussion of Dowel, Dobet and Dobest.[27] It was the B poet who tried, without marked success, to shape it in such a way as to fit the title *Visio de Dowel,* while the C poet seems to have had another try at the same business,[28] with, possibly, somewhat more success. Since a consideration of all the multitudinous revisions in this part of the poem is hardly possible, I shall limit myself to the question, as applied to C, of what Dowel is. This is the

[27] MSS TUDH2 agree in closing Passus VIII of the A text with a colophon suggesting that the subsequent part of the poem will concern Dowel, Dobet and Dobest together. Thus T reads, in part, *incipit vita de do-wel do-bet et do-best secundum wyt et resoun.* The next two passus are labeled in TH2 *de dowel, &c.,* while U omits, probably accidentally, *&c.* The abbreviation is also omitted after the heading of Passus XII in URJ. See EETS, I. xxv. 137; EETS, IV. 857. Dunning, pp. 167–184, argues that the A *Vita* is complete. Though I cannot agree with his major premise, he does make it clear that A treats all three lives together.

[28] While the headings of B and C MSS vary greatly, the presence of individual sections for Dowel, Dobet, and Dobest are clearly indicated. See Skeat's footnotes.

question which, in all texts, the Dreamer asks again and again and to which he gets answers from virtually all hands. Yet none of the explicit definitions that he hears succeeds in satisfying him or the reader, so that we are forced to search beyond the explicit for an implicit definition. For the B text the most commonly accepted interpretation is, I suppose, that expressed by Chambers: Dowel is the active life, embodied here by Haukyn, Activa Vita,[29] just as in the *Visio* it was embodied, though on an ideal level, by Piers. There is much evidence for this theory and it would be difficult to refute it. I have, however, already mentioned my belief that the Dowel section contains two not wholly congruent ideas considered simultaneously: on the one hand Dowel as the external active life, on the other Dowel as the first stage of the internal contemplative life—on the one hand the moral and social, on the other the spiritual. As Dunning has shown, this contrast between moral and spiritual definitions is perceptible in the A text, where Wit and Study present one side, while Thought and Clergye present the other. [30] It is also present in the B text, where, however, the personifications do not so neatly express one point of view or the other.[31] And it is present in the C text. In the definition—not so much expressed as achieved by an accumulation of effects—that C accepts for Dowel lies, as I have said, the chief difference between the B and C Texts in the Dowel section. In B, the solution is found in the person of Haukyn, the moral aspect of Dowel. But in C, it is worked out in Dowel's spiritual aspect as the first stage in the contemplative life which he must pursue who would be perfect. What the name of this stage is we shall see shortly.

[29] *Mind*, pp. 149 ff.

[30] Dunning, p. 173: ". . . the three 'lives' mentioned by Thought as Dowel, Dobet and Dobest are not subjective but objective states of perfection or well-doing." Idem, p. 174: "Wit . . . defines Dowel, Dobet and Dobest as subjective states of perfection or well-doing." See idem, pp. 178–179, for Clergye's and Study's definitions.

[31] Dunning, pp. 191–192, notes that B obfuscates Wit's definition.

We have long been accustomed, in literature, to hearing wisdom spoken from the mouths of fools and idiots. Yet we can hardly help being shocked when the approaches to a highway leading toward perfection are shown to us by someone bearing the deplorable name of Recklessness. But this is precisely what occurs in the C text. In the B version, Recklessness appears apparently just in order to give the Dreamer some bad advice (which the Dreamer follows) and then disappears, having spoken a total of eight lines (B. XI. 33–40). He seems to be merely another one of those reprehensible characters that surround Fortune, a suitable fellow for Childishness and the trio who, according to St. John, make up the sum of things in this world—Lust of the Flesh, Lust of the Eyes and Pride of Life (1 John 2:16). Thus Chambers is fully justified in referring to Recklessness as one of the "sins of passionate youth."[32] In C, Recklessness appears in the same company earlier than he does in B[33] and takes over all the Dreamer's monologue about predestination, the salvation of the heathen and the value of learning—the famous rebellious monologue with which the A poet broke off the poem.[34] In C Recklessness then gives the Dreamer the bad advice (C. XII. 304–309) and afterward, becoming as it were coalesced with the Dreamer, follows the advice in the Dreamer's person.[35] He reappears after the interlude of the pursuit of Fortune and, still inhabiting the Dreamer's body, harangues Clergye steadily for five hundred lines.[36] Of this speech part is new in the C text, while the rest is, in B, assigned by Skeat to Lewte,[37] though on doubtful evidence. The B poet, or possibly an early B scribe, left out the speaker's identity. In

[32] *Mind,* p. 134.

[33] At C. XII. 195, in time to rejoin B at B. X. 375, more than a hundred lines before his appearance in B.

[34] A. XI. 250–303, B. X. 372–474, C. XII. 200–303.

[35] Cf. C. XIII. 4 with XIII. 12. In the first line, Covetousness-of-Eyes gives Recklessness advice which in the second line the Dreamer follows.

[36] C. XIII. 88 through XIV. 128.

[37] See EETS, II. 176, sidenote to XI. 148.

C, however, the speech is expressly assigned to Recklessness, although the assignment is made at its end rather than at the beginning.[38]

The most arresting thing about this speech is its extremely eloquent praise of the virtues of patience and poverty, or, to be more accurate, the virtue of patient poverty. One should, perhaps, hyphenate the expression, since the noun and adjective seem to combine to make one distinct idea. I shall, however, follow the poet's lead and refer to "patience" and "patient poverty" as meaning, in this context, the same thing. The poet himself seems clearly to have been following the lead of the author of *Patience* in yoking the two virtues thus inseparably, although, inevitably, he is less clear than his forerunner on how the two virtues come to be yoked under a single *significatio*.[39] No speech in *Piers Plowman* is more filled with New Testament quotations and New Testament paraphrases on the subject of apostolic poverty than this of Recklessness. In rapid succession we get Matthew, Mark, Luke and John—Gospel and Epistles —as well as Paul[40] and, though Skeat does not mention it, a good bit from the fifth chapter of the Epistle of James[41]. Indeed, the passage would serve as a guide book for any one who is looking for authority to cast his burdens upon the Lord and to renounce all anxiety for the affairs of this world. By

[38] See C. XIV. 129 and Skeat's note, EETS, IV. 278.

[39] See *Patience,* ll. 1–60. The relationship has not, of course, been established, but seems to me highly probable. See Menner, ed., *Purity,* pp. xxix–xxx, and *Patience,* H. Bateson, ed., 2d ed. (Manchester, 1918), pp. xxiv–xxviii, with which compare his first edition (1912), pp. 20–25, 67–70.

[40] Matt. 19:29 at C. XIII. 159; 19:21 at XIII. 166; Mark 16:16 at XIV. 87; 12:43 at XIV. 98; Luke 14:12 at XIII. 102; 10:40 at XIII. 136; 10:42 at XIII. 139; 14:33 at XIII. 170; 12:20 at XIII. 215; John 8:34 at XIII. III; 12:24 at XIII. 178; 16:20 at XIII. 207; II Cor. 6:10 at XIV. 4; Gal. 6:2 at XIV. 78; I John 3:14 at XIII. 98; James 2:10 at XIV. 122; and the part of the Athanasian Creed which forms Piers' pardon at XIII. 118.

[41] Cf. James 5:10–11 with C. XIV. 20–25; 5:11 with XIII. 200–203. C. XIII. 198–199 closely translates James 5:7. The apostrophe to the rich at XIII. 219 ff. echoes James 5:1 ff.

the same token, the passage is a storehouse of quotations that set forth the distinction between the active and contemplative lives, although the poet lays the emphasis not on the two lives but on poverty and riches. Thus even the story of Mary and Martha is used, not in its classic medieval sense to illustrate Christ's preference for the contemplative life, but to illustrate the superiority of a life of patient poverty over a life of wealth.[42] In both B and C the speech is an excellent one. But in C, where there is added the well-sustained metaphor of the merchant and the messenger, the poet attains an even greater degree of eloquence than is apparent in the B text.

It is this speech which, I believe, first sets the reader upon the trail leading to C's definition of Dowel: patient poverty, the first stage in the soul's journey to perfection. Though the idea has never been without influence on the earlier conduct of the poem, it receives here its fullest expression and, as we shall see, holds the stage for most of the remainder of Dowel in the C text. But before we can continue on the path to perfection, we must pause to consider the nature of the traffic policeman who set us upon it. Who, and what, is Recklessness? An obvious explanation may be based upon the etymology of his name. Recklessness is the quality of not caring. In English, and in Middle English, the sense of the noun seems to have been universally pejorative.[43] But the sense of the verb upon which the noun is ultimately formed is less one-sided. *To reck* (Middle English *recchen*) means, among other things, "to take heed for," "to be anxious for," and might conceivably be used to translate the Latin *esse solliciti* in the phrase, "Take no thought

---

[42] C. XIII. 135–139, B. XI. 242–246. The poet concludes the story of Mary and Martha by observing (B), "Ac pouerte god put bifore and preysed it þe bettre."

[43] See *OED, recklessness,* and *reckless,* a. The use of the adjective in *Gawain and the Green Knight,* 1. 40, seems, however, to point to a nonpejorative sense in Middle English. Arthur's court is described as indulging in "reckless" mirths—surely innocent merriment, though carefree.

for the morrow."[44] By extension of this meaning into that of the derived noun, recklessness might come properly to be ascribed to the apostles who, casting their burdens upon the Lord, forbore to suffer anxiety for worldly things. Such, indeed, is Burdach's conception of the character in *Piers Plowman*.[45] And, upon the basis of Recklessness' speech on patient poverty, this seems to be what the character came to mean for the C reviser.

Such a development of the personification we meet in the B text is, to say the least, unexpected, for in B there is no quality apparent in Recklessness that would make us admire him. And, strangely enough, the C poet, when in his elaboration of B he first introduces Recklessness, takes some pains to make him appear as bad as possible. Thus he describes him as speaking "in ribaldry" and repeats a rumor to the effect that he is kinsman of Sir Wanhope.[46] The mention of wanhope,

---

[44] See *OED, reck*, v., I, b. The word is not used for Matt. 6:34 in either Wyclif Bible, where the locution *be busy* is preferred. The poet, however, uses *reck* in precisely the same sense at C. XVII. 315, where Liberum Arbitrium says of Charity that "of rentes ne of richesses . . . reccheþ he neuere."

[45] I had developed my theory of the character of Recklessness before I realized that it had already been put forward by Burdach, who (*Ackermann,* p. 310) describes Recklessness as "die 'Sorg- und Sorgenlosigkeit,' die nicht rechnet und zählt und frei ist von der Unruhe der Gewinnsucht." Burdach continues: "In der Komposition des ganzen Werkes spielt ihr Auftreten und ihre Ermahnung eine vorbereitende Rolle, die künstlerisch wohl durchdacht ist. Von allen Reden, die den mit ihr erscheinenden Personifikationen in den Mund gelegt werden, ist keine mit dem Grundproblem des Gedichts enger verwachsen als ihre weitgreifende Belehrung über die Prädestination und namentlich über den Segen der Armut, über das Verderbenbringende des Reichtums. Durch drei Passus des Gedichts führt sie das Wort. Ihr umfassendes Lob der Armut weist hin auf das Vorbild, das Christus in seiner menschlichen Niedrigkeit gegeben hat." Burdach normally deals with the poem through the B text and gives notice when he is speaking in terms of C. In this case, however, although presumably he is discussing B, the context indicates that he is thinking of C, since it would be difficult to apply his remarks to B's Recklessness. Burdach does not consider the seamy side of the character.

[46] C. XII. 198–199. Later he is "in a rage." See XIV. 129.

however, may be a clue leading to a solution of the problem of what C was about. Chambers has shown that the A poet broke off his poem in despair—wanhope—because he was unable to solve the riddles posed by predestinarianism and the dogma concerning the damnation of the righteous heathen.[47] In the statement of these riddles, the central question seems to be, what sort of men are, in God's eyes, most worthy to receive His saving grace? Arbitrarily and, indeed, recklessly, the poet makes several rapid conclusions: since learning (Clergye) is historically seen to be no more attractive to grace than is ignorance, it follows that the will of God is inscrutable; and since the will of God is inscrutable, one may as well take a chance and lead one's life as one's will, or even whim, dictates. In this mood the poet broke off the A text and in this mood in the B text the Dreamer conducts his unfortunate experiment with Fortune. When he returns to his search, with his fingers burned, the question of who is worthy to receive the grace of salvation is once more introduced. But now there is advanced a positive, instead of a negative, argument. Grace is given to the man who, like Trajan, is filled with love and justice, or to the man who imitates in his life the patient poverty of Christ. (The Poet of *Piers Plowman,* like the poet of *Patience,* seems to have possessed the virtue of poverty.) We might observe that in the reopened argument of B Clergye still is not presented as being especially attractive to grace, but the inferiority of learning is now presented less for its own sake than in order to exalt patient poverty:

> Ac grace ne groweth nouȝte · but amonges lowe;
> Pacience and pouerte · the place is there it groweth,[48]

---

[47] *Mind,* pp. 130–131.

[48] B. xii. 62–63. C. xv. 24–29 alters and expands the lines into a consideration of preventing grace. See George Sanderlin, "The Character 'Liberum Arbitrium' in the C-text of *Piers Plowman,*" *MLN,* lvi (1941), 453 and n. 13, for a discussion of the change.

Poverty—patient poverty—is the chief means to grace and Recklessness in C seems to have the same sentiments toward Clergye and Scripture that the poet has in B, even though these are not directly expressed in the earlier text.

> Ac me were leuere, by oure lorde · a lippe of godes grace
> Than al the kynde witt that ȝe can bothe · and connynge of
> ȝoure bokes.[49]

Who is actually responsible, in the B text, for the long speech which carries on the reopened discussion of grace—the speech on patient poverty? Despite its ascription by Skeat to Lewte, and despite the ambiguous line that follows its conclusion, I am convinced that the passage really belongs to the Dreamer. And so, apparently, was Chambers.[50] If this ascription is correct, then the B text helps us to explain the change that Recklessness' character undergoes in C. In B one man advances a certain argument, draws a rash conclusion from it, acts upon his decision—foolishly, as it turns out—and then, chastened, returns to the argument in order to draw from it a more constructive conclusion. But it is the same man all the time—the Dreamer, or the poet himself. In C, precisely the same thing occurs, only the man is called Recklessness. If we turn from an objective to a subjective consideration of his character we may see that, just like the man of the B text, Recklessness fulfills a separate one of his potentialities (even if they are only etymological potentialities) in each of the two phases of the discussion of grace: first the recklessness of wanhope, second the reck-less-ness of St. Francis. He is an entity with extension in two directions, while a human being is an entity with extension in an infinite number of directions. One does not ordinarily label

---

[49] C. XII. 226–227. This sentiment is, in C, echoed by Conscience, who tells Clergye at C. XVI. 179–180, Me were leuere, by oure lord · and ich lyuye sholde,/ Haue pacience parfitliche · than half thy pack of bokes!

[50] *Mind,* p. 136: "Then our dreamer goes on to contrast with this standard of patience and poverty the avarice and ignorance of priests."

each of the various extensions of a man, but one may of a personification. For us, with our natural tendency to regard all personifications as static, and with some years of bitter experience with reckless drivers behind us, the essential unity of Recklessness may be hard to perceive. But if nowhere else, we should be able to see it in the ragged clothes in which he first stands forth (see C. XII. 195): they are, on the one hand, the badge of a man who doesn't give a damn; and, on the other, the banner of the apostles whom Christ ordered to take but one coat with them on their travels.[51]

It is impossible to guess exactly why the C poet made the change. The reader who compares the B and C versions of Dowel will notice that most of B's autobiographical material, particularly in the section dealing with Imaginatyf, is omitted from the later version, so that it would be impossible to derive from C what Chambers derived from B relative to the A poet's reasons for abandoning the poem after the third passus of Dowel. Those biographical details are not necessary to the main sense of the poem and at first glance, in the present matter, it looks as if the C poet were pursuing a policy of omitting biography by having the Dreamer swallowed up by Recklessness. But anyone who uses that explanation after observing the magnificent abandon with which Recklessness is identified with the Dreamer is giving the C poet credit for less skill than he deserves. The two characters are fastened together with transparent tape. The C poet was careful that the reader should see through it and perceive at once the Dreamer and Recklessness.[52] Though pointing out a joke that only oneself has seen is a risky business (and from the solemnity with which *Piers Plowman* is sometimes handled, pointing out humor in it at all might be considered offensive), I suggest that the C poet was having a sort of double-edged joke, first in the loose identification of the Dreamer with Recklessness, second in the surprising

[51] Mark 6:9; Luke 9:3.
[52] See p. 148, n. 35, above.

154

development of Recklessness from one who is made to appear a very bad actor to one who exemplifies, to some extent, the virtue of patient poverty. I do not think that Joyce was the first artist to discover that a pun might both be entertaining and at the same time accomplish a serious purpose. It occurs to me that just as in Dobet the poet rings the changes on charity through Liberum Arbitrium (Anima in B), the Tree of Charity, the Samaritan and ultimately, Christ, so here he is beginning to ring the changes on patient poverty in the person, as well as through the words, of Recklessness. As we shall see, he goes on to develop the idea fully in the character of Patience and in Piers. Recklessness, then, introduces a dominant theme of Dowel.

After this detour during which we have examined Recklessness, let us return to the highway to perfection and investigate patient poverty in its relation to that strangely unsuccessful minstrel, Haukyn the active man. In both B and C we come to Haukyn by way of the banquet given by Conscience in honor of the fat Doctor of Divinity, a social event which the Dreamer and a new acquaintance of his, Patience, are permitted to attend. Although the two texts diverge in significant ways, the dominant theme throughout the banquet scene is, in both, patience: *Patientes vincunt.*[53] With this virtue Conscience is so impressed that he vows to accompany the character bearing its name in order to learn its nature at first hand.[54] And so, after dinner, the two depart, accompanied, of course, by the Dreamer. Straightway they encounter Active, or, as he is more frequently called in B, Haukyn. With this encounter the two texts diverge altogether. In B, Haukyn makes his long confession that includes instances of each of the deadly sins in turn. Following

---

[53] The phrase occurs at B. XIII. 134, 171; C. XVI. 138, 157; also at B. XIV. 33, 52; C. XVI. 255. Skeat EETS, IV. 308, connects it with Matt. 10:22, *qui autem perseveraverit usque in finem, hic salvus erit,* and with similar expressions in the Cato books. See Burdach's interesting note, *Ackermann,* p. 226, n. 1. See also the verses from James quoted on p. 162, n. 66, below.

[54] C. XVI. 184, "With pacience wol ich passe, parfitnesse to fynde."

this, Conscience, acting as Haukyn's confessor, speaks of contrition, confession and satisfaction (defining them, incidentally, as Dowel, Dobet and Dobest) (B. XIV. 16–21). Then Patience begins to speak and, employing the phrase *Ne solliciti sitis* (B. XIV. 33) which Piers had used after the Priest impugned his pardon, promises that, given an opportunity, he himself will feed Haukyn and those who rely on Haukyn for provisions, if the penitent will renounce the life he has been leading. Twice again we hear the phrase *Patientes vincunt* (B. XIV. 33, 52). Patience goes on to emphasize the importance of contrition, confession and satisfaction (B. XIV. 81–96) and then, after an interruption by Haukyn, launches into a long speech in praise of poverty, terminating with the nine *distinctiones paupertatis* (B. XIV. 103–319). Haukyn is overcome with grief, apparently because Patience has made him feel the futility of his way of life. He laments for his existence, asking why, after his baptism, he

> . . . ne hadde ben ded and doluen   for Doweles sake!
>
> (B. XIV. 321)

And the Dreamer awakes to the sound of Haukyn's lament.

It is, as I have said, generally agreed that in Haukyn the representative of the average sort of active life, the Dreamer of the B text finally comes to know Dowel and what he had thought would be gold turns out to be mere dross. Twice before the Dreamer has favored active life over any other means of salvation: once when it was exemplified in Piers and once when the Dreamer's inability to solve the riddle of grace had driven him back toward his earlier conclusion.[55] But Haukyn's devastatingly complete confession, along with his lament, seems to settle once and for all the question of the value of the active life: if it is Dowel, then we must Dobet. The phrase *Ne solliciti sitis* serves, as it has before, as a signpost pointing toward a con-

---

[55] See A. XI. 293–303, B. X. 452–474, C. XII. 286–303.

templative life. Thus in the B text Haukyn's confession is the essential element that gives dramatic validity to the direction the poem is about to take: the search for Dobet.

The C reviser makes a drastic simplification of the Haukyn incident. In the first place, the entire confession is omitted, or transferred to the confession of the Deadly Sins in the *Visio*. The incident thus ceases to be a climactic representation of the inadequacy of active life and Haukyn, instead of embodying Dowel, tends to become just another character like Clergye, holding a place in the poem merely in order to serve as a foil to patient poverty. This transformation is accomplished directly. Whereas in the B text Patience does not begin to speak until after Haukyn's long confession and until after Conscience has told the penitent about the importance of contrition, confession and satisfaction, in C Patience takes the stage almost immediately.[56] Haukyn, in his introductory speech, tells of the duty he has of providing food for all mankind. This leads him, by a somewhat devious path, to assert that the degeneration of the people of Sodom was caused by an overabundance of edibles. Patience at this point shows himself quite the opposite of his name:

> 'Pees!' quath Pacience · 'ich praye the, syre Actyf!
> For thauh neuere payn ne plough · ne potage were,
> Prude wolde putte hym-self forth · thauh no plouh erye.
> Hit am ich that fynde alle folke · and fram hunger saue,
> Thorgh the heye helpe of hym · that me hyder sente.'
> (C. xvi. 234–238)

Having maneuvered the conversation around to where he wants it, Patience starts off on a long speech on his favorite theme, a speech which parallels, though sometimes very roughly, the passage assigned to him in the B text. In the course of the revision the C poet removes most of the emphasis that B placed on the three parts of penitence. In place of Conscience's clear definition of Dowel as contrition, Dobet as confession and

[56] Haukyn begins to speak at C. xvi. 194, Patience at C. xvi. 234.

Dobest as satisfaction, Patience makes a rapid definition which seems intended to equate the sum of the two triads rather than their parts.[57] Furthermore, where in B the relation between penitence and patience is not clear, C makes an effort to express it:

> *Cordis contricio, oris confessio, operis satisfactio;*
> These thre with-outen doute · tholen alle pouerte,
> And lereth lewed and lered · heh and louh to knowe,
> Ho that doth wel other bet · other best a-bouen alle;
>
> (C. XVII. 33–35)

C's alterations seem to place the emphasis squarely upon patient poverty. In B, patient poverty also figures prominently. Thus it is patient poverty, which is obviously understood as a manifestation of a contemplative life, that is recommended as a cure for the evils attendant upon active life.[58] But in B this theme shares the poet's attention on a more or less equal basis with penitence and with Haukyn's active life. In C, however, patient poverty is the paramount theme and the others are reduced to the barest minimum. This shift in emphasis, occurring as it does at the end of the vision where, if ever, we should expect to find Dowel defined, suggests to me that the C reviser intended to accomplish an almost complete redefinition of Dowel: instead of the active life, Dowel is patient poverty. Someone may excusably object here that this is all a sort of verbal quibble, since if patient poverty is better than the active life in both texts, why may not the former play Dobet to the latter's Dowel in C as well as in B? Reduced to grammatical terms, the objection is, indeed, unanswerable. But there are two other reasons against it: the first I shall glance at briefly in my remarks on Dobet; the second, which is rather more formidable, will be found in C's presentation of the banquet scene, to which we shall now turn.

---

[57] See C. XVII. 25–32.
[58] See especially B. XIV. 28–33, where Patience promises to feed mankind if Haukyn foregoes his endeavors in that direction.

I have already had occasion to mention Coghill's theory that Piers Plowman embodies Dowel, Dobet and Dobest in turn. That Piers should do so—though not, I am sure, vocationally—was, I think, the intention of the C as well as of the B poet. Yet in C Piers makes an appearance in the section concerning Dowel, whereas B excludes him from this part of the poem. His appearance occurs during the banquet scene, where, in the B Text, he is only mentioned.[59] The banquet begins in much the same manner in both texts. Patience appears at the gate, is welcomed by Conscience and is seated with the Dreamer at a side table reserved for the socially unelect. While the Doctor of Divinity[60] at the head table stuffs himself with rich dainties, Patience and the Dreamer are served sour loaves of *agite penitentiam* and other allegorical foodstuffs. The Dreamer, his resentment at this disparate treatment at first held in check by Patience, is finally allowed to ask the Doctor his usual question about the three lives. The answer that he receives is really not a bad one, but the Dreamer in furious indignation hurls it back into the teeth of the speaker. Desperately trying to make conversation in this inclement social atmosphere, the host Conscience asks Clergye for his definition of Dowel, Dobet and Dobest. But Clergye requests that he be excused from answering, since Piers Plowman has impugned all learning except love alone, taking for his text *Dilige deum et proximum* and *Domine, quis habitabit*. At this moment, in the C text, Piers—who we did not know was present at the banquet—suddenly begins to speak, saying,

> ... '*pacientes uincunt.*
> By-for perpetual pees · ich shal preoue that ich seide,
> And a-vowe by-for god · and for-sake hit neuere,
> That *disce, doce, dilige · deum* and thyn enemye;

[59] B. XIII. 21–219, C. XVI. 26–184.
[60] Wells on p. 297 of his translation indicates that Clergye and the Doctor of Divinity are the same character. But the distinction is clearly made at B. XIII. 198–199, C. XVI. 176–177.

> Hertely thou hym helpe · emforth thy myȝt,
> Cast hote coles on hus hefde · of alle kynde speche,
> Fonde thorgh wit and with worde · hus loue for to wynne,
> And ȝif hym eft and eft · euere at hus neede;
> Conforte hym with thy catel · and with thy kynde speche,
> And leye on hym thus with loue · tyl he lauhe on the;
> And bote he bowe for this betynge · blynd mote he worthe!
>
> (C. xvi. 138–148)

Having thus spoken, Piers vanishes so quickly and mysteriously that no one knows where he has gone. Reasoun, who only in C attends the banquet, disappears in search of him.

Now if what I have said about C's identification of patient poverty is true, and if Coghills' conclusions about the significance of Piers' epiphanies may be applied to the C version, then Piers should represent patience here. And, indeed, that seems to have been the author's intention, for he prepares us for such an identification—ambiguously and in a rather misty way—with the lines introducing Patience:

> Pacience as a poure thyng cam · and preide mete for charite,
> Ylike to Peers Plouhman · as he a palmere were.
>
> (C. xvi. 33–34)

Since Patience is like Piers, it is quite in keeping with the poet's usual way of thinking that Piers should be patience. Furthermore, Piers' speech is, of course, based upon that of Patience in the B text.[61] It is, however, undeniable that this speech concerns charity. In order to account for this apparent inconsistency, we have to turn back to B. After Clergye's refusal to discuss Dowel, Conscience calls on Patience, observing that

> Pacience hath be in many place · and perauntre cnoweth
> That no clerke ne can · as Cryst bereth witnesse;
> *Pacientes vincunt, &c.*
>
> (B. xiii. 133–134)

That is, since Patience is successful—and knows what no clerk

---

[61] Cf. C. xvi. 138–148 with B. xiii. 136–147.

(Clergye) knows—perhaps Patience can help us out with a definition of Dowel. And that is precisely why, in C, Piers is qualified to speak: *Patientes vincunt,* he says, "The patient are successful." Hence,

> By-for perpetual pees ich shal preoue · that ich seide.
>
> (C. xvi. 139)

The explanation for Piers' special knowledge about charity lies in the fact that he is himself patience, to which special insight, particularly in regard to charity, is given. The idea that patience is the ground in which charity grows—suggesting St. Paul's definition, *Charitas patiens est, benigna est* (1 Cor. 13:4)—is of course repeated many times in *Piers Plowman,* but nowhere expressed more clearly than in the B lines which describe the Tree of Charity,

> Pacience hatte the pure tre · and pore symple of herte,
> And so, thorw god and thorw good men · groweth the frute Charite.
>
> (B. xvi. 8–9)

In the banquet scene we have an implicit representation of the patience-charity relationship. Though Piers speaks—prophetically, as of something to be realized in the future—of charity, he is patience. And if we may apply Coghill's theory to the C text, then Piers is here embodying Dowel and Dowel is patience. Reasoun, as I have said, goes off in search of Piers, while the other dominant personification, Conscience, utterly rejecting the claims of Clergye, goes off with Piers' *alter ego,* Patience, in order to find perfectness.[62] The Dreamer has good company in his search for Dowel.

Burdach has pointed out in the Epistle of James a possible source for the banquet scene.[63] Reproving his flock for admir-

---

[62] C. xvi. 178–184. Conscience's repudiation of Clergye is less conditional in C than in B and further enhances the importance of patience.

[63] *Ackermann,* p. 224 and n. 2. James 2:2 ff.

ing riches rather than poverty, James says that in their meetings they accord greater honor to a man wearing a golden ring and a clean garment than they do to a poor man, giving the one a prominent place and the other at best a stool. That the poet had, perhaps, the Epistle in mind as he wrote the incident seems also indicated by the fact that the Epistle repeats, shortly after the lines concerning the rich and poor man, a text similar to *Dilige deum et proximum,* which Clergye ascribes to Piers Plowman.[64] Following Burdach's lead one finds, as I have observed before, that the discussion of patient poverty in *Piers Plowman* bears many echoes of the Epistle—which may, indeed, have shared with *Patience* responsibility for the inseparable yoking of poverty with patience.[65] The verse which Burdach suggests may have provided the seed from which the Tree of Charity in Dobet grew seems also, along with its companion verse, to have reference to the present matter:

> Patientes igitur estote, fratres, usque ad adventum Domini. Ecce agricola expectat pretiosum fructum terrae, patienter ferens donec accipiat temporaneum et serotinum. Patientes igitur estote et vos, et confirmate corda vestra, quoniam adventus Domini appropinquavit.[66]

A little later the prophets, in particular Job, are put forward as examples of true patience and suffering.[67] It occurs to me that

[64] C. xvi. 135. See James 2:8.

[65] See p. 000, n. 41, above. The fifth chapter of the Epistle of James begins (1–6) with a dire warning to the rich, and then continues (7–11) with instructions to James' brethren to be patient. Although the brethren are not expressly said to be poor, there is a strong implied contrast between them on the one hand and the rich on the other, and it would be easy to read into the Epistle praise of patient poverty, rather than solely of patience.

[66] James 5:7–8. See Burdach, *Ackermann,* p. 221 and n. 2.

[67] James 5:10–11: "Take, my brethren, the prophets, who have spoken in the name of the Lord, for an example of suffering affliction, and of patience. Behold, we count them happy which endure [cf. *patientes vincunt*]. Ye have heard of the patience of Job, and have seen the end of the Lord; that the Lord is very pitiful, and of tender mercy."

Piers in his epiphany as C's Dowel may, in the anagogical sense, stand for the prophets who waited patiently for the coming of Christ—the coming, that is, of charity, the all-comprehending importance of which Piers has vowed that he will prove and which, in the person of Christ, he does prove in Dobet. Traces in the poem of the historical view of Joachim of Flora have been noted before.[68] It is my suggestion that just as in Dobest Piers is St. Peter in the era following the coming of Christ, and in Dobet the human nature of Christ himself at the time of the Incarnation, so here he may stand for the prophets in the era before Christ's coming. And just as morally charity proceeds from patience, so anagogically charity was the end of patience, in that the coming of Christ was the fulfillment of the prophets' patience—the fulfillment of the law. So Dobet springs from Dowel.

IV. *DOBET: PIERS, LIBERUM ARBITRIUM AND ANIMA*

It is generally agreed, I believe, that the subject of B's *Visio de Dobet* is charity and that, for all practical purposes, B's definition of Dobet is charity.[69] That the same is true of the C version of Dobet will become apparent as we examine the major changes that the C poet made in his revision of the section. But aside from the major changes, there is one aspect of the C poet's revision that should receive some comment here. We have seen how in B one of the cures for the ills of active life was found in patience, which in turn produces charity. In going from the Dowel of the active life to the Dobet of charity, therefore, the B poet did not allot any special section for a consideration of patience by itself. What he did do was constantly associate it with its fellow virtue, charity, both at the end of Dowel and at the beginning of Dobet. The C poet, however, shifted the definition of Dowel from active life to patience, and in so doing he enabled himself to cover the subject of patience

---

[68] See Wells, p. 129, above.
[69] See Chambers, *Mind*, p. 154; Burdach, *Ackermann*, pp. 195, 311.

completely before turning to charity—to effect a logical separation of the two virtues while retaining, of course, the sense of their relationship. This fact accounts for several rather surprising changes. Thus where in the B version of Dowel, Haukyn is permitted to ask where Charity dwells, C, who is presenting patience as Dowel and wants to save charity for Dobet, alters the question to read, "What is perfect patience?"[70] Similarly, where in Dobet Anima gives examples from the lives of the saints to show the importance of patient poverty, the C poet, who apparently felt that the topic had already been adequately treated, altered the passage so that these examples serve merely to prove that it is impossible for anyone who would live in charity to make his living by begging.[71] And when B describes the Tree of Charity initially as a tree of patience from which grows the fruit charity, C omits the lines.[72] But we must bear in mind that these are not alterations in doctrine but rather rearrangements of material. Once again we must be careful not to misunderstand C by adhering too closely to the parallel-text method of reading the poem.

We come now to the major alterations made by the C poet in the *Visio de Dobet*. Probably the most interesting of these is the omission of Piers Plowman from the dream which has to do with the Tree of Charity. Before we proceed to a discussion of this, however, we should call to mind that in the B text Piers makes two appearances in this part of the poem: one as proprietor of the garden in which the tree grows and another as Christ during Holy Week.[73] The second appearance occurs in the last passus of Dobet. The poet, who has experienced a long, unhappy waking interval after the dream in which he converses with the Samaritan, finally goes back to sleep to find himself

---

[70] Cf. B. xiv. 97–98 with C. xvi. 276.
[71] Cf. B. xv. 263–266 with C. xviii. 1–8.
[72] B's lines are quoted on p. 160 above.
[73] B. xvi. 21 ff. and xviii. 10 ff.

in Jerusalem on the first Palm Sunday. There he tells us that he saw

> One semblable to the Samaritan · and some-del to Piers the
>   Plowman,
> Barfote on an asse bakke · botelees cam prykye.
>
> (B. xvii. 10–11)

Faith, standing at a window, cries, "Hail, Son of David!" The Dreamer, bewildered, asks Faith what is taking place and who it is that is going to joust in Jerusalem. "Jesus," Faith answers,

> 'And fecche that the fende claymeth · Piers fruit the
>   Plowman.'
>
> (B. xviii. 20)

"Is Piers here?" the Dreamer exclaims. Faith replies,

> 'This Iesus of his gentrice · wole Iuste in Piers armes,
> In his helme and in his haberioun · *humana natura;*
> That Cryst be nouȝt biknowe here · for *consummatus deus,*
> In Piers paltok þe plowman · this priker shal ryde
> For no dynte shal hym dere · as *in deitate patris.*'
>
> (B. xviii. 22–26)

These lines, which stand almost unaltered in the C text,[74] clearly identify Piers with Christ—but, we must note, not with the divine nature of Christ but with Christ's human nature, with the Son of Man, not the Son of God. In one sense, since Christ did take mankind's and Piers' nature, Piers may be said to represent Christ, for Christ was not part God and part man, but wholly God and wholly man. But in another sense, and perhaps the more important one, Piers stands for no more than all mankind in the era between the Creation and the Incarnation, the mankind whose nature Christ took. Thus we must not lose sight—as it is probable the poet never did—of the mystical doctrine which comprehends simultaneously the duality and the

---

[74] Before B. xviii. 22, C adds at xxi. 20, *"Liberum dei arbitrium . . .* for loue haþ vndertake That þis iesus, etc."

unity of Christ's nature, the doctrine that is most effectively presented in the lines quoted above.[75]

In the B text, a suggestion that Piers is to be identified with Christ is made much earlier in the poem, even before Piers' introduction as proprietor of the Tree of Charity. In his dream following that of the confession of Haukyn, the Dreamer encounters a strange tongueless and toothless person who introduces himself with nine names, the most important of which seems to be Anima (B. xv. 13 ff.). Anima discourses upon various topics related to the general subject of patience and charity. The latter, upon the Dreamer's request, Anima defines as a person of so agreeable a nature that the Dreamer's enthusiasm is roused:

> 'By Cryst, I wolde that I knewe hym,' quod I · 'no creature
> leuere!'

To this Anima rejoins,

> 'With-outen helpe of Piers Plowman, . . . 'his persone
> seestow neuere.'
>
> > (B. xv. 189–190)

"Do clerks know him?" the Dreamer asks.

> 'Clerkes haue no knowyng,' quod he · 'but by werkes and
> bi wordes.
> Ac Piers the Plowman · parceyueth more depper

---

[75] The nature of Piers' metamorphoses are discussed at length by Burdach, some of whose observations are of extraordinary interest. See especially *Ackermann*, pp. 304–305, 311–314. The background of Langland's conception of the character is carefully considered, idem, pp. 314–357. Burdach is most insistent that Piers remains distinct from the divine nature of Christ: "Immer aber bleibt *Piers plowman* von der göttlichen Natur Christi unterschieden." Idem, p. 312. Mention should be made of another interesting study of Piers' significance, that by H. W. Troyer, "Who Is Piers Plowman?" *PMLA,* xLvii (1932), pp. 368–384. In many respects Troyer seems in accord with Burdach. I agree entirely with his statement, "The unity of the Piers symbol lies . . . in the humanness of all of its variants. Piers is man" (p. 371). But I find it hard to believe that within the unity of the symbol there is so much variety as Troyer suggests.

> What is the wille and wherfore · that many wyȝte suffreth,
>> *Et vidit deus cogitaciones eorum.*[76]

Anima then gives two examples of men who successfully conceal from the general public the fact that they have not charity, concluding,

> There-fore by coloure ne by clergye · knowe shaltow hym
> neuere,
> Noyther thorw wordes ne werkes · but thorw wille one.
> And that knoweth no clerke · ne creature in erthe,
> But Piers the Plowman · *Petrus, id est, Christus.*
>> (B. xv. 203–206)

These three mentions of Piers certainly seem to accomplish his identification with Christ, and I think that many of us find it difficult not to agree with Skeat in his note to the second passage, "Here *Piers the Plowman* is completely identified with *Jesus Christ.*"[77] Assuming that the identification has been made, we must also go on to admit that it may emphasize the divine rather than the human nature of Christ. The first passage may, indeed, be read as meaning that charity will never have corporeal existence on earth until Christ assumes Piers' nature, but the other two, in citing Christ's ability to see into the hearts of men, seem to be dealing with an attribute of God rather than of man.

If we accept the identification, we should, in reading on in the B text, be fully prepared upon our next meeting with Piers to recognize him as Christ. The meeting occurs in the dream-within-a-dream in which the Dreamer is permitted to see the Tree of Charity.[78] The allegory is, as the reader will recall,

---

[76] B. xv. 192–194. Cf. Matt 9:4; Luke 11:17.

[77] EETS, iv. 347, note to B. xv. 193.

[78] See B. xvi. 1–89 and cf. C. xix. 1–123. Mabel Day, "Duns Scotus and 'Piers Plowman,' " *RES, III* (1927), 333–334, argues that the source of the tree is in Duns Scotus' *De Rerum Principio.* But the tree in Duns is not much more like the tree in the poem than is the tree in St. Augustine (see *Migne,* xxxiv, 379–380), which Burdach describes, *Ackermann,* pp. 285–287. The history of trees in religious allegory seems very complex. See Burdach's note, idem, p. 285, n. 2.

extremely elaborate. Piers, proprietor of the Garden of Heart where the tree whose fruit is charity grows, has farmed out the land to Liberum Arbitrium. The tree itself is supported by three props, which represent the three persons of the Trinity. Piers explains that against the attacks of the world and the flesh he defends the tree by means of the first two props, God the Father and God the Son. Against the devil Liberum Arbitrium, Piers' lieutenant, is sometimes effective in his own right. And against a concerted attack by the world, the flesh, and the devil, Liberum Arbitrium uses the third prop and pulls down the devil with the aid of grace and the Holy Ghost. After receiving this exposition from Piers, the Dreamer starts to question him about the tree upon which the three props grew. Piers answers brusquely that the tree is called the Trinity and indicates that further questions upon that subject are unnecessary. The Dreamer then expresses curiosity about the fruit of the Tree of Charity, which is now seen to represent the conditions of human life, although earlier it had consisted of charitable works. At the Dreamer's request, Piers causes some of the fruit to fall, and the fruit lying thus scattered on the ground is recognized as the Old Testament prophets. These the devil gathers together and bears away to limbo, unopposed. Whereupon Piers, once again acting in "pure teen," seizes the second prop, *Filius Dei,* and strikes out after the thief, thus precipitating the Incarnation. The dream then dissolves into a vision of the Nativity.

It is difficult to adhere steadily throughout this account to an identification of Piers with Christ, even if we limit the identification to Christ's human nature. One could hardly deny that there is some awkwardness in hearing Piers, if he stands for Christ, explain to the Dreamer,

> Thanne sette I to the secounde pile · *sapiencia-Dei-patris,*
> That is, the passioun and the power · of owre prynce Iesu.
> (B. XVI. 36–37)

Piers' action in bringing down the fruit himself also seems strange if he is indeed the Savior. Furthermore, though the scene begins, apparently, in an allegory depicting the spiritual condition of man in the fourteenth century, thirteen hundred years after the Atonement, it ends, with no explicit transition, in an allegory depicting the condition of man between his fall in Eden and the birth of Christ—who alone could rescue the souls of the patriarchs and prophets from Satan. Therefore at the end of the vision when he strikes out with the second prop, Piers could not very well represent the human nature of Christ, since Christ had not yet assumed human nature, although he could represent the human nature which Christ was to assume, or, less effectively, the second person of the Trinity before the Incarnation. The latter, however, seems sufficiently symbolized by the second prop. On the other hand, since a few lines later the poet uses the phrase *plenitudo temporis,* one might argue that he had in mind St. Paul's statement, *At ubi venit plenitudo temporis, misit Deus Filium suum,*[79] and that Piers stands for God the Father. I do not know what conclusion to draw from the statement that Piers taught the Christ child leechcraft. The point is a doctrinal one, with its roots heaven knows where. The concept does, however, suggest a separation between two parts of Christ's nature and possibly means that Piers has at length assumed the form of Christ's human nature. Another explanation has, however, been offered.[80]

[79] B. xvi. 93, C. xix. 127. See Gal. 4:4.

[80] Miss Day identifies Piers in his capacity as Christ's instructor as the Logos and traces the conception to Duns Scotus (334). But it seems contrary to the evidence to take Piers as the divine rather than the human part of Christ. In C it is Liberum Arbitrium who teaches Christ. According to Miss Day, "The Revisions of 'Piers Plowman,'" *MLR,* xxiii (1928), 23–24, C misunderstood B's Scotist conception of Piers when he permitted him to be replaced by Liberum Arbitrium, who is introduced as man's free will and therefore could not rightly act in place of the Logos. The point about the "misunderstanding" is valid only if we allow the identification of Piers with the Logos in B, which seems to me arbitrary. See Sanderlin's explanation of C's change, 452–453; also p. 173, n. 88, below.

It is obvious, of course, that allegory must not—indeed cannot—be read with the intellect alone, but must be interpreted by a sympathetic imaginative process. Even so, we cannot altogether ignore the demands of logical consistency, and it is necessary for us to make as much sense as possible of what we read. The Christ-Piers identification does not fit the vision of the Tree of Charity and it seems necessary to modify our views. An alternate interpretation has been put forward by Burdach, who, in his commentary on the poem, insists that the B lines which seem to accomplish the identification of Piers with Christ, and in particular the Latin phrase, *Petrus, id est, Christus,* do not do so at all. On the evidence of I Cor. 10:4, wherein St. Paul says of the water-giving rock from which the tribes of Israel drank, *petra autem erat Christus,* and on the evidence of what Burdach calls an old "speculation" that St. Peter is a source of life for men's souls, Burdach hazards the belief that the reference is not so much to Christ as to St. Peter.[81] That is, Piers is identified not with Christ but with Peter, who had received from Christ some of His effectiveness as a source of spiritual life. So far as the ability to see into men's hearts is concerned, Burdach denies that it is an exclusively divine attribute, since it was also given to the prophets.[82] Unfortunately, the

[81] *Ackermann,* pp. 311–312. Because Burdach's line of reasoning is obscure and possibly capable of another interpretation, I reproduce it here in full: "Hier fällt nun auch einem Blitzlicht gleich das Wort: *Petrus id est Christus.* Das darf man nicht verstehen, als sollte damit die Identität des Pflügers Peter mit dem göttlichen Heiland behauptet werden. Man darf es auch nicht einfach herleiten aus einem Willkürakt der Mystik, d. h. der in Typologie und Tropik schwelgenden, allegorisierenden Auslegung, die bekannt ist als interpretatio mystica. Vielmehr ist hier mit Petrus der Apostel Petrus gemeint auf Grund von 1. Cor. 10, 4. Und dieser Gleichsetzung des Menschen Christus mit dem in der Wüste Lebenswasser spendenden Fels, den der Stab des Moses öffnete, liegt eine alte vielverzweigte Spekulation zugrunde, die auch neben und nach Paulus fortlebte bis ins Mittelalter hinein. Der Apostel Petrus ist ein Quell des Lebens für die Gemeinschaft der menschlichen Seelen, die Gott suchen." Burdach goes on to say that the donation of Constantine was believed to have deprived Peter's successors of Peter's capabilities. This would explain why clerks are unable to recognize charity. See also idem, p. 341.

[82] *Ackermann,* p. 312, n. 1.

details of Burdach's reasoning are not altogether clear, nor does he cite any medieval authority in support of his theory. Wells, however, seems to have arrived at the same conclusion independently, although he does not develop the argument.[83] The suggestion is extremely attractive, inasmuch as it enables us to continue to regard Piers as a man throughout the vision of the Tree of Charity and gets around some, if not all, of the difficulties enumerated in the last paragraph.

With Piers as a man, it becomes possible to reinterpret the vision. Miss Owen and Burdach have suggested, independently, that the scene is not, as I have described it, twofold, giving first an allegory of the state of man after the Incarnation and then an allegory before the Incarnation, but a single allegory dealing with the pre-Christian era.[84] Such an interpretation is strongly supported by the image of the Trinity as three similar shafts— an image derived from the legends concerning the prehistory of the cross.[85] Nevertheless, there are several serious obstacles to its acceptance, the most troublesome being the mention of the Passion in Piers' description of the second prop, the wisdom of God the Father (B. XVI. 36). On the other hand, the part of Piers himself is somewhat clarified. He is mankind, or rather that elevated portion of mankind which includes the patriarchs and prophets—Moses, Abraham, David, Adam and the others

[83] See H. W. Wells', translation of *Piers Plowman,* p. 298, where he says that the phrase, *Petrus, id est, Christus,* "almost certainly" refers to the Pope.

[84] See D. L. Owen, *Piers Plowman: a Comparison with Some Earlier and Contemporary French Allegories* (London, 1912), pp. 123–124, and Burdach, *Ackermann,* p. 228: "Die Vision des Lebensbaumes umfasst also nur das Leben der Menschheit bis zum Erlösungswerk Christi."

[85] For the prehistory of the cross, see the references listed by Skeat, EETS, IV, 373–374, and by Burdach, *Ackermann,* p. 229, n. 1. Particularly interesting is the study, cited by Burdach, by Wilhelm Meyer, "Die Geschichte des Kreuzholzes vor Christus," *Abhandlungen der philoso-phisch-philologischen Classe der königlich bayerischen Akademie der Wissenschaften,* XVI (1882), II, 101–166. The best English version of the legend is that of the expanded Northern Passion, edited from MS Harleian 4196 by Richard Morris under the title "The Story of the Holy Rood," in *Legends of the Holy Rood,* EETS, 46 (London, 1871), pp. 62–86.

who prefigured Christ before the Incarnation just as St. Peter became Christ's vicar after the Ascension. The pre-Christian elements are perhaps enhanced by the earlier allusion to the rock which Moses smote to bring forth water (*Petrus, id est, Christus,* or *petra autem erat Christus*) and the later one to the tree of the Trinity, from which grew both the rod with which Moses smote the rock and, ultimately, the cross itself.[86] Considered in association with such details, the scene as an allegory of the pre-Christian era seems fairly satisfactory, if also extremely subtle. Piers is a man throughout, or at least until the moment when he hits out after the fiend with the second prop, thus beginning the Incarnation. At that moment he is, probably, still man, but man about to enter into a combination with God and hence almost divine himself. The poet comes close to the doctrine of deification.[87] After the moment when Piers' anger is aroused he ceases to be human nature in insolation and becomes the human nature of Christ, the Son of Mary who, herself human, nevertheless gave birth to the Son of God.

There remains the objection that if Piers is to be understood as man in the vision of the tree, then man is thrice represented —once in Piers, once in the fruit of the tree and once by Liberum Arbitrium, man's free will. With respect to the first two, it is possible to regard Piers as the abstract ideal of the prophet-

---

[86] Morris, p. 74, ll. 439–456.

[87] Miss Hort, . . . *Cont. Rel. Thought,* p. 81, speaks of another passage in the poem as "suggestive of the paradox that man, if he remains man, ceases to be man; while if he tries to live according to the divine spark which is in him, he will become more than man, though still remaining man. But Langland has not pursued this line of thought to its conclusion —it would have led him straight on to the mystical doctrine of deification." And concerning B's conception of *Liberum Arbitrium* (discussed below) she notes: "And again . . . we see how near Langland came to the doctrine of deification; the only thing wanting is its explicit formulation. Nothing . . . is good except a good will, because a good will is God himself (p. 115). This is even more true of the C text, in which Liberum Arbitrium, man's free will, becomes Libera Voluntas Dei. See C. xix. 118–125 and the discussion below.

patriarch and his fruit as the souls of individual men. But this still leaves in doubt the part of Liberum Arbitrium. Up until the end of the vision, Liberum Arbitrium is described as performing much of the defense of the tree. What this division of labor between Piers and free will signifies I do not clearly know. One might suppose that Piers, inasmuch as he can make use of the first two persons of the Trinity, might also make use of the third; or, conversely, since Liberum Arbitrium can avail himself of the third prop, that he might also use the other two.[88] Twentieth-century inability to comprehend fourteenth-century allegory possibly accounts for some of our bewilderment, but one wonders whether it was not shared by a good many unsubtle, literal-minded medieval readers—whether, indeed, the incident of the Tree of Charity as it dictated itself to the B author in terms of poetry is altogether susceptible of satisfactory rational explanation. The allegory seems too complex, too crowded. Although Burdach's interpretation of the phrase *Petrus, id est, Christus* lacks the documentation I should like to see supporting it, it is, I believe, substantially correct. But even though it clears up some of the difficulty, there are still a number of curiously shaped pieces that do not fit into the puzzle. Piers remains ambiguous and even redundant. One can only conclude that in his composition B got hold of an idea of such poetic splendor that he became blinded to its remoter ramifications and particularly to its extension into the field of logic.

---

[88] While grace, which is sought by man's free will, is considered an attribute of the Holy Ghost, I cannot find that in orthodox thought it was ever held to be exclusively the attribute of the Holy Ghost, and in C Liberum Arbitrium avails himself of all three props of the Trinity. Miss Day objects that "man's free will could not have brought into action the power of the Father and the passion of Christ" ("The Revisions of *P.P.*," 23–24). Sanderlin suggests that C held with St. Anselm that *liberum arbitrium* is a faculty that seeks rectitude as its end, and hence that there is nothing wrong with representing a self-perfecting (or self-perfected) will as using all three piles to attain this end, or as acting as Christ's instructor (451–453).

We have had cause to notice before a strongly apparent tendency in the C poet to shut the doors to uncertainty that the B poet left open and to confine the sense of the poem within the walls of logic. Probably in no other part of *Piers Plowman* did the B poet leave more doors open than in the vision of the Tree of Charity and no more strenuous effort in shutting them was required of the C poet anywhere else. His revision was drastic. Instead of redefining Piers more clearly and setting forth in exact terms his relation to Liberum Arbitrium, the C poet took the bold step of eliminating Piers altogether and replacing him by his former coworker, Liberum Arbitrium. Nor does the attempt to cast light on obscure matters stop there. The conversation between the Dreamer and his Instructor about the tree upon which the three props of the Trinity grew, a pluralizing of the tree image that threatens to turn the garden into a forest, is omitted.[89] That the Tree of Chrity is also the Tree of Human Life is made evident at the very beginning of the vision, where the tree is given the name Imago Dei,[90] in B, this transition from one aspect of the tree to another is unlabeled. Since Piers is entirely replaced by Liberum Arbitrium, the division of labor between the two necessarily disappears. Also deleted is the puzzling statement that Liberum Arbitrium alone may sometimes suffice to ward off the devil, and the companion statement that the third prop is brought into use against the combined attacks of world, flesh and devil. Moreover, the substitution of Elde for the proprietor of the garden as the agent in knocking down the apples seems a happy one.[91] Finally, with the elimination of Piers the problem of whether the incident is a pre- or post-Christian allegory becomes less insistent. I believe, however, that one can read it as a pre-

[89] We should observe that under discussion in B. XVI. 55–63 is an entirely different tree from that over which Piers is watching. It is upon this second tree that the props of the Trinity grew.

[90] C. XIX. 6–7. "Euene in the myddes · an ympe, as hit were,/ That hihte *Ymago-dei* · graciousliche hit growede."

[91] Cf. C. XIX. 106 with B. XVI. 75.

Christian allegory without encountering too many inconsistencies. In all these alterations the C poet seems to be endeavoring to get rid of difficulties; and if we grant that Liberum Arbitrium is a proper substitute for Piers, the incident as it is told in the C version seems, on the whole, more intelligible than it does in B.

Clarification, however, must be judged as much by what is introduced as by what is deleted, and Liberum Arbitrium is a personage whom most of us find every bit as puzzling as his predecessor, and who certainly would win no popularity contest for characters in *Piers Plowman*. For all his changing significance, we are apt to feel at home with Piers himself, always recognizing in him (as, I am sure, the author intended us to do) the simple farmer to whom Truth sent a pardon. Liberum Arbitrium, on the other hand, is a formidable creation who owes his existence to scholastic theology—a not very ingratiating paternity. Of course the C poet did not have to go far to find him, since he was already there, prefabricated by B, as Piers' lieutenant in the garden. All the C poet had to do was promote him, albeit to a rank we might not suspect him worthy to receive—from Piers' lieutenant to Active's leader.[92] Let us examine his qualifications for this promotion in order to determine what was in the C poet's mind when he made the substitution of Liberum Arbitrium for Piers.

St. Bernard of Clairvaux, discussing in their relationship to man the three types of freedom that God possesses perfectly— freedom of counsel, freedom of enjoyment and freedom of choice—makes the following observations which seem pertinent to an understanding of the C poet's conception of the character of Liberum Arbitrium:

> Puto autem in his tribus libertatibus ipsam, ad quam conditi sumus, Conditoris imaginem atque similitudinem contineri: et imaginem quidem in libertate arbitrii, in reliquis autem duabus bipartitam quamdam consignari similitudinem. Hinc est fortassis,

---

[92] C. XVII. 158: "Thenne hadde Actyf a ledere · that heyhte *Liberum-arbitrium*."

quod solum liberum arbitrium sui omnino defectum seu diminutionem non patitur, quod in ipso potissimum aeternae et incommutabilis divinitatis substantiva quaedam imago impressa videatur. Nam, etsi habuerit initium, nescit tamen occasum, nec de justitia vel gloria capit augmentum; nec de peccato sive miseria detrimentum. Quid aeternitati similius, quod non sit aeternitas?[93]

Now I do not think that the C poet was in any way directly acquainted with the theology of Bernard, although Skeat records two quotations from the Saint in *Piers Plowman*.[94] But I am entirely certain that some such doctrine about the will as this—whether Bernard's or some other medieval theologian's —transmitted, probably, through other minds, not all of them accurate, was known to the poet and that his creative imagination had grasped some of its essentials. According to the Bernardine system, *liberum arbitrium,* man's free will, or free choice, as it is better translated, is that part of man which bears the impress of the image of God to which man was created.[95] Although man has lost through sin some of the likeness originally inherent in the image, he may, by proper spiritual exercise, restore it. In the C text, the Tree of Charity, which is also the Tree of Human Life, bears another name: Imago Dei, the Image of God. Indeed, it is by this name that the tree is first known. And if, acting upon this hint, we read the passage while associating Liberum Arbitrium with a Bernardine concept of the will,[96] the scene in the Garden of Heart will become

---

[93] *Migne,* CLXXXII, 1016. From chap. ix of Bernard's treatise, *De Gratia et Libero Arbitrio.*

[94] At C. XII. 165, B. XI. 2; C. XVII. 221, B. XV. 59.

[95] For a discussion of this point, see Etienne Gilson, *The Mystical Theology of St. Bernard,* trans., A. H. C. Downes (New York, 1940), pp. 45–54.

[96] Sanderlin, 453, n. 14, has pointed out that Liberum Arbitrium's self-description at C. XVII. 177, "a wil with a reyson," recalls St. Bernard's definition: *Porro voluntas est motus rationalis. . . . Habet sane, quocunque se volverit, semper rationem comitem, et quodammodo pedissequam: non quod semper ex ratione, sed quod nunquam absque ratione moveatur.* See *Migne,* CLXXXII, 1003. From chap. ii of *De Gratia.*

more comprehensible and more suggestive. As Imago Dei, the tree signifies mankind. Simultaneously it signifies charity, the first example of which, so far as man is concerned, was his own creation by a loving God. The three props signify, of course, the Trinity. And the intermediary who can call upon the Trinity for defense against man's enemies is that faculty in man by which he most nearly approaches the Deity, Liberum Arbitrium, who in his very nature bears the image of God, the full likeness of which he may yet restore.

Another Bernardine concept may have been present in the C poet's mind when he decided to make Liberum Arbitrium, rather than Piers, proprietor of the Tree of Charity. We must never forget that the poem as a whole amounts to a long, many-sided consideration of the problem of salvation. The scene in the Garden of Heart provides in a very real sense the turning point in the poem. Hitherto, the discussion has dealt in general and specific terms with a wide variety of topics related to the problem of salvation: with grace, with predestination, with the status of the heathen both before and after Christ, with the relative merits of learning and ignorance, the active life and patience. But from the moment the Holy Ghost speaks in Mary's ear the poem begins to deal with the first great cause of salvation, both directly in the Incarnation and in the organization whose aim is to perpetuate the effects of the Incarnation, the Church. The central figure in the turning point is Liberum Arbitrium. There is a peculiar appropriateness in the choice of this character if we suppose the poet to have been familiar, in one form or another, with a conception like Bernard's of the role *liberum arbitrium* plays in salvation:

Quid igitur agit, ais, liberum arbitrium? Breviter respondeo: Salvatur. Tolle liberum arbitrium, et non erit quod salvetur: tolle gratiam, non erit unde salvetur. Opus hoc sine duobus effici non potest: uno a quo fit; altero cui, vel in quo fit. Deus auctor est salutis, liberum arbitrium tantum capax: nec dare illam, nisi Deus; nec capere valet, nisi liberum arbitrium. Quod ergo a solo

Deo, et soli datur libero arbitrio; tam absque consensu esse [al. effici] non potest accipientis, quam absque gratia dantis. Et ita gratiae operanti salutem cooperari dicitur liberum arbitrium, dum consentit, hoc est dum salvatur. Consentire enim salvari est.[97]

As George Sanderlin has said in an interesting but all too brief note on C's Liberum Arbitrium, the passage in C's vision of the tree is "an allegory of the cooperation of grace and free choice in the defense of the righteous soul against evil" (453). It is also, of course, something more than this. But viewed solely as an allegory of grace and free will it fits perfectly into its position in the poem.

With a Bernardine Liberum Arbitrium the scene in C unrolls comprehensibly and even with certain artistic improvements over the B version. The description of the use of the three props is given in its simplified form, with Liberum Arbitrium as the agency that makes use of all three. The elaboration of the discourse concerning the fruit of the tree we could do without; still, it is characteristic of the C poet while cleaning up B's canvas to smear his own a little. The truly impressive moment comes after Liberum Arbitrium, at the Dreamer's request, has bidden Elde shake down some fruit from the tree. The devil is lurking in readiness, and as soon as the fruit falls he gathers it up and bears it away to limbo. And while the Dreamer's eyes, like our own, are on the fiend, a great alteration has taken place in Liberum Arbitrium:

Thenne meuede hym mod · *in maiestate dei,*
That *Libera-Voluntas-Dei* · lauhte the myddel shoriere,
And hitte after the fende · happe hou hit myghte.
Filius, by the faders wil · flegh with *Spiritus Sanctus,*
To ransake that rageman · and reue hym hus apples,
That fyrst man deceyuede · thorgh frut and false by-heste.
    And thenne spake *Spiritus Sanctus* · in Gabrielis mouthe
To a mayde that hihte Marie . . . .[98]

[97] *Migne,* CLXXXII, 1002. From chap. i of *De Gratia.*
[98] C. XIX. 118–125. See p. 172, n. 87, above.

The sudden transformation of Liberum Arbitrium from man's free will to God's free will, paralleling what in the B text I take to be the development of Piers from human nature to the almost divine nature that Christ was about to assume, has its own special grandeur. Doubtless such a transformation would find no sanction in Bernardine epistemology. Yet the creative mind, translating a mystical system into concrete images, could, if it so desired, render the metamorphosis easy. All one has to do is to make man's free will a sharer in the divine free will, a step that seems logically to follow Bernard's question, *Quid aeternitati similius, quod non sit aeternitas?*

I do not wish to imply that the C poet superimposed upon the B text a Bernardine idea of the will without taking into consideration what the B poet's original idea of the will was. Liberum Arbitrium had, after all, been introduced in B, and there is reason to suppose that when the C poet developed the character in the manner we have seen he was well aware of what it had meant to the B poet. In order to show this, let me refer to an excellent analysis that has been made of the part Liberum Arbitrium plays in B. Miss Hort, discussing the significance of the vision of the Tree of Charity, makes the following comments:

> The most important thing about man is his free will; it is that which is his final guard against evil. While man is in the process of growing into perfect charity, he is supported and helped by the power of God and by the wisdom of God; but when he is at length near his attainment, then the only thing that can help him and preserve him from sin is his own free will. He who sins against the Holy Ghost is he who sins of his own free will, by deliberate choice. However, free will can only overthrow the evil one by grace and through the help of the Holy Ghost. (pp. 113–114)

Miss Hort goes on to observe that the relation between free will and the Holy Ghost is not clear in the B text. She believes, however, that the obscurity may be cleared up. The poet, in a later passage, identifies the Holy Ghost as the free will of the Father and the Son.[99] If we relate this fact to those already given us, we arrive at the conclusion that the B poet "uses the term Liberum Arbitrium for the Holy Ghost in man, and that the meaning of the whole passage is that Liberum Arbitrium, the most important thing about man, is the Holy Ghost; that it is the Holy Ghost in man, helped by the Holy Ghost outside man, which finally leads man to salvation."[100] The identification of Liberum Arbitrium with the Holy Ghost is, as Miss Hort notes, apparently idiosyncratic and the C poet omits it, along with the special connection between the two in the vision of the tree. He retains, however, more than a little of the B poet's individuality and in particular his tendency to deify free will—Active's "leader," as the C poet calls it. This is apparent when Liberum Arbitrium becomes, without explanation, Libera Voluntas Dei—a transition which, whatever its relation to the Bernardine doctrine, would seem to have required impetus from elsewhere.[101] In B, man partakes of divinity in the possession of free will, which is the portion of the Holy Ghost that resides in him. In C, man also partakes of divinity in the possession of free will which is, apparently, itself a portion of the free will of God. It needs only to introduce into C the B poet's definition of the Holy Ghost as the free will of God to bring the two texts into complete agreement. And even though the C poet omits this, we certainly have a striking resemblance between them, since things equal to the same thing are equal

---

[99] B. xvi. 220–224: "Þus in þre persones is perfitliche manhede, Þat is, man & his make & moillere her children, And is nouȝt but gendre of o generacioun bifor Ihesu cryst in heuene, So is þe fader forth with þe sone, and fre wille of bothe; *Spiritus procedens a patre & filio;* Which is þe holygoste of alle, and alle is but o god."

[100] Miss Hort, . . . *Cont. Rel. Thought,* p. 115.

[101] Miss Day seems to object to this development in the character of Liberum Arbitrium . . . ("Revisions of 'P.P.,'" 24). But for Langland's tendency toward the doctrine of deification, see p. 172, n. 87 above.

to each other. We should observe, therefore, that on the matter of the almost unlimited importance of Liberum Arbitrium, the B and C poets are in accord, despite the latter's drastic revision. This suggests to me that the B poet's conception of free will, as well as C's, derives ultimately from some doctrine similar to that of St. Bernard.

It is time to speak briefly about the C poet's substitution of Liberum Arbitrium for B's Anima as the character who serves in the capacity of Prologue to Dobet. The explanation for this alteration provides us, I believe, with one more reason for the substitution of the same character for Piers and at the same time illustrates the C poet's tendency to develop the poem upon lines already laid down in the B text. Let us first recall that the dominant theme of Dobet is charity and then let us turn to B to find how charity is there defined. The definition is drawn from Anima by the Dreamer's somewhat cynical question through which he lets us know that his name is Long Will. Charity, Anima explains, is a childish thing,

> With-outen fauntelte or foly, a fre liberal wille.
> (B. xv. 146)

"A free, liberal will": the phrase seems almost to be a punning translation of *liberum arbitrium,* as if the poet, along with later translators,[102] realized the inadequacy of the English "free will" to render the full sense of the Latin and took advantage of the relation between the adjectives *"liber"* and "liberal" to point his own translation in the direction of charity. The importance of the will as the emotional faculty, the faculty capable of experiencing love, is further emphasized by the B poet in the repeated statement of Anima that charity is to be seen only in the will and hence is perceptible to none but Piers. It seems

---

[102] See G. B. Burch, ed., St. Bernard's *The Steps of Humility* (Cambridge, 1940), pp. 13–14; also *The Treatise of St. Bernard, Abbat of Clairvaux, concerning Grace and Free Will, trans.,* W. W. Williams (London, 1920), p. xi.

likely that the C poet, desirous of emphasizing charity to the utmost, took the hint from B to make Liberum Arbitrium, the emotional faculty of the soul, serve as the prologue to a dramatization of charity. In adopting B's notion of the will as the love-making faculty, the C poet was also following the lead of the theologians, including Bernard,[103] from whom either the B or C poet might have derived it. What C failed to do was to have Liberum Arbitrium expressly define himself as the seat of love—the sort of failure that is typical of both poets. Nevertheless, if we again call into service the axiom that things equal to the same thing are equal to each other, then Liberum Arbitrium seems an appropriate person to play the part he does in Dobet.

The substitution is attended, however, by one superficially troublesome alteration and by another which seems more serious. The first of these occurs in the introductory speech by the Dreamer's interlocutor in the vision preceding that of the Tree of Charity. In the B text the interlocutor, Anima, calls himself by nine names which describe the faculties of the soul according to a catalogue that goes back at least as far as Isidore of Seville,[104] from whom the B poet directly quotes. Because of its antiquity we are apt to think of the catalogue as an invariable entity, like a listing of the fifty states of the Union. Thus the C poet's addition of a name not included in B's list, Liberum Arbitrium, the most important of all the names in C, may seem to us, as it did to Skeat,[105] a violation of the laws of common sense. But we err if we assume that Isidore's catalogue formed any generally accepted summary of the soul. Alcuin, for instance, has another catalogue that varies in important respects from Isidore's,[106] and Sanderlin has pointed out that the list in C is exactly the same as that appearing in John of Damas-

---

[103] Burch, p. 12.

[104] See Skeat's note to C. XVII. 201, EETS, IV, 338.

[105] Ibid.: "It is hard to see how all these various names can be applied to Free Will."

[106] Skeat, ibid., gives a Middle English translation of Alcuin's catalogue.

cus,[107] as reputable an authority as Isidore. I do not think that the change suggests that the C poet was a partisan of a different school of theological thought from the B poet. Lists of the faculties of the soul seem to have been popular in medieval times and were apparently used as exercises in intellectual virtuosity. Thus a translation of Alcuin's appears in isolation in Lambeth MS 306;[108] the B poet's sufficiently delighted Drayton that he turned it into an amiable, if rather implausible, sonnet;[109] and one John Cok took the trouble to copy C's in its entirety.[110] Possibly the B poet found Isidore's in isolation in some MS. or other and the same happened with respect to C and John Damascene's. Furthermore, while the catalogue B used may have been the best he could find, it does not, we should observe, really fit the requirements of the B text. *Liberum arbitrium,* which turns out to be "the most important thing about man," is omitted, and the list does not even contain a good substitute. For no one, I think, would be willing to accept *animus,* the closest thing to will in the B list. The C poet was fortunate in running across the description he did, for what he needed— and what B needed, too—was a description wherein *liberum arbitrium* should appear as a universal power of the soul. And this, as Sanderlin has said, is precisely what John Damascene's description provides (450).

The second alteration is more difficult to explain, inasmuch as it seems to involve a genuine doctrinal difference. In B, Anima tells the Dreamer that love, which exists only in the will,

---

[107] 450–451. Sanderlin quotes the pertinent passage from John of Damascus as follows: *Libero ergo arbitrio appetit, et libero arbitrio vult et scrutatur, libero arbitrio inquirit et iudicat; libero arbitrio disponit, libero arbitrio eligit, et libero arbitrio impetum facit et libero arbitrio agit et operatur semper in his que secundum naturam sunt.*

[108] Originally printed by F. J. Furnivall, *Political, Religious, and Love Poems,* poet's rev. ed., EETS, 15 (London, 1903), p. 65.

[109] Reprinted by Skeat, EETS, IV, 338.

[110] See Carleton Brown and R. H. Robbins, *The Index of Middle English Verse* (New York, 1943), p. 119, item 745.

may not be perceived in works. In C, Liberum Arbitrium, who as will is the seat of charity, tells the Dreamer that love may be perceived in works and even emphasizes the fact.[111] Now it may be that this is a direct change of heart. On the other hand, the C poet may have been driven to the alteration by the exigencies of logic: whereas it is proper for Anima to say that charity is perceptible only in the will, there is something rather awkward in having will say the same—the subtilization approaches absurdity. Actually, the B poet's insistence upon the invisibility of charity seems an aberration from his normal trend of thought, since nowhere else does he even suggest that there is any flaw in the doctrine of good works. Furthermore, it is interesting that C, who affirms the value of works as an index of charity, is able to take over without modification B's description of charity—that is, his description of the external forms that charity takes. Thus the B poet, having denied the validity of works as an index, is forced by logic to drop the subject then and there or else implicitly to deny his denial. It was the second of these courses that he chose to pursue.[112] I do not know what the source of the B poet's idea was; it seems to be a curious, rather perverse extension of one of St. Paul's observations, "Though I bestow all my goods to feed the poor, and though I give my body to be burned, and have not charity, it profiteth me nothing" (1 Cor. 13:3). The C poet, however, was able to find a scriptural passage of equal authority and straightforward sense to support his point of view: *Operibus credite,* the means by which Christ told His followers that they might recognize His divinity (John 10:38). Whatever the motive for it, the C poet's alteration seems to have improved the logic

---

[111] Cf. C. XVII. 339 "Ac thorw werkes thou myght wite · wher forth he walketh; *Operibus credite.* · with B. xv. 203–204: There-fore by coloure ne by clergye · knowe shaltow hym neuere,/Noyther thorw wordes ne werkes · but thorw wille one."

[112] The description of Charity in B. xv. 210–252 is, of course, necessarily objective: Charity is known by his works.

of B and to have made the poem more consistent with what both the B and C poets show elsewhere were the dominant tendencies of their thought.

Reading the C version of the *Visio de Do-Bet* with a sympathetic rather than a hostile heart, it is possible for one to work out sensible explanations for the alterations that the C poet made. Of artistic improvement there may not be a great deal and the lover of poetry will probably still prefer the B version of Dobet. But taken as a thing in itself, the C version should prove esthetically satisfying, and if we possessed only C's Dobet we should still be aware that we had a splendid piece of Middle English poetry. Furthermore, even on a comparative basis, the lover of clarity might prefer the later text. Let us take as a single illustration the C poet's handling of Piers. Back in Dowel, in the banquet scene, we were given a glimpse of him prophesying charity while representing, apparently, patience. Piers then passes from the poem for a long time. During the last passus of Dowel and the earlier ones of Dobet we hear nothing about him except a single fugitive reference made by Liberum Arbitrium. This replaces the B poet's three emphatic, and misleading, couplings of Piers with Christ which culminate in the phrase *Petrus, id est, Christus;* it consists of the single suggestive Latin line (also in B), *Et vidit deus cogitationes eorum,* following the statement that Piers has most perfect knowledge of charity (C. xvii. 337). We do not, in C, have to worry whether or not this identifies Piers with Christ, for when Piers finally takes the stage again it is in one body with Christ. Meanwhile the discussion has treated charity—Dobet—on various levels: through Liberum Arbitrium, the faculty which is alone capable of love; through the Tree of Charity, which reflects God's love for man in the relation between free will and salvation; in the Incarnation, when Christian charity came to earth; in the Samaritan, who as a symbol of charity becomes one with Christ and Piers Plowman; and ultimately in the Atonement, the supreme act of charity. It is in the Atonement that Piers is seen again. After the long interval since he appeared as Dowel he reappears as Dobet. The patience is rewarded, the law fulfilled, and Piers, who had impugned all learning but love and truth, has made good his promise,

> . . . ich shal preoue þat ich seide
> And a-vowe by-for God and for-sake hit neuere.

V. SUMMARY

Near the beginning of this essay I spoke of the similarity of the structure of the C text of *Piers Plowman* to the incident recounted by St. Matthew concerning the rich young man who asked Christ two questions about salvation. I suggested that the first of the two answers he received—*Keep the commandments* —formed the subject of the *Visio de Petro Plowman,* while the second, beginning *If thou wilt be perfect,* formed the subject of the *Vita de Do-Well, Do-Bet et Do-Best;* and that the first section of the poem dealt with the moral and social aspects of life, while the second dealt with its spiritual aspects. In the study of the C poet's revisions of the religious allegory I have tried to show, among other things, that his interest in active life virtually ended with the conclusion of the *Visio* and that the *Vita* takes up in turn various stages of a contemplative life. The first of these stages is patience (Dowel) and the second charity (Dobet). It is time to face the issue which I originally avoided of trying to equate these stages of contemplative life with some known medieval triad comprehending the steps by which the soul may attain perfection.

I have presented at some length the evidence for believing that the C poet was familiar with certain manifestations of a theological system similar to St. Bernard's, and it is to Bernard that we may look for an analogue to the C text's steps to perfection. According to the thinker who represents perhaps the fullest flowering of the contemplative school, the anagogical path consists of the three steps of humility, charity and unity.[112] It is a peculiarity of the poet that in his long discussion of the first step he only occasionally describes it in terms that associate it directly with humility. Nevertheless, the names by which he calls the first step, poverty and patience, are aspects of humility —practical aspects of humility, one might say. St. Bernard was thinking in terms of monks,[113] with whom the problem of poverty, at least theoretically, did not occur. But the author of *Piers Plowman* was not, I am sure, a monk, and was endeavoring to point out the path of perfection not to monks but to anyone who was interested in finding it. Therefore his translation of humility into the more objective patience, and retranslation of patience into the undeniably objective patient poverty, seems only natural. With charity, there is no similar problem, except that the poet of C emphasizes its external aspects more than the theologian does. For the final step on the path, unity, we are left without guidance: the C poet made no alterations in the *Visio de Dobest*. Perhaps he was satisfied with it as it stood, or perhaps he died before he could undertake its revision. I incline toward the second alternative. As it stands, Dobest does not seem to contain much that is suggestive of the vision of God of St. Bernard. Nevertheless, in the section as it stands there are elements suggestive of the unitive condition of the soul, just as in B's Dowel there is a good deal about patience and in B's Dobet the main theme is charity. Specifically, there is the constant repetition of the word *unity,* even though it usually signifies the Church.[114] But I am unable to make much out of this. Progress along the anagogical path is, of course, a gift of grace, both in Bernard and in *Piers Plowman*. As the

[112] See Burch, pp. 101–107. This book contains a most useful summary of St. Bernard's epistemology.

[113] Idem, p. I.

[114] See C. XXII. 330 ff., B. XIX. 325 ff. Especially significant are the lines B. XX. 211–212 (C. XXIII. 212–213): ". . . I comsed to rowme spout Thorw Contricioun and Confessioun · tyl I cam to Vnite." Professor Meroney first called my attention to this passage.

poem ends in the B text, and hence in C, this progress seems to have stopped short of its goal:

> 'Bi Cryste,' quod Conscience tho · 'I wil bicome a pilgryme,
> And walken as wyde · as al the worlde lasteth,
> To seke Piers the Plowman · that Pryde may destruye,
> And that freres hadde a fyndyng · that for nede flateren,
> And contrepleteth me, Conscience; · now Kynde me auenge,
> And sende me happe and hele · til I haue Piers the Plowman!'
> And sitthe he gradde after grace · til I gan awake.[115]

Perhaps if the C poet had lived he might have had the grace to continue on the path.

With respect to the question of authorship, the evidence considered in this chapter establishes nothing conclusive for either theory. It is altogether possible that a second poet should have revised the religious allegory of B in the manner we have seen. But if there was a second poet, the evidence points to his having been one of large capacities, both intellectual and artistic— a worthy successor to B. Furthermore, he seems to have had an extraordinarily thorough knowledge and understanding of the poem that he was rewriting, since the majority of his revisions have their source and their sanction in B. On the negative side, there is no evidence that the C poet in any way perverted the meaning of the poem so that B would not have approved of it, no question of two different schools of theological thought. Rather, the C poet developed lines of thought that were latent in B. St. Augustine's comment on certain discrepancies between the snyoptic Gospels is perhaps relevant here: *Nihil obstat narrandi diversitas, ubi eadem dicuntur, maxime quum quisque evangelistarum eo ordine credat se dicere, quo Deus voluit.*[116] If we alter *"evangelistarum"* to *"poetarum,"* the remark seems applicable to B and C. Since the

---

[115] B. xx. 378–384 (C. xxiii. 380–386).
[116] Quoted from *Corpus Iuris Canonici,* ed., E. L. Richter, 2 vols. (Leipzig, 1922), II, 913.

similarities between the texts far outweigh the differences, even where drastic revision has taken place, I believe that we have to deal with but one poet, who remained ever discontent with what he had accomplished and, to the end of his life, kept striving to write in the way God wished—*eo ordine quo Deus voluit.*

7

PIERS PLOWMAN AND
SCRIPTURAL TRADITION*

D. W. Robertson, Jr. and Bernard F. Huppé

I. THE METHOD

IN MEDIEVAL SCHOOLS students were taught to read books on three distinct levels. The procedure was definite and systematic. First, a work was considered in terms of its grammatical structure and syntax. When this preliminary was thoroughly mastered, the students were led to consider the obvious meaning of what they had read. If it were narrative, for example, the second step would be to learn the outline of the narrative. Finally, students were taught the higher meaning, the doctrinal content, or, as we might call it, the theme of what they had read. These three levels were called *littera, sensus* and *sententia,* respectively. The first two levels were preliminaries to the third, for the importance of any work was thought to lie in its higher meaning, or as Chaucer would have said, in its *sentence.*[1] If medieval

* Reprinted by permission of Princeton University Press from D. W. Robertson, Jr. and Bernard F. Huppé, *Piers Plowman and Scriptural Tradition,* Copyright, 1951, by Princeton University Press. London: Geoffrey Cumberlege, Oxford University Press. Reprinted here are Chap. I, pp. 1–16, and Chap. IX, pp. 234–248. Excisions have been made as required to present these chapters as a two-part independent essay.

[1] See G. Paré, A. Brunet and P. Tremblay, *La renaissance du xiie siècle: Les écoles et l'enseignement* (Paris and Ottawa, 1933), pp. 116–117. The four senses of Scriptural commentary were developments of the *sentence.*

readers considered the works they read in this way, it is only natural that medieval writers should have deliberately composed their works with a definite *sentence* in mind. In other words, the medieval writer or reader would never have been content, as the modern naturalist professes to be, with a "slice of life." The underlying meaning, the theme, had to be always clear. It should be understood that this meaning was not a fortuitously applied "moral." On the contrary, it was frequently integrated skillfully with the matter of the work itself so that it formed the dominant unifying element. The relative importance of matter and *sentence* is indicated by Chaucer's Nun's Priest, who compares the matter of his tale to the chaff, its *sentence* to the fruit. As an allegory, *Piers Plowman* is directly concerned with a higher meaning in the medieval sense.

The existence of a large body of Scriptural quotations in the text of the poem furnishes a key to the ultimate source of its allegorical meaning. These quotations are not haphazard, decorative or macaronic but are connected intimately with the *sentence* of the poem. The truth of this observation is not clear until it is understood that the Bible did not exist alone in the Middle Ages. It was surrounded by a nexus of traditional interpretation which was the source of the homiletic and liturgical offices by means of which the ordinary Christian learned the Catholic doctrine. Biblical exegesis was at the same time the culmination of all scholastic exercises. Even theology was at first but an aid to a true understanding of the sacred text.[2] It

---

[2] Ibid., pp. 257–258, Cf. Beryl Smalley, *The Study of the Bible in the Middle Ages* (Cambridge, 1941), pp. xiv–xv. For a systematic survey of biblical exegesis, see C. Spicq, *L'exégèse latine au moyen age* (Paris, 1944).

For the reader who wishes to follow the biblical references in an English text, it should be noted that references are to the Vulgate throughout this study. Since neither Ecclesiasticus (Ecclus.) nor Sapientia (Sap.) appears in the King James Version and since the numbering of the Psalms differs in the two Bibles, the Douay Bible should be consulted for references to these three books.

is to this nexus of interpretation that the poet directs us when he tells the reader to consult the "glose." Like vernacular literature, Scripture was read on three levels[3] with the further elaboration that the highest level, or *sentence,* might be developed in three ways. The distinction between the level of the sense and that of the *sentence* was again sharply defined. As Spicq puts it:

> Le sens littéral ou historique se distingue du sens spirituel ou allégorique comme l'humanité visible du Christ de sa divinité invisible, ou plus prosaïquement comme l'écorce de l'amande. . . . L'emploi des vocables est significatif de l'estime réciproque que l'on a pour l'un et l'autre sens. L'exégèse littérale est qualifiée de "carnaliter, secundum sensus corporeos, secundum superficiem, etc. . . . ," l'interprétation spirituelle est "secundum mysterium, secundum symbolum, spiritualiter, secundum intelligibilem sensum" ou "intelligence mystique, intérieure" et "spirituelle"; en un mot, les deux exégèses s'opposent, selon la dichotomie paulinienne, comme la lettre à l'esprit. (p. 19)

Rind and core, chaff and fruit, the letter and the spirit in Paul, are expressions indicating the supreme importance of *sentence* in the study of the Bible. The three levels by means of which this *sentence* might be elaborated, although they varied somewhat among authorities, were tropological, allegorical and anagogical. The tropological meaning was that which applied to the individual so that it was frequently moral in application. The allegorical sense was used originally to interpret the Old Testament in the light of the New, or to interpret it as it applies to the Church. The anagogical sense is concerned with the heavenly mysteries. These three levels may be regarded as the classical division.[4] The Scriptural quotations in *Piers Plowman* should be examined in the light of the exegetical tradition which developed on the basis of this technique. Moreover, throughout the poem, even in passages unsupported by direct

[3] See Paré, *et al.,* p. 228; Spicq, pp. 99–100.
[4] See Spicq's discussion and the references he gives, pp. 21–25.

quotation from the Bible, the author had the *sentence* of Scripture constantly in mind. This *sentence* as it appears in traditional exegesis forms a completely objective test of the meaning of the allegory of the poem. . . .

The medieval student of theology was thoroughly trained in the interpretation of Scripture so that he would command several traditional interpretations of any important Scriptural passage. In his study, he would not confine himself to any single commentator, but would deliberately familiarize himself with the tradition of patristic comment and with such subsequent comments as he had available or considered important. Indeed any commentary he might have consulted, from the summarizing *Glossa ordinaria* to the fullest commentary, such as Bonaventura on Luke, would have enforced the necessity for richness and flexibility of selection. Almost any page of a typical commentary like Peter Lombard on the Psalms, where differing authoritative interpretations are set down side by side as permissible variants, would have made clear the existence and importance of alternative interpretations. Moreover, the poet might have had available not only concordances to the Vulgate, but what amount to alphabetical concordances of key words from Scripture arranged either according to the senses of Scripture or according to variants in patristic interpretations. The variations are accompanied by citations or quotations from the biblical text. In general, these *répertoires exégétiques,* as Spicq calls them, served as a guide to the biblical *sentence* of important objects or conceptions. For example, in the twelfth-century *Allegoriae in sacram scripturam,* the word *dormitio* is given seven meanings: the quietness of contemplation, spiritual torpor, death, sickness, blindness, falling into sin, sexual embrace.[5] Clearly, the number of possible meanings for the con-

---

[5] *PL,* 112, 913. The work is erroneously attributed there to Rabanus Maurus. See Spicq, p. 63. There is an extensive discussion of the *répertoires* in Chapter 3.

cept sleep is large and various. A poet using one of them in an allegory would make his selection clear either through the context of his own work or by the citation or suggestion of a determining text in Scripture. In *Piers Plowman,* for instance, the notion of sleep is used in the sense of spiritual torpor at the beginning of Passus I and in the sense of the quietness of contemplation at the beginning of Passus XVI. These meanings are obvious in relation to the context of the poem. In composing his allegory, therefore, the poet was forced to select from a variety of possibilities.

The selection of explanatory materials [should be] in part determined by the character of the poem itself and by its position in a definite theological and ecclesiastical tradition. Piers Plowman represents in part what Konrad Burdach described as the "Urbild und Vorbild des Apostels Petrus und seiner Päpstlichen Nachfolger."[6] We should say, however, that he represents God's ministry on earth in the *status praelatorum;* that is, the patriarchs, the prophets, Christ, the disciples and the subsequent representatives of the apostolic tradition, who are, in the secular tradition, the popes, the bishops and the parish priests. Piers is the ideal, actualized in Christ, of what the men in this status should be. An important theme in the poem involves the fact that the function of those in the *status praelatorum* has been usurped by certain members of the *status religiosorum* with the result that God's hierarchy has been upset, to the detriment of the Church as a whole. Specifically, the function of Piers has been usurped by the friars, who maintained what the poet thought of as invalid pretenses to the apostolic succession. The criticism of the friars in *Piers Plowman* is not, however, simply a matter of conventional abuse based on observation; it is rather a clear and definite continuation of the strug-

[6] *Vom Mittelalter zur Reformation,* III, 2 (Berlin, 1926–1932), p. 189. Cf. pp. 294–314. We consider the remainder of Burdach's definition, only part of which is quoted here, to be misleading.

gle between the seculars and the friars having as its focal point a debate on the states of perfection. This debate reached a climax in the thirteenth century when William of Saint-Amour made a spectacular attack on the position of the fraternal orders. It is significant that the central point in William's argument corresponds exactly with the position taken by the author of the poem:

> Il établit que ceux-là seuls ont la droit de prêcher qui en ont reçu la mission; il oppose à la hiérarchie traditionnelle, sans les nommer, les Ordres nouveaux qui n'ont point charge d'âme et veut établir que le Souverain Pontife lui-même n'a pas entendu leur donner dans l'Eglise une mission générale qui serait au détriment de celle confiée déjà aux évêques et aux prêtres séculiers.[7]

Apart from the thesis that the friars have unjustly usurped the apostolic tradition, there are striking parallels in detail between William's argument and the poem. In the Prologue the friars stand accused of false preaching, of false "clothing" or outward status, of abusing confession. The poet warns that unless the friars are brought in line with Holy Church, the greatest mischief will ensue (ll. 58–67). In Passus III, a friar calls on Lady Mede and indicates that he is more interested in the temporal reward she offers than in any attempts to reform her.

---

[7] Maurice Perrod, *Etude sur la vie et sur les œuvres de Guillaume de Saint-Amour* (Lons-le-Saunier, 1902), p. 157. Cf. p. 159. On the beginnings of the subsequent quarrel over perfection, see P. Glorieux, " 'Contra Geraldinos.' L'enchainement des polémiques," *Rech. Théol. anc. med.,* VII (1935), 129–155; K. Schleyer, "Disputes scolastiques sur les états de perfection," ibid., X (1938), 279–293. The opening remarks of Schleyer's discussion, p. 279, are instructive: "Parmi les grands problèmes agités par les penseurs scolastiques, de la moité du XIIIᵉ au début du XIVᵉ siècle, se range la question du *status perfectionis.* Les partis en présence étaient d'un côté les maîtres séculiers, de l'autre les ordres mendiants. Tous deux prétendaient posséder dans leur état la plus haute perfection, c'est-à-dire le rang le plus élevé dans l'ordonnance hiérarchique de l'Eglise. Il est évident qu'il ne s'agissait pas ici d'une revendication purement théorique. L'opposition entre le clergé séculier et les ordres mendiants s'étendait bien au delà des universités."

Indeed, he professes himself willing to serve her evil purposes in corrupting knights and clerks (ll. 35–63). In Passus VIII, two Minorites meet Will and indicate their fraternal pride in announcing that Dowel has always and will always live with them. They illustrate, moreover, the easy repentance which the friars offered (ll. 8–56). In Passus XIII, a Dominican, proud to be a "master," takes a place at the head of the table and demonstrates himself to be an arrant hypocrite.[8] He is attacked in the poem on the basis of a text which William of Saint-Amour used to great advantage in his own attack on the friars, *periculum est in falsis fratribus* (ll. 33–97). Finally in Passus XX, the friars are shown to be followers of Antichrist, as William of Saint-Amour implied, and their entry into Holy Church is shown historically from a secular point of view. In illustrating the result of their seizure of control, the poet goes even further than William of Saint-Amour by having Conscience turn aside from the church in pursuit of Piers. These detailed accusations may be found in William of Saint-Amour's writings. The poet's added conclusion would have been out of place in the *De periculis,* since it warned of dangers not yet fully realized. The poet described what he considered to be the results of a failure to heed that warning.[9]

Historically, William's doctrines were condemned in a council held before the Pope. Assembled to refute him was an imposing task force of authorities, including Humbert de Romans, Albertus Magnus, St. Thomas Aquinas and St. Bonaventura. William was not allowed to defend his position, perhaps because of the fame of his eloquence. In spite of the condemnation and

[8] On the title "master" and the desire of the friars to dominate, see the letter of the University of Paris in Denifle and Chatelain, *Chartularium,* I, 252–258.

[9] The details of William of Saint-Amour's attack may be found conveniently described in the works of Perrod, Glorieux and Schleyer mentioned in the notes above, and in the excerpts from the *De periculis* in Bierbaum, *Bettelorden und Weltgeistlichkeit,* Franziskanische Studien, Beiheft II (Munchen, 1920). Specific references to the more striking correspondences are given in our notes.

the cleverness of the opposition, he did not recant. Indeed, his position was maintained in direct succession by Gérard d'Abbeville and by Godefroid de Fontaines and by Jean de Pouilli at Paris.[10] In England, the central traditions of secular theology were defended vigorously against the friars throughout the thirteenth and fourteenth centuries:

> The quarrel in Oxford was in truth but a symptom of the great feud between the friars and the seculars which divided the whole church of England—indeed the whole church of Europe— throughout the fourteenth century. In England as in France the universities were but the organs of the secular clergy at large. . . . Occasional bickerings between the secular masters and the friars continued, however, to be among the normal incidents of university life.[11]

Among the most prominent of the secular apologists was Archbishop Richard Fitzralph, who died defending his cause at Avignon in 1360.[12] A typical and easily accessible fourteenth-century attack on the friars is the *Contra querelas fratrum* of Uhtred de Boldon.[13] It is not to be expected that William's successors who, it must be emphasized, represented the central traditions of scholastic theology,[14] should have regarded the

[10] The quarrel continued at Paris well into the fifteenth century. See F. M. Powicke and A. B. Emden, eds., *Rashdall's Medieval Universities* (Oxford, 1936), I, 396–397. See "Jean de Pouilli," *Dictionnaire de théologie catholique.*

[11] Powicke and Emden, II, 74, 76.

[12] Ibid., II, 75. Cf. Aubrey Gwynn, S. J., *The English Austin Friars in the Time of Wyclif* (Oxford, 1940), pp. 79–89. He says concerning the B text of *Piers Plowman* that the complaints against the friars are "in the familiar tradition of Guillaume de Saint-Amour, Jean de Pouilli, and Richard Fitz-Ralph."

[13] Mildred Marcett, ed., *Uhtred de Boldon, Friar William Jordan, and "Piers Plowman"* (New York, 1938), pp. 25–37.

[14] Pierre Glorieux, "Pour une édition de Gérard d'Abbeville," *Rech. Théol. anc. med.,* IX (1937), p. 56, has this to say of William's immediate successor: "Gérard d'Abbeville est, plus et mieux que tous autres, le type du théologien du maître séculier du XIIIᵉ siècle. Il encarne en quelque sorte 'l'Ecole'; non point l'école thomiste à laquelle ce nom

men who condemned William and their doctrines with the veneration accorded them by certain moderns. In vernacular literature, the importance of the secular tradition is well attested in the popularity of such works as the *Roman de la Rose,* where Jean de Meun not only openly defends William but attacks the friars violently in the character of False-Semblaunt. The accounts of the friars in the *Roman de la Rose* and in *Piers Plowman* have much in common. For these reasons we [should avoid] commentaries by friars, except when they repeat exegetical commonplaces without controversial purpose. . . .

The antifraternal attitude in the poem does not limit the scope of *Piers Plowman* any more than the Dominican attitude of St. Thomas, for example, limits the scope of the *Summa theologica.* The attitude is an important attribute of the tradition in which *Piers* was written; it is by no means the whole of the poem. In the poem are expressed most of the guiding ideas of the central tradition of medieval Christianity since the poet's object is not only to show the evils of the church but to place these evils against a background of positive ideals and aspirations. . . .

The most fundamental doctrine of medieval Christianity is that the end of all biblical study is the promotion of *caritas,* the love of God and of one's neighbor. As perfect charity is the end of Christian behavior, so it was felt to be the ultimate *sentence* of the Bible. St. Augustine explains this principle clearly in the *De doctrina:*

> Omnium igitur quae dicta sunt, ex quo de rebus tractamus, haec summa est, ut intelligatur Legis et omnium divinarum Scripturarum plenitudo et finis esse dilectio rei qua fruendum est, et rei quae nobiscum ea re frui potest. . . . Quisquis igitur Scripturas

passera par la suite; mais la scolastique officielle, l'enseignement traditionnel qui trouvera en lue son expression le plus exacte." As a result of the special interests of most modern scholars, almost no attention has been paid to the traditions of the "scolastique officielle" after the lifetime of St. Thomas.

divinas vel quamlibet earum partem intellexisse sibi videtur, ita ut eo intellectu non aedificet istam geminam charitatem Dei et proximi, nondum intellexit. Quisquis vero talem inde sententiam duxerit, ut huic aedificandae charitati sit utilis, nec tamen hoc dixerit quod ille quem legit eo loco sensisse probabitur, non perniciose fallitur, nec omnino mentitur.[15]

What was not in accord with charity was automatically erroneous. Charity is thus an informing principle of medieval thought, providing the inspiration for and controlling the bent of all written attempts to set forth truth. For truth is charity, and like charity must be approached through faith and hope, as St. Paul reveals. Clearly the opposite of charity is *cupiditas,* the love of one's self or the world. There are thus two loves, each representing a direction in which the human will may turn. As Rabanus Maurus points out, the Holy Scripture inculcates charity and condemns cupidity:

Non enim praecipit Scriptura nisi charitatem, nec culpat nisi cupiditatem; et eo modo informat mores hominum. Charitatem voco motum animi ad fruendum Deo propter ipsum, et se atque proximo propter Deum, Cupiditatem autem motum animi ad fruendum se et proximo, et quolibet corpore non propter Deum.[16]

Passages in the Bible which do not literally promote charity must be interpreted figuratively:

Ergo in locutionibus figuratis regula sit hujusmodi ut tam diu versetur diligenti consideratione quod legitur, donec ad regnum charitatis interpretatio perducatur. Si autem hoc jam proprie sonat, nulla putetur figurata locutio. Si praeceptiva locutio est, aut flagitium, aut facinas vetans, aut utilitatem aut beneficientiam jubens, non est figurata. Si autem flagitium aut facinus videtur jubere, aut utilitatem et beneficentiam vetare, figurata est.[17]

---

[15] I, xxxv, xxxvi; PL, 34, 34. See also Peter Lombard, *Sententiae,* II, xxxVIII, PL, 192, 743: "Omnia praecepta divina referuntur ad charitatem." Cf. Paré et al. pp. 214–215.

[16] *De cler. inst.* III, xiii, PL, 107, 389. These words are quoted from St. Augustine, *De doctrina Christiana,* by Rabanus.

[17] Ibid., c. 390.

Since charity is the New Law which Christ brought to mankind, the commentators felt that this Law should be revealed in both the Old Testament and the New. Charity is the end of the human will; it is the basis of perfection in any status. Symbolically, from the Father and the Son springs the Holy Spirit, or charity, so that man, the image of God, is thereby inspired to charity.[18] Thus the Christian has faith and hope that he may achieve charity. Conscience and intellect direct the will to strive for charity.[19] But the will, directed by conscience and intellect, cannot turn toward charity unaided; an act of divine Grace is necessary.[20] Furthermore, the will must be directed within the Church which Christ established, where perfection may be sought in three states: *conjugatorum,* or active, *viduarum* or contemplative, *virginum sive martyrorum* or prelatical. Perfection may be reached through charity in any one of these.[21]

Obversely, cupidity is the end of human failing, descending from the love of the world and a love of the flesh to a union with the Devil in his struggle against charity, that is the sin

[18] Cf. Peter Lombard, *Senteniae,* I, x, PL, 192, 549: "Spiritus sanctus amor est, sive charitas, sive dilectio Patris et Filii. Unde Aug., in lib. 15 de Trin., c. 17, ait: Spiritus sanctus nec Patris est solius, nec Filii est solius, sed amborum; et ideo communem qua invicem se diligunt Pater et Filius, nobis insinuat charitatem."

[19] Cf. ibid., III, xxv, PL, 192, 811: "Cor accipit pro intellectu, et conscientiam pro spe. Qualis, inquit, charitas est finis praecepti procedens de corde puro, id est de puro intellectu, ut nihil nisi Deus diligatur; et conscientia, id est, de spe bona et fide non ficta, id est non simulata. Non ergo charitas fidem et spem, sed fides et spes charitatem praecedere videntur." The authority is Augustine.

[20] Ibid., II, xxxix, PL, 192, 746: "Dici enim quod homo subjectus peccato facit quod non vult, quia naturaliter vult bonum. Sed voluntas haec semper caret effectu, nisi gratia Dei adjuvet et liberet."

[21] See Hugh of St. Victor, *Miscellanea,* VI, xxv, PL, 177, 825: "Triplex est descriptio: Alii ad conjugium, alii ad continentiam, alii describuntur ad virginitatem. In his tribus est tota descriptio Christi: qui non est in aliqua istarum non est Christi, sed potius ad censum diaboli pertinet." On the possibility of perfection within any status see Godefroid de Fontaines (Louvain, 1932), 140–141.

against the Holy Spirit.[22] Against the love of God stands the love of one's self, Augustine's *amor sui*. In the ignorance of conscience and the weakness of intellect, the misguided will turns inward on its own desires so that it is filled with cupidity. Thus there are two ends to human life: charity and cupidity. These two ends are most generally symbolized in the figure of the two cities, Jerusalem and Babylon, which grow out of charity and cupidity respectively.[23] Human living is ideally a pilgrimage from Babylon to Jerusalem. The two cities stand as ends of human living, and specifically each has its levels of significance. Rabanus Maurus describes the four conventional meanings of Jerusalem as follows: historically, the city itself; allegorically, the church of Christ; anagogically, the Heavenly City; tropologically, the soul of man praising God.[24] Babylon too is historically a city. In the *Allegoriae in sacram scripturam* its meaning on the three levels of the *sentence* appear: allegorically, the church of the Gentiles; anagogically, Hell; tropologically, the corrupted spirit.[25] The idea of human life as a pilgrimage is beautifully illustrated in one of Gregory's homilies on Ezechiel, where he discusses the meaning of the Prophet's admonition to his people that they leave Babylon. The Prophet must be understood for his *sentence*, declares Gregory. Whoever falls

[22] See Peter Lombard, *Sententiae*, II, XLIII, PL, 192, 756: "Si quis vero sancti Spiritus dignitatem, majestatem et potestatem abneget sempiternam, et putet non in Spiritu Dei ejici daemonia, sed in Beelzebub, non potest ibi esse exhortatio veniae, ubi sacrilegii plenitudo est. . . . Peccatum enim in Patrem id intelligitur, quod fit per infirmitatem, quia Patri Scriptura frequenter attribuit potentiam; peccatum in Filium, quod fit per ignorantiam, quia sapientia Filio attribuitur; tertium expositum est. Qui ergo peccat per infirmitatem vel per ignorantiam, facile veniam adipiscitur, sed non ille qui peccat in Spiritum sanctum. Cum autem una sit potentia, sapientia, bonitas trium, quare Patri potentia, Filio sapientia, Spiritui sancto bonitas saepius assignetur, superius dictum est."

[23] St. Augustine, *Civitas Dei*, XIV, XXIX.

[24] *In Gal.*, PL, 112, 331.

[25] PL, 112, 872. Of course other meanings of Babylon are given here, but they are simply variations of the above: civitas reproborum, peccatum, impii, caro nostra, hic mundus.

from right doing to wrong doing comes to the confusion of Babylon from the peace of Jerusalem:

> Quod vero ad transmigrationem populi admonendam propheta mittitur, non solum ea transmigratio debet intelligi quae ejus populi erat in corpore, sed etiam quae facta fuerat in mente. A Jerusalem quippe ad Babyloniam venerat. Et quid Jerusalem nisi visio pacis, quid Babylonia nisi confusio vocatur? Quisquis vero a rectis operibus in perversis actibus cadit, quoniam a bono studio ad vitia defluit, quasi ab Jerusalem ad Babyloniae civitatem venit. Culmen enim bonae contemplationis deseruit, atque in transmigratione confusionis jacet. Quod illis solet saepe evenire qui cum bona agunt, in his de sua virtute gloriantur.[26]

Central in this symbolic edifice is the will of man turned toward Jerusalem or toward Babylon, but the will alone cannot turn toward Jerusalem without Christ's Redemption. The lesson of the Redemption is imparted to the will through the succession which Christ founded to lead His bride, the church. The human will must be directed in its pilgrimage by Peter, in our poem the plowman who sows in the human heart the seed of Scripture, the word of God. The church is in itself insufficient to the guidance of the true wayfaring Christian. It must be a church informed and guided by the successors of Peter in the *status praelatorum*. As the church is the bride of Christ, it must also be the bride of Piers Plowman. If it is not, the will can never find the straight road to Jerusalem. . . .

II. SOME CONCLUSIONS

. . . To understand *Piers Plowman* we must be prepared not only to see it in terms of the bitter controversy between the friars and the seculars or in the light of the tradition of Biblical commentary; we must understand its full human import, the permanent symbolic value of the search for Piers Plowman. If the thought of *Piers Plowman* is demonstrably clear, if the

---

[26] PL, 76, 894. The two cities have their most famous exposition in Augustine's *Civitas Dei*.

poem reveals intellectual integrity and if it reflects a great tradition of Western civilization, it must reveal something of the
human heart for all time.

The poem opens with a preliminary vision of the folk of the
world, viewed in the perspective of eternity, wandering in the field
of the earthly Church between the ditches of Babylon and the
hill of Jerusalem. Pitifully few are approaching the tower on
the hill. Implicit in the vision is the question of the Psalmist:

> Lord, who shall abide in thy tabernacle? who shall dwell in
> thy holy hill?

Also implicit in the vision is the answer to this question, Christ's
warning: "Few are chosen." The members of the ecclesiastical
hierarchy for the most part seek the transitory satisfactions of
the flesh, pretending to offices which they make no effort to
fulfill. And the laymen have corrupted their institutions in the
interests of self-love. The words of Christ, "I am that bread of
life," are lost in shouts of "Hot pies!"

In this picture of confusion lies the fundamental problem of
the poem. When the fourteenth-century poet looked around
him he saw only the shadow of what once had been. The ideals
that had motivated Innocent III in his attempt to bring the new
theology of the sacraments to every remote parish, the feeling
for a natural hierarchy under Divine Law that had inspired the
the Magna Charta, the penetrating intellectual elaboration of
the doctrine of charity developed in the thirteenth-century universities, the operative piety exemplified by such kings as
Alfred and St. Louis—all these were now only empty forms.
Men walked in the shadows of the great cathedrals, and on
some of them work continued, but the spirit which produced
them was gone. Structures like the cathedral at Chartres would
grow no more in a soil that had become spiritually sterile. The
Prologue to *Piers Plowman* gives us a glimpse of this sterility.
The poem itself analyzes its causes and describes in detail the
ideals which must be reactivated if the Christian world is ever

to go again on the greatest of all crusades, the pilgrimage to the heavenly Jerusalem.

To understand the poem in its relevance to ourselves, we must attempt to recapture some of the old enthusiasm for this goal. In many respects, the elaboration of Biblical teaching developed in the thirteenth-century schools was history's most significant intellectual achievement. It was the result of centuries of continuous philosophical tradition supported by cumulative pastoral experience. Both the speculative tradition of the schools and the empirical tradition of the parishes were maintained by a single institution so that one could interact freely with and control the other. Philosophers might differ in detail, but in general they agreed on a hierarchy of values the elements of which could be grasped by even the most ignorant and at the same time could win the profound respect of the most culti-vated. Medieval thinkers realized to the full that without some concept of value it is impossible to lend the events of everyday existence significance beyond animal satisfaction. To the poet it was of the utmost importance that the system of values which he found symbolized in Jerusalem be maintained, lest the vision fade away entirely from the sight of men. The fears of the poet were justified. What the poet was witnessing and attempting to counteract was the beginning of the great intellectual chaos which produced the Waste Land, a country which has become so much more terrifying than the poet's Field of Folk that the modern reader is apt to overlook as insignificant some of the poem's bitterest portrayals of evil. *Piers Plowman* is the epic of the dying Middle Ages.

The basic structure of *Piers Plowman* rests on contrasts which express in various ways the medieval ideal and its corruption. The clarity of these contrasts is largely dependent upon an understanding of the application of the traditional levels of meaning. Each level has a symbolic context appropriate to it. The allegorical level, for example, is concerned with the church, and the basic classification of persons in the poem under Dowel,

Dobet and Dobest rests on the traditional division of persons in the church as active, contemplative and prelatical. More exactly, Dowel, Dobet and Dobest represent the ideals which persons in these states should follow. Actual persons either exemplify these ideals of their corruption. To illustrate, one may classify the chief characters in the Prologue allegorically or externally as follows:

	GOOD MINSTRELS	JANGLERS
Dowel	The mice who wish to bell the cat	King, council, lawyers, etc.
Dobet	Anchorites and hermits who do not "kairen aboute."	Hermits who wish "her ese haue," friars etc.
Dobest	The good plowmen	False plowmen who follow pride, evil priests, bishops etc.

A similar table may be made for almost any episode in the poem if one remembers that the poet sometimes wishes to stress the absence of one or more of the classifications. The table below presents some of the more striking representatives on the allegorical level of the various classes, active, contemplative and prelatical, taken from the poem as a whole.

	SEED OF ABEL	SEED OF CAIN
Dowel	The Knight who helps Piers (VI)	The Extortionate Lord (XIX)
Dobet	True Religious "Folis" (XX)	The Friars
Dobest	The Lewd Vicar	The Priest (VII)

One of the principal objects of the poem is to give the various states' inner content. For this reason, the tropological level, which indicates the inner moral qualities of individuals and their moral duties is of especial importance. A general scheme of the tropological level may be represented in terms of the three parts of the image of God in man: the memory, the intellect and the will. Any individual in any of the three allegorical states ideally preserves the image in terms of faith, hope and charity.

	THE IMAGE OF GOD	THE COR- RUPTED IMAGE
Memory	Faith	Oblivion
Intellect	Hope	Ignorance
Will	Charity	Cupidity

Although each status has as its end charity, the tropological duties of the members of the various external statuses vary. To illustrate the special duties of each status, the poet uses several symobls. For example, the relationship of the various statuses to the world is indicated progressively by the terms *conjugatos, viduatos, virgines*. Again, the person in the active status must learn, the contemplative must teach and the prelate must practice the highest form of charity in self-sacrifice for his flock: *disce, doce, diligere*. The members of all three states must direct themselves toward charity. Anima explains charity in terms of three levels which suggest its functions in the three states (xv, 171–178). When it consists simply in desiring and receiving spiritual food, it symbolizes Dowel. When it includes this and acts of devotion accompanied by the function of teaching, it is Dobet. Finally, when it includes both of these and the apostolic act of washing away sin, it symbolizes Dobest. When they practice charity, the three states are related to the world in terms of ascending degrees of self-denial; they are related to society in terms of ascending degrees of service:

	RELATION TO THE WORLD	RELATION TO SOCIETY
Dowel	Conjugatos	Disce
Dobet	Viduatos	Doce
Dobest	Virgines	Diligere

Charity is the basis for perfection in any state, but charity was brought to man by Dobest in its highest form, Christ. Only through teaching of charity in the apostolic succession can it be continued on earth, so that the existence of Dowel and Dobet is dependent on the function of Dobest. Thus the person in the active state who wishes to attain the ideal of Dowel must be aided by Dobest. This fact is illustrated in Conscience's instruction of Haukyn, the active man who asks how he may cleanse his soiled robes of innocence. The cleansing may be accomplished through penance in all of its three parts: *contritio, confessio, satisfactio.* But each of the three parts may be considered a function of Dobest. Contrition, the waking of the mind from oblivion in faith, is encouraged by the priest through preaching and example. The searching of the conscience in oral confession, the casting out of ignorance in hope, is the function of the priest as teacher. Finally, the setting of penance and the granting of absolution, the direction of the will away from cupidity toward charity, is a function of the priest exercising his apostolic powers. In Christ all three states find their highest example. Dobest, in the imitation of Christ the Redeemer, teaches the imitation of Christ in the other two states.

When the mind is governed by cupidity rather than by charity, there is a progression of evil beginning with the sin against the Father in oblivion continuing with the sin against the Son in ignorance and culminating with the sin against the Holy Spirit and the triumph of cupidity over the will. These conditions may be considered as opposites of the ideals represented by Dowel, Dobet and Dobest. They reveal increasing degrees of desire for worldly satisfaction and with relation to society increasing degrees of disservice to mankind:

	RELATION TO THE WORLD	RELATION TO SOCIETY
Sin against the Father	Concupiscence of the Flesh	False Witness
Sin against the Son	Concupiscence of the Eyes	Usury
Sin against the Holy Spirit	Pride of Life	Taking Reward against the Innocent

On the anagogical level are revealed the ultimate sources of good and its corruption. The forces of good are symbolized by Holy Church, the bride of Jerusalem; those of evil are symbolized by Lady Mede, the Whore of Babylon:

HOLY CHURCH	LADY MEDE
The Father	The World
The Son	The Flesh
The Holy Spirit	The Devil

These levels form the ultimate frame of reference around which the others are constructed. For example, on the tropological level, the memory, the intellect and the will are governed either by the Father, the Son and the Holy Spirit respectively, or by the world, the Flesh and the Devil. The tropological corruption of these levels produces the opposites of Dowel, Dobet and Dobest. Dowel is characterized by obedience to the Father, Dobet by the removal of the sin against the Son and Dobest by the maintenance of the Holy Spirit or charity.

The various spiritual levels are exemplified externally and particularly on the historical level with characters from the Bible and the modern Church:

PIERS PLOWMAN	SE IPSOS AMANTES
Patriarchs	Cain
Prophets	Pharisees
Christ and the Apostles	Antichrist and the Friars

The basic contrast lies between the true priesthood of God and the ministry of Antichrist. The patriarchs and prophets could not find salvation in the Old Law; only through the New Law of charity were they able to leave Hell. Similarly, Dowel and Dobet cannot be saved without Piers, who bears the tradition of the Redemption. The tragedy of the poem is that the human will seeking salvation cannot find Piers in the Church. The place of Piers has been usurped by the Friars under the guidance of Antichrist.

It is through the character Will that we see these contrasts operating on various levels. Will is many-sided because he has the flexibility of the faculty he represents which moves between the opposites of willfulness and charity. Because the poet has been successful as a poet, he has created in Will so appealingly human a character that through interest in him many have lost sight of the fact that Will is merely a device by means of which the poet may set off the actual against the ideal in the poem and so develop his major theme. For this purpose Will is portrayed at the beginning as one among the wolves in sheep's clothing. His clothes reflect the manner in which he has been misled. They improve as Will, serving as a hypothetical example, is brought nearer his ideal goal. The persons who mislead him typify the misleading forces of the actual world. But the forces which bring about his ultimate rise to a state of grace are not actual forces in the earthly Church; they are the forces which should operate there. Similarly, the pattern of Will's salvation is a pattern of what should be, not of what is. Thus Will is instructed first not by an actual priest but by the anagogical church itself who reveals her own nature to him and the nature and operation of her opposite, the Whore of Babylon. Actually, a successor to Piers Plowman should be the one who explains to the human will the ideal which the heavenly Jerusalem represents and the origin of its corruption on earth; the fact that Holy Church herself instructs Will is a negative intimation of the theme that Piers Plowman is absent from the church militant. Will's Vision of the struggle against Lady Mede carried on by the King who calls Reasoun and Conscience to his aid is only a vision of the possible, a suggestion as to the means by which the earthly community may be made to resemble its eternal counterpart. Will himself does not take part in the vision, and it is obvious that it is not a picture of anything the poet could see around him or reasonably predict in the near future. As a result of Reasoun's teaching, Repentance moves the will of the folk to weep, and they confess in a manner which prepares them for the guidance of Piers Plowman. The vision of the Half Acre is an ideal vision of God's ministry, demonstrating the lesson of good works in the earthly church. Even in the episode of the Half Acre, which is an ideal vision, the salvation of the folk of the field is not shown to be assured. Indeed it becomes clear that confession without satisfaction through good works is unavailing. Though the commons assent to the rule of Reasoun through their confessions, they must implement their faith and hope through the works of charity. But humans are lazy and are repelled by the need to work; in the face of work many of those who had confessed prefer to sing "Trolli-lolli" in a ditch. Piers attempts to bring them back through spiritual hunger and the threat of eternal punishment, but these threats have only temporary effectiveness. Finally, salvation through pardon is suggested, but the pardon of Piers Plowman is an affirmation that faith, hope and the labors of charity in the field are necessary, that the way of Piers is the right way. Positively, the pardon shows that only through the fulfilment of the obligation to the redemption is salvation possible. But the position of the earthly church is made apparent at once in the person of the Priest who neither recognizes nor understands his pardon. It is significant that in spite of Will's vision, his position at the end of it is exactly that of the Priest. The human will, although it naturally desires the good, unguided by Piers is incapable of understanding the basic contrast between Jerusalem and Babylon or the means by which the earthly church may be made to resemble its heavenly counterpart.

In the *Vitae,* which are concerned with the way Will may find the truth of Piers Plowman, there is a similar series of contrasts between the actual and the ideal. There is no steady progression toward salvation. Those episodes which are concerned with the exposition of the ideal move to the point at which it becomes clear that what is needed in the church militant is Piers Plowman. Thereupon the poet develops the unhappy conclusion that Piers is not present in the earthly church and the ideal is succeeded by a picture of the corrupt actuality.

Although Will has seen Piers in the *Visio,* he does not in Dowel begin his search with instruction by a true priest. Instead he meets two friars. As a result of their ministrations, Will's thought is confused and misled so that he cannot properly act upon the possibilities of both good and evil presented by Wit, the speculative intellect. Although Will still desires the good, he proceeds to corrupt the teaching of the intellect, learns nothing through Study and Clergye, finally corrupts Scripture through his own willfulness and falls into the sleep of the Land of Longing. Will's progressive descent from being simply misled by the friars to his abandonment of the true good typifies what the human will actually faces in the Church militant. Through God's providence he sees the evils of the friars who have comforted him in his evil life. Through his knowledge of evil he finds loyalty to the true church. With Loyalty, Scripture's teachings become effective and Will is able to profit by the vision of Nature and the teaching of Imaginatyf. But Piers must direct the human will in its study of Scripture and in the understanding of the truth which makes conscience operative, so that the poet is here again concerned with the ideal pattern of the development of the human will. When Conscience comes to guide Will, he must, of course, guide him within the church. Again the poem turns to the actual church from the vision of the ideal to discover that the place of Piers has been usurped by the Master Friar. The result of this usurpation is shown to Will in the figure of Haukyn the active man. Haukyn cannot perform true penance without Piers. Although Conscience teaches him what true penance should be, he makes it clear that true penance without Piers Plowman is impossible. The *Vita de Dowel* ends on the same desperate note as does the *Visio.* Unless the prelatical status reflects Dobest, unless Piers Plowman is in the church, those in the active status face inevitable and tragic doom.

In the *Vita de Dobet,* Will does find Piers Plowman, but he does not find him on earth. He learns through Anima what is wrong with the Church militant. When he asks her where he may find Piers, he is told that Piers guards the Tree of Charity. In other words, he may be seen only in a spiritual vision. Will's vision again pictures the ideal. In this episode, the high point in the poem, Will is shown in one supreme figure the ideals of Dowel, Dobet and Dobest combined. Moreover, Will learns his relation in the image of God to the other faculties of the human mind. He learns that together the three faculties must live in charity. But when he hears the Easter bells tolling, he understands that he must worship God in the Church. Again the poem reaches the place at which it is necessary to look for Piers Plowman in the Church militant: the life of prayer and contemplation also needs Piers Plowman. But in the *Vita de Dobest* it is made perfectly clear that the force which is alone able to bring salvation is absent from the Church militant. Piers has been supplanted by a host of friars under the leadership of Antichrist. The only hope left for the human will is the collective force of the Christian Conscience insisting that in its priests the image of Piers be found. We remember that the evil of the friars had this much of good; it succeeded in awakening Will to Loyalty. The purpose of the poet was not simply to expose the evil of the friars; it was to arouse his readers to a realization of the immediacy of their danger in the hope that they would be stirred to action so that Piers might again walk on earth.

In the figure of Will we have seen one of the chief means by which the poet achieves coherence in *Piers Plowman*. In what Will does and in his reactions are developed the progressive contrasts which contribute materially to the structural integrity of the poem. In the *Visio* these contrasts are based on the most general of possible symbols for good and evil. In the *Vitae* they become particularized and progress in scope and significance until we reach the poet's crowning picture of the Redemption and his description of the historically progressive corruption of the church militant culminating in the vision of the perils in those late days which came through the friars. As the movement of the poem develops naturally from the needs of the human will represented by the dreamer, the structure of the poem may be shown to develop naturally out of the needs of the folk in the field as pictured in the Prologue. The Prologue contains, in fact, all of the major themes of the poem. It sets at once the basic contrast between true and false prelates and suggests the discrepancy between the ideals of the three states and their actual counterparts. The Babylonian confusion of the Kingdom ruled by self-love implies by contrast the vision of Peace which appears immediately in Passus I in the figure of Holy Church descending from the mountain. It is this same Babylonian kingdom with which is contrasted the Kingdom governed by Reasoun and Conscience. The members of the Prologue's realm are those who mislead Will in the *Vitae,* and in the closing episode of the poem the poet explains in detail the source of the Babylonian confusion. Meanwhile, the positive ideas developed as ideals or as ideal patterns of conduct stem from the theme of Holy Church's sermon: *Deus caritas.*

There are certain images set in the Prologue, those of food and clothing for example, that are used to give coherence to the poem. The clothing of the plowmen is contrasted with that of the followers of pride as Holy Church's clothing is contrasted with that of Lady Mede. Will's clothing has progressive symbolic value, notably in the change from his early clothing to the "dear robes" of Passus XIX. The clothing of Haukyn is of central importance in Dowel. The clothing image is reflected in the armor of Piers in which Christ fights. Holy Church uses Lot's drunkenness in illustration of the misuse of temporal goods. Piers employs Hunger to frighten the wasters who seek to forget their spiritual hunger in the pleasures of the flesh. The feast placed before Patience and Will is sharply contrasted with the dainty worldly fare of the Master Friar, who must drink before he preaches. In the final passus Will is concerned with the problem of sustenance in the world. There are many other such images repeated and elaborated in Passus XIX. The Plant of Peace introduced by Holy Church becomes central in Anima's instruction of Will. The image of the tower set in the Prologue is reflected in Holy Church's sermon, in the instructions of Piers to the pilgrims, in Wit's discussion of the castle of Caro and finally in the Barn of Christendom. These images and others are used so consistently and repeatedly that it is impossible to do more than supply a few illustrations here. Indeed, we may make the generalization that the structure of the poem is based largely on the repetition and contrast of symbols which are progressively elaborated and developed.

The development by symbolic repetition may sometimes be obscured by the fact that the connection between symbols is often made through an understood Scriptural nexus. Thus Piers' half-acre is closely related to the Barn of Christendom through the parable of the gathering of the harvest (Matt. 13:24 ff.). The tower of Truth, which is the end of man's search, is related to the Castle of Caro through the implied biblical idea of man made in the image of God. The imagery when taken with the symbolic values it acquires from biblical contexts serves as a means of poetic condensation in the maintenance of the major themes of the poem. Similarly, the Scriptural quotations when taken on the level of the *sentence* as developed in traditional exegesis furnish a key to wider vistas of meaning which relate the parts of the poem in much the same way that the parts of the Bible were related by the commentators. It would not be surprising if a reader ignorant of the fact that Piers Plowman represents the central tradition of Christ's ministry might be led to suppose that there was a lack of connection between the parts of the poem, each of which is united to the other in an increasing emphasis on the tragic absence of the traditional figure from the Church. If the identification of Holy Church with the heavenly Jerusalem and of Lady Mede with the Whore of Babylon is not kept steadily before the mind's eye, it is possible to fail to see the relationship between the sermon of Holy Church and what follows. Altogether, when the poem is read on the level of the *sentence,* the development of its themes becomes clear and it is seen to progress logically and coherently to its conclusion.

Like any great work of art *Piers Plowman* has a quality which defies critical analysis. It is possible to repeat the testimony of others who have felt the varied powers of the poet from the ecstatic verse with which he describes the Redemption to the realistically powerful picture of Glutton in the tavern. It would be possible to add further testimonial to the way in which in individual passages we have been moved to wonder and delight, to the quietness of spirit which is the particular effect of the greatest poety. But that has not been the service which we have hoped to render here. We have wished first to show that the charge that the poem as a whole is chaotic and formless is false. Then we have wished to show the greatness of the ideal presented in *Piers Plowman* and to demonstrate the intellectual grandeur and clarity with which the great ideal is developed. It is true that the architecture of the poem is not so obvious to the modern reader as that of the *Divine Comedy,* but when the principles governing that architecture are known, it becomes clear that the English poem is no less perfect structurally than the Italian. Many of the most startling poetic effects of the poem are achieved through its deliberate Scriptural connotations. The picture of Holy Church descending from the mountain is striking in itself, but its Scriptural connotations make the picture more than merely striking, suggesting as they do the Transfiguration in the Gospel, the Bride of Christ in the Apocalypse, and Sion and Jerusalem throughout the Scriptures. If the *Divine Comedy* is an expression of the ideals of the thirteenth century, *Piers Plowman* is a projection of those ideals against the actuality of fourteenth century life. The English poem is representative of its turbulent and critical age and place, but it is also an expression of some of man's most cherished ideals. Society is still being misled by false leaders. Modern man, like Will, is still searching for leadership which will embody traditional belief with human compassion, which can reformulate and activate the principles of charity and bring the world a little nearer the Vision of Peace. In short, the heirs to the tradition of medieval England may add to the annals of their literature a work of epic scope with only one peer in any other medieval vernacular.

8

THE ART OF READING MEDIEVAL PERSONIFICATION-ALLEGORY *

Robert Worth Frank, Jr.

THE MODERN READER of medieval allegories must often agree with Mrs. Malaprop that nothing is so headstrong as an allegory, on the banks of Nile or elsewhere. It seems the most intractable of forms. He is told it must be interpreted, with the implication that its true meaning accompanied the author to his tomb these many centuries ago. And he is further discouraged when he sees all kinds of writing labelled "allegory," until almost everything written in the Middle Ages seems to belong in this locked bookcase. But reading an allegory, especially one with personifications, is not the mysterious process which critics may have made it appear to be. A few simple principles are all the reader needs.

First, he must not confuse one kind of allegory with another. He most certainly will make this confusion, however, if he listens to the careless cataloguers and literary historians. He will read the *Divine Comedy,* in which characters and significant details are concrete and have a second meaning, that is, are *symbols;* and he will be told this is an allegory. Then he will read *Piers Plowman,* in which characters and significant details are abstractions and have only one meaning, that is, are *per-*

* Reprinted, by permission, from *ELH, XX* (1953), 237–250.

sonifications; and he will be told that this, too, is an allegory. Obviously the two poems are two different kinds of writing. If they are both allegories, they are different kinds of allegory. The first thing to do is to distinguish between them. For that purpose, distinct terms are needed.

Since Hegel's day many critics have referred to Dante's kind of allegory as "symbolism" and to Langland's as "allegory."[1] These terms, however, are not completely satisfactory. One critic has observed that, in addition to violating medieval usage, the term "symbolism" is too inclusive for allegory as a whole, let alone one kind, and "allegory" is too inclusive for a narrative using personifications, for such a narrative is merely one kind of allegory. He suggests "allegory" for Dante's kind of poem and "personification allegory" for Langland's.[2] But calling the *Divine Comedy* "allegory" has the defect of using a generic term for what is one species of the genus. Another student objects to using the conventional terms "allegory" and "symbolism" for the two types because "*allegory* is a word used to describe a work of art as a whole (as *pastoral* is), and *symbol* is a word used to describe a particular kind of ingredient in a whole work of art." In other words, he says, "symbolism" and "allegory" do not differ as a play of Shakespeare's differs from a play of Rowley's, but as a line of verse differs from a play.[3] I propose here to sacrifice euphony to clarity and call

[1] The history of the terms has been traced by Leo Leonard Camp, *Studies in the Rationale of Medieval Allegory,* 1942, an unpublished doctoral dissertation in the University of Washington Library, p. 36. I am greatly indebted in this article to Camp's work, and I am happy to have the opportunity to call attention to it. It deserves a better fate than to lie forgotten in the Limbo of unpublished dissertations. For a published summary, see *Abstracts of Theses and Faculty Bibliography, 1942–1943, Publications of the University of Washington, Theses Series,* VIII, June, 1944, 93–96.

[2] Ibid., 4–5, 58, 62.

[3] Paul Pickrel, *Religious Allegory in Medieval England: an Introductory Study Based on the Vernacular Sermon before 1250,* an unpublished doctoral dissertation in the Yale University Library (1944), p. 10. This dissertation contains a brilliant first chapter on the nature of allegory—primarily symbol allegory.

Dante's type of allegory "symbol-allegory," and Langland's type "personification-allegory."

Although the reader can thus distinguish between the two forms, the medieval writer often complicates matters slightly by employing both forms in the same piece of writing. He had little sense of these literary forms as *forms*. To him both were methods of expressing the truth. The medieval Church constantly stimulated his imagination with both symbols and abstractions. In giving allegorical interpretations to the Scriptures and to beasts, flowers, jewels, etc., the Church created a mode of thought which encouraged symbol-allegory. In raising to supreme importance the soul of the true believer and in picturing the world as a place where vices and virtues struggled for that soul, the Church gave abstractions a dramatic significance which encouraged personification-allegory. Medieval preaching, for one, employed both forms and helped give them currency.[4] Late medieval writers of personification-allegory saw nothing incongruous about introducing symbols into their work. The rose in the *Roman de la Rose* and the tower on the toft and the dungeon in the dale in *Piers Plowman* are symbols. But the reader can easily distinguish between a personification and a symbol, and all he must do when the devices appear side by side is to read a passage of symbol-allegory in one way and a passage of personification-allegory in another.

How should he read each kind of allegory? He gets no help from the Middle Ages themselves, for they were not interested in this kind of literary criticism.[5] The definition of allegory commonly accepted then, one inherited from the ancients, will cover both types: "Allegoria est enim, sicut saepe jam dictum est, quando aliud dicitur, et aliud significatur."[6] The rules must be worked out empirically.

[4] Cf. G. R. Owst, *Literature and the Pulpit in Medieval England,* Cambridge, England, 1933, pp. 56–109; Paul Pickrel, *passim.*

[5] This fact emerges clearly in J. W. H. Atkins, *English Literary Criticism: the Medieval Phase* (Cambridge, England, 1943).

[6] Cassiodorus, on Psalm xxxi. 13, Migne, PL 70, col. 223. Similar definitions are given by Isidore of Seville, *Etymologiarum Libri XX,*

In symbol-allegories characters and significant details are presented in concrete form. In addition to their literal value they have a figurative value. The cross symbolizes Christ; Virgil, in the *Divine Comedy,* is not only the shade of the Augustan poet but also the power of human reason. The interpretative problem is to find, first, the other meaning of the symbols employed and, second, the other meaning of the pattern of relationship between the symbols and the action in which they are engaged, if there is action.[7] What is the other meaning of the ship and the rudder in the poem *On the Death of Edward III?*[8] And what is the other meaning of the relationship between rudder and ship?

Migne, PL 82, col. 115; and "Prothemata Glossae Ordinariae," Migne, PL 113, col. 63. Migne lists the patristic definitions in PL 219, Index XLVI, cols. 123 ff. Since the problem of "allegory" seems to be a semantic problem as much as anything, the reader had better be warned of a pitfall in the use of the word "allegoria" by the medieval commentators. In addition to being used in the generic sense illustrated by the definition just cited, "allegoria" was used as the term for one of the four levels of meaning possible in the Scriptures. The much repeated rhyme will make the point clear:

> Littera gesta docet, quid credas allegoria,
> Moralis quid agas, quo tendas anagogia.

(Migne, PL 113, col. 28) This more specific meaning of "allegoria" is itself somewhat slippery. Most frequently, "allegoria" as a level of meaning in Scripture refers to the figurative or typological sense of Scripture, by which persons, things and occurrences recorded before the earthly life of Christ prefigure similar matters in the gospels. "It assumes a mysterious harmony between the Old Testament and the New, the 'types' of the former anticipating and conforming to the 'antitypes' of the latter." (Karl Young, *The Drama of the Medieval Church* [Oxford, 1933], II, 265.) This is the sense of "allegoria" given by Nicolas de Lyra: ". . . si res significatae per voces referantur ad significandum ea quae sunt in nova lege credenda, sic accipitur sensus allegoricus. . . ." (Migne, PL 113, col. 28.) Sometimes the commentators are careful when using "allegoria" in this restricted sense to use phrases like "sensus mysticus" or "sensus spiritualis" in referring to the nonliteral in general. The reader had better check the context before deciding what sense "allegoria" carries in any particular passage.

[7] In my discussion of symbol-allegory I am indebted to Pickrel, pp. 5–20.

[8] *Minor Poems of the Vernon MS,* II, ed. F. J. Furnivall, EETS, o.s. 117 (London, 1901), pp. 715–718.

How is the reader to solve this problem? Usually the problem is solved within the text itself. Contrary to popular opinion, the medieval allegorist was not intent on baffling his reader. His purpose was to communicate. Frequently he explained his symbol-allegory explicitly. The Middle English *Bestiary,* for example, gives the "significatio" of each animal in detail. In the poem *On the Death of Edward III,* the reader is told that the ship was the knights of England, the rudder was Edward III. Holy Church in *Piers Plowman* carefully explains the meaning of the tower and the dungeon, and the Samaritan explains the "other" meaning of the scene in which he helps the wounded traveler,[9] familiar as this other meaning was. The explanations of the "allegorical" sense were sung as part of the play of Isaac and Rebecca.[10] The writer, of course, does not always explain. Sometimes he may feel it is artistically clumsy to explain. Sometimes it might be dangerous (true of political symbol-allegory in particular).[11] Sometimes he can rely (or thinks he can) on his audience to understand his other meaning.[12] Sometimes he may wish to be understood by a select few and no one else.[13] Or finally, sometimes he is a mystic and cannot describe his experience literally, symbols are his only language.[14]

[9] *The Vision of William concerning Piers the Plowman . . . ,* Text B, edited by W. W. Skeat, EETS, o.s. 38 (London, 1869): I. 12 ff.; XVII. 90–123. . . . I have used *Piers Plowman* for most of the examples of personification-allegory in this study, since it is the most discussed and the most successful of the medieval English personification-allegories.

[10] *Drama of the Medieval Church,* II, 258–264.

[11] Cf. the symbol-allegory of the belling of the cat in *Piers Plowman.* Langland says he dare not explain the story: Pr. 208–209.

[12] This would probably be Chaucer's attitude in using what little symbol-allegory there is in *The Book of the Duchess.*

[13] Jefferson Butler Fletcher believes this is the motivation for Dante's symbol-allegory: *Symbolism of the Divine Comedy,* (New York, 1921), pp. 2–4.

[14] Edward A. Bloom, "The Allegorical Principle," *ELH,* XVIII (1951), 174–175, has an interesting statement on obscurity in allegory (i.e., symbol-allegory). A certain degree of obscurity, he points out, is inseparable from the form, but obscurity has never been considered an attribute of allegory.

In all such symbol-allegories where the figurative meaning is not stated, the other value for the symbols and their pattern of relationship (and activity) must be worked out from either the narrower context of the work itself or the wider context of relevant biographical and historical facts and contemporary ideas and ideologies. This wider context must be recreated accurately and, sometimes, in considerable detail, with the proper emphasis of elements in the context. This is one of the most important and most demanding tasks of historical criticism.

My primary interest is not in symbol-allegory, and so I shall not analyze further the method for reading such allegories. What must be remembered, however, is that they utilize concrete images and not abstractions. When a concrete image has an abstract value it is stated elsewhere or revealed by the context, never explicitly in the symbol itself. If it were, the symbol would cease to be a concrete image and so would cease to be a symbol.

Personification-allegory is quite different. Its essential characteristic is that it uses abstractions as though they were concrete substances—people, places, things.[15] Strife in *Le Songe d'Enfer* is a tavern bully; Righteousness is a sword with which the Pilgrim in the *Pèlerinage de Vie Humaine* defends himself. The mistake the reader usually makes in reading this kind of allegory is the mistake of looking for more hidden meanings than the form allows. Personification-allegories are closer to the literal than symbol-allegories. This point was made by the late Leo Leonard Camp, who insisted that the form is allegoric

---

[15] Bertrand H. Bronson, replying to C. S. Lewis' obvious preference for symbolism over allegory, asserts that: "Symbol and personification are not opposites. The two terms are not even commensurate, for the first includes and transcends the second. A personification is but one among many kinds of symbol." ("Personification Reconsidered," *ELH*, XIV [1947], 167.) Personification and symbol may not be opposites, but they do differ from one another, if by personification one means an abstraction used as though it possessed concreteness and if by symbol one means a concrete person, place, or thing used to mean something other than itself.

only under certain conditions. In the Middle Ages, he believed, it was written and read as literal narrative.[16] His conclusions are worth summarizing. When a personification merely talks, as when Nature speaks in the *De Planctu Naturae,* the situation is not usually allegoric: "The intention is to give direct discourse on a subject. This would be literal."[17] When moral types, types of character or passion, act according to their character, their action will be literal. The action of Glutton in *Piers Plowman,* for example, has no double significance. It is simply the conduct proper to such a type. "Personified types . . . may or may not act allegorically, and perhaps most often they act literally."[18] The action of a moral or social type is allegoric when "it is the metaphoric action of a type which is treated as if it had only a mental existence."[19] Personification-allegory is clearly allegoric when abstractions engage in action: "The behavior of any abstraction, except a moral or social type, would be utterly absurd if it did not have a second sense."[20] Camp summarized his discussion of the form as follows: "A personification is thus allegoric by its action and not because it represents something different from itself [which it does not]; it is the action which carries the secondary meaning, which differs from the one apparent."[21]

I would suggest a slight modification of Camp's position. The reader may feel that the situation is also allegoric when a personification speaks or when a moral or social type acts according to type. There is no such entity as Nature with the power of speech. The poet *really* means that this is what man can or should learn from nature (whatever he may mean by "nature"). Likewise Gluttony is not an entity that talks or acts. The poet

[16] *Studies in the Rationale of Medieval Allegory,* p. 84.
[17] Ibid., pp. 58, 75.
[18] Ibid., p. 64.
[19] Ibid., p. 76
[20] Ibid., p. 61.
[21] Ibid., p. 62.

really means that gluttony leads to talk or action of this kind. The reader must go beyond the poet's literal statement here to some extent, however simple and immediate the process of understanding the *real* meaning may be. The metaphoric action of moral types and the action of abstractions are more clearly allegoric, I believe, because the process by which the reader understands the real meaning is more conscious and complex and involves interpretation of each detail of the action. If the allegorist says Drunkenness spends his evenings noisily in a tavern and falls in a ditch on the way home, the reader has only to see that the allegorist really means drunkenness causes this kind of action. There is no other meaning to the noisy evening or the action of falling in a ditch. These are literal. But if the allegorist says Drunkenness lures Reasoun into an ale-house, befuddles him with drink and persuades him to go off with a tart named Sensuality, each detail must be interpreted. The relationships and the actions are not to be taken literally. The reader must see that the allegorist really means that drunkenness may corrupt man's reason and lead to sensuality.

The great value of Camp's analysis is that it narrowly circumscribes the area of the allegoric in personification-allegory and points out the considerable degree to which the form is literal narrative. Only the action is allegoric, and often not that (or only in a most limited way). Characters are never allegoric. They are literal; they mean what their names say they mean. The error which the reader is most likely to make is to treat the personifications as though they were symbols and "interpret" them. And so he wastes time puzzling over what is really meant by a character called Desire, and, what is worse, sometimes discovers, he thinks, what it really means.[22] Actually, of

[22] For example, Greta Hort, *Piers Plowman and Contemporary Religious Thought* (London, Church Historical Society [1937?]), pp. 69 ff., treats some of the personifications as "allegorical" characters and says the character Truth is really *"synderesis"; Kynde Wit is really "lex naturalis."*

course, the allegorist meant "desire" and nothing more. That was why he gave the character that name.[23]

The fundamental difference between the method used in reading symbol-allegory and that used in reading personification-allegory may be stated as follows. In symbol-allegory, the reader must make two interpretations before he can understand the "other" meaning of the narrative. He must interpret, first, the symbols, and second, their pattern of relationship and activity. For example, the reader must translate the characters of Virgil and Dante into their other meaning. Virgil also means the human reason; Dante also means mankind in general. Next, the reader must translate their relationship and activity. In the *Inferno* Virgil acts as Dante's guide through the various circles of Hell. This pattern of relationship and activity means that the human reason can lead mankind to a knowledge of what is evil and what sins should be avoided. Not until he has made two translations—of the symbols and of their relationship and activity—can the reader understand the symbol-allegory. In personification-allegory, on the other hand, the reader must make at most *one* translation to understand the allegory. He does not have to find a second meaning for the personifications in the allegory, for they have none. Their names—Thought, Wit, Nature—express their one and only meaning. What the

---

[23] Absolute inflexibility on this point is probably unscientific. Bernard Huppé has argued, for instance, that in the Lady Mede episode in *Piers Plowman,* the abstractions Lady Mede and Conscience are literal, i.e., are meed (reward) and conscience, but at a second level are at times historical characters: Conscience is John of Gaunt, Lady Mede is sometimes Alice Perrers, sometimes Piers Gaveston. ("The A-Text of *Piers Plowman* and the Norman Wars," *PMLA,* LIV [1939], 37–64, especially 61–62, n. 46.) Possibly. The action or speech of a personification might be intended to *suggest* the action or speech of a particular historical character; a personification might even be intended to *suggest* a historical character. But that a personification would be intended to *represent* a historical character seems less likely, since real characters and symbols may be used in a personification-allegory. Certainly a personification cannot stand for a concept or quality other than that expressed by the name of the personification.

reader must sometimes do is to find the second meaning for the pattern of relationship and activity in which the personifications are placed. In *Piers Plowman,* Dame Study is introduced as Wit's wife. This relationship of the characters *really* means something else: that the activity of study is closely related to the faculty of wit, the faculty of sensory intelligence. But this one translation—of a relationship or activity—is the only translation the reader must make. In other words, in symbol-allegory the reader translates characters (and significant details) *and* relationships and actions. In personification-allegory, he translates *only* relationships and actions.

(There is, of course, another process which the reader must perform in reading personification-allegory, but it cannot be called translation or interpretation in the sense in which I have just used these words. Since the relationship or actions of abstractions usually express a general idea—for example, that worldly riches corrupt man's moral powers—the reader has the problem he has with any generalization: he must understand what the generalization means. This is not always easy. If, for example, in a personification-allegory two characters called Anger and Patience build a castle called Gluttony—I improvise here—the reader will probably be puzzled. The allegorist is saying that anger and patience give rise to gluttony. But neither his experience nor any body of ideas the reader is familiar with supports this generalization. The problem here, however, would be one in the author's psychology or biography, or in literary sources or the history of ideas. It would not be a problem in the interpretation of personification-allegory *as allegory.*)

Certain more specific observations may be made about reading personification-allegories. The names of the characters are all-important, for it is through them that the allegorist states a good part of his meaning. The reader must therefore understand what a character's name means, for that will be the key to his speeches and actions.[24] If the reader thinks that "imaginatyf" means "imagination" and nothing more, he cannot properly understand that portion of *Piers Plowman* in which the character Imaginatyf acts and speaks. The names also may give the reader a key to the theme or problem being dramatized. The writer of a personification-allegory did not choose his abstractions at random. His choice was governed by the body of ideas or the facts of the situation which he was treating. Like any writer dramatizing a theme or problem, he considered the aspects of that theme and gave each its place in the narrative, presenting it in the form, usually, of an abstraction. The meanings stated in the characters' names, when considered as a unit, will help the reader to see the central issue of the personification-allegory. For example, the personifications Thought, Wit, Clergye (Learning), Dame Study, Dame Scripture (Writings) and Imaginatyf in the first vision of Dowel in *Piers Plowman* suggest that the central issue here is some question or problem about the human intelligence and human learning.

Another point to note is that all the characters in a personification-allegory need not be abstractions. C. S. Lewis complains that not all the characters in the *Roman de la Rose* are aspects of the lover's or the lady's thought and emotion. Jalosie represents the interference of the lady's relatives; Amis, the typical friend, is hardly a personification at all; and the Nurse or Duenna is a specific individual, not an abstraction.[25] Lewis' Complaint is unjustified. It arises, I believe, out of his preoccupation with the portrayal of states of mind in some medieval personification-allegories.[26] He seems to feel no other matter is appropriate for the form. Although the inner life was often effectively treated in the form, the form was not used for this

[24] Cf. on this point W. Roy Mackenzie, *The English Moralities from the Point of View of Allegory*, Harvard Studies in English, Vol. II (Boston, 1914), p. xi.

[25] *The Allegory of Love* (Oxford, 1938), pp. 118, 119.

[26] Cf. ibid., pp. 30, 69, 113.

purpose alone, as Lady Philosophy, Genius, Grace Dieu and fourscore other nonsubjective personifications prove.[27] Guillaume de Lorris knew more about the form than C. S. Lewis, and he included the characters Lewis objects to because they belonged. He was writing, not about the minds of lovers, but about a love affair, of which the lady's and the lover's states of mind, relatives, friends and duennas were all a part. In placing a real person (the Duenna) in the poem, he was well within his rights.[28] The form is a very elastic one. Personifications of states of mind and of categories of objective reality, moral types, specific individuals—the reader must accept them all as characters and try to relate them to the theme which the writer is developing.

It is also useful to remember that there is generally a relationship between the writer's meaning and the physical form and activity of his personifications. An obvious example is the portraits of Hate, Felonye, Vilanye, Coveitise, etc., on the wall encircling the garden in the *Roman de la Rose*. The fact that they are grouped together means they are a unit. The fact that they are part of the wall encircling the garden means these qualities are walled out of the garden and a young man possessing them would be barred from the fashionable, idle society within, from the world of courtly love.

The intention to communicate meaning by the physical form and activity of the personification occasionally leads to another kind of elasticity. The physical form or activity ascribed to the personification may shift as the allegorist endeavors to indicate what concrete realities his abstraction applies to. Envy, in the

[27] Cf. Ernest Langlois' amusing comment: "On ne personnifiait pas seulement les vices, les vertus, les arts, les facultés de l'âme, mais aussi les saisons, les plantes, les animaux, les fleuves, les montagnes, les éléments, les aliments, etc." *Origines et Sources du Roman de la Rose* (Paris, 1891), p. 66.

[28] Mackenzie, p. 3, pointed out that when God or the Devil appears in a morality, he is neither an abstraction nor a type; he is God, or he is the Devil.

228

confession scene in *Piers Plowman,* seems now a man, now a woman. There is no need for the reader to be confused. The poet has not lost control of his personification. It is merely his way of showing envy at work among both men and women. The name remains the same, and so the reader knows that envy is the theme, for all the shifts of form and action.[29]

One final word of warning. It is sometimes argued that since the medieval exegetist and the medieval writer of symbol-allegory were both concerned with the nonliteral, the writer must have been influenced by the exegetist. Even as the exegetist *read* four levels of meaning into the Scriptures, the writer *wrote* four levels of meaning into his work—a truly virtuoso performance. It is easy, however, to overestimate the prevalence of the fourfold method in medieval exegetical work. An investigation of the use of allegory in English sermon literature before 1250 has noted that preachers ordinarily discussed only one allegorical level in a Scriptural passage and applied the fourfold method infrequently.[30] It is also a fact that interest in the fourfold method of interpretation waned in the later medieval period. Nicholas of Lyra, for example, though not denying that the four levels of meaning (or three levels, or two) were sometimes present in the Scriptures, stressed the importance of the literal sense and condemned the heavy layer of "mystical" interpretation which, he said, almost smothered the literal text and made an understanding of it well nigh impossible.[31] Some-

[29] Owst, among others (pp. 88–89), thinks this practice a defect in *Piers Plowman.* Although I am concerned in this article with the exegesis of personification-allegory, not the aesthetics of the form, Langland's device of giving a shifting concrete content to an abstraction, a kind of montage technique, seems to me an effective technique for giving some variety and subtlety to a personification and for overcoming the tendency of the form to become static.

[30] Pickrel, pp. 50–51, 84.

[31] Migne, PL 113, col. 30. De Lyra and other commentators pointed out that Scripture did not always have four levels of meaning; sometimes it had only a literal sense; sometimes it had no literal sense, properly speaking; sometimes a literal and a moral sense only, etc. cols.: 33–35.

thing more substantial than an offhand allusion to "the four fold method in the medieval period" must be supplied before the reader should feel obliged to look for four levels of meaning in a medieval symbol-allegory. He may even content himself with finding only a "second" meaning in the *Divine Comedy*. The argument remains to be proved for Dante's use of the fourfold method, even though he referred to the method in discussing the Canzoni and again in discussing the *Divine Comedy*.[32]

Weak as the case is for symbol-allegory, it is weaker still for personification-allegory. For one thing, the form developed without any historical connection whatsoever with Scriptural exegesis.[33] And its literal nature renders it an impossible medium for the fourfold method. The meaning of a character is expressed in its name. It cannot, therefore, mean two or three other things as well. It is just possible, I have noted, for a personification to refer to or suggest a specific person.[34] An abstraction named Hope, for example, might suggest, say, the

De Lyra himself announced that he would concentrate on the literal sense. The changes of emphasis in medieval Scriptural exegesis are described by Beryl Smalley, *The Study of the Bible in the Middle Ages* (Oxford, 1941), *passim,* a most readable and humane study of a forbidding subject; and P. C. Spicq, *Esquisse d'une Histoire de l'Exégèse Latine au Moyen Age* (Paris, 1944), *passim.*

[32] An early, very general essay suggesting that the fourfold method of interpretation be applied to Dante is S. Udny, "The Interpretation of Dante," *Living Age*, CCXXXVII (1903), 735–744. Opposed are C. S. Lewis, p. 48, and L. L. Camp, pp. 17, 203. A massive attempt to apply the method to Dante was made by H. Flanders Dunbar, *Symbolism in Medieval Thought and its Consummation in the Divine Comedy* (New Haven, 1929). C. H. Grandgent, in his review of Dunbar's book (*Spec.,* V, [1930], 111), expressed strong doubts that the method should be applied to Dante. Camp, pp. 203–209, analyzes specific errors of Dunbar's method. Charles S. Singleton's contention that the literal level in *The Divine Comedy* is a truth, not a fiction, need not concern us here. But he apparently discusses the poem in terms of only two levels of meaning, the literal and the allegorical: "Dante's Allegory," *Spec.,* XXV (1950), 78–86.

[33] Dunbar, p. 278.

[34] See note 23.

Black Prince. But Hope cannot also have other, distinct abstract meanings like good thoughts and salvation. I raise the issue because the fourfold method of interpretation has been suggested for at least one personification-allegory, *Piers Plowman,* and, less vigorously, for another, the *Roman de la Rose.* Nevill Coghill has argued that the method should be applied to Langland's poem: "All these four meanings [the literal, the allegorical, the moral or tropological, and the anagogical] are to be found in *Piers Plowman.* They are sometimes simultaneous, sometimes interlinked, sometimes single; but on all four planes the poem is complete, and all understanding of it must move poetically among them all."[35] If at this point the reader throws up his hands in despair, it is small wonder. Coghill's suggestion would make of the poem a hopelessly complex design. If *Piers Plowman* deals with the anagogical at any point, that fact will be evident from the names of the personifications and their speeches and actions. The speeches and actions will pertain to matters anagogical, the celestial mysteries, and the personifications will be aspects of these celestial mysteries. There will be no need to appeal to the fourfold method to perceive the anagogical sense. No need, and no excuse. The method is impossible for the form, and the reader should put it out of his thoughts.

If the reader, in short, will remember that personification-allegory is primarily designed to make the meaning explicit and is very close to the literal in its statement, the form *as form* will cause him little difficulty.

[35] "Introduction," *The Vision of Piers Plowman,* newly rendered into modern English by Henry W. Wells, New York, 1935, p. xvii. Coghill has repeated this view in later writings on *Piers Plowman.* Camp., p. 4, criticizes Coghill on this point, as does Morton W. Bloomfield in his review of Coghill's *The Pardon of Piers Plowman* in *Spec.,* XXII (1947), 463. Recently Coghill seems to have suggested that the fourfold (or rather, the threefold) method should be applied to the *Roman de la Rose;* see his *The Poet Chaucer* (The Home University Library of Modern Knowledge, 185), New York, 1949, pp. 12–13.

9

LANGLAND, HILTON AND THE THREE LIVES*

S. S. Hussey

IN THE SECOND part of *Piers Plowman*—the *Vita* as it is usually called—the Dreamer engages in a search for Dowel, Dobet and Dobest, three abstractions of which he knows neither the whereabouts nor the meaning. Furthermore, the colophons of the manuscripts divide the *Vita* into three parts, with the general titles *Vita de Dowel, Vita de Dobet, Vita de Dobest.* Critics of the poem have been at least as puzzled as the Dreamer and have sought to elucidate these terms, often by equating them with standard triads in medieval religious thought. The present paper is offered as an investigation of the work of these critics, in the hope that, by sifting the evidence, we might reach a better understanding of the concepts.

Late nineteenth-century criticism of *Piers Plowman* saw it as a great "social document," without fully realizing its importance as a great poem, and in the early years of this century it was still possible to speak of the looseness and non-co-ordination of the work.[1] It was in an attempt to show that *Piers Plowman*

---

* Reprinted, by permission of the Clarendon Press, Oxford, from *The Review of English Studies,* N.S., *VII* (1956), 132–150.

[1] On the alleged looseness of construction see, for example, E. D. Hanscom, 'The Argument of the *Vision of Piers Plowman*', *PMLA* ix (1894), 412; C. W. Stubbs, *The Christ of English Poetry* (London, 1906), p. 77; E. Legouis, *A History of English Literature* (London, 1926), p. 71.

is in fact carefully planned beneath a somewhat rough surface that H. W. Wells advanced the view that Dowel, Dobet and Dobest are the principal organizing factors in the poem, and are to be equated respectively with the active, contemplative and mixed lives of the mystics.[2] N. K. Coghill took up the same idea using different terminology (the "lewed" life of Dowel, the "clerkly" life of Dobet and the "episcopal" life of Dobest) and argued that Piers was a personification of each life in turn, representing Dowel in the *Visio,* and Dobet and Dobest in the sections of the poem that bear those titles. *The Vita de Dowel,* Coghill thought, was a moral consideration of all three lives.[3] Wells, however, protested against what he called an over-literal approach by Coghill. He restated his original thesis with the proviso that Dowel, Dobet and Dobest should not be iden-tified with vocational callings but should be interpreted as men-tal states, which, although the names suggested an ascending scale, could be experienced in greater or less degree by every Christian, no matter what his social position.[4] To this R. W. Chambers agreed.[5]

Since the time of Chambers, and partly as a result of his great authority in *Piers Plowman* scholarship, the view of Do-wel, Dobet and Dobest as active, contemplative and mixed lives has become the standard critical interpretation. It is important to note, however, that Chambers was supporting Wells' second article: that the concepts are psychological not sociological, states not estates; but later discussion has often tended to fol-low Coghill's designation of them as "lewed," "clerkly" and "episcopal." This idea gained currency by means of Coghill's

[2] "The Construction of *Piers Plowman,*" pp. 1–21 above.

[3] "The Character of Piers Plowman considered from the B Text," pp. 54–86 above. I cannot agree that the *Vita de Dowel* sets out to expound the moral nature of all three lives. Piers does not make an appearance in this section, but Dowel seems still to be the author's main concern. The colophons (whoever supplied them) appear to me to be adequate descriptions of the progress of the poem.

[4] "The Philosophy of Piers Plowman," above, pp. 115–129.

[5] *Man's Unconquerable Mind* (London, 1939), esp. pp. 102–106.

British Academy Lecture of 1945.[6] A still more recent view, that of D. W. Robertson and B. F. Huppé, also derives from the articles of Wells:

> The allegorical level, for example, is concerned with the church, and the basic classification of persons in the poem under Dowel, Dobet, and Dobest rests on the traditional division of persons in the church as active, contemplative, and prelatical. More exactly, Dowel, Dobet, and Dobest represent the ideals which persons in these states should follow. Actual persons either exemplify these ideals or their corruption.[7]

The vagueness of the language here allows more scope to the poet than the views of Wells, Coghill and Chambers, who give the impression (perhaps unintentionally) that Langland simply repeated standard teachings of the Doctors of the Church as passed on by fourteenth-century writers. But Robertson and Huppé are really making only a somewhat less extreme statement than those of their predecessors, and if they, as specialists, are somewhat more circumspect, the general view of the meaning of Dowel, Dobet and Dobest is still repeated in books which do not discuss the poem in detail:

> Do-wel is the active life, the life of the good layman; Do-bet is the contemplative life, the life of the man of a religious order; Do-best is the life of the highest human responsibility made possible by the union of activity and contemplation, the life of the Bishop.[8]

The error, I think, lies in the type of criticism that, having perceived some correspondences between Dowel, Dobet and Dobest and the active, contemplative and mixed lives, proceeds to equate the two triads, thereby limiting the interpretation of

[6] "The Pardon of Piers Plowman," *Proc. Brit. Acad.* xxxi (1945), 303–357.

[7] *Piers Plowman and Scriptural Tradition* (Princeton, 1951), pp. 236–237.

[8] E. M. W. Tillyard, *The English Epic and its Background* (London, 1954), p. 166.

the former. The present article does not seek to invalidate Coghill's contention that Piers makes three grand appearances in the poem—one for each kind of life—but discusses what these three lives represent.

In support of this argument Wells brought evidence from St. Thomas Aquinas and the *Meditationes,* wrongly attributed to St. Bonaventura but certainly translated into English by Nicholas Love in the early years of the fifteenth century.[9] Chambers sought support from the writings of Walter Hilton, particularly *Mixed Life.*[10] In his article in *Medium Ævum* (pp. 54–86 above), Coghill listed the various definitions of Dowel, Dobet and Dobest given in the poem. It ought to be possible, therefore, to test these arguments by examining whether the definitions in *Piers Plowman* suggest an equation of Dowel, Dobet, and Dobest with active, contemplative and mixed lives as defined by the writers mentioned above. It is doubtful how far the writings of St. Thomas can be used to interpret *Piers Plowman.* Coghill says that he was "certainly known, at least by hearsay, to Langland."[11] M. W. Bloomfield, on the other hand, speaks of a "vague anti-Thomism" in Langland's work, but his references do not seem very conclusive.[12] Miss Hort considers it unlikely that Langland had read the *Summa,* but thinks that he had picked up something of its teaching by talking to those

[9] P. 15 above. The passage from the *Summa Theologica* is: "Vita contemplativa simpliciter est melior quam activa quae occupatur circa corporales actus: sed vita activa, secundum quam aliquis praedicando et docendo contemplata aliis tradit, est perfectior quam vita quae solum est contemplativa: quia talis vita praesupponit abundantiam contemplationis. Et ideo Christus talem vitam elegit" (Part III, Qu. xl, A. I). The *Meditationes* is now attributed to a thirteenth-century Franciscan, possibly John de Caulibus; see E. Zeeman, "Nicholas Love—A Fifteenth-Century Translator," *RES* vi (1955), 117 and references given there.

[10] Pp. 104–106.

[11] "The Pardon," p. 322.

[12] "Was William Langland a Benedictine Monk?" *MLQ,* iv (1943), 58, 60.

who had.[13] Father Dunning makes extensive use of St. Thomas, but only on points of doctrine generally accepted in the Middle Ages.[14] It is interesting to note that Robertson and Huppé refuse to use the *Summa Theologica* to interpret *Piers Plowman* because of Langland's constant criticism of the friars.[15] As far as I can discover, Langland never quotes directly from St. Thomas, although where St. Thomas is passing on the teaching of earlier writers he may seem to echo him. Love's translations of the *Meditationes* (licensed for reading by Archbishop Arundel in 1410) was later than *Piers Plowman*. Hilton, though, seems a much more valuable witness. As Chambers states, he was probably an exact contemporary of Langland, and it is on Hilton's *Mixed Life* that Chambers chiefly relies:

> The three kinds of good life, as there defined by Walter Hilton, were common knowledge; Langland could not have missed them, and they are the three kinds of good life which in *Piers Plowman* are named Do-well, Do-better, and Do-best. (p. 105)

The date of composition of *Mixed Life* is not known. According to Miss Jones[16] the earliest manuscripts are late fourteenth century and the remainder fifteenth century. *The Scale of Perfection* recognizes two lives only, active and contemplative, and the idea of mixed life is similarly absent from *The Cloud of Unknowing* and the works of Rolle. All these were, of course, meant for an audience different from that of *Mixed Life*. Whoever read them subsequently, they were composed for recluses, not for the devout man of secular estate who (as early printed texts tell us) was addressed in *Mixed Life*.[17] But unless we have been particularly unfortunate in the survival of manu-

---

[13] G. Hort, *Piers Plowman and Contemporary Religious Thought* (London, 1938), pp. 56–59.

[14] T. P. Dunning, *Piers Plowman; An Interpretation of the A-Text* (London, 1937), p. 14.

[15] P. 10.

[16] D. Jones, *Minor Works of Walter Hilton* (London, 1929), pp. xviii-xx.

[17] Jones, pp. xxii, xxvi, xxviii, xxxi.

scripts, mixed life does not seem to have become popular in England until the end of the fourteenth century. There were the teachings of the Fathers, particularly of St. Gregory who recognized all three lives although he never called the mixed life by that name, but it seems to have needed Hilton, writing in English at the end of the fourteenth century, to bring the third life to the attention of a wider audience. Love cites him as the exponent of the idea, and presumably he is referring to *Mixed Life:*

> Where of and othere vertuouse exercise that longeth to contemplatyf lyuynge/ and specially to a recluse. and also of medled lyf/ that is to saye somtyme actyfe and somtyme contemplatyf as it longeth to dyuerse persones that in worldely astate hauen grace of goostly loue/ who so wole more pleynely be enformed and tauʒt in Englisshe tonge lete hym loke the tretys that the worthy clerke and holy lyuere maister Walter hyltoun/ the chanoun of thurgartun/ wrote in englische by grace and hiʒe discrecioun. and he schal fynde there/ as I leue/ a sufficient scole and a trewe of alle thise.[18]

Langland, however, mentions Dowel, Dobet and Dobest as early as A. IX, composed, according to the latest scholarship, in the late 1360's.[19] In view of this, Chambers' assertion that Langland "could not have missed" a knowledge of all three lives is probably too strong. And whereas in his earlier arguments, for example the discussion of selective or nonselective charity, Langland quotes "authorities" to support each view,[20] he does not quote authorities to support his definition of the three

[18] *The Mirrour of the Blessed Lyf of Jesu Christ . . . by Nicholas Love,* ed. L. F. Powell (Oxford, 1908), pp. 164–165.

[19] See: O. Cargill, "The Date of the A-text of *Piers Ploughman,*" *PMLA,* XLVII (1932), 354–362; B. F. Huppé, "The A-Text of *Piers Plowman* and the Norman Wars," ibid., LIV (1939), 37–64; J. A. W. Bennett, "The Date of the A-text of *Piers Plowman,*" ibid., LVIII (1943), 566–572.

[20] For Langland's use of authorities see Hort, pp. 28–43, and for the specific problem of selective or nonselective charity, E. T. Donaldson, *Piers Plowman, the C-Text and Its Poet* (London, 1949), pp. 130–134.

lives,[21] as though he either did not know them or deliberately dispensed with them in an attempt to argue out the answer for himself. The search for a direct source, either patristic or contemporary, seems to go against Langland's own inclinations.

In discussing Hilton's view of the three lives, Chambers has to admit that they do not tally exactly with Dowel, Dobet and Dobest.[22] Hilton does not definitely place the mixed life above the contemplative life. Chambers calls this one of the "minor differences" between Hilton's view and Langland's. I submit that the difference is important enough to make it doubtful that the two writers were dealing with the same idea. Early in his treatise, Hilton sets out the alternation between the active and the contemplative life that results in the mixed life:

> Þe thredde lif þat is medled lonketh to men of holi chirche as to prelates and oþere curates wheche hauyn cure and souerente oure oþere men for to kenne þem and rewle þem boþen þere bodies and principaly þere sowles in fulfellyng of þe dedys of mercy bodely and gostely. Vn to þese men it longeth sumtyme for to vse werkes of mercy in actife lyf in helpe and sustenaunce of þemselfe. and of here sogetes and of oþere also. And sumtyme for to leuyn alle maner besynesses outward and ȝeue þem vn to prayers and meditacioun as redyngge of holy wrytte and to oþere gosteli occupaciouns after þat þei fele þem disposed. Also it longeth to summe temporal men þe wheche hauyn souerente with meche auer of werdly goodes and haue also as it were lordschepe ouer oþer men for to gouerne and susteyne þem as a fader haþ ouer his children. a maister ouer his seruantes. and a lord ouer his tenauntes. þe wheche men hauen also resseyued of oure lordis gifte grace of deuocioun and in partye sauour of gostely occupacioun. Vnto þese men also longeth medled lyf þat is bothe actif and contemplaif. (f. 3ʳ.)[23]

---

[21] Except St. Paul at B. xii. 30, but this is too general to be useful.

[22] P. 105.

[23] Quotations are from MS. Cambridge University Library Ff. 5. 40 of *Mixed Life*. Miss J. Russell-Smith, who is preparing a critical text, kindly informs me that this is the best MS. of the longer version of this treatise.

But he goes further than this. His argument is that God has placed some men in a particular worldly state which prevents them from living a fully contemplative life. It is because of the obligations of these men to those they govern—obligations of charity if seen from a religious standpoint—that they are exhorted to adopt a mixed life:

> Þou schat nouth vtterly folwen þin desire for to leuen occupacioun and besynesses of þe werd qweche ben nedful to vsen in rewlynge of þin selfe and of alle oþere þat ben vndyr þin kepyng and ȝeue þe holly to gostly occupacioun of prayers and meditacions, as it were a frere or a monk or an oþer man þat were nougth bounden to þe werd be chylderen and seruantes as þou art for it falleth not to þe. and if þou dost so þou kepist nougth þe ordre of charite. Also if þou woldest leuen vtterly gostly occupacioun namely now after þe grace þat god haþ ȝouen vn to þe and sette þe holly to þe besynesse of þe werd to fulfellyng of werkes of actif lyf as fully as an oþer man þat neuere felede deuocioun. þou leuest þe ordre of charite for þin state askeþ for to done bothe ilkone of þem in dyuerse tyme. þou schat medele þe werkes of actif lif with gostely werkes of lif contemplatif þanne dost þou wel. (f. 2^r.)

Hilton, if forced to an absolute order, would seem to place contemplative life highest of all:

> And sothely for swich a man þat is in spiritualte souereynte as prelates and curates ben or in temporel souerente as werdely lordis and maistres ben I holde þis lif best medeled and most behouely to þem as longe as þei arn bounden þer to. Bot to oþere þat ben fre nouth bounden to temporal ministracioun ne to spirituale I hope þat lif contemplatife alone. if he myghte come þere to sothfastely were best most spedful. most medful. most fayr and most worthi to þem for to vsen and for to holde. (f. 4^v.)

Hence Hilton, writing for a limited class of men, of whom his "devout man of secular estate" is one, says that absolutely contemplative life is best, but not all men who wish may follow it. Langland, in a poem meant for anyone who would read it, suggests, by his very names, an ascending order: Dowel, Dobet,

Dobest. The identification of these with active, contemplative and mixed lives is not borne out by a careful reading of *Mixed Life*.

It is time to turn to the poem itself. Langland mentions only active and contemplative lives, the mixed life never being named. At A. vii. 234 (B. vi. 249, not in C) he mentions both active and contemplative life but without any idea of progress from one to the other:

> For Kuynde Wit wolde that vche mon wrouhte
> With techinge or with tilynge or trauaylynge of hondes,
> Actyf lyf or contemplatyf Crist wolde hit alse.[24]

This reference Coghill dismisses by the assumption that at that stage of the poem Langland had not fully worked out the allegory of the *Vita*.[25] A. xi. 179–184 is more serious, as it would seem to equate Dowel with active life:

> 'Hit is a wel lele lyf', quod heo, 'among the lewed peple,
> Actif it is ihoten, hosebondes hit vsen;
> Trewe tilieris on erthe, taillours and souteris,
> And alle kyne crafty men that cunne here foode wynne,
> With any trewe trauaille toille for here foode,
> Diken or deluen, Dowel it hatte.'

Thus, for Coghill, active manual labor becomes an essential part

---

[24] Quotations from *Piers Plowman* are from Skeat's Parallel Texts edition (Oxford, 1886). I assume that one author, probably called William Langland, wrote all three texts, and therefore quote from whichever text seems most relevant. In abandoning Skeat's caesural stop, I have used additional punctuation, although not to such an extent as to change the interpretation. In the above passage, Knott and Fowler, *Piers the Plowman, A Critical Edition of the A-Version* (Baltimore, 1952), place a semicolon after *contemplatyf,* thus making the third line parallel with the second. If the semicolon is placed after *hondes,* the third line (referring to the Martha-Mary story) would mean that Christ too wished all men to be engaged in some useful occupation. However it is read, the text gives no hint that the two lives are to be equated with Dowel and Dobet.
[25] "The Pardon," p. 336.

of Dowel.[26] If this was the intention of A at this point, it is noteworthy that the rest of the triad is not given. Dobet and Dobest do not signify contemplative and mixed lives, as we might expect, and this particular definition does not recur in B or C. A similar difficulty is met with in the case of Haukyn who is actually called *Activa-Vita:*

> 'I am a mynstral', quod that man, 'my name is *Actiua-vita,*
> Alle ydel ich hatye, for of actyf is my name'.

Chambers, in his discussion of this part of the poem,[27] sees in Haukyn "the inferior type of Active Man as Hilton defines him —ignorant, rough, untaught, with no savour of devotion, yet with a fear of God, and good will to his fellow-Christians"; and he states that "Hawkyn, Active Life, stands for all, from the lowest to the highest, who are too 'fleshly and boisterous,' too much cumbered with the world, to undertake the life of Contemplation, Poverty and Charity." But if Haukyn is to represent active life, even a lower type of active life, and if active life equals Dowel, it seems strange that he should be guilty of all the sins in the calendar—after all, most writers (including Hilton, and Langland as just quoted) regarded it as sufficient for salvation[28]—and that Haukyn himself after his confession wishes that he "hadde ben ded and doluen for Doweles sake" (B. XIV. 321). I have sometimes thought that Langland was not using "Activa-Vita" as a technical term here, for Haukyn twice (B. XIII. 225, 238) defines himself as "hating idleness," a definition which seems to savor more of etymology than of mysticism, but I should not insist upon this.

---

[26] "The Pardon," p. 325.

[27] B. XIII. 224–225. Chambers, pp. 151, 154.

[28] I have changed Skeat's *feir* at A. XI. 179 (read by MS. V only) to *lele* (most of the other MSS. including T). For the meaning of *lele* ("just allowable") see Donaldson, pp. 65–66. Cf. also Skeat's misgivings about Haukyn, "Activa-Vita": "The minstrel here described was very far from being an honest man, and was hardly justified in giving himself so honest a name." (EETS edition, IV. 313.)

Some lines found only in the C text (VIII. 209–306) are also difficult:

> Thenne was ther on heihte Actif, an hosebounde he
>   semed:
> 'Ich haue ywedded a wyf', quath he, 'wel wantowen of
>   maners;
> Were ich seuenyght fro hure syghte, synnen hue wolde,
> And loure on me and lyghtliche chide and seye ich loue
>   anothere.
> For-thy, Peers plouhman, ich praye the telle hit Treuthe,
> Ich may nat come for a Kytte, so hue cleueth on me;
>   *Vxorem duxi, et ideo non possum uenire.'*
> Quath Contemplacion, 'by Crist thauh ich care suffre,
> Famyn and defaute, folwen ich wolle Peers.'

Donaldson sees these lines as foreshadowing Piers' transition from Dowel to Dobet, made absolute in the Pardon Scene.[29] This raises the question of the significance of Piers' tearing of the Pardon. To suggest, with most critics,[30] that he renounces the active life absolutely in favor of the contemplative (even if we admit that these are the proper meanings of Dowel and Dobet) seems to me too drastic, for it implies that the first is unworthy of the good man. All men had to begin in active life, and most writers (including, incidentally, Hilton)[31] are tolerant to those unable to progress farther. The Pardon is sent as a reward to Piers, and it promises that those who do well shall go to Heaven. Piers, therefore, here symbolizes Dowel, perhaps more completely than at any other point in the poem. As Frank says,[32] it is a strange practice that makes Piers, just as his significance becomes clear, immediately pass on to represent something else.

[29] Pp. 166–168.

[30] For a discussion of critical opinion, see R. W. Frank, "The Pardon Scene in *Piers Plowman*," *Spec.*, XXVI (1951), 317–331, and J. J. Lawlor, "*Piers Plowman*; The Pardon Reconsidered," *MLR* XLV (1950), 449–458.

[31] E.g., *Scale of Perfection* (ed. Sitwell, London, 1953), pp. 96–98, 163–165.

[32] P. 325.

It will have been noticed that the argument so far has been concerned principally with Dowel and Dobest. I should not object to a rough equation of Dowel with the idea of the active life, although I believe that Langland was not thinking of the technical term and that the resemblance is coincidental. The first stage in any progression must be described in general terms, and in such triads as these must refer to the majority of Christians who have no special religious calling. But if this is to be allowed, we must dismiss any idea of limiting active life to the performance of manual labor. Hilton's definition was much wider than this; it covers much of what Langland's critics usually assign to Dobet:

> Be þis bodely werkyng þat I speke of may þou vnderstonde alle maner of goode werkes þat þin soule doth bi þe wyttes and þe membres of þin body vn to þin selfe as in fastynge. wakynge and and in refreynynge of fleschly lustes bi oþer panaunce doynge or to þin euencristene bi fulfellynge of þe dedes of mercy bodely or gostly. or vn to god be suffrynge of alle maner bodely myscheues for þe luf of rythwysnes. Alle þese werkes don in trouthe be charite plesen god withoute whiche þei ben nouth. (f. I^v.)[33]

I have already stated that I consider the idea of mixed life too limited to apply it to the idea of Dobest. The most difficult of the three equations is that of Dobet and the contemplative life.

There seems, first of all, to be some confusion of thought here, since the critics sometimes refer to Dobet as the contemplative life, sometimes as the "clerkly life." Obviously not all clerics were contemplatives. The difficulty lies in the question: did the practice of the contemplative life demand complete renunciation of the world and enclosure of some sort? If it did, Dobet cannot be equated with the contemplative life. If contemplation is only an occasional practice in a life otherwise

---

[33] Cf. *Scale of Perfection* (I quote from B.M. MS. Harley 6579): 'Also apartie of actife lif lith in grete bodili dedes. wilk aman doth to hym self. as gret fastynge. mikel wakynge. and oþer scharp penuance doynge' (f. 2^v) and the remarks of Frank, pp. 324–327.

passed in the world, we seem (on the evidence of the same critics) to be dealing not with Dobet but with Dobest. Abbot Butler sets out well the ambiguity in the use of the term:

> 'Contemplative life' has two meanings. It has an objective meaning: a manner of corporate life ordinated with the primary object of facilitating and promoting the exercise of contemplation, by removal or reduction of the usual obstacles. And it has a subjective or personal meaning, according to which, whatever be the external conditions, that man is leading a contemplative life who effectively practises contemplation. In this sense, whatever be his calling or manner of life, a contemplative is leading a contemplative life: it is a matter of personal experience, not of external conditions.[34]

The question of what Hilton meant by "contemplation" is worth further investigation. Early in *The Scale of Perfection* he distinguishes three degrees of contemplation. The first is not true contemplation; it is governed by the reason and does not include any inward experience of God. The second has two stages: a lower stage which Hilton states may, by a special gift of grace, be experienced briefly in active life, and a higher stage possible only to those who, after long bodily and spiritual exercise, come to tranquility of body and soul. The third, distinguished by the approach to perfect knowledge and love of God and completed only in Heaven, is usually reserved for the enclosed contemplative.

In Book II of *The Scale of Perfection*, Hilton seems to have abandoned these rigid definitions, though the substance of his teaching remains the same[35] He never states that enclosure is absolutely necessary for the practice of contemplation. There may be many approaches to contemplation, but only one door:

> Þer mown be mony sundry weies. and sere werkes ledend sundry soules to contemplacioun. for after sundry disposynges of men

---

[34] E. C. Butler, *Western Mysticism* (London, 1922), p. 290.

[35] For Hilton's different treatment of this subject in Books I and II, see Sitwell p. 9, n. 1. Cf. also *Eight Chapters* (ed. Jones), pp. 95–97.

and after sundry states. as are religious and seculers þat þei are in. are diuers exercices in wirkynge. Nerþeles þer is no gate bot on for what exercice it be þat a soule haf bot if he may come bi þat exercice to þis knowynge and to a meke felynge of him self. . . . soþly he is not ȝit come to reformynge in felynge ne naþ not fully contemplacioun. (f. 96ᵛ.)

Mixed Life, however, perhaps because Hilton's later view became again more crystallized, or perhaps because in that book, meant for a secular audience, he was anxious to give clear-cut definitions, seems to demand some sort of enclosure:

Contemplatif lif a lone longeth to swiche men and wymmen þat for þe loue of god forsaken alle open synnes of þe werd and of here flesch and alle besynesses charges and gouernaunses of werdly goodes and make þem self pore and naked to þe bare nede of þe bodely kynde and fre from souereynte of alle oþere men to þe seruise of god. (f. 3ʳ.)

The point which seems to emerge from Hilton's teaching on this subject is that even in the lower stage of the second degree of contemplation of his earlier definition—the one most favorable to an identification of Dobet with the contemplative life— he demands enclosure of the mind, if not of the body, to an extent which Langland does not recognize. Furthermore, in Hilton's definitions of contemplation, assiduous and devout prayer is a constant feature, and, as Father Sitwell says, he seems to have visualized contemplation as a growing awareness of the life of sanctifying grace within the soul.[36] Langland, in the *Vita de Dobet,* does not stress this side of contemplation, whereas it is the predominant aspect with Hilton. Moreover, there is in Langland nothing about the "lightsome darkness" and the "rich nought" of *The Scale of Perfection* or of *The Cloud of Unknowing,* still less of the sensuous imagery of Rolle. The definitions of Dobet in *Piers Plowman* seem to stress practising what one preaches or helping or teaching others. "To love friend and foe," "to suffer," "to suffer for the good of

[36] p. xi.

your soul all that the Book, by the Church's teaching, bids," "Doce," "Confession"—the definitions are taken from Coghill's table (pp. 75–77 above)—how can these be equated with the contemplative life as defined by Hilton?

There are two further pieces of evidence which, although not proof in themselves, help to make suspect the equation of Dowel, Dobet and Dobest with active, contemplative and mixed lives. The first was, in fact, noticed by Chambers. It is that whereas Hilton represents Christ as living the mixed life, *Piers Plowman* B. XIX. 104 ff. shows Christ practicing Dowel, Dobet and Dobest in turn.[37] The second is that the Middle Ages, drawing inspiration largely from St. Augustine and St. Gregory, had standard scriptural illustrations for the active and contemplative lives: Martha and Mary, Lia and Rachel, St. Peter and St. John, Moses' ascent of Mount Sinai. Such comparisons are common in medieval mystical writings. Hilton uses those of Martha and Mary and Lia and Rachel in *Mixed Life*.[38] So common was the use of the former story as an illustration of active and contemplative lives, that Pecock, who wishes to draw a rather different moral, has to justify at some length his departure from the views of "manye holy doctouris."[39] But when Langland quotes the story of Martha and Mary he uses it, not to illustrate Christ's praise of the contemplative life above the active, but to exalt poverty:

> Martha on Marye Magdeleyne an huge pleynte she made,
> And to owre saueour self seyde this wordes,
> *Domine, non est tibi cure quod soror mea reliquit ne solam ministrare, etc?*
> And hastiliche god answered and eytheres wille folwed,

---

[37] Chambers, p. 105. Huppé in *Spec.* XXII (1947), 619, remarks on the difficulty of Christ apparently representing Dobet, an intermediate virtue.

[38] *Mixed Life* (ed. Jones), pp. 10–11, 32–34. See also: *Ancrene Riwle* (EETS, o.s. 225), p. 189; *Cloud of Unknowing* (EETS, o.s 218), pp. 47ff.; *Scale of Perfection,* ed. Sitwell, p. 26; Love, *Mirrour,* ed. Powell, pp. 156–165, 174–175, 200–201.

[39] Pecock, *Reule of Crysten Religioun* (EETS, o.s. 171), pp. 488–493.

Bothe Morthaes and Maries, as Mathew bereth witnesse,
Ac pouerte god put bifore and preysed it the bettre;
Maria optimam partem elegit, que non auferetur ab ea.[40]

This seems a strange moral to draw, and stranger still for any writer who had read treatises explaining the active and contemplative lives.

The probabilities, therefore, seem to be against a direct identification of Dowel, Dobet and Dobest with active, contemplative and mixed lives. This has been noticed before, but has not, I believe, been demonstrated in detail. Meroney, finding the triad active, contemplative and mixed lives unsatisfactory as an explanation of the three "lives" in *Piers Plowman,* suggested that they might be understood in terms of another triad: purgative, illuminative and unitive lives, a triad possibly originating with St. Augustine and having been developed by pseudo-Dionysius.[41] Meroney's article lacks the detailed illustrations from the poem which one would like to see, and appears to place too heavy a stress on the single line B. xx. 212:

> I comsed to rowme
> Thorw Contricioun and Confessioun tyl I cam to Vnite.

The third stage of this triad seems to come rather late in the poem. It may be objected that the final stage of the mystical progress was only begun on earth and completed in Heaven. But the ending of *Piers Plowman* gives no indication of this, for the final pilgrimage of Conscience in search of Piers apparently takes place on this earth.

Two critics, Father Dunning and Professor Donaldson, have considered that not one but both of the triads mentioned above

[40] B. xi. 242–246. Noticed also by Donaldson, p. 171.
[41] H. Meroney, "The Life and Death of Longe Wille," ELH, xvii (1950), 8–15. On pseudo-Dionysius see: P. Pourrat, *Christian Spirituality* (London, 1922), i, 220, n. 1, and P. Hodgson, "Dionysius the Areopagite and Christian Mystical Tradition," *Contemporory Review,* clxxvi (1949), 281–285.

might be applied to the elucidation of the poem. Dunning says that in the A text Thought and Clergye define Dowel, Dobet and Dobest in terms of objective states of perfection (active, contemplative, and mixed lives) whereas Wit defines them more subjectively as purgative, illuminative and unitive states, teaching that perfection does not depend on a man's position in life but on the state of his soul.[42] I believe Dunning is correct in seeing that the triad active, contemplative and mixed lives will not fit all the definitions of Dowel, Dobet and Dobest, and in stressing that the latter have to do with the individual conscience much more than with rank. But once again we get the best answer with respect to Dowel. It is roughly equivalent to purgation as it is to active life, because the rooting out of sin is as much an initial stage in a man's reformation as is living according to the Commandments. However, after Wit's first definition (A. x. 76–80) Dowel does not come particularly close to the purgative state, and at the end of all his instruction the Dreamer seems as puzzled as ever:

> 'Ʒet am I neuere the ner, for nouʒt I have walkid,
> To wyte what is Dowel witterly in herte.'
> (A. xi. 250–251)

And Dunning admits that in this matter the evidence from the B text runs contrary to that from A.[43]

Professor Donaldson, too, believes that Dowel, Dobet and Dobest sometimes come close to active, contemplative and mixed lives, and sometimes to the purgative, illuminative and unitive states:

> . . . the *Vita* handles two basically different concepts at the same time and sometimes in the same terms. The chief difference between the concepts is that the first, as applied to the life of the individual, seems to develop in a sequence from outwardness (the active life) to inwardness (the contemplative life) to inward-

[42] Pp. 173–174, 179, 182.
[43] Pp. 191–192.

outwardness (the mixed life), while the second develops in a sequence of three stages of inwardness, all of which, of course, have also appropriate outward manifestations and all of which are, incidentally, open to men of all vocations.[44]

He goes on to demonstrate that C's particular modification of this general idea was to emphasize Dowel as the first stage in a more subjective spiritual life. As this paper has shown, I cannot agree with the part of the argument which deals with active, contemplative and mixed lives, but Donaldson's sensitive and thorough discussion of the metamorphosis of B into C seems essentially correct. But although I agree that C in particular contains some of St. Bernard's philosophy, I cannot agree that evidence of his mystical teaching is to be seen there also. The triad humility, charity and unity, as set out by St. Bernard, does not seem to correspond with Dowel, Dobet, and Dobest. Donaldson himself does not appear to be completely sure of his thesis, admitting that Dobest contains little suggesting St. Bernard's idea of union with God, and resorting to a rather unsatisfactory line of argument to change St. Bernard's humility into C's "patient poverty."[45]

But how did the Church in general view the relationship between the active, contemplative and mixed lives and the purgative, illuminative and unitive states? This question has fortunately been considered by Father Pepler. We have, he points out, to distinguish between an exterior station of life, fixed by rule and obligation, and an interior life of progress common to all Christians, but it is perfectly possible to fit the two together:

> . . . there are three exterior states for a Christian to follow— the active, the mixed, and the contemplative—and these remain permanently according to his obligations. But within the interiority of his mind and heart he lives a simple Christian life which

44 P. 159.
45 P. 196.

begins by being active in desire and by preference but concludes by being firmly fixed in contemplative love.[46]

The interior life may be seen further in terms of a progression: purgation, illumination and unity (or, as they were sometimes called, the stages of the *incipientes, proficientes* and *perfecti*). The exterior contemplative state may assist the interior life by providing circumstances favorable to contemplation, but it should not be regarded as a merit in itself, for in Heaven real reward comes as a result of the interior life and only accidental reward as a result of the exterior. The troublesome mixed life can now be seen not as a true stage of the interior life, but an exterior state. It is properly a combination of the exterior active state and the interior contemplative life. A man's interior life must be either active or contemplative. In a bishop, the stock example of the mixed life, it is contemplative, just as St. Thomas' mixed life will be seen to be more contemplative than active. But a bishop need not have reached the highest type of life, that of union with God.

These are valuable distinctions, expressing more fully what had been pointed out earlier by Abbot Butler (who was not, of course, dealing with fourteenth-century writings) and I have dealt with them at some length, since attempts to fit together one type of interior life and another external state and to label the result Dowel, Dobet and Dobest, have resulted in false criticism of *Piers Plowman*. But I cannot agree with Father Pepler when he suggests that Dowel, Dobet and Dobest represent the three stages of the interior life, albeit in a different way from that suggested by Meroney:

> Langland classed the active life in its lowest form as a purely 'natural' living according to the flesh and at best as something approaching the well-meaning busy life usually described by the mystical writers as 'active'. On the other hand his three, Dowel, Dobet and Dobest, are the types of good life, supernatural rather

[46] C. Pepler, "The Divine Specialists," *Life of the Spirit,* v (1951), 395.

than natural, guided by the Holy Spirit. The first stage may be to some extent identified with the better sort of active life; but on the whole all three could be regarded as contemplative in so far as they are supernatural and devoted ultimately to God. He does in fact describe three stages of the beginner, the proficient and the perfect in the devout life. This is characteristically active concerned directly with fellow human beings though based on God and the love of God. Such an active conception of the three ways was perhaps inevitable in a poem cast in so essentially social a mould.[47]

Langland does not make a specific distinction between a lower and a higher level of active life, as Hilton, for example, does. Such a distinction would have to be inferred from the characterization of Haukyn as opposed to the early Piers. But the question seems to be one of two completely different books, written by two very different men. Hilton, the Augustinian canon and director of souls seeking mystic union with God, saw and applied the distinction between active, contemplative and mixed lives and purgative, illuminative and unitive interior states, as Pepler notes. But Langland, the wanderer, the talker, dealing primarily with Heaven as reflected in the things of this world, does not seem to be continuously aware of the difference. Pepler, and Meroney also,[48] illustrate their argument by quoting C. XIX. 68 ff., a discussion of the fruit of the Tree of Charity (or *Ymago-dei,* to give it its proper title in C):

> 'Adam was as tree and we aren as hus apples,
> Somme of ows sothfast and some variable,
> Somme litel and some large, like apples of kynde.
> As weddede men and wedewes and ryȝt worthy maidenes,
> The whiche the *Seynt Esprit* seweth, the sonne of al heuene,
> Conforteth hem in here continence that lyuen in
>   contemplacion,
> As monkes and monyeles, men of holichurche;
> These hauen hete of the Holi Gost, as crop of treo the sonne.

---

[47] C. Pepler, "Langland's Way to Unity," *Life of the Spirit,* I (1947), 202–203.

[48] Pp. 14–15.

Wedewes and wedeweres that here owen wil forsaken
And chast leden here lyf ys lyf of contemplacion,
And more lykyng to oure lorde than lyue as kynde asketh,
And folwe that the flessh wole and frut forth brynge,
That lettered men in her langage *Actiua Uita* callen.'
'Ȝe, syre', ich seide, 'and sitthen ther aren bote two lyues
That oure lorde aloweth, as lered men ous techeth,
That is *Actiua Uita* and *Uita Contemplatiua*,
Whi groweth this frut in thre degrees?' . . .

These lines are puzzling, partly because of the syntax. I believe that "The whiche" in line 72 refers only to "ryȝt worthy maidenes," and that lines 72–75 are a parenthesis. But, however we read the passage, the Dreamer objects that there are three degrees of fruit, yet only two permissible ways of life. Pepler argues that Langland classes the three degrees of good life (signified here by Matrimony, Widowhood and Virginity) all together as contemplative, and places the active life outside of this. But both he and Meroney appear to overlook the fact that this passage appears toward the end of the poem. From the beginning Langland had heard of active and contemplative (and possibly mixed) lives, but while writing the C text, he added this passage to a poem which, as Donaldson states, already dealt to a much greater extent than B with the individual conscience. Langland came to see that these terms were not satisfactory, even as a temporary definition of Dowel, Dobet and Dobest. He was unable, that is, to carry out the sort of equation that the theories of Wells, Coghill and Chambers logically demand of him: three degrees of fruit equal active, contemplative and mixed lives, which in turn equal Dowel, Dobet and Dobest. It would have been an excellent chance to make this intention clear. So, as usual, he argues out the difficulty in his poem. By so doing, he has perceived a possible ambiguity in the terms which Hilton and the mystics employed much more precisely. But he does not use the specialized terms purgation, illumination and union to describe the interior progress of the soul. (The fact that the barn Unity is called "holicherche on Englisshe" (B. XIX. 325) seems to fix this as a nontechnical use of the word.) Nor does the passage contain a permanent solution to the problem. If Langland was satisfied, the same solution would surely appear elsewhere, not only in the closing passus of C—unless, of course, he died, and so was unable to do more than state his difficulty. His immediate solution was to adopt a third triad: Matrimony, Widowhood and Virginity, which at least was not ambiguous.

I have suggested that neither the triad active, contemplative and mixed lives, nor the triad purgative, illuminative and unitive states, nor a combination of the two is completely satisfactory as a definition of Dowel, Dobet and Dobest, and that the proposed equations break down especially in the case of the second elements, that is, that Dobet equals the contemplative life or the illuminative state. There seem, therefore, to be two possible solutions to the problem. The first is that Langland had a source not yet identified for the ideas of Dowel, Dobet and Dobest. The second is that he used those names to represent a composite system, an amalgam his own mind had made from ideas which were "in the air"; perhaps he himself had not fully assimilated these concepts, or perhaps he considered that the ordinary Christian would not follow, or would not need, the complexities of contemporary thought. I think that we should recognize the importance of solutions of this second type in any study of the history of fourteenth-century ideas. Obviously we must first separate and understand the various systems, but having done so, we ought not to expect that the result will provide a ready-made guide to the thought of a great writer, particularly of a great poet. And, as several critics have pointed out, Langland seems to have been a talker and a listener rather than a student, either of philosophy or of mysticism. His probable way of life, and his methods of organizing and presenting his poem (with its numerous digressions) both point in this direction.[49]

I consider, however, that there is a third possibility: that

[49] See Donaldson, pp. 159–160 and the references given there. For Langland's probable way of life see the final chapter of Donaldson's book.

the ideas themselves were originally fairly simple, nontechnical ones. This approach is seen in part in the criticisms of the poem by F. A. R. Carnegy and G. H. Gerould. Carnegy quotes Mensendieck to the effect that Dobet is not an ideal superior to Dowel but simply a life conducted according to the precepts of Dowel; the only man able to live Dobet fully was Christ. Hence Dobest is the foundation and perfect rule of the Church on earth, according to the example of Dowel and through the redemption of mankind by Christ (Dobest).[50] Gerould asks:

> . . . is it necessary to ascribe fixed limits to those states of right living? Are not the three simply different aspects of the way of life to which any Christian may aspire, however much he may fail to reach it?[51]

These suggestions, however, do not fully allow for the progression inherent in the concepts of Dowel, Dobet and Dobest.

I would not deny the possibility that Langland's idea of the nature of Dowel, Dobet and Dobest underwent certain modifications as he progressed from the A text to the B text and from B to C, but I believe that his main ideas remained constant. I believe further that by the close of *Piers Plowman* Langland's readers have a good, though vague, idea of what Dowel, Dobet and Dobest represent, although, like the poet, they might be hard put to it to make a comprehensive, all-inclusive definition of them in a few lines. At one point, indeed, Langland almost gives up the idea of definitions:

> 'And seith that Dowel and Dobet aren two infinites,
> Whiche infinites, with a feith, fynden oute Dobest,
> Which shall saue mannes soule', thus seith Piers the Ploughman,
> 'I can nouȝt her-on', quod Conscience. . . .
>
> (B. XIII. 127–130)

---

[50] F. A. R. Carnegy, *The Relations between the Social and Divine Order in William Langland's "Vision of William concerning Piers the Plowman"* (Breslau, 1934), pp. 34–35, 38–39.

[51] "The Structural Integrity of *Piers Plowman*, B," *S.P.*, XLV (1948), 74.

As earlier critics have stated,[52] the various definitions in the poem are not mutually exclusive but complementary. Langland may, while feeling his way toward a solution, have tried temporary equations of Dowel, Dobet and Dobest, with various triads: contrition, confession and satisfaction; matrimony, widowhood and virginity; or (less likely) active, contemplative and mixed lives. But I believe that such definitions were not systematic and that we should beware of limiting Langland's terms by equating them with titles like "contemplative life" with their restricted meanings.

The first mention of Dowel is at the close of the Pardon Scene.[53] It is obviously a translation of the *qui bona egerunt* of the pardon itself. But it has already been suggested in Holy Church's advice to the Dreamer in Passus I of the B text:

> And alle that worche with wronge wenden hij shulle
> After her deth day and dwelle with that shrewe.
> Ac tho that worche wel, as holiwritt telleth,
> And enden as I ere seide in treuthe, that is the best,
> Mowe be siker that her soule shal wende to heuene,
> Ther treuthe is in Trinitee and troneth hem alle.
> (B. I. 126–131)

with which we may compare C. XIII. 117–118:

> And euery man help other for hennes shulleth we alle
> To haue as we han deserued, as holychurche wittnesseth,
> *Et qui bona egerunt, ibunt in uitam eternam; qui vero*
> *mala, in ignem eternum.*

and B. XIX. 191–193:

> And demen hem at domes daye bothe quikke and ded;
> The gode to the godhede and to grete Ioye,
> And wikke to wonye in wo withouten ende.

---

[52] Coghill, p. 78 above; Wells, pp. 13 and 119–120 above; Dunning, p. 170; G. Kane, *Middle English Literature* (London, 1951), pp. 240–241.
[53] A. VIII. 97; B. VII. 113; C. X. 289.

Thus the idea of Dowel (if not the name) is implicit throughout the poem.

Now Langland's sudden mention in Thought's speech of two further degrees, Dobet and Dobest, has puzzled several critics. But we ought not to be so surprised at this, especially when we notice that Dowel is sometimes defined alone (B. IX. 107, XI. 402, XII. 30, XIII. 104, XIV. 87). This suggests that Dowel was Langland's main concern throughout the poem, and that by it he meant something like "living a good life in whatever state you are called." This seems to be his main message. All good men, including good bishops (who cannot signify Dobest which has not been mentioned at this point), share in Piers' pardon. Early in the poem bishops and priests are exhorted to concentrate on the spiritual welfare of their flocks, just as knights are told that their task is to enforce efficient administration of their estates.[54] The same teaching is present in the episode of the ploughing of the half-acre, and is repeated by Grace in the final stage of the poem:

> 'Thowgh some be clenner than somme, ȝe se wel', quod Grace,
> 'That he that vseth the fairest crafte, to the foulest I couth
>   haue put hym,
> Thinketh alle', quod Grace, 'that grace cometh of my ȝifte;
> Lok that none lakke other, but loueth alle as bretheren.'
>   (B. XIX. 246–249)

It is Dreamer's own defence when Reasoun questions him:

> Yf ich by laboure sholde lyue and lyflode deseruen,
> That labour that ich lerned best therwith lyue ich sholde:
> *In eadem uocatione in qua uocati estis, manete.*
>   (C. VI. 42–43)

Once the idea of Dowel is clear, Dobet and Dobest follow naturally, not as different "lives" or "states" but as degrees of the same thing. To use the metaphor employed earlier in this

---

[54] A Prologue 90–95; A. I. 92 ff.

paper, we have a simple equation with one unknown and two multiples of it, not a compound equation of three unknowns in uncertain relationship. Of course, as Imaginatyf told the Dreamer, there were plenty of books to teach men what Dowel, Dobet and Dobest meant, not only books like *Mixed Life,* but much more generally, books about how to live a good life.[55] And if you live a good life, you can go on to live a better and best life, helping others as well as helping yourself, and finally accepting a measure of responsibility for their spiritual welfare. As Wit says (A. x. 119–123), Dobest comes from Dowel and Dobet—the progression is a natural one.[56] Let us finally return to the first definition of Dowel, Dobet and Dobest, that of Thought, a passage substantially the same in all three texts:

> Whoso is trewe of his tonge and of his two handes,
> And thorugh his laboure or thorugh his londe his lyflode
>   wynneth,
> And is trusti of his tailende, taketh but his owne,
> And is not dronkenlew ne dedeignous, Dowel hym folweth.
> Dobet doth ryȝt thus, ac he doth moche more;
> He is as low as a lombe and loueliche of speche,
> And helpeth alle men after that hem nedeth;
> The bagges and the bigurdeles he hath tobroken hem alle
> That the erl Auarous helde and his heires;
> And thus with Mammonaes moneie he hath made hym
>   frendes,
> And is ronne into Religioun and hath rendred the bible,
> And precheth to the people seynt Poules wordes
>   *Libenter suffertis insipientes, cum sitis ipsi sapientes.*
> 'And suffreth the vnwise with ȝow for to libbe',
> And with gladde wille doth hem gode, for so god ȝow
>   hoteth.
> Dobest is aboue bothe and bereth a bisschopes crosse,
> Is hoked on that one ende to halie men fro helle.

---

[55] B. XII. 17–19. Cf. A. XI. 265–267 where information about Dowel is said to be found in the Solomon and Aristotle; there is no mention of contemporary works on mysticism.

[56] Cf. A. XI. 86–91.

A pyke is on that potente to pulte adown the wikked
That wayten any wikkednesse Dowel to tene.
(B. VIII. 80–97. Cf. A. IX. 71–89, C. XI. 78–98)

Here it is stated that Dobet includes all that Dowel does but much more and that Dobest is above both—not necessarily superior in rank or in mystic communion with God, but in the practice of the good life leading to salvation which I believe it was the Dreamer's (and so the poet's) chief concern to find.[57]

[57] I wish to thank Professors P. Hodgson and G. Kane for their helpful discussion and criticism of the subject-matter of this article. They are not, of course, committed to the views expressed. My thanks are also due to the authorities of the British Museum and the University Library, Cambridge for permission to quote from manuscripts in their possession.

10

STRUCTURE OF THE B TEXT OF
PIERS PLOWMAN

T. P. Dunning, C.M.

IT IS NOW very generally agreed that the organizing factors in the B text of *Piers Plowman* are the concepts of the active, contemplative and mixed lives as distinguished by the medieval theologians and spiritual writers. There is, however, no general agreement as to how these factors operate in determining the structure of the poem.[1] Certain questions still present themselves, of which the most insistent is concerned with the relationship between the two main parts into which the poem is divided, the *Visio de Petro Plowman* and the *Vita de Dowel, Dobet et Dobest.* If Dowel, Dobet and Dobest represent the active, contemplative and mixed lives, with what aspect—if any—of the spiritual life

---

Reprinted, by permission of the Clarendon Press, Oxford, from *The Review of English Studies,* N.S., VII (1956), 225–237.

[1] For an excellent summary of the different interpretations of these concepts proposed by critics of the poem, see E. Talbot Donaldson, *Piers Plowman: The C-Text and its Poet* (New Haven, 1949), pp. 156–161; and for an admirable discussion of the various views, see S. S. Hussey, "Langland, Hilton, and the Three Lives," pp. 232–258. Hussey reaches the conclusion that "neither the triad active, contemplative and mixed lives, nor the triad purgative, illuminative and unitive states, nor a combination of the two is completely satisfactory as a definition of Dowel, Dobet and Dobest . . ." (p. 253). The present article will suggest that the definitions of the active, contemplative and mixed lives so far put forward by critics of *Piers Plowman* have not fully taken into account the connotation of those terms in Langland's time.

of man is the *Visio* concerned? And in what sense and to what extent do the three divisions of the *Vita* represent the traditional divisions of the spiritual life?

I hope to show that a closer examination of the terms "active," "contemplative" and "mixed" lives in their fourteenth-century connotation will throw some further light on these questions.

I.

It is first useful to recall that Langland had a vast body of uniform spiritual teaching on which to draw. One of the many services which Pantin's recent work on the English Church in the fourteenth century has accomplished for students of medieval English literature is to make clear how the teaching of the Fathers and doctors had, by that time, become available to a very wide public in a great number of semipopular and popular manuals and compendia.[2]

To understand properly the poet's use of this body of teaching on the Christian life, which is essentially the inner life of the individual, one must take into account the scope and purpose of the poem. The one is indicated in the Prologue, the other in Passus I. From the beginning, Langland shows that his subject is Christian society, or the Church, and that his concern is with the reform of society. It would seem that he largely takes for granted the traditional teaching on the spiritual life of

---

[2] W. A. Pantin, *The English Church in the Fourteenth Century* (Cambridge, 1955), pp. 189–262. I should like to mention three works in particular which became vade mecums of the clergy during the fourteenth century and which I have consulted for this paper: Hugh of Strasbourg's *Compendium Theologicae Veritatis,* a summary of St. Thomas' *Summa,* mentioned by Richard Rolle, and popular for over three hundred years; John of Freiburg's revision of Raymond of Peñafort's *Summa Confessorum,* a useful and most popular compendium of Canon Law, recommended by the pope to every priest engaged in pastoral work; and William of Pagula's *Oculus Sacerdotis,* written *c.* 1320, of which some fifty manuscripts survive in England (Pantin, pp. 195–202; L. E. Boyle, "The *Oculus Sacerdotis* and some other works of William of Pagula," *Trans. Royal Hist. Soc.,* 5th Series, v [1955], 81–110).

the Christian: and while using this as the framework of his poem in such a way as never to distort its systematic character, he constantly modifies it to reflect his preoccupation with (1) Christian society and (2) the society of his own time and its peculiar problems. Two examples may serve to illustrate the point.

The first is from Passus XIX. Here Langland has come to the final stage of the spiritual life: we have moved from contrition, confession and satisfaction through patience and poverty to faith, hope and charity; and now to the Cardinal Virtues. According to the traditional *schema,* the final element of the spiritual equipment is the seven Gifts of the Holy Ghost. But instead of describing these gifts—wisdom, understanding, and the rest, which guide the soul to the higher flights of mysticism —Langland describes the gifts of the Holy Ghost as the talents each man receives for a particular work in the world; and he makes the giving of these gifts the starting point for building up again at the end of his poem that composite picture of Christian society we saw in the Prologue. This time, in Passus XIX, first the ideal, and then, as in the Prologue, the contemporary. And so his end, like Eliot's, is in his beginning.

The other example is from the *Vita de Dowel.* This represents the beginning of the spiritual life proper, and a principal feature of such a beginning, according to all the spiritual writers, is coming to know oneself. In the *Benjamin Major,* for instance, Richard of St. Victor points out in some detail how the knowledge of oneself is first necessary if one wishes to lead a spiritual life worthy of the name. The diversity of our human faculties, the multiplicity of affections, the perpetual mobility of the mind are elements which must be understood if one wishes to control them. Besides, concupiscence having veiled the eye of the intelligence, how are we to distinguish the good from the bad, how can we judge the movements of the heart, how discern their provenance? A reconnaissance of the terrain where one is to exercise the inner life is indispensable. Richard judges that *discretio* and *deliberatio* take charge of that necessary

261

work.[3] It seems that Passus VIII–XII really constitute that phase of the Christian's development where the Dreamer comes to know himself. Scripture says at the beginning of Passus XII, "Multi multa sciunt sed seipsos nesciunt," and the same point is underlined by Imaginatyf throughout Passus XII. One might also refer to the effects of concupiscence on the intelligence, vividly described in Passus XI. This is, however, the framework. Within this framework, Langland has embodied two of the main intellectual preoccupations of his day: the place of learning in the good life and the problem of predestination.[4] These are represented as the chief clouds which obscure the Dreamer's vision of the ground he has to cover.

Such manipulation of the body of traditional teaching presupposes among the poem's first readers a familiarity with the main lines of that teaching. The same assumption underlies the poem's outward structure. Its significance may be better understood by examining the terms "contemplation" and "action."

II.

"The traditional doctrine of the two ways of life, the one of Action, the other of Contemplation, is so clearly suggested in the incident of Martha and Mary that it must be considered to have its origin in the Gospel itself."[5] Nevertheless, during the early centuries, especially at Alexandria, Christian thought on the subject was profoundly influenced by neo-Platonic philoso-

[3] *Benj. Maj.* iii, c. 23, 132 B–C–D. Summarized and discussed in G. Dumeige, *Richard de Saint-Victor et l'idée chrétienne de l'amour* (Paris, 1952), pp. 54–56. "Le 14e siècle est tributaire de la notion de contemplation élaborée durant les siècles précédents: à travers les définitions et les classifications de saint Thomas et de saint Bonaventure, on a conservé notamment la trace de Hugues et de Richard de Saint-Victor" (François Vandenbroucke, *Dict. de Spiritualité* (Paris, 1952), II. 1988).

[4] Discussed in Pantin, pp. 123–135. See also T. P. Dunning, "Langland and the Salvation of the Heathen," *M.Æ.,* XII (1943), 45–54.

[5] H. Bérard, "Action et Contemplation," *Le Vie Spirituelle,* XX (1929), 135. The most comprehensive discussion of this complex subject is in the *Dict. de Spiritualité,* II. 1643–2193. See also P. Pourrat, *Christian Spirituality*, 3 vols., trans. (London, 1922–1926); Dom Cuthbert Butler, *Western Mysticism,* 2nd ed. (London, 1927).

phy. In the pagan tradition, the contemplative life meant a life of study, consecrated to philosophical speculation; the active life, one devoted to external works and especially to political affairs. The influence of this tradition on the Christian theologians at Alexandria may be seen in the high speculative quality they attributed to the contemplative life, by reason of the *gnosis,* which for them distinguished the perfect Christian. Cassian, on the other hand, in resuming the teaching of the Egyptian monks on Christian perfection, puts forward a somewhat different view. The life of the Egyptian cenobites was, in fact, not contemplative in the Alexandrian sense, being very little speculative and very much given up to manual labor. In his fourteenth *Conference,* Cassian divides the contemplative life into two parts, actual and theoretic. By the theoretic (*theoria*), he means the act of contemplation itself. He is quite clear that this act is not continuous: one cannot, as it were, *live* this kind of life. One achieves the act of contemplation from time to time. The actual life is the cultivation of virtues. This is, as it were, the setting of the contemplative life. Cassian does not seem greatly concerned with the precise character of this setting: it may be a hermitage; but it may also be the reception and care of strangers—what we should now call active good works.[6]

It would seem that the teaching of St. Gregory on the spiritual life, from which the Western tradition chiefly derives, is a development of these ideas of Cassian. For "Gregory, the great clerk," as Langland calls him, the active and contemplative lives are not lived separately by two distinct categories of people but should be united in the lives of everyone, for the life of pure contemplation is quite beyond the power of human nature.[7]

[6] Cassian, *Conferences,* tr. Robert (London, 1847), II. Conf. xiv.

[7] St. Gregory's teaching on the spiritual life is to be found chiefly in his *Homilies on Ezechiel* and in his *Morals on Job.* The latter book was written for monks, and Langland refers to it in regard to monks, in Clergye's speech in x. 292–299. The *Homilies,* however, were not addressed to monks, but to the ordinary people of Rome, and they embody the same teaching. In the present article I am indebted to Dom Butler's study of St. Gregory's teaching in *Western Mysticism,* pp. 91–133.

In his view, contemplation is an act wherein the mind, having disengaged itself from the things of this world and fixed its attention on spiritual things, is by a great effort raised above itself to a direct and simple intuition of God, not by a process of reasoning but by a close union of love. This perception of the "unencompassed Light" "as through a chink" is momentary; and then the mind, exhausted by the effort and blinded by the vision of the Light, falls back wearied to its normal state, to recuperate its spiritual strength by exercising the works of the active life, till in due time it can again brace itself for the effort of another act of contemplation.[8]

The contemplative life, then, in St. Gregory's mind, is not that solely which excludes the external works of the active life to devote the greater part of the time to actual contemplation: it is that which has contemplation for its proper end, abstracting altogether from the amount of time given respectively to external works and to prayer. Contemplation is possible in a life crowded with external activity—as were, no doubt, the lives of many of those whom St. Gregory addressed; as were, for instance, the lives of St. Catherine of Siena and St. Bridget of Sweden and other contemporaries of Langland who achieved the highest Christian perfection. St. Gregory's distinction is based on the principle that in the moral order it is the end which specifies the acts. So was begun the great Western tradition of spirituality. St. Bernard, the Victorines, St. Bonaventure and St. Thomas Aquinas are fully in accord with St. Gregory.[9]

[8] *Homilies on Ezechiel,* II. ii, tr. Butler, pp. 93–95. Cf. II. v: Butler, pp. 98–101.

[9] St. Thomas' teaching on the subject is very substantial, comprising not only forty-eight articles in the *Secunda Secundae* of the *Summa,* but also a number of *opuscula* on the Religious Life and the Religious State, ed. R. M. Spiazzi, *Opuscula Theologica S. Thomae Aquinatis, II: de re spirituali* (Rome, 1954). For an analysis of two treatises contemporary with Langland, see W. A. Pantin, "Two Treatises of Uthred of Boldon on the Monastic Life" in *Studies in Medieval History Presented to F. M. Powicke* (Oxford, 1948), pp. 363–385.

The importance of this teaching is that contemplation is open to all: the contemplative life is conceived as the perfection of the ordinary Christian life, charity in a high degree.[10] Some Christians, such as monks and hermits, lead a kind of life which is deliberately ordered toward contemplation as its end: their state will be often referred to as "the contemplative life." Nevertheless, their lives, too, must necessarily be a blend of action and contemplation. And contemplation is not confined to those in the monastic state.

The perfection for which man can hope on earth is, however, only relative, because "as long as we are on earth, there is always room in us for an increase of charity." Hence, "if the perfecting of our spiritual life be nothing else than growth in justice and charity, then its essential law will be progress."[11] This concept of progress brings forward the notion of stages on the journey. These stages were discussed and analyzed by the doctors from early Christian times, and by Langland's time the notion of three main stages in the progress of the soul toward God had become a traditional view. These stages constitute one aspect of the triple division Dowel, Dobet and Dobest.

Since, in St. Gregory's view, the good Christian life at even its highest stage on earth is a blend of action and contemplation,

---

[10] Hence St. Gregory says: "The contemplative life means the keeping of charity towards God and our neighbour, and the fixing of all our desires on our Creator," *Mor. in Job,* vi. 18 (tr. mine). This is the main theme of Langland's poem. "Loue is leche of lyf," says Holy Church at the end of Passus I, "and also the graith gate that goth into heuene" (B. 202–203). Not merely is this theme constantly reiterated throughout the poem and especially stressed when the poet is defining Dowel, Dobet and Dobest, but there will be found a progressive strengthening and deepening of the teaching on Charity, culminating in the speech of the Samaritan in Passus XVII (note particularly ll. 250–292), and having as its climax the Passion and Death of Christ and its redemptive effects, as described in Passus XVIII. Cf. Vandenbroucke in *Dict. de Spiritualité* ii. 1988: "A la suite de saint Bonaventure, sans doute, l'amour prendra au 14e siècle une place prépondérante dans la notion de contemplation."

[11] Pourrat, I, 186–187.

in what sense can Dowel be considered to represent the active life? Or in what sense, if any, does the *Visio* represent the active life, as Coghill would have it?[12]

It must be noted that the terms "action, "active life," as used by St. Gregory, St. Bernard, St. Thomas and other spiritual writers, refer to the *spiritual life:* the "action" denoted is not any kind of action, such as manual labor, but the active practice of virtue. The distinction is not between *otiosa* and *negotiosa:* the good works of the active life are works of religion and devotion.[13] In other words, the active life is the ascetical life.

The active life may be considered under two aspects. First, these good works—vocal prayer, mortification, the service of the neighbor, the practice of the virtues—constitute the normal conditions under which the spiritual life is lived on no matter how high a plane. Whether the spiritual life of any individual have the character of active or contemplative does not depend on the absence of activity but on the presence of contemplation.[14] Secondly, the term active life is used in a more restricted sense. The spiritual writers are agreed that to achieve union with God in prayer we must remove in ourselves the obstacles to the working of God's grace in us. This we do by severe self-discipline in the spiritual formation of our character—that is, by the good works of the active life. In this sense, the active life is a state in which contemplation is not yet present. And in this restricted sense, the active life is conceived as a stage of the spiritual life, the beginning of the spiritual life proper: Dowel. The transition from Dowel to Dobet is the transition from action to contemplation; this is indicated in Passus xv, the Prologue to

[12] "The Character of Piers Plowman," See above, pp. 54–86.

[13] Wells already noted this important point in "The Construction of *Piers Plowman,*" pp. 1–21 above; but it seems to have been largely overlooked by some later writers on the same subject.

[14] Butler, p. 323.

Dobet, though Langland is careful also to indicate that the good works of the active life do not cease to be performed.

Now, there are other works which man must perform which are not works of the spiritual life at all. A consideration of this aspect of man's situation gives us the key to the *Visio*. As St. Paul says, "prius quod animale, deinde quod spirituale" (1 Cor. 15:46). Man is not a pure spirit, but a being composed of soul and body. He therefore finds himself compelled to take thought for the needs of the body. This primary necessity gives rise to the arts and crafts—the provision of food and clothing and all those major occupations which absorb most of the energies of men in civil society. We have only to live to become aware of the imperious demands of this necessity: and *necessitas* is the term St. Bernard, for example, uses for this care or love of the body: a necessity *quae urget nos*. It is to these facts of life Holy Church refers in Passus I. 17–57. This necessity must be distinguished—as Lady Holy Church points out—from another form of carnal love which arises from concupiscence and for which the technical term is *cupiditas*—a cupidity *quae trahit nos*. "As the normal state of the body is health, so the normal state of the heart is purity," or *simplicitas*. "It is unhappily a fact that human desire only very rarely observes the limits of either. Instead of remaining canalized in the bed of natural necessity"— within the limits, that is, set out by Holy Church in Passus I. 20–60—"the will goes off in pursuit of useless pleasures; that is, of pleasures not desired because required for the due exercise (*in mesurable manere*) of the functions that preserve life, but pleasures desired for their own sake as pleasures." That the will has overstepped the limits of natural necessity may be recognized when it has no longer any right reason for its desires: "For riȝtful reson schulde rewle ȝow alle."[15]

---

[15] B. I. 54. See E. Gilson, trans., *The Mystical Theology of St. Bernard* (London, 1955), pp. 40–42, to which I am much indebted in this paragraph.

The first stage, then, in the spiritual journey of man is the limiting of his natural appetites, by reason, within the limits of the *necessitas quae urget nos*—'Measure is medicine', as Lady Holy Church says: and the rejection of Lady Mede, *quae trahit nos* by her meretricious beauty. Most of the folk in the field have been drawn to Lady Mede; but guided by Reasoun, they repent and go to Confession, and then set out in a body to seek St. Truth. Their guide is, appropriately at this stage, a poor ploughman, himself concerned with the provision of the basic necessities of life and whose condition is not one in which he is greatly tempted by cupidity. The way he outlines to Truth is the way of the commandments, the first stage of the active life, the lowest plane of the spiritual life. But having been only just converted from servants of Mede to seekers after Truth, the folk in the field, before they can advance at all, must first be grounded in that carnal love which is of necessity and is therefore legitimate. They must be taught the lesson of Lady Holy Church's opening lines. And so, before the pilgrimage can start, we have in the ploughing of the half-acre an exposition of how the different ranks of society are to be provided with food and clothing in a measurable manner *so that* they may serve God. But the service of God in a positive fashion has not yet begun.

Two points may be noted at the end of B. Passus VI:

(1) It is true that Piers began by outlining a way to Truth; it is, however, merely the beginning of the way, the way of the commandments, the way of those who, as Guillaume de St. Thierry says, "being either moved by authority or stirred by example . . . approve the good as set before them without understanding it."[16] The next stage is where the spiritual life proper begins, when a man starts to progress along this way by

---

[16] *The Golden Epistle of Abbot William of St. Thierry,* tr. Shewring, ed. Dom Justin McCann (London, 1930), p. 27. Cf. Ruysbroeck, *The Seven Steps of the Ladder of Spiritual Love,* tr. F. Sherwood Taylor (London, 1943), pp. 40–43.

beginning to understand the import of some of the truths in which he believes (an understanding that comes to Piers only as a result of Truth's "Pardon," at the very end of the *Visio*). Thus he moves from the *animale* to the *spirituale* and becomes a "rational" man in the spiritual life, as Guillaume puts it. And he moves forward, not merely by the practice of virtues, but "by the progressive understanding of himself and of those things which in the teaching of the faith have been laid before him."[17] This development takes place during the long debates of the *Vita de Dowel*.

(2) The second point to be noted is that the pilgrimage outlined by Piers does *not,* in fact, take place in the *Visio*. The reason is, I think, because the reform of society is not possible on a corporate basis: it is achieved when each individual reforms himself. For Langland, Christian society is the Church, and the reform of the Christian is the beginning and growth of a truly fervent spiritual life. Now the spiritual life by definition is the *inner* life of the individual. This pilgrimage to Truth must be made by each of the folk on his own. It is the *Vita de Dowel, Dobet et Dobest.*

The Pardon episode in Passus VII seems to be clearly a call by God to Piers to lead a truly spiritual life—to move on from the way of the commandments: to do well, in the sense in which St. Gregory and St. Bernard, St. Thomas and St. Bonaventure would interpret *bona agere:* to spend more time in prayer and penance; that is, to progress in Charity by the mortification of desires and the practice of virtue. And the message seems to bring to Piers in a flash a new understanding of old truths: *Fuerunt michi lacrime mee panes die ac nocte. . . . Ne solliciti sitis. . . .* The pardon initiates a new kind of pilgrimage: the progress of the soul in the spiritual life.

The *Visio*, then, is concerned with the *animalis homo* and with the first stage in his regeneration. The *Vita de Dowel, Dobet et Dobest* is concerned with the spiritual life proper. And

[17] *The Golden Epistle*, p. 28.

at the end of Dowel, the people in the plain of Passus V are recalled in the person of Haukyn,[18] and we are reminded that the pilgrimage to Truth has been, in fact, for some time under way, but in a different mode—the only possible one. In this manner, the two parts of the poem are intimately bound together as one whole.

III.

We now come to consider the significance in the poem of the threefold distinction of Dowel, Dobet and Dobest. The poet has guided us here by a number of definitions, for the *Vita* begins with the Dreamer's search for Dowel and his questioning of various characters as to its nature. The definitions which are given may be divided into two main classes. Outside this division fall two definitions which may be termed accidental, and one rather mysterious definition given by Piers Plowman, who reappears in the *Vita de Dobet* as a symbolic figure, representing the human nature of Christ.[19]

First, to consider the two definitions which I have termed "accidental," since they define Dowel in a particular case. The first of these is the tentative definition of the Dreamer toward the end of Passus XI. Dowel, he says, "is to see much and suffer more." Imaginatyf, who has just appeared, tells him that if he *had* suffered, Reasoun would have further explained to him what had already been told him by Clergye. There is clearly no finality about this definition (B. XI. 398–429). The second comes in Passus XIV where Conscience identifies Dowel, Dobet and Dobest with the three parts of the sacrament of Penance —contrition, confession and satisfaction (XIV. 16–24). The meaning appears to be that at this stage the sacrament of Penance is what is most essential for Haukyn. For the sinful man,

---

[18] On the relationship between Passus XIII, XIV and the *Visio,* see the very stimulating article by Stella Maguire, "The Significance of Haukyn, *Activa Vita,* in *Piers Plowman,*" RES, XXV (1949), 97–109.

[19] Piers's definition is reported by Clergye, B. XIII. 118–129.

regeneration begins with this sacrament, which restores the infused virtues of faith, hope and charity, to the soul.[20] And we note that immediately afterwards Conscience does in fact begin to exhort Haukyn to a higher life, to patience, poverty and charity—to the life to which Piers Plowman was called in the *Visio,* by the "Pardon."

To turn now to the two main classes of definitions. The first class consists of:

(1) Definition of Friars, VIII. 18 ff.;
(2) Definitions of Wit, IX. 94–97; 199–206.;
(3) Definitions of Study, X. 129–134; 187–188;
(4) Definitions of Imaginatyf, XII. 30–40.;
(5) Definitions of Patience, XIII. 136–171.

All develop the first definition of the Friars, for all define Dowel, Dobet and Dobest as growth in charity. Patience's definitions not merely end this series, but end the whole series (apart from a reference to Dowel, Dobet and Dobest in the life of Christ in Passus XIX. 104–193). These definitions, then, furnish one aspect—and the chief aspect—of the threefold division of the second poem in the *Liber de Petro Plowman.* The *Vita* is essentially concerned with spiritual reform; this must be the spiritual progress of the individual. We have reference here, then, to the distinction of three main stages in the Christian's progress in the love of God, whether considered, as St. Bonaventure considers them in his book *De Triplici Vita,* as the purgative way, the illuminative way, and the unitive way; or, in the terms of an earlier distinction, the condition of *incipientes,*

---

[20] See, for example, Uthred of Boldon, *De perfectione vivendi:* "Man's *via* is twofold: (1) of first innocence, (2) of *reparacio graciosa* through Christ. By sin, man was wounded in his natural and intellectual powers, and despoiled of gratuitous and moral virtues (cf. *Sent.* dist. ii, c. xxv); by penitence the theological virtues are regained. Perfection consists in the practice of the three theological virtues." (Summary by Pantin, *Studies . . . Presented to F. M. Powicke,* p. 375.)

of *proficientes* and of *perfecti*. The purgative way of St. Bonaventure is concerned with the expulsion of error and sin and leads to peace; the illuminative way is concerned with the deeper knowledge and more exact imitation of Our Lord; the unitive way is the achievement of union with God through the operation of the Holy Ghost.

The second class of definitions comprises:

(1) Those given by Thought in VIII. 78–102;
(2) Wit's first definition—leading on from Thought—in IX. 11–16;
(3) The definitions given by Clergye in X. 230–265;
(4) The definitions of the Doctor, XIII. 115–117.

To these may be added the distinction of Dowel, Dobet and Dobest in the life of Christ, XIX. 104–193.

In considering Langland's point of view in these definitions, we shall be helped by recalling that the phrase "contemplative life" may also denote a manner of corporate living ordered to the primary end of facilitating and promoting the exercise of contemplation; such a state of life is created by the stable observance of the evangelical counsels, by means of vows, publicly taken. This objective state is referred to juridically as "religion" and the members of such a society as "religious."[21] The contemplative life is not the exclusive prerogative of such persons, but in virtue of their vows they are constituted in an objective state of perfection: in *statu perfectionis acquirendae*.[22] Hence they are in the *Vita de Dobet,* but they are not the only persons there: Langland never identifies the *Vita de Dobet* with the religious state. (See Passus XV, Prologue to *Dobet.*)

A higher state than the religious life is the office of a bishop or abbot or other ecclesiastical prelate. This is the most perfect

---

[21] These canonical terms had already become colloquial by the fourteenth century. Langland frequently uses them: see, for example, B. X. 312–313.

[22] St. Thomas Aquinas, *S.T.,* II–III. clxxxiv. 5.

state of all. And here we come to the *only* sense in which the majority of the doctors will use the notion of a "mixed" life of action and contemplation. As we have seen, the contemplative life as actually lived—even in religion—*is* a mixed life, but the relation between action and contemplation in the life of a prelate is a very special one. The function of a prelate is to exercise *spiritual* authority: it is, therefore, as John of Freiburg expresses it, a *magisterium perfectionis* and presupposes perfection.[23] That is to say, it ought to be the overflowing of contemplation. *Contemplata tradere* is the phrase St. Thomas uses of true ecclesiastical government,[24] and the phrase is often repeated in the *Specula* and *Compendia* used in the fourteenth century. Hence a prelate is said to be constituted in *statu perfectionis acquisitae:* in the *Vita de Dobest.*

Priests with the care of souls share in the authority of the bishop, but since they may resign their care at any time (and he may not, unless in very exceptional circumstances), they are not constituted in an objective state of perfection. Juridically, they are in the active life. However, by reason of their functions they are bound to be in a subjective state of perfection.[25] Hence we meet them often in the *Vita de Dowel,* but their functions are discussed with those of religious in the Prologue to *Dobet.*

Walter Hilton inevitably comes in here, but I suggest that in regard to the meaning of Dowel, Dobet and Dobest he will bring only confusion. In the *Scale of Perfection,* written for a religious sister, Hilton distinguishes merely two kinds of life, the active and the contemplative. In his treatise *Mixed Life,* written for a wealthy man living in the world and apparently exercising

---

[23] "Status religionis ad professionem pertinet quasi quedam via tendendi in perfectionem. Status autem episcopalis ad perfectionem pertinet tanquam quoddam perfectionis magisterium." Joannes de Friburgo, *Summa Confessorum,* lib. III, titl. xxviii, questio iiii. Cf. *S.T.* loc. cit., art. 7.

[24] *S.T.* II–II. clxxxix and clxxxv.

[25] *S.T.* II–II. clxxxiv. 8.

a good deal of temporal sovereignty, Hilton seems to liken his reader's state to that of a bishop; and in thus confounding the two, seems to deny to prelates the most perfect state of all.[26] This may be a compliment to his reader, or it may be simply an example of somewhat loose thinking in a popular treatise.[27] Whatever the explanation, Hilton's concept of the mixed life seems not to be found in Langland: a surer guide to Langland's view is given in the extract from the *Meditationes Vitae Christi,* quoted by Wells.[28]

If we now consider the second class of definitions of Dowel, Dobet and Dobest, we may see, foreshadowed in them, the blending in the structure of the *Vita* of the two traditional concepts: the three stages of the soul's progress in the love of God, and the three objective states of life—the active life, the religious life and the life of prelates.

Thought distinguishes the three objective states clearly. In Wit's first definition, Dowel and Dobet are defined in subjective terms, but Dobest is "a bisschopes pere" (IX. 14). We are moving toward the more important concept, that of progress in love, and Wit's further definitions in Passus IX belong to this class. Clergye again defines Dowel and Dobet in general fashion—the contemplative life is not the special prerogative of religious

---

[26] *Mixed Life,* ed. D. Jones in *Minor Works of Walter Hilton* (London, 1929), ch. v, 16–17; ch. vi, 22–23. S. S. Hussey clearly illustrates the discrepancy between Hilton and Langland (esp. pp. 236–240, 242–247). Hussey, however, is surely mistaken in treating Hilton's definition as authoritative: as he notes himself, St. Gregory "recognized all three lives although he never called the mixed life by that name" (p. 237). So did many other doctors, whose views St. Thomas synthesizes in *S.T.* II–II. clxxix–clxxxii. For a writer contemporary with Langland in the same tradition, see Uthred of Boldon in Pantin, pp. 374–380.

[27] It is unlikely that Hilton is here recalling an earlier definition of the mixed life given by St. Augustine, discussed and dismissed—as an unnecessary distinction—by St. Thomas, *S.T.* II–II. clxxix, "Of the division of life into the Active and the Contemplative." See also Butler, pp. 291–304.

[28] Wells, 134–135. The passage is from chap. xlv. See Pseudo-Bonaventure, *Meditations on the Life of Christ,* tr. Sister M. Emmanuel, O.S.B. (London, 1934), pp. 219–220.

nor of priests—but Dobest includes "alle manere prelates" (x. 267). The Doctor's definition in Passus XIII is a general statement of the three juridical states, as we might have expected.

From this examination, it seems that Langland begins in the *Vita* by indicating the pilgrimage of the soul toward God. The first stage in the spiritual life of any individual is an emergence alike from intellectual error and moral disorder. This is the *Vita de Dowel.* I have earlier referred to the dissipation of intellectual error in the first part of *Dowel,* Passus VIII–XII. In Passus XIII we meet moral disorder in the person of Haukyn, and the situation described in Passus V is recalled. As in Passus V, but now in a more explicit manner, this disorder is repaired by the sacrament of Penance. The moral virtues which will sustain Haukyn and also help him to make progress are put before him: Poverty, or the spirit of poverty in some degree, and Patience.[29]

With the Prologue to *Dobet* (Passus XV) we have already progressed. Priests and religious come in for a large share of the discussion, for they make proclamation of leading the con-

---

[29] Of Patience, St. Gregory says: "Perfection springs out of patience. He that maintains patience possesses his soul, in that henceforth he is endued with strength to encounter all adversities so that by overcoming himself he is made master of himself." (*Morals on Job,* v. 33. Oxford tr. i. 266–267). Echoed by St. Thomas in *S.T.* II–II. cxxxvi. 2, ad 2. Langland has already brought out that it is the hardships of life which make it difficult for Haukyn to keep from deadly sin. There is another reference in St. Thomas to patience which seems to indicate the background of Langland's mind here and the link which binds Passus XIII and XIV with V and VI: "The inclination of reason," St. Thomas says, "would prevail in human nature in the state of integrity. But in fallen nature the inclination of concupiscence prevails, because it is dominant in man. Hence man is more prone to bear evils for the sake of goods in which the concupiscence delights here `and now, than to endure evils for the sake of goods to come which are desired in accordance with reason; and yet it is this that pertains to true patience" (*S.T.* II–II. cxxxvi. 3 ad 1. Dominican tr.) Here we have the point of Reasoun's entry into the vision of Mede (Passus IV), and of Reasoun's sermon in Passus V, leading to repentance. Now, Patience is put forward as the virtue which will render his teaching stable and make progress along the road to Truth possible.

templative life. Langland summarizes the discussion conducted through Passus X–XII on the place of Learning in the good life and applies the conclusions to the obligations of the clergy in Christian society. The highest evangelical ideal of poverty, put by Patience before Haukyn, is here presented in practice, in the lives of religious, anchorites and hermits.

We are thus led on to a more comprehensive view of Charity in the *Vita de Dobet*. Perfection is represented in the redemption wrought by Christ and is rightly conceived as a growth in faith, hope and charity in the speech of the Samaritan. Piers Plowman appears as the human nature which the Wisdom of God assumed to redeem mankind.

Then, instead of leading us on to the third stage of the spiritual life, as do Rolle and Hilton, Tauler and Suso, the mystical stage in which the Holy Ghost works unimpeded in the soul, the poet, in the *Vita de Dobest,* quietly turns—as the definitions of Wit and Clergye had foreshadowed—to the third objective state, the life of prelates.

There is no sharp break. There is a gradual moving away from the figure of the Dreamer's progress during the latter part of *Dobet* to the meaning for all men of the Passion and Death of Christ. This is reflected in the objective fashion in which these events are narrated. After the Samaritan's speech to the Dreamer, the objective tone becomes apparent and continues right through Passus XVIII. There the language takes fire, as Langland describes the Redemption by Christ and the Harrowing of Hell in memorable verse, ending with the debate between Mercy and Truth, Peace and Righteousness—a debate traditional since St. Bernard but which again Langland retells in his own way. Then, in the *Vita de Dobest,* while dedicating Passus XIX to the activity of the Holy Ghost and thereby indicating one aspect of Dobest, Langland describes how the Holy Ghost through the agency of Piers builds up the structure of the Church. For unlike Tauler and Suso and Hilton, Langland's concern is not with religious sisters, but with Christian Society.

Piers in XIX and XX represents the ideal pope, in whom Christ continues to be represented on earth, and our attention is drawn to the government of the Church. The blending of the two traditional triple distinctions in the concepts of Dowel, Dobet and Dobest has been extremely well done, and it has been made to serve the poet's purpose in the poem.

The beginning of Dowel is love; by love, love is increased until we come to the perfection of love, which is Dobet; while Dobest is superabundant love, overflowing into the works of the apostolate, cultivating the Christian life in the souls of men and raising the edifice of the Church. Such is the ideal. And it is a traditional one. Almost at once, in Passus XX, Langland recalls the real: the siege-scarred Christendom of his own time, first pictured in the Prologue. And the poem ends with the poet going out into the world to seek, apparently, a true pope who will effect a reform: the Piers Plowman described in *Dobest*.

11

THE IMAGINATIVE UNITY OF
PIERS PLOWMAN*

John J. Lawlor

I.

IT IS TO be hoped that the considerations advanced by Fr. T. P. Dunning in a recent article will win general assent.[1] Fr. Dunning has given in brief space an account of the unity of theme in *Piers Plowman* which should safeguard us from exploring false paths and repeating old errors. In particular, his identification of "active life" with "the spiritual life" will prevent that confusion of "active life" with mere activity, action as opposed to contemplation, in which a good deal of comment upon *Piers Plowman* has been entangled. Much of the difficulty over the "definitions" of the three lives might have been spared if those who followed Wells' decisive lead had observed, as he did, that, in Fr. Dunning's words, "the good works of the active life are works of religion and devotion" (p. 266). There is thus room for the blending of two traditional triads—active, contemplative and "mixed" lives, and purgative, illuminative and unitive ways. Indeed, so far from rejecting the one to provide for the other,[2]

---

* Reprinted, by permission of the Clarendon Press, Oxford, from *The Review of English Studies,* N.S., VIII (1957), 113–126.
    [1] "The Structure of the B-Text of *Piers Plowman"* above, pp. 259–276.
    [2] Professor Howard Meroney, insisting upon the spiritual life as the poet's dominant concern, finds it necessary to reject the triad of "lives" as

we must see their very interdependence if we are to advance at all with the Dreamer. But confusion came from another source, namely Walter Hilton's special conception of mixed life: and here, too, Fr. Dunning does a notable service by showing that "in regard to the meaning of Dowel, Dobet and Dobest [Hilton] will bring only confusion" (p. 273). The recent contribution of S. S. Hussey, in which Hilton's views are taken as authoritative, illustrates the difficulties which beset *Piers Plowman* criticism.[3] Hussey perceives well enough that "active life" must include "much of what Langland's critics usually assign to Dobet." But for him this serves only to throw doubt on any claim for the three lives as truly satisfactory equivalents of Dowel, Dobet and Dobest, a doubt which is reinforced when "the idea of mixed life" (that is Hilton's idea of it) is correctly seen to be "too limited" to apply to Dobest (pp. 232–258 above). The root cause is plain: it is the definitions of the active, contemplative and mixed lives so far put forward by Langland's critics that are at fault.[4] Hussey's contribution is more valuable for his criticism of those definitions than for any firm conclusions he himself can offer, for, correctly understanding the nature of "active life," he cannot see its applicability to Langland's Dowel, a term which, he holds, "must refer to the majority of Christians who have no special religious calling" (p. 243). We are back, though by a less familiar route than usual, at that central stumbling-block of *Piers Plowman* interpretation, the connection between the *Visio* and the *Vita*. There is no possibility of advance until we see that the "doing well" which refers to *all* Christians consists in that conformity to the rule of "riȝtful reson" which the Plowman of the *Visio* at once exemplifies and helps to bring about. This is the necessary con-

"a false and mischievous analogy which has stultified *Piers Plowman* criticism for twenty years." ('The Life and Death of Longe Willie,' *ELH,* xvii [1950] 1–35.)

[3] "Langland, Hilton, and the Three Lives." See pp. 54–86.

[4] Cf. Dunning, p. 259, n. 1.

dition of and the preparation for that further "doing well" which, while it is open to all Christians, is essentially the progress of the individual soul in the spiritual life and thus admits of degrees of "perfection." Hussey is, I am sure, wholly right to stress the penetrating simplicity which invests Langland's term Dowel and hence the progression, Dobet, Dobest. It is evident, above all, in that concern for the *practice* of the Christian life which I comment on below. But we shall be making an impossible demand if we insist that the Christian life, as the Dreamer begins to inquire into it in the *Vita,* must involve no complexities. The truth is that Langland's Dowel is no invariable term. His concern is with right conduct, a "doing well" which, first apprehended as the obedience to God's law required of all men, is deepened into awareness of the spiritual life—that life which may be expressed as obedience to the counsels rather than the commandments, conformity to God's will in the spirit of a son rather than a servant. As such, Langland's "doing well" joins with and becomes indistinguishable from the "doing well" of the spiritual life, and the progression to a "better" in this sphere is easily and naturally achieved. But it is the lasting appeal of Langland's work that in the conclusion he turns aside from the ideal, the "best" of the spiritual life, to the real, the leadership which is required by the suffering and sinful humanity we first encountered in the Prologue. Langland's poem has thus a design all its own: and we rightly reject those "definitions" that would "provide a ready-made guide" to his thought.[5] But we shall make no headway with Langland's thought until we grasp the connection between the "doing well" that is enjoined upon the folk of the *Visio* and the prospect of "doing well" that is revealed to their leader, the Plowman. Fr. Dunning has, I believe, given us the firmest ground we have yet been offered for resolving the purely "doctrinal" question, what is the "theme" or "content" of the *Liber de Petro Plowman* and

[5] Hussey, p. 254.

what is the relationship in those terms between the *Visio de Petro Plowman* and the *Vita de Dowel, Dobet et Dobest?* Langland's theme is "doing well," an insistent probing of man's capacity for the good life; and this is prepared for by presenting in the *Visio* the *animalis homo* and "the first stage in his regeneration."[6]

If this is the relation between *Visio* and *Vita* in terms of Langland's thought we may be better enabled to ask how is this relation effected in the poem?—and thus, of *Piers Plowman* as a whole, by what distinctive appeal to imagination does the poet initiate and conduct the "argument" of his poem? Fr. Dunning has very well demonstrated how Langland, employing "as the framework of his poem" "the traditional teaching on the spiritual life of the Christian," modifies it to his purpose, "his artistic preoccupation with (*a*) Christian society, and (*b*) the society of his own time and its peculiar problems" (p. 261). What that "artistic preoccupation" may be is not part of Fr. Dunning's immediate purpose to inquire. But it should be a question worth raising, for *Piers Plowman* is not a treatise, remarkable only for clothing deep truth and penetrating observation in memorable verse. To be sure, some who have perceived poetry in *Piers Plowman* have yet witheld the designation "poem." C. S. Lewis has praised Langland for "sublimity," and for a "largeness" of vision which pertains to "the intellectual imagination." But Langland, he concludes, "is confused and monotonous, and hardly makes his poetry into a poem."[7] Similarly, G. Kane speaks of a "paradox of total greatness and local failures."[8] A unity of theme, or "doctrine," and hence a mutual relationship of the major parts of the work, will not, assuredly, of themselves serve to counter these objections. We must try to clarify the imaginative appeal of Langland's work—to find, if we can,

---

[6] Dunning, p. 269.

[7] *The Allegory of Love* (Oxford, 1936), pp. 160–161.

[8] *Middle English Literature* (London, 1951), p. 185.

the focus of imaginative attention, the vantage point from which we, with the writer, look out upon his world.

It should be the more useful to make this inquiry in as far as the poem, if there is one, may need to be rescued from over-much elucidation. A work as long as *Piers Plowman,* in its B and C texts, and as comprehensive in its main issues may well reward approaches from widely differing standpoints. But critical evaluation is likely to fare ill in this pressure of interests.[9] There is a further consideration. Readers—not always untutored—who have been conscious of the explorations as well as the affirmations that the work contains have thought of *Piers Plowman* as a kind of spiritual autobiography, in which the author hammers out his best understanding of what often appears to puzzle and even, sometimes, to elude him. Against these, there have not been lacking interpreters who, rightly insisting upon a body of traditional teaching informing Langland's thought, seem at times to come very close to suggesting that Langland is a writer of clear purpose, involving his readers in perplexities that were for him only apparent, in order to win their better understanding. It is, unless I am greatly mistaken, to the second group that Fr. Dunning belongs, in his maintaining that Langland "largely takes for granted the traditional teaching on the spiritual life of the Christian" (pp. 260–261). The question here is not one of degree (the mere extent, covered by Fr. Dunning's "largely," to which Langland might be thought *not* to "take for granted" traditional teaching) but rather of kind, the kind of activity we are to envisage in the writer. It would require a considerable hardihood on our part to discredit Langland when he tells us of his setbacks and vexations, the problems he cannot

[9] As Kane observes, "To consider *Piers Plowman* as a poem is not only the safest but also the most fruitful means of studying it, and should precede the detailed consideration of its single features and qualities." It may, however, be felt that Kane's attempt "to isolate the main features" of the poet's "personality" is itself allowed, unhappily, to precede consideration of the poem (pp. 185, 192).

solve as well as the truths he can confidently affirm. Yet it is true that his "teaching" at all points appears conformable to what had long been maintained and was more generally accessible in his own day than has always been realized.[10] The question is, finally considered, insoluble: but in its present terms it is certainly ill put. The mere dichotomy—"Poem or Autobiography?"—will never take us very far, but with some kinds of poem we can hardly apply it all. If, then, we can see what imaginative unity *Piers Plowman* may have, we must go on to determine the kind of poem we have been dealing with.

II.

It will be best to begin with the *Vita de Dowel,* not only because it is, by common consent, one of the most difficult parts of the whole work, but because in it we are given some account of the Dreamer himself, pondering the significance of what has been seen in the *Visio,* and in that pondering some of the problems which the Dreamer presents as vexing him are well to the fore. What deserves our notice at once is the series of rebuffs the Dreamer receives from the authoritative persons he interrogates after his first colloquy, that with the Friars. From the Friars he has received practical counsel in the parable of the man in the storm-tossed boat—counsel which is designed to turn the inquirer away from the high theoretical question— how shall a man avoid sin?—to the humbler recognition of common experience implied in the distinction between sins of frailty and deliberate sins. The Dreamer is not content, and seeks to know more; but we should note, in view of the scold-

---

[10] Fr. Dunning (p. 260) draws attention to W. A. Pantin's account of manuals of instruction for parish priests and vernacular religious and moral treatises (*The English Church in the Fourteenth Century* [Cambridge, 1955], pp. 189–243). Pantin's general observation (p. 189) is especially worth pondering: "It is impossible to exaggerate the importance of the educated layman in late medieval ecclesiastical history." For a treatment of the "intellectual history" thus involved, see G. de Lagarde, *La Naissance de l'esprit laïque au déclin du Moyen Age* (Paris, 1934–).

ings he is to receive, that all he seeks to know is where he can find Dowel, so that, as he humbly says, he may learn of these high matters by direct observation: "if I may lyue and loke. I shal go lerne bettere" (VIII. 58).[11] It is a sentiment which is repeated after Thought's "explanation":

> I coueite to lerne
> How Dowel, Dobet, and Dobest · don amonges the peple.
>
> (VIII. 108–109)

Wit's account of the matter is no more helpful to this Dreamer who seeks examples from practice. In the wooden allegory of Sir Dowel inhabiting the Castle of Kind, we may detect a similarity to the Plowman's allegory of the ten commandments, delivered to the Pilgrims of the *Visio*. In either case, the predicament of the listener is the same. Like the Pilgrims, the Dreamer seeks a living embodiment of the good, not mere discourse, however apt. It is therefore a striking irony that Dame Study, waiting with unconcealed impatience for the end of Wit's discourse, should soundly berate the Dreamer as a seeker after mere knowledge. But the irony is deepened when we perceive that the Dreamer is eventually drawn into debate, so that Study's warning against high speculation, unfairly levelled at the Dreamer on first encounter, is later amply justified. Her very words, "Non plus sapere quam oportet" (x. 116), are repeated at the end of the *Vita de Dowel* by Anima, rebuking a Dreamer who has sought to know all (xv. 63–67). Similarly, Imaginatyf is able to point, unopposed, the moral of the Dreamer's experience:

> for thine entermetyng · here artow forsake,
> *Philosophus esses, si tacuisses.*
>
> (XI. 406)

We see very readily that, in his being drawn into debate, the Dreamer has fulfilled Clergye's prediction:

> The were lef to lerne · but loth for to stodie.
> Thou woldest konne that I can · and carpen hit after,

---

[11] Except as otherwise indicated, all references are to the B text.

Presumptuowsly, parauenture · a-pose so manye,
That hit myȝthe turne me to tene · and Theologie bothe.

(A. XII. 6–8)

As Miss Maguire has remarked, in an article which firmly grasps
the tension between the speculative and the practical in the *Vita
de Dowel,* the Dreamer we meet at the beginning of Passus
XIII "still seems to hold to his faith in the possibility of an intellectual resolution of his problems." So, as she observes, the
turning point must come with the entry of a moral virtue, Patience, upon the scene of the Banquet.[12] But we should not fail
to notice that experience itself has already given the Dreamer
a foretaste of patience. At his meeting with Imaginatyf he could
ruefully contribute his own finding concerning Dowel: "To se
moche and suffre more · certes', quod I, 'is Dowel!' (XI. 402).
If we look back, we see that the Dreamer is one who has been
drawn aside from his original purpose, from the question where
is Dowel to discourse upon what is Dowel. But the situation in
which he was placed, *vis-à-vis* Wit, Study etc. is not simple;
rather, it is one of cross-purpose. Just as his interlocutors mistrusted him, a seeker, as it appeared, after mere knowledge, so
the Dreamer mistrusted them, the learned and authoritative.
Christ was a carpenter's son; what, then, is the place of learning in the good life? In this, of course, Langland is echoing
controversies of his own day,[13] but it is his achievement to communicate the universal sense of unchangeable cross-purpose
between authority and the ardent inquirer. So we follow a
Dreamer who, meeting no direct answer to the over-simple
question he proposes, finds himself involved in debate, to reach
that point of ultimate weariness, foretold by Study, where all
exercise of reason threatens to appear as profitless subtilizing:

The more I muse there-inne · the mistier it semeth

[12] "The Significance of Haukyn, *Activa Vita,* in *Piers Plowman,*"
RES, xxv (1949), 99–100.
[13] See Pantin, pp. 123–135.

And the depper I deuyne · the derker me it thinketh;
Is is no science for sothe · forto sotyle inne.

(x. 181–183)

He must learn to be constant to his own initial purpose, the search for a truth revealed in practice, but it is no easy matter. It is his final lesson, at the hands of Anima, that the search for knowledge may be not merely immoderate but even positively harmful: for

the more that a man · of good mater hereth
But he do ther-after · it doth hym double scathe.

(xv. 57–58)

In all this the Dreamer has been less fortunate than the repentant sinners of the *Visio*. They found a guide in the Plowman who is "of flessh oure brother." The Dreamer's questioning will avail him little until, all subtilizing exhausted, he is brought to contemplate Incarnate Deity, the Savior who

wole Iuste in Piers armes,
In his helme and in his haberioun · *humana natura*.

(xviii. 22–23)

It is the last irony that those he had interrogated at the very outset of his journey had given a sufficient answer to his desire to find examples from practice:

'I have no kynde knowyng', quod I · 'to conceyue alle ʒowre
wordes,
Ac if I may lyue and loke · I shal go lerne bettere'.
'I bikenne the Cryst', quod he · 'that on the crosse deyde'.

(viii. 57–59)

The imaginative appeal of the *Vita* in its whole extent resides not in any answer to the Dreamer's inquirings, though there is, as we have seen, a decisive turn in the *Vita de Dowel* when the shift is made from speculative to practical considerations. The truly imaginative appeal is in the very failure of inquiry so long as the initiative is with the Dreamer. It is he, who at the outset insisted on the practice of the good life, who is in the end brought to understand what his earlier interlocutors had doggedly maintained as the ground of their reserve toward him —that practice is all. Then, and only then, is he ready to apprehend as vision what eluded him as discourse. And this, in its turn, will mean that his search, so far from ending, must have a new beginning.

III.

If this is the imaginative appeal, what is its focus? What particular aspect of human nature serves as an entry upon and sustains the *Vita*? To answer that question, we may with advantage turn back to the beginning of Langland's work as a whole, not only to see afresh the relation of *Visio* and *Vita* but to place the rebukes of the *Vita de Dowel* in their full setting. In the Prologue, the Dreamer has acutely observed a world whose law is self-interest; now, in the first Passus of the *Visio,* Holy Church is to "explain." In doing so she will encounter questions from the Dreamer which are inappropriate to his understanding, for the Dreamer desires all-embracing answers, but his gaze is directed outwards, while the real situation requiring redress is within the heart of man. The colloquy deserves to be taken in some detail, for it contains indications which are central to our inquiry.

Holy Church, as yet unknown to the Dreamer, begins with the simple and sufficient statement that to do right is to live according to Truth's teaching, and this is at once given its particular application to the world the Dreamer has seen—men are to observe "mesure" in the use of creature comforts. The Dreamer at once asks a large question—and this is to be characteristic of him: to whom does the wealth of the world belong? The answer is, as was Holy Church's first statement, that the individual is to look to himself: he is to render unto Caesar the things that are Caesar's. As she concludes her "explanation" of the "field," the Dreamer asks her who she is, and the reply he receives carries its own mild reproof:

'Holicherche I am', quod she · 'thow ouȝtest me to knowe,
I vnderfonge the firste · and the feyth tauȝte'.

(I. 75–76)

The Dreamer at once cries to be taught how to save his soul. Holy Church's answer is in keeping with baptismal simplicity. Those who do good and purpose no evil to their fellow men shall have their reward. What she adds is very important for the implications that are later to come to the Dreamer of the *Vita de Dowel;* the truth she has uttered is common knowledge to all men, Christian and Pagan alike: "cristene and vncristne. clameth it vchone" (I. 93). We should not miss the gentle rebuke that this implies. But it is not dwelt upon: Holy Church continues by emphasizing the obedience to Truth which all men must give and concludes that those whose actions show their true faith will go to heaven where Truth is enthroned. Nothing simpler or more directly connected with the practice of the individual soul could be conceived. But the Dreamer responds with another of his large questions—how does Truth come to man— and disclaims any natural knowledge upon the point; he does not know "By what craft in my corps. it comseth and where" (I. 137).[14] Now Holy Church is less gentle: how stupid, she declares, to say he does not know something revealed by common experience! This is the first scolding the Dreamer receives, and the first of many that are to come in the *Vita de Dowel*. An apparently radical question has been asked, and the answer is, in effect, "look in your heart." Something known to all men has been overlooked by this searcher after knowledge:

'It is a kynde knowyng', quod he · 'that kenneth in thine herte
For to louye thi lorde · leuer than thi-selue;
No dedly synne to do · dey thouȝ thow sholdest.'

[14] The C text has the sadder recognition, "By what wey hit wexith and wheder out of my menyng."

288

The Dreamer's question is foolishness indeed. But he is not left without one concession to his desire for knowledge. Holy Church concludes,

> 'This I trowe be treuthe · who can teche the better,
> Loke thow suffre hym to sey · and sithen lere it after.
> For thus witnesseth his worde · worche thow there-after.'
>
> (i. 140–145)

The lesson should be clear to the reader, if it is long in coming to the Dreamer. There is something "better" than this "treuthe" —not better than truth, absolutely considered, but better than the truth that is all that can be revealed to the Dreamer in his present condition. And in the moment that Holy Church withholds the "better" she gives her reasons for doing so: it is a teaching which must be carefully attended to, and it must be *practiced*. At the outset of the work, the Dreamer is established for the purposes of the poem in one line by both the neat glance at his impetuosity—"suffer hym to sey"—and the sterner counsel to pass from theoretical inquiry to earnest application. We are prepared for the last lesson the Dreamer of the *Vita de Dowel* is to grasp. In him the desire to intervene, to search out the imagined heart of the problem, consistently overbears the simple and prior necessity of an individual attempt to practice the life about which he would know all. Again, the vexation of Holy Church with this inquirer who overlooks the knowledge written ineffaceably in his own heart may remind us of the "pure tene" of the Plowman when realization[15] breaks upon him. The focus of imaginative attention in *Piers Plowman* is upon our habitual incapacity to grasp that what we know as doctrine bears directly upon us, and hence our search for a truth which shall be comprehensive while in fact, and all unwittingly, we would exclude ourselves from the reckoning.

---

[15] I keep this term "realization" throughout in order to stress the imaginative appeal the poet achieves. In terms strictly applicable to the spiritual life, the word "conversion" may be used, always provided that it is not misunderstood as a "turning from" unbelief to the Christian faith.

What I have called the "focus" of imaginative attention is therefore perfectly adapted to the doctrines the poet communicates. As Fr. Dunning observes, a "principal feature" of beginning "the spiritual life proper" "according to all the spiritual writers, is coming to know oneself." Some men, at the outset, will "approve the good as set before them without understanding it"; and progress is made when a man begins "to understand the import of some of the truths in which he believes." When the transition is made from the *animale* to the *spirituale,* man moves forward, "by the progressive understanding of himself and of those things which in the teaching of the faith have been laid before him" (pp. 261, 268–269).

We begin to see that Langland's work offers a remarkable combination. His theme is of the greatest solemnity: man is a creature destined for regeneration. Hence we have the distinctive appeal to imagination—vision must show forth what remains hidden to discursive thinking. But it is Langland's genius to initiate and conduct his poetic argument by showing us man as determinedly ratiocinative, seeking the causes of all things and overlooking what lies nearest home. The kind of poem we are dealing with is thus not easily determined. If we approach it by asking what is the poet's dominant faculty, we must answer, in however unfashionable terms, the satiric intelligence.

IV.

The satire abounding in the *Visio* is not always squarely faced by critics elaborating a claim for the unity of *Piers Plowman.* True, there is general recognition that the perception of widespread wickedness prompts, by a natural reaction, the question "how may I save my soul?" But the connection between *Visio* and *Vita* may be thought to go deeper. Certainly, if we are to claim for *Piers Plowman* an imaginative unity, we must ask again how the work of the satirist is related to the thinker's task of construction. Some critics may feel that the satire of the *Visio* is an involuntary concession to the age in which Langland wrote, and it is noticeable that as scholarship has attended closely to *Piers Plowman* it has become increasingly absorbed in the matter of the *Vita* in its three great divisions. We are so much concerned with the issues Langland unfolds that we may be in danger of neglecting the simplicity with which he begins. Lewis states clearly what is implied by others when he invites us to consider Langland in these terms:

> He is writing a moral poem, such as Gower's *Miroir de l'homme* or Gower's Prologue to the *Confessio Amantis,* and throwing in, as any other medieval poet might have done, a good deal of satire on various "estates." (p. 158)

This is a striking reaction from those earliest critics who, dwelling with satisfaction on the poet's more obvious satirical targets, hailed him as a great reformer and thus, in Fuller's phrase, "by *Prolepsis* a Protestant." But each side misses the mark, for Langland's satire is more radical than Lewis allows, and covers a wider range than Fuller perceived. What is central to Langland's whole design is the observed discrepancy between what we believe and what in fact we are. His poem has its focus in this aspect of the human condition. He therefore proceeds at the outset of the poem by way of external observation—the misdeeds of others—until he has amply shown the necessity of repentance. At this stage, he advances a step farther in the whole inquiry by bringing forward the one good man the world of his poem can produce in its deepest need—only to humble him. In the realization that comes upon Piers we may see that we have not reached a final limit when goodness is found—for the goodness is now seen to be relative: the only absolute is Perfection. The Plowman who began by instructing others in the way of law (the stiff, signpost-like allegory of the commandments in Passus v) has perceived that the law condemns unless it is perfectly fulfilled. He therefore turns—or rather, he is turned—away from justice to the Divine Mercy, and his "confession of evil works" is, in St. Augustine's phrase, "the beginning of good works." For Piers there has opened a road to the Promised Land which leads beyond Sinai.

The satire of the *Visio* is emphatically not "thrown in." Langland, indeed, begins well within the customary usages of satire. But his genius is to carry the argument beyond those limits. If all men profess the truth and few appear to practice it, we must pass from censure to inquiry, for this universal condition must make us ask, what is man's capacity for the good life? It is in that light that we see the shortcomings of the best man the world of the *Visio* could produce, the Plowman whose pardon brings an equal and undeviating assurance of reward and punishment. And it is thus that we are prepared for the next appearance of "Piers Plowman"; for it is the Redemption, perfectly fulfilling inexorable law, which allows the Plowman to seek a mercy which is also justice. But the satiric intelligence has not done: what we have seen in the *Visio* is slow to declare itself to the Dreamer of the *Vita de Dowel*. In Langland, imagination and logic are uniquely joined: his characteristic capacity is to imagine absolutely. The pardon that is a "pardon" only on condition that law can exact no punishment reveals the external world for what it is in the moment that we pass beyond it. There remains the Dreamer, hitherto the observer, on whom realization is yet to fall, and throughout the *Vita de Dowel* there is the continual play of a satiric intelligence that comes upon us at many turns and with a varying range of effect—from tonic scorn and impassioned rebuke to the practiced facility of the dialectician in whose mind there is always ready to start up the *contra!* of swift objection. Langland appears to have solved a capital problem, to communicate in imaginative and poetic terms the central riddle of our experience. It is not only that we everywhere approve and seldom practice the good: much more, it is that the realization of our own predicament is the last discovery we make. The Dreamer searches long and confusedly for what the Plowman saw in a moment: but the Plowman was ready for this knowledge, by reason of his long perseverance in simple well-doing. The strength of the *Vita de Dowel, Dobet et Dobest* is that the Dreamer in his turn is *brought* to know the truth when all his efforts have been apparently fruitless. He must contemplate Incarnate Deity before his ultimate questioning is at rest. But he is then freed to continue his own pilgrimage, long postponed, to find the human creature who comes closest to the ideal. Langland's poem propounds an answer not to the simple, though profound, question—how do we know ourselves?—but to the question which lies closer to real experience—how shall we be brought to know ourselves?

To put the primary difficulty in Fr. Dunning's words,

> ... how are we to distinguish the good from the bad, how can we judge the movements of the heart, how discern their provenance? A reconnaissance of the terrain where one is to exercise the inner life is indispensable. (p. 261).

Langland's "answer" is in effect twofold. Firstly, that we "distinguish the good from the bad" all too easily—where others are concerned. This is his *Visio,* where the reader, with the Dreamer, is the spectator of vice and folly. But when we think we have found a good man, then the standard that is at once in question will surprise us into examining not the vices of others, but our own. The reader is involved in this development in a way comparable with that employed in *Gulliver's Travels.* In each instance, the standpoint of the observer is decisively shifted. Dislodged from a comfortable vantage point, our guide, and thus, find ourselves involved, no longer able to interpose between ourselves and reality that "glass wherein beholders do generally discover everybody's face but their own." But what for Gulliver comes as a progressive understanding in a world of sober discourse comes to the Dreamer all at once as action on the part of the Plowman—an action which continues to perplex the Dreamer until action is perfected in the Crucifixion and made triumphant in the Harrowing of Hell. The logical imagination of Langland can move easily from sardonic observation to exalted wonder. The quality of his poetry is an unswerving fidelity to the facts of particular experience: for its center is in the hard fact that the human condition is to find self-knowledge the all-but-impossible undertaking. Of this kind of poem we are tempted to say that the poet succeeds by calling Reasoun to the aid of Imagination.

V.

Piers Plowman, then, appears to traverse two major kinds of poetry to which we are accustomed. On the one hand, its greatest things, as Lewis has observed, come from the region of "the 'intellectual imagination.' " So, we may add, does its continuing energy, the play of a logical imagination in a predominantly satiric mode. But this introduces us to the other aspect in which the poem must be viewed. The satire is concerned with the truths we claim to know and yet do not apprehend: so, at the turning points, vision must play the decisive part. Thus, for some modern readers great Romantic poetry may be the best entry upon the complexity of experience to which *Piers Plowman* is faithful—the penetrating simplicity of "realization," and its uncovenanted nature, the sharpness of the sense of defeat—which at once redoubles awareness of what we seek while it falsifies all our contriving—and, rarely but centrally, the exaltation of vision. We must not classify Langland's work with the poetry that merely expounds a system of beliefs. It is in its essentials more like that genuinely new "kind" for which the treatise poem of the eighteenth century prepares a way—a poety which is concerned not with the exposition of doctrine as a contribution to the reader's knowledge but with the individual reader's apprehension of truth, his growing into awareness, as the poem proceeds, of a path inescapably opening before him. These different kinds may resemble each other at certain points, and we run the risk of confusing them whenever we paraphrase for discussion their "content." It could hardly be otherwise when the poet himself cannot adequately safeguard from misinterpretation his theme of "Imagination,"

> Power so called
> Through sad incompetence of human speech.

But there is yet a difference between *The Pleasures of Imagination* and *The Prelude* which is not merely the difference between a greater poet and a less. Fr. Dunning does well to recall us from an unreflecting acceptance of *Piers Plowman* as spiritual autobiography. But we must not be diverted from the real center of imaginative excitement, the difference between "knowledge" and "realization," between the doctrines so long accepted and the significances at last apprehended. We may well, if we choose, identify the poet behind the Dreamer, maneuvering the reader through his guide until vision is inescapable. But we should be very sure that we allow for the activity of the poem itself, bringing to the poet, in the act of telling, new relations and significances. Our criticism will be beside the mark if we do not see that the poem succeeds by communicating the mind, not behind, but *in* the poem—a poem which is always, in a sense, unfinished. As it is a poem piercingly clear in its central issues, so it is multiple in its implications.

It is with those "implications" that we encounter the charge of passages that are "confused and monotonous," the "paradox of total greatness and local failures"; and we shall do well to heed Tillyard's warning that it is possible to be "too tolerant of Langland's repetitions and irrelevant moralising."[16] Not everything in Langland can be defended: indeed, one would wish to hear less in some modern criticism of Langland as a mastercraftsman of multiple allegorical meanings, perception of which will somehow enable us to see merit in what might otherwise appear otiose or redundant. But before judgment is given on such particular passages as appear faulty, it would be as well to

---

[16] *The English Epic and its Background* (London, 1954), p. 168.

place them in the setting of Langland's whole endeavor. His undertaking must be not merely to state the apparent perplexities and nearly insoluble difficulties, but to communicate the very sense of weariness and apparent purposelessness that any stage of the journey may afford, if it is looked at neither from the end nor the beginning, but as it was encountered. Perhaps, too, our modern practice of concentrating upon the *Vita de Dowel, Dobet et Dobest* increases the difficulty of apprehending the whole work serially, experiencing its crises as they occur and not as they may be extracted from their setting for the purposes of cross-reference and detailed comparison. It is the merit of Langland's poem that we share the sense of confusion and apparent repetition of experience, for how otherwise shall we see that man must be brought to simple practice? But this is not to claim that Langland works of set purpose and in thorough detail, like a modern artist who would communicate the sense of reality as complex and ambiguous by fostering a degree of complexity and ambiguity in the very communication itself. There is no question of that capital verdict of criticism, *pauper videri Cinna vult et est pauper.* Langland is faithful to a central purpose, our blindness to what resists all our inquiry until we are brought to practice it, and for this fidelity we may be thankful. When penetrating clarity and largeness of vision are found side by side with the very taste of purposelessness we may feel that what is monotonous and confused is the necessary, but excessively rare, complement of those heights of "intellectual imagination" which thereby gain in authenticity and are saved from any suspicion of the merely austere.

In the same way, our understanding of Langland will be sounder if, as we come to judgement, we can concern ourselves less with the doctrines with which the Dreamer wrestles and more with the nature of his progress toward his goal. The poem deals in mysteries, but the focus of attention is not upon man's ignorance of what is too dark for him; it is upon his insentience of what has been brought into the light of common day. Langland's poem thus succeeds in communicating not a cumulative effect of discursive thinking, but the very pressure of experience itself. However it may have been with Langland himself, his Dreamer is one who is forced, in the words of a later allegorist, "not to propound, but to live through, a sort of ontological proof."[17] Langland's hand is there, certainly: but it is his greatest single achievement that at the turning points we see that the preparation is not the creature's but the Creator's. Until the living example is set before us, all our inquiries serve only to mislead. So the Plowman, and after him the Savior Himself, are sent to meet our need. It is thus fitting that the Dreamer goes forth at the end to seek a true exemplar. Langland's last and most individual stroke is in deepest conformity with his whole design. By it he draws that design conclusively away from a formal into a truly imaginative unity.

[17] C. S. Lewis, *The Pilgrim's Regress* (London, 1943), p. 10.

12

THE *VISIO* AND THE PARDON SCENE*

Robert Worth Frank, Jr.

THE TWO VISIONS of the first part [of *Piers Plowman*] quite obviously form an artistic whole. Their title, the *Visio,* is evidence of this unity. They have, also, unity of place and time. The Dreamer falls asleep in the Malvern Hills at the beginning of the first vision and awakens there, "meatless and moneyless," when the second vision has ended.[1] We hear no more of the Malvern Hills in the poem. Moreover the field of folk is the scene on which the curtain rises for both visions;[2] we never see the field again. The action of these two visions takes place within a single day. The Dreamer falls asleep on a May morning, with the sun in the east, wakens for a moment, dreams again, and wakens from the second dream in the late afternoon, with the sun setting "in the south."[3] These unities bind the two visions.

This artistic unity is the reflection of a thematic unity. It is a

* Reprinted, by permission, from *Piers Plowman and the Scheme of Salvation: An Interpretation of Dowel, Dobet, and Dobest* (New Haven: Yale University Press, 1957), pp. 19–33.

[1] A. Pr. 5, VIII. 130; B. Pr. 5, VII. 141; C. I. 6, X. 295.

[2] A. Pr. 17, I. 2, V. 10; B. Pr. 17, I. 2, V. 10; C. I. 19, II. 2, VI. 3.

[3] This is the time scheme in A and B: cf. A. Pr. 5, 13, V. 5–8, VIII. 129; B. Pr. 5, 13, V. 5–8, VII. 140. The unity of time is destroyed in C by the long interlude between the first and second visions: C. VI. 1–108. But as in A and B the Dreamer falls asleep for the first vision in the morning (C. I. 6, 14) and awakens after the Pardon Scene in the late afternoon (C. X. 294).

view of man and his world that we have in the *Visio*. Its theme is man working in this world toward an eternal punishment or reward. The two visions are a dramatization of the way to damnation and the way to salvation. The theme is introduced figuratively in the field of folk and explicitly in the speech of Holy Church. The field of folk midway between the tower and the dungeon are the people of this world, Holy Church explains, their lives bounded by good and evil. The way to salvation is to follow Truth—that is, to love God and man. The way to damnation is to follow Wrong or False; specifically, to follow Lady Mede, to love worldly reward above all else (I. I–II. 50). The poet is stating the basic Christian doctrine: "These two loves, Charity and cupidity, are the two poles of the medieval Christian scale of values."[4]

Mede is for the poet the most evil and specific form which cupidity assumes in this world. Throughout Holy Church's speech, which is a guide to the doctrinal content of the *Visio,* Truth (the law of love) and money are the polar elements. Money belongs to Caesar; it is not God's. The polarity is most evident in the play on the word "treasure." Treasure is money, meed, worldly reward, but treasure is also the greatest good, truth.[5] In the narrative of Lady Mede, the poet dramatizes this pernicious and pervasive desire for worldly reward. There is an obvious contrast between the two ladies the Dreamer meets: Holy Church, the purveyor of right doctrine, "A Loueli ladi of lere in lynnen yclothed," and Lady Mede, the seductress of mankind, clothed in a rich scarlet robe lined with fur and covered with gems.[6] Holy Church warns the Dreamer against Lady

[4] D. W. Robertson, "The Doctrine of Charity in Medieval Literary Gardens: A Topical Approach through Symbolism and Allegory," *Spec.,* XXVI (1951), 24.

[5] I. 45, 56, 70, 83, 85, 133, 135, 205–206. See the discussion of *temporalia* in Robertson and Huppé, *Scriptural Tradition,* pp. 38–48, for some of the Church's teachings on the subject.

[6] I. 3; II. 7–17. There is an interesting discussion of Lady Mede's clothing in Robertson and Huppé, pp. 50–52.

Mede and tells him charity and meed are antithetical and inimical principles:

> And what man be merciful · and lelly me loue,
> Schal be my lorde and I his leef · in the heiȝe heuene.
> And what man taketh Mede · myne hed dar I legge,
> That he shal lese for his loue · a lappe of *caritatis*.
>
> (II. 32–35)

The specific charge against Lady Mede is that she corrupts law in this world, and a good part of the narrative develops this charge. Many of the characters and personifications introduced belong to the machinery of law; (II. 58–63, 163–164 ff.) judges are bribed; (III. 12–25) Peace, who has a complaint against Wrong, is bought off with a present "al of pure golde";[7] and the narrative ends with a judgment handed down by Reasoun (IV. 113–148). But the corruption of man-made law by Mede suggests, if it does not symbolize, Mede's corruption of divine law. And in fact the narrative and the speeches are constantly reaching out to show the evil influence of Lady Mede in other aspects of human life. Most striking is the scene where Mede corrupts the friars and the sacrament of confession (III. 35–63). In his speech rejecting Lady Mede, Conscience attacks her as a universally destructive force, not as a corrupter of law alone; and he analyzes meed as the cause of the damnation of human souls and contrasts it with another kind of meed, salvation. This larger implication of the Lady Mede episode is evident in what might be called the poet's text for the vision, the fifteenth Psalm (fourteenth in the Vulgate):

> Domine quis habitabit in tabernaculo tuo? aut quis requiescet in monte sancto tuo? Qui ingreditur sine macula, et operatur iustitiam: Qui loquitur veritatem in corde suo, qui non egit dolum in lingua sua: Nec fecit proximo suo malum, et opprobrium non accepit aduersus proximos suos. Ad nihilum deductus est in conspectu eius malignus: timentes autem Dominum glorificat: Qui

---

[7] IV. 47–103, esp. 94–103.

iurat proximo suo, et non decipit, qui pecuniam suam non dedit ad vsuram, et munera super innocentem non accepit: Qui facit haec, non mouebitur in aeternum.[8]

The issue in the Lady Mede episode, therefore, is more than political and legal reform. The issue is salvation, and worldly reward is condemned because it leads to damnation. The conclusion of the episode, in which Wrong is punished and Mede is driven out by Conscience and Reasoun (IV. 171–195) preaches the lesson that mankind can control the desire for worldly reward and check the drift toward damnation by following the dictates of conscience and reason. In this way man will keep the divine law. At the same time he will keep man-made law. (The machinery of law, and the king himself, must be ruled by these faculties of reason and conscience.) Both Conscience and Reasoun in their speeches before the king describe the day when meed no longer rules as an era of universal peace and love, in which the divine law of love will be maintained on earth:

> Shal na more Mede · be maistre, as she is nouthe,
> Ac loue and lowenesse · and lewte togederes,
> Thise shul be maistres on molde · treuthe to saue.[9]

The second vision of the *Visio* shows how the field of folk can begin to follow Truth and move toward salvation. First there must be repentance, the necessary prologue to all right action. Repentance comes in response to the voice of reason, which exhorts man to mend his ways, perform dutifully the tasks to which God has called him in this world, and follow Truth (v. 11–60). Repentance's work is the great confession of the deadly sins, where man's evil ways are spread before him until he weeps for forgiveness, promises to reform and begs to know the way to Truth. (v. 61–519).

---

[8] The edition of the Vulgate used in this essay is *Biblia Sacra Vulgatae Editionis,* ed. P. Michael Hetzenauer, 2d ed., rev. (Ratisbon and Rome), 1922.

[9] III. 288–290. For the whole passage see 282–322

The confession scene is dramatic rather than doctrinal. Its vivid portraits and realistic sketches of medieval life have made it a grab bag of quotations for the social historian. The long scene does more than illustrate and entertain, however. Lady Mede's scandalous career was a vision of cupidity; the confession scene is larger in scope than this: its theme is sinfulness. Cupidity may be at the root of all or much of this sinfulness, but the confessions reveal, not cupidity alone, but sin in all its variety. At the same time the scene individualizes sinfulness and roots it in the human heart. Without the confession of the deadly sins, the appeal to individual reform which follows would lack emotional power, and the move from the negative first vision to the positive second, from "do not evil" to "do well," would be anticlimax. It is a vision of evil work to motivate and balance the summons to good work of Piers the Plowman.

The confessions testify to the need for forgiveness and reform. Repentance's prayer at the close of the confessional contains the poet's double hope for mankind: God's mercy and love for man, and man's close kinship with God, the semidivinity of human nature coexistent with its sinfulness.

> "Now god," quod he, "that of thi goodnesse · gonne the worlde make,
> And of nauȝte madest auȝte · and man moste liche to thi-selue,
> . . . . .
> And madest thi-self with thi sone · and vs synful yliche,
> . . . . .
> And sith with thi self sone · in owre sute deydest. . . .
> . . . .
> And al that Marke hath ymade · Mathew, Iohan, and Lucas,
> Of thyne douȝtiest dedes · were don in owre armes;
> *Verbum caro factum est, et habitauit in nobis.*
> And bi so moche, me semeth · the sikerere we mowe
> Bydde and biseche · if it be thi wille,
> That art owre fader and owre brother · be merciable to vs."[10]

[10] v. 488–489, 494, 495, 507–511.

Thirty lines later Piers the Plowman, the symbol of man's semidivine nature, makes his first appearance in the poem to show mankind God's way. Piers knows the way to Truth: Meekness, obedience to conscience and good deeds, especially the observance of the ten commandments, lead to Truth's castle; grace enables one to enter; and if grace be lacking, entrance may be secured through the mercy of Christ and Mary (v. 570–638). But before man can begin his journey toward Truth he must do his feudal duties in this world (vi. 3–113)—an obligation he is often reluctant to perform (vi. 114–172). Although hunger drives the lazy and rebellious to labor, it vanishes with the harvest and they return to idleness (vi. 173–321). To Piers and to all men who do perform their duties, however, Truth grants a pardon:

> Et qui bona egerunt, ibunt in vitam eternam;
> Qui vero mala, in ignem eternum.[11]

Like the first vision with its picture of legal corruption, the second vision presents a problem in the poet's own world and time, the problem of feudal duties and labor. His interest in this problem is real and intense. But like the first vision, the second vision also gives this immediate issue a spiritual significance. The good work of this world is also in some measure the good work of salvation. The poet's method is not symbolic. At most, the scene of the plowing of the half-acre is suggestive of this value. The faithful laborers in the field may suggest—certainly they parallel rather than contradict—the image of the man of good works. But the scene is to be read literally.[12] The poet treats the issues of feudal duty, rebellious laborers, beggars

[11] vii. 1–3. The Latin is given after vii. 3.

[12] For an allegorical or symbolical interpretation of the scene in the half-acre, see Robertson and Huppé, pp. 83–91. I cannot accept this or their other "allegorical" readings of the poem. See Morton W. Bloomfield's review in *Spec.*, xxvii (1952), 245–249. Robertson and Huppé do, however, quote an interesting passage from Bede (PL, 91, col. 995) on the necessity of work for salvation (p. 87).

and famine with the passion of an inspired pamphleteer. The vision as a whole is something more than a political poem, not because it has a second meaning, but because the poet also talks of salvation.

The talk about matters spiritual is not extraneous to his doctrine of work. It grows out of his conviction that there is an intimate and indissoluble alliance between labor and spirituality. This conviction is embodied, as I have said, in the figure of Piers himself. It appears again and again in this vision. Truth is attainable only by the faithful laborer; one must faithfully perform his duties in this world before he can do those spiritual works essential for salvation. Piers, the good plowman, serves Truth, and only he can show mankind the way to Truth (v. 544–562). And before mankind can perform the spiritual work which Piers had described for them, they must join him in work on the half-acre (vi). Truth grants His pardon only to Piers and those who help him:

> And alle that halpe hym to erie · to sette or to sowe,
> Or any other myster · that myȝte Pieres auaille,
> Pardoun with Pieres plowman · treuthe hath ygraunted.
> (vii. 6–8)

Was not mankind commanded to labor by God?

The doctrine of the pardon, do well, i.e. do good works and be saved, is a logical culmination of the doctrine of labor in the vision. It sums up at the same time a line of thought running through the entire *Visio*. At the very beginning Holy Church advised man to lead a good life, in words which are almost a translation of the Latin pardon:

> And alle that worche with wronge · wenden hij shulle
> After her deth day · and dwelle with that shrewe [Lucifer].
> Ac tho that worche wel · as holiwritt telleth,
> And enden as I ere seide · in treuthe, that is the best,
> Mowe be siker that her soule · shal wende to heuene,
> Ther treuthe is in Trinitee · and troneth hem alle.[13]

[13] I. 126–131 (cf. A. i. 117–122 and C. ii. 130–134).

She further advised kings, knights, rich men and clergy to conduct themselves properly if they would follow Truth.[14] Reasoun gave similar advice to priests, religious, kings, popes and lawyers, and less directly to the common folk.[15] Do well, too, is the lesson of the confession scene.

The meaning of the pardon and the pardon scene, however, has been a matter of debate and dissension among the critics, largely because of Piers' quarrel with the priest. The priest tells Piers his pardon is no pardon at all; and Piers, in anger ("pure tene"), tears up the document. He quotes from the Psalter and says he will not work so hard to feed his belly anymore, but make prayers and penance his plow, as the Psalter and Evangels advise. The priest sneers at his learning, they quarrel, and the noise awakens the Dreamer, who concludes, after reflecting on the scene, that pardons from popes may be of some help, but Dowel is a more certain way to salvation (VII. 112–200).

The scene does have its confusing aspects, particularly the priest's statement that the pardon is no pardon, Piers' action in tearing the pardon, and his description of the change he proposes to make in his mode of life. There have been a variety of interpretations for these difficulties, but there is considerable agreement on two main points: the pardon is not a valid pardon, and Piers' words to the priest contain a rejection of the active life for the contemplative life. Both points, I believe, are mistaken and misleading.[16] The pardon is valid, and Piers affirms, not the superiority of the contemplative life over the active life, but, within the active life, the doctrine of what I shall call *ne solliciti sitis.*

Those who are skeptical about the pardon say either that it has no real validity or that it is valid only for Piers, not for the

[14] I. 94–101; 173–201.

[15] v. 42–60, 24–41.

[16] I have reviewed at greater length the various views concerning the Pardon Scene in "The Pardon Scene in *Piers Plowman,*" *Spec.,* XXVI (1951), 317–331.

rest of mankind.[17] Since the poet's theme was the salvation of mankind, this makes the pardon of only limited value. But there is evidence in the text, apart from Piers' puzzling words and actions, which proves the poet intended his audience to accept the pardon as valid for all men. And Piers' words and actions can be interpreted to confirm, not contradict, this view of the pardon.

I have already pointed out that the message of the pardon, do well, is a logical culmination of the doctrine of labor and good works preached throughout the *Visio*. If the pardon is no pardon, if do well is not the way to salvation, the reader has been led down the garden path by a most irresponsible poet. The objection of some critics that the *Visio,* although it may teach that doing good merits salvation, also shows mankind incapable of good works, simply will not hold. They have been blinded by the moralist's inevitable practice of preaching more about men's sins than about their virtues. There are good men in the field of folk and in the scene of the plowing of the half-acre; and the long account of the kinds of men to whom the pardon applies is pointless if the poet believes mankind incapable of goodness. Piers Plowman himself is a symbol of man's

---

[17] Skepticism about the value of the pardon is expressed in one form or another by the following critics: Wells, "Construction," pp. 3–4, 11 above. Chambers, *Mind,* pp. 119, 121. Coghill, pp. 64–65 above and *The Pardon,* pp. 17–19. George Winchester Stone, "An Interpretation of the A-Text of *Piers Plowman," PMLA,* 53 (1938), 666. Francis A. R. Carnegy, *The Relations Between the Social and Divine Order in William Langland's "Vision of William Concerning Piers the Plowman"* (Breslau, 1934), pp. 17–18, 44. John Lawlor, " 'Piers Plowman': The Pardon Reconsidered," *MLR, 45* (1950), 449–458: Lawlor argues that the *Visio* shows, first, that society can produce only one good man, Piers, and second, it shows through the pardon how far that good man falls short of the standard enjoined upon all men, "Be ye perfect." The tearing of the pardon is an act of acceptance; it shows Piers aware of his imperfection and resolved to pursue a better life, the contemplative. Robertson and Huppé, pp. 92–94, find the pardon valid; they interpret it as the grace of the Redemption. They go so far beyond the text, however, that I cannot follow them.

capacity for good. Finally, the text leaves no doubt that the Dreamer himself accepts the pardon. If the poet had wanted to strip the pardon of its value, he would hardly have ended the *Visio* with the Dreamer's words of acceptance. It is, he says, a pardon "alle the peple to conforte."[18] Although he expresses the conventional doubts about the trustworthiness of dreams, and worries over the relative value of papal indulgences and good works, he concludes that dreams can reveal the truth and that doing well is superior to indulgences. With a bow to orthodoxy he concedes some value to pardons from Rome, but concludes,

Ac to trust to thise triennales · trewly me thinketh,
Is nouȝt so syker for the soule · certis, as is Dowel.
    ·   ·   ·   ·   ·

For-thi I conseille alle Cristene · to crye god mercy,
And Marie his moder · be owre mene bitwene,
That god gyue vs grace here · ar we gone hennes,
Suche werkes to werche · while we ben here,
That after owre deth-day · Dowel reherce,
At the day of dome · we dede as he hiȝte.
(VII. 179–180, 195–200)

This is the way the *Visio* ends, with a bang, not with a whimper. There are no doubts here. The pardon is valid: all men should heed it.

This evidence of the text is supported by the authority which the pardon possessed. It is not only that the pardon was given by Truth (and by Truth, as the poem makes clear, is meant God). The lines of the pardon come from the well-known Athanasian Creed.[19] Popular because of the succinctness with which it stated the essential beliefs of the Church,[20] the Creed

---

[18] VII. 146. Not in A. In C. x. 300 it is "the puple to gladen."
  VII. 179–180, 195–200.

[19] First noted by Burdach, *Ackermann*, p. 267, n. 1.

[20] Cf. J. Tixeront, "Athanase (Symbole de Saint)," *DTC*, I, Pt. II, 2186–2187.

answers in forthright fashion the question which the poem itself seeks to answer: What shall a man do to be saved: "Quicumque vult salvus esse" are the words which open the Creed; and immediately after the article which is quoted as Piers' pardon in the poem, the thirty-ninth, the Creed closes with a blunt assertion of its authority: "Haec est fides catholica: quam nisi quisque fideliter firmiterque crediderit: salvus esse non poterit."[21]

Although the poet did not say the pardon came from the Athanasian Creed, the Creed was so well-known there can be little doubt that both he and his audience knew the source. The Creed was not only a creed but also a part of the liturgy and was actually considered a psalm, known familiarly as the "Quicumque vult." It was recited as part of the service at Prime and was as familiar as the Psalms to the poet and his contemporaries.[22] There was also a Middle English translation of the Creed.[23] Finally, there is some evidence that the particular lines of the Creed quoted as Piers' pardon may have had, as Nevill Coghill suggests, "some vogue as a catch-phrase about salvation towards the end of the fourteenth century and a little later."[24]

[21] For the Latin text of the Creed see Philip Schaff, *Creeds of Christendom* (New York, 1877), II, 66–70.

[22] The frequency with which it was recited at Prime varied according to custom. The Symbolum Athanasium is used at Prime on Sundays in the Roman Rite, daily at Prime in many Roman derivatives (e.g. the Sarum) and in the Ambrosian Rite: Henry Jenner, "Creed, Liturgical Use of," in *The Catholic Encyclopedia* (New York, 1913), IV, 479. According to the Sarum Breviary it was recited daily except from Maundy Thursday to the end of Easter Week: William Chatterley Bishop, "A Plain Introduction to the Structure and Arrangement of the Salisbury Breviary," *Breviarium ad Usum Insignis Ecclesiae Sarum* (Cambridge, Eng., 1882–1886), *3*, xxxi. In the Psalterium of the York Breviary, the Creed is prefaced with these instructions: "dictur de feria: vel ferialiter de dominica." *Breviarium ad Usum Insignis Ecclesie Eboracensis,* Publications of the Surtees Society, *71* (Durham, 1880), I, 882.

[23] See George Hickes, *Linguarum Vett. Septentrionalium Thesaurus* . . . (Oxford, 1703–1705), I, 233–235; and W. Heuser, "Eine Vergeseene Handschrift des Surteespsalters und die dort eingeschalteten Mittelenglischen Gedichte," *Anglie,* XXIX (1906), 405–408.

[24] *The Pardon*, p. 19, n. 2.

They were used, he points out, at the climax of the last scene of the *Castle of Perseverance*.[25]

This evidence both within and outside of the text is not canceled out by Piers' reactions in the Pardon Scene. To argue that it is would ascribe to these reactions more importance than they deserve. The fact that they are dropped completely in the C text[26] suggests that the essential meaning of the scene is communicated without them. An unquestionably dramatic passage was removed because it was confusing. To the Dreamer, even in B, Piers' reactions do not bear the message of the scene. He comments on them not at all, only on the pardon and the priest's impugning of it. The only issue for the Dreamer is the one raised by the priest's rejection of the pardon: which gives greater promise of salvation, the good life or papal indulgences.

But, although one may deny that Piers' reactions carry the principal message of the scene, there is no denying their presence in A and B. What, therefore, do these reactions mean? If Piers is rejecting the pardon, the rejection can only be the poet's way of showing how the Church's practice of selling indulgences leads men astray, a point he wants to make.[27] The view that Piers rejects the pardon has, however, this great difficulty: it contradicts the main purpose of the scene and the symbolic value already given Piers. As the Dreamer's comments reveal, the purpose of the scene is to advocate doing well and to attack papal indulgences. The priest supports indulgences. To give the priest a convert weakens the poet's attack. And to make the

[25] *The Macro Plays,* ed. F. J. Furnivall and A. W. Pollard, EETS, e.s. *91* (London, 1904), 186. Cf. also the use of the lines in a fourteenth-century sermon: *Sermons,* p. 29.

[26] Cf. C. x. 284–294.

[27] Cf. R. W. Chambers, "Long Will, Dante, and the Righteous Heathen," *Essays and Studies by Members of the English Association,* IX (Oxford, 1924), 53: "When the priest, representing current ideas, refuses to accept it [the pardon], the poet is brought up against the contrast which he feels so bitterly, between his own sense of justice, and that which seems to him to prevail in the current practice of the Church."

convert Piers, the symbol of right conduct, the follower of Truth, confuses the message and destroys the value of Piers as a symbol. Also, this would put Piers on the priest's side at one moment, but at loggerheads with him a moment later. And in C Piers opposes the priest and so supports the pardon. The view that Piers accepts the pardon creates too many difficulties to be tenable.

Piers' reactions, as a matter of fact, can be interpreted to signify his acceptance of the pardon. The act of tearing the pardon, so often understood as an act of rejection, implies this only so long as one disregards the special nature of his pardon. When Coghill and Chambers say that Piers decides not to put his trust in a piece of parchment, to bulls with seals,[28] they overlook something. Just as Piers' Testament is not really a will but a device for communicating an ethical message dramatically by means of the contrast between the conventional form and its novel content, so too the pardon is not really an orthodox pardon but a device for stating an ethical principle dramatically. The clash between form and content is even sharper here, for this pardon contains a message which is by implication an attack on pardons and which does in fact lead to such an attack by the Dreamer. How, then, can we speak of it as we would of a conventional pardon, as a piece of parchment, a bull with seals? That is precisely what it is not. In accepting its message, Piers is rejecting bulls with seals. In tearing the parchment, Piers is symbolically tearing paper pardons from Rome. One had to possess such pardons to receive their supposed benefits. But this pardon, once its message has been read and taken to heart, has served its purpose and is only a worthless piece of paper. (And so, the implication may be, are all pardons. The poet could not afford to condemn pardons too overtly.) Piers has lost nothing by tearing it. The act, then, because of the special character of the pardon, was intended as a

[28] *Mind,* p. 119; *The Pardon,* pp. 17–20.

sign that Piers had rejected indulgences and accepted the command to do well. Unfortunately, it was a very confusing sign.[29]

Once the act of tearing the pardon is seen as no act of rejection, Piers' other reactions can easily be explained to imply acceptance of the pardon. Piers' "tene" may be directed against himself, as Chambers suggests: he may be vexed to discover that he has wasted precious time being busy about his belly-joy.[30] But it is more reasonable to assume that it is directed against the priest. He is angry with him a few lines later. And the poet is angry with him, the supporter of papal indulgences, the misleader of souls. The priest is the one logical object in the scene for Piers' anger.

Piers' words also support the pardon. His quotation from the Psalter, " 'si ambulauero in medio vmbre mortis, non timebo mala; quoniam tu mecum es' " (Psalm XXII in the Vulgate), was interpreted by several medieval glosses as an affirmation of faith, and it is certain the poet knew a gloss on the line.[31]

---

[29] Glunz, *Literarästhetik,* p. 529, says the pardon serves a double function in the poem. It indicates to the various classes in the ploughing scene that they are on the right road, in which each serves the community. Piers symbolizes the perfect man, who satisfies the common weal as well as the individual good. But Piers tears the pardon at the moment when this first goal is reached. He has fulfilled one command to do good, to do good for the community. Now he hears another command to do good: to prove his worth as an individual in personal righteousness. The tearing of the pardon signifies the end of one condition and the beginning of another for Piers. Glunz' reading seems an accurate description of the direction in which the poem is moving at this point. I would object only to his confining the issue in the second vision to the economic good of the community—the salvation of mankind is the implicit issue of the second vision. And I would object to his reading so much into the simple act of tearing the pardon, especially when the action is omitted in C. The action, it seems to me, must be related to the issue of the relative value of pardons and good works.

[30] *Mind,* p. 121.

[31] R. W. Chambers pointed out that the poet quotes the same verse at B. XII. 289, and adds, " 'The glose graunteth vpon that vers a gret mede to treuth. . . .' ": "Incoherencies in the A and B texts of 'Piers Plowman' and Their Bearing on the Authorship," *London Mediaeval Studies,* I (1937), 34.

Although there are several glosses on the verse, the one he most probably knew was that which appears in both the *Glossa Ordinaria* and in Peter Lombard's *Commentarius in Psalmos Davidos*.[32] It interprets "mecum es" as meaning (following Augustine), "In corde per fidem, ut post umbram mortis ego tecum sim." The poet clearly associates the verse with the idea of reward to the faithful man, for when he quotes it again at B.XII.289, it comes after a discussion of men of steadfast belief; and immediately preceding the verse is another Latin line: "Deus dicitur quasi dans vitam eternam suis, hoc est, fidelibus." If the line is an expression of Piers' firm faith, what is Piers resolved to have faith in? If the line has any relevance to the dramatic situation in which it occurs, it must mean either that Piers will have faith in the priest or that he will have faith in the pardon. The poet would hardly have Piers quote the Psalter to support papal indulgences. There is no difficulty if he quotes it in support of the Athanasian Creed. He is resolved to have faith in the pardon, in spite of the priest's objections. Faith, for the poet, always meant what the pardon preached: moral action, doing well. So he has Piers announce at once that he will do prayers and penance, which would be considered good works,[33] and which imply a rejection of papal indulgences.

If the pardon is valid and Piers accepts it, then the way of life he proceeds to describe and which he determines to follow is the "do well" enjoined by the pardon:

"I shal cessen of my sowyng," quod Pieres · "and swynk nouȝt so harde,
Ne about my bely-ioye · so bisi be namore!
Of preyers and of penaunce · my plow shal ben herafter,
And wepen whan I shulde slepe · though whete-bred me faille.
The prophete his payn ete · in penaunce and in sorwe,
By that the sauter seith · so dede other manye;

[32] PL, *113,* col. 876; PL, *191,* col. 243.
[33] Cf. Dunning, p. 147.

That loueth god lelly · his lyflode is ful esy:
   Fuerunt michi lacrime mee panes die ac nocte.
And, but if Luke lye · he lereth vs bi foules,
We shulde nouȝt be to bisy · aboute the worldes blisse;
Ne solliciti sitis · he seyth in the gospel,
And sheweth vs bi ensamples · vs selue to wisse.
The foules on the felde · who fynt hem mete at wynter?
Haue thei no gernere to go to · but god fynt hem alle."

(VII. 117–129)

Just what kind of life is described here? A good many critics, as I have mentioned, say this is the contemplative life, to which Piers is turning from the active life. The view depends in part on the assumption that the pardon is rejected. It rests also on several other assumptions, all of them mistaken.

First, there is the assumption that Dowel is the kind of bodily labor seen in the plowing scene. Since Piers says that hereafter he will not do so much bodily work, he must be rejecting Dowel and moving on to Dobet (and it is assumed that Dobet is the life of contemplation). But the poet never calls bodily labor "Dowel." He uses the phrase for the first time when the priest translates the pardon and when the Dreamer comments on its message. So Dowel must be something more than bodily labor. (Also, it is unreasonable to assume the poet has Piers move on to something better than Dowel at the very moment when the reader first hears about Dowel.)

There is also the assumption that Piers is abandoning bodily labor completely. As Father Dunning observed, Piers "does not say that he will work no more: he merely says he will not work *so hard,* nor be *so busy* about providing himself with means of sustenance. . . . Piers merely declares that he will give the interests of his soul a decided preference over the interests of the body."[34]

---

[34] *Piers Plowman,* p. 149. Father Dunning has a sound analysis of the Pardon Scene (pp. 145–152), except that he tries to establish that the priest accepts the pardon.

313

There has been, as I have already observed, some misunderstanding of the nature of the active and the contemplative life among the students who have seen these lives as major patterns in the poem. The misunderstanding appears in their interpretation of this speech. The prayers and penance which Piers says he will perform do not prove that he is taking up the contemplative life. Prayers and penance are not confined to contemplatives, nor do they distinguish the contemplative life from the active. In Walter Hilton's *Epistle on Mixed Life,* "bodely werkes," the appropriate religious activities of those leading the Active Life ("worldly men & wymen the whiche lefully vsen worldly goodes, & wylfully vsen worldly besynes"), are contrasted with the activities of contemplatives. These "bodely werkes" include "al maner of god werkis þat thy soule doth by þe wyttes & þe membris of thy body," such as fasting, waking, restraining of fleshly lusts by doing penance, doing deeds of bodily or spiritual mercy to one's fellow Christians, and suffering bodily harm for the love of righteousness.[35] The program for those in the active life recommended in Hilton's piece *On Daily Work* is even more rigorous.[36] The active life, then, is not physical labor, but just the kind of activity that Piers pledges himself to: prayers and care for his spiritual profit. Of the contemplative's withdrawal from the world, being quiet from outward action, and hope to see the face of God there is no hint in Piers' speech.

Perhaps it is not quite accurate to say that the active life is "just the kind of activity that Piers pledges himself to." It is, however, a way of life that can be realized within the active life. I cannot agree with Chambers when he says Piers' determination not to worry about food any longer is "the Contemplative Life as Walter Hilton defines it: when men forsake 'all business,

[35] *Yorkshire Writers, I,* 264–266. Father Dunning has material showing that the command to do good refers to "the good works of a virtuous life." *Piers Plowman,* pp. 146–147.

[36] *Yorkshire Writers, I,* 137–156.

314

charges, and government of worldly goods, and make themselves poor and naked to the bare need of the bodily kind. . . .' "[37] The doctrine which Piers states is the doctrine of *ne solliciti sitis,* not of the contemplative life. The Gospel passages Piers quotes are not interpreted as a summons to the contemplative life. According to the *Glossa Ordinaria,* the verses say, not that man shall not labor, but that he shall not be *too solicitous* about his food: "non prohibet providentiam, per quam in sudore vultus panis praeparatur, sed vetat sollicitudinem quae mentem perturbat et ab aeternis revocat."[38] God will provide for the righteous man, even as he has provided for the fowls of the air: "Qui dedit majora, id est vitam et corpus, dabit et minora, id est victum et vestes. In his promissis veritatis nemo dubitet: Sit homo quod esse debet, mox adduntur ei omnia propter quem sunt facta."[39] The *Catena Aurea* expresses precisely the meaning of the lines: "Be not withdrawn by temporal cares from things eternal."[40]

The line comes from the Sermon on the Mount, which is, if not the source of several of the leading ideas in the poem, at least the authority the poet appealed to in support of them— the *Beati pauperes* of the *Beatitudes* for the doctrine of poverty, *fiat voluntas tua* from the Pater noster for the same doctrine and for *ne solliciti sitis, dimitte nobis debita nostra* from the Pater noster for the doctrine of *redde quod debes.*[41] The passage in the Sermon where *ne solliciti sitis* appears states the injunction at great length and with considerable power:

> Ideo dico vobis, ne soliciti sitis animae vestrae quid manducetis, neque corpori vestro quid induamini. Nonne anima plus est quam esca: et corpus plus quam vestimentum? Respicite volatilia caeli,

[37] *Mind,* p. 124.
[38] On Luke 12: 22: PL, *114,* col. 296.
[39] On Matt. 6:25; PL, *114,* cols. 105–106.
[40] 1, 251. See also Dunning, *Piers Plowman,* pp. 148–151.
[41] For *Beati pauperes* cf. xiv. 214; for *fiat voluntas tua* cf. xiv. 48 and xv. 174; for *ne solliciti sitis* cf. xiv. 33; for *dimitte nobis debita nostra* cf. xix. 384–392.

quoniam non serunt, neque metunt, neque congregant in horrea: et pater vester caelestis pascit illa. Nonne vos magis pluris estis ills? Quis autem vestrum cogitans potest adiicere ad staturam suam cubitum unum? Et de vestimento quid soliciti estis? Considerate lilia agri quomodo crescunt: non laborant, neque nent. Dico autem vobis, quoniam nec Salomon in omni gloria sua coopertus est sicut unum ex istis. Si autem foenum agri, quod hodie est, et cras in clibanum mittitur, Deus sic vestit: quanto magis vos modicae fidei? Nolite ergo soliciti esse, dicentes: Quid manducabimus, aut quid bibemus, aut quo operiemur? haec enim omnia gentes inquirunt. Scit enim pater vester, quia his omnibus indigetis. Quaerite ergo primum regnum Dei, et iustitiam eius: et haec omnia adiicientur vobis. Nolite ergo soliciti esse in crastinum. Crastinus enim dies solicitus erit sibiipsi. sufficit diei malitia sua.[42]

Sollicitudo, as Konrad Burdach has pointed out, was a catchword of Christian ethics. It is the continual concern for worldly goods, greediness for gain, avarice.[43] Burdach's investigation of the doctrine of *ne solliciti sitis* in the Old and New Testament and in Augustine and later medieval religious thinkers proves the doctrine was not peculiar to the *Piers Plowman* poet.[44] He further shows that the doctrine, together with the doctrine of poverty preached more explicitly in *Dowel,* was associated with the idealization of labor, not with the contemplative life.[45] *Ne solliciti sitis* was for the poet the solution to a fundamental question: how to provide for the body without destroying the soul. The answer is: Care for the soul, and God will provide if necessary for the body. The essence of the doctrine, Burdach says, is that a faithful devotion to God, an inner freedom from

[42] Matt. 6.

[43] *Ackermann,* p. 270.

[44] Ibid., pp. 268, 269–283, 308–310, 310 n. 2, 351–358. See also the quotation from Wyclif, p. 306, n. 1.

[45] Ibid., pp. 294 (point three, on the cult of poverty and Wyclif's poor priests) 294–296 (point six, on the moral duty of active work), 295–296, n. 1 (the quotation from Wyclif), 351–354. The doctrine of the importance of work appears in the arguments against the begging friars. Cf. Richard Fitzralph's *Defensio,* pp. 86–87, 88–89, 89–90.

care about gain, and an easy mind which calculates nothing must be the basis of all work and all activity which merits God's grace. It alone gives the soul the serenity and the power to love which is due man as God's image, and which leads him to God.[46]

This doctrine will appear at greater length in the visions which follow. What Piers says here is the merest hint, a preparation for the fuller development to come in *Dowel,* especially at its climax, the scene with Haukyn. That is why the Dreamer does not mention it after the vision ends, and why it could be dropped in C. It is the first glimpse of Dowel, the first suggestion of what Piers' pardon means. The poet quite properly concentrates, as the *Visio* ends, not on this foreshadowing, but on the merit of the pardon, Dowel's superiority over indulgences. As we have seen, there is no denial of the pardon. It is valid for mankind, and Piers accepts its message. It states the basic rule that man must follow if he would be saved. This rule is that he must do well. The rule is stated in a form (the unorthodox pardon) designed to show the falseness of the contrary view, that man can purchase salvation. The attack in the Pardon Scene on the philosophy of money applied to the scheme of salvation is paralleled and to some extent prepared for by the attack on the philosophy of money applied to the social order in the Lady Mede episode. Similarly, the support in the plowing scene of the philosophy of work applied to the social order parallels and prepares for the support of the philosophy of work applied here to the scheme of salvation. For the pardon says man must "work" (do well) to be saved, and it is offered to, and accepted by, the personification of the good workman, Piers Plowman. The doctrine of the spiritual value of physical labor blurs the line between "work" and "good work" and makes them a unity. The way to Truth, which Piers described for the pilgrims, involved activities ethical and religious in nature; but first the half-acre must be plowed. This prerequisite of "work" having

---

[46] *Ackermann,* pp. 351–352.

been described, the poem proceeds in *Dowel, Dobet and Dobest* to an examination of the *good* work, which, together with work, leads to salvation. The *Visio* has dramatized the principles of good and evil and shown a sick society which needs to be purged and reformed. The remainder of the poem will show what man must do in order to do good, and how he is able to do it—that is to say, it will convey the poet's view of the scheme of salvation.

13

PATRISTIC EXEGESIS IN THE CRITICISM OF MEDIEVAL LITERATURE: THE DEFENSE*

R. E. Kaske

INTERPRETATION OF THE Vulgate Bible occupied a central place in the intellectual life of the Middle Ages. Its results are preserved systematically in the abundant commentaries on the Vulgate itself, as well as in various encyclopedic collections of exegetical commonplaces; they are embodied piecemeal in many other traditional Christian forms, such as sermons and homilies, the Latin hymns and sequences, the liturgy of the Church and the pictorial arts. In the course of the Middle Ages, the allegorizing technique which formed an important part of biblical exegesis was increasingly extended to nonbiblical material as well —notably by the mythographers and by encyclopedists like Rabanus Maurus, Thomas of Cantimpré, John of San Geminiano and Pierre Bersuire, who allegorize also phenomena drawn directly from the natural sciences.[1]

* Reprinted, by permission, from *Critical Approaches to Medieval Literature,* ed. Dorothy Bethurum (New York: Columbia University Press, 1960), pp. 27–48, 60, 158–159.
[1] For the exegetical writers mentioned here and throughout, as well as for medieval exegetical writers generally, the basic reference work is Friedrich Stegmüller, *Repertorium Biblicum Medii Aevi* (Madrid, 1940–1955), Vols. II.-V. Biblical exegesis from its beginnings through the thirteenth century is surveyed by Beryl Smalley, *The Study of the Bible in the Middle Ages* 2d ed. rev. (Oxford, 1952); from the eighth through the fourteenth centuries, by Father C. Spicq, *Esquisse d'une histoire de*

The whole of this sprawling exegetical tradition, it seems to me, can make broadly two kinds of contribution to our understanding of medieval literature. The first, which has been recognized to some extent in modern scholarship, is that of explaining the medieval interpretations underlying obvious biblical quotations or allusions. A second contribution—potentially greater, though it has been relatively little exploited in the study of medieval English literature—derives from the role of the entire exegetical tradition as a sort of massive index to the traditional meanings and associations of most medieval Christian imagery. I refer, of course, not to the venerable pastime of source hunting, but to the close analysis of the traditional associations which such imagery usually brings with it into literary works, and the interpretation of whatever artistic use has been made of them. At the risk of introducing a note of tedium into a hitherto attractive controversy, the main part of my paper will demonstrate the interpretation of exegetical imagery and allusion by a series of examples from Langland and Chaucer.* . . .

Before settling down to cases, however, let me clarify a few of my own premises, which may disagree at some points with those of other scholars whatever their attitudes toward exegetical interpretation. There is, it seems, a certain emotional objection to this exegetical approach, in the belief that any such concentration on what are loosely thought of as "religious" allusions must regiment all medieval writers into a row of humorless proselytizers, preaching a monotonous gospel to later emancipated generations. Without denying the fundamental didacticism of most medieval literature, I think there is an important

l'exégèse latine au Moyen Âge, Bibliothèque thomiste, Vol. xxvi (Paris, 1944). Since the completion of the present paper, two other general works of comparable importance have appeared. Father Robert E. Mc-Nally, _The Bible in the Early Middle Ages,_ Woodstock Papers, No. 4 (Westminster, Md., 1959); and, especially, Father H. de Lubac, _Exégèse médiévale: Les quatres sens de l'Ecriture_ (Paris, 1959), 2 vols.

* For purposes of this anthology, the examples from Chaucer have been omitted. See Professor Kaske's original essay, pp. 48–60 [Ed.].

distinction to be made here. Even in basically didactic works, "religious" imagery or allusion need not be employed in simple evangelic frenzy, like a series of vendor's cries; one expects as a matter of course that a civilized Christian writer will use it with objective artistry, as a meaningful, evocative and perhaps unique image for what he is trying to express. Particularly would this be true in a civilization which seems to have distinguished much less sharply between "religious" and "secular" thought than does our own. So used, I do not see that exegetical imagery is more limited in its range of possible effects than imagery or allusion of any other kind. If this principle is sound, however, it has an important converse application: the interpreter of such imagery must not be content to reduce it indiscriminately to the most inclusive and uniform terms, but must analyze carefully its precise meanings in its particular contexts. Not every exegetical image or allusion is most fruitfully interpreted by direct recourse to *charitas* and *cupiditas,* accurate though the formula may be as universalizing commentary.

Another objection sometimes made to the exegetical approach is that few medieval writers—particularly fourteenth-century laymen, like Chaucer—would have had so much knowledge of biblical exegesis; and that in any case their audience could have understood few allusions to it. If I may invoke a few truisms: it is a notorious fact that a poet needs considerably less systematized information than do—ideally, anyway—the scholars of a later day who pursue him, since where he chooses to lead, we must follow; we may spend years in accumulating and sifting out what he has picked up painlessly in a conversation, a sermon or an evening's casual reading. I suppose it is equally obvious that poets do not always write to be wholly understood by readers or hearers less sophisticated than themselves, or to be wholly understood with ease by any audience; one might profitably ask, in fact, whether the use of exegetical allusion really involves a greater intrinsic improbability, or creates a more demanding kind of literature, than does the allusion of Donne or Eliot. There remains, as a final problem, that abstraction about whom we admittedly know next to nothing—the "sophisticated fourteenth-century English audience." Now according to our own common experience of human capacities for informal knowledge, surely no one would deny that such an audience *might* have been aware of a fairly large body of unsystematized exegetical lore. On the one hand, I know of no concrete evidence that has ever been brought forward for the absence of this awareness; while on the other hand there is some strong indirect evidence for its presence: for example, Chaucer's casual mention of Peter Riga's great exegetical poem the *Aurora;* the freedom with which Langland, Chaucer and others employ references to glossing and the general apparatus of biblical commentary, often as the vehicle of metaphor; and, most significant of all, the thousands of obviously exegetical allusions to be found in medieval art, medieval homiletic literature and the medieval liturgy including the hymns and sequences.

Such external arguments—including even the valuable supporting evidence of medieval poetic theory, so far as it can be ascertained—must in themselves be ultimately inconclusive; but they do imply that if we can find convincing and important examples of exegetical allusion in medieval literature, we need not shut our eyes to them in the simple faith that they could not possibly be there. The normal discipline of scholarly argument, of course, demands that exegetical interpretation of an individual figure or allusion be supported by well-documented parallels from the exegetical literature itself, somehow embracing enough peculiar features that to consider them accidental would outrage probability. More extended exegetical allusion in a given work must be supported by an accumulation of parallels large enough, or by a pattern complex enough, that to consider it accidental would outrage probability. But if this is so, the same scholarly discipline seems to dictate that the only conclusive evidence for the absence of exegetical allusion in a work—a few extraordinary cases apart—will be a demonstrable absence of such parallels.

Like almost any new line of scholarly inquiry, the exegetical approach to medieval literature has before it inevitably several large problems, some of them extremely complex. For example, to what extent do medieval writers actually draw their material, their governing outlooks and their means of literary expression, from the exegetical tradition? What theory, if any, underlies their use of it? Where it does seem to be consistently used, to what extent does it produce a connected level of meaning beyond the literal, and to what extent merely a number of separate allusions? To what extent, if any, do medieval writers employ creatively the famous "four levels" of biblical exegesis? If a substantial literary use of the exegetical tradition can be recognized, what major channels made it a part of the cultural repertory of medieval writers and their audiences? On most of these questions there would still be considerable disagreement, even among scholars convinced of the general validity of the discipline itself. My own opinion is that although they are obviously important questions, they are not the most immediately profitable ones; I would suggest, in fact, that these are the very questions scholarship is not yet equipped to answer. What we need first is a really prodigious amount of minute, systematic research centered on individual medieval works, with the immediate aim of showing the precise contributions made by the exegetical tradition to the meaning of descriptive details, figures of speech, characters, limited passages and so on.

For no medieval English work that I know of has this basic research ever been done, though a bold beginning has been made by D. W. Robertson and B. F. Huppé in *Piers Plowman and Scriptural Tradition*. Reviewers have pointed out serious errors and weaknesses in their work, for the most part justly. Rather less acknowledgment has been made of their positive contributions: the number of passages and details for which they convincingly show an exegetical background, and the consequent attention they have called to the large questions already mentioned. For our present discussion, however, the most significant weakness of their book is its tendency to proceed from general assumption to the explanation of particulars, instead of vice versa; the resulting paradox is that it does not make intensive enough use of the exegetical tradition which is its distinctive tool. This weakness, I take it, grows out of a situation not altogether under the authors' control—that is, lack of the solid foundation of preliminary scholarship referred to earlier, on which their own comprehensive interpretation could be partly based. An interpretation of *Piers Plowman,* supported by whatever is most relevant from the immense and still imperfectly conquered exegetical tradition, is hardly a task to be begun *ex nihilo* by two scholars and brought to perfection within the covers of a single book; if it were, the book would be one we might all have to get a year's grant to read. In this important way, the work of Robertson and Huppé is like a pinnacle without a sufficiently wide base. And except for their own contributions, the lack that existed when they wrote exists today. It seems less accurate, then, to say that the approach to *Piers Plowman* by way of the exegetical tradition has failed, than that it has not yet been painstakingly tried. Hence, in part, the examples which follow.

My first passage is a single extended simile from *Piers Plowman,* occurring within Will's first inner dream, in a speech uncertainly assigned in the B text, in a discussion of poverty:

> And alle the wyse that euere were · by auȝte I can aspye,
> Preysen pouerte for best lyf · if pacience it folwe,
> And bothe bettere and blisseder · by many-folde than ricchesse.
> Al though it be soure to suffre · there cometh swete after;
> As on a walnot with-oute · is a bitter barke,
> And after that bitter barke · (be the shelle aweye),
> Is a kirnelle of conforte · kynde to restore;
> So is, after, pouerte or penaunce · pacientlyche ytake.
> For it maketh a man to haue mynde in gode . and a grete wille

To wepe and to wel bydde · wher-of wexeth mercy,
Of which Cryst is a kirnelle · to conforte the soule.

(B. XI. 247–257)

This figure is derived from medieval interpretations of two biblical verses: Canticles 6:10, "I descended into the garden of nuts"; and the miraculous production of almonds or nuts by Aaron's rod in Numbers 17.8. Both verses have a variety of interpretations, all beginning with the ancient division of the nut into bitter hull, hard shell and sweet kernel, found in Philo and Pliny. Langland's figure on poverty blends together two of the most common of these interpretations. The general pattern of the first may be illustrated from the twelfth-century comment of the Cistercian Thomas of Citeaux on Canticles 6.10:

> . . . just as the nut has a most bitter hull and is girded about with a most hard shell, and when the harsh-tasting and hard parts have been taken away a most sweet fruit is found, so all the chastisement and labor of restraint by which Holy Church is exercised seems bitter indeed while it is present, but in the future brings forth most sweet fruit.

Later commentators apply the same pattern to those who patiently bear external hardships but have the sweetness of divine consolation within, and to those from whom harsh lives have called forth compassion, mercy, and true devotion.

Langland's final reference to Christ as a "kernel" touches on a second traditional interpretation of the two biblical verses, which makes the nut or almond signify Christ Himself—as, for example, in Adam of St. Victor's great Christmas sequence *Splendor Patris et figura,* where the hull and the shell are associated with Christ's physical sufferings during the Crucifixion, the kernel with the hidden sweetness of His divinity for mankind. In uniting these two traditional exegeses of the nut, then, Langland has utilized their spiritually meaningful common ground: the interpretations of the kernel, in which the sweetness that follows tribulation and the sweetness of internal devotion are both merged with the sweetness of Christ—probably to be thought of, accordingly, both as man's eternal reward and as man's internal dweller and counselor. Seen thus, in its exegetical context, the figure gains not only in the purposefulness of its own inner structure, but also in the metaphysical allusiveness that can distinguish medieval religious poetry at its best.

Such small and clear-cut uses of exegetical imagery are frequent in *Piers Plowman*. Leaving this specimen to stand for them all, I proceed to more complex examples. A passage which so far as I know has never been interpreted, either within itself or in its relation to the rest of the poem, is the abrupt speech of Book just before the Harrowing of Hell:

> Thanne was there a wiʒte · with two brode eyen,
> Boke hiʒte that beupere · a bold man of speche.
> 'By godes body,' quod this Boke · 'I wil bere witnesse,   [230]
> That tho this barne was ybore · there blased a sterre,
> That alle the wyse of this worlde · in o witte acordeden,
> That such a barne was borne · in Bethleem citee,
> That mannes soule sholde saue · and synne destroye.
> And alle the elementz,' quod the Boke · 'her-of bereth witnesse.
> That he was god that al wrouʒte · the walkene firste shewed;
> Tho that weren in heuene · token *stella comata,*
> And tendeden hir as a torche · to reuerence his birthe;
> The lyʒte folwed the lorde · in-to the lowe erthe.
> The water witnessed that he was god · for he went on it;   [240]
> Peter the apostel · parceyued his gate,
> And as he went on the water · wel hym knewe, and seyde,
>   *Iube me venire ad te super aquas.*
> And lo! how the sonne gan louke · her liʒte in her-self,
> Whan she seye hym suffre · that sonne and se made!
> The erthe for heuynesse · that he wolde suffre,
> Quaked as quykke thinge · and al biquashte the roche!
> Lo! helle miʒte nouʒte holde · but opened the god tholed,
> And lete oute Symondes sones · to seen hym hange on rode.
> And now shal Lucifer leue it · thowgh hym loth thinke;
> For *Gygas* the geaunt · with a gynne engyned   [250]
> To breke and to bete doune · that ben aʒeines Iesus.
> And I, Boke, wil be brent · but Iesus rise to lyue,
> In alle myʒtes of man · and his moder gladye,

And conforte al his kynne · and out of care brynge,
And al the Iuwen Ioye · vnioignen and vnlouken;   [255]
And but thei reuerencen his rode · and his resurexioun,
And bileue on a newe lawe · be lost lyf and soule.'

(B. xviii. 228–257)

Let us begin by recalling that from a Christian point of view, Book's speech falls within the most suspenseful brief period in human history: the time between Christ's apparent defeat by Death and the conclusive vindication of Christianity by the Harrowing of Hell and the Resurrection. More specifically, the speech stands about as squarely as possible between the period of the Old Law and that of the New, introduced as it is between the completion of the Atonement with the death of Christ and its first fruits as manifested in the Harrowing of Hell. The Debate of the Daughters of God immediately preceding it presents a conflict of claims incompatible under the Old Law; the Harrowing of Hell which immediately follows is a dramatization of the reconciling of these claims and of the change to the conditions of the New Law. In accord with this crucial placing, the speech of Book is designed not only as literal comment on the career of Christ and its climax in the present stupendous world-moment, but also as a kind of double-surfaced mirror reflecting the essential truth of both past and future—just as, according to medieval commentary, the essential truth of both past and future is reflected in the letter of the New Testament. This controlling pattern is developed primarily by the use of themes taken from the exegetical tradition.

The most obvious of these exegetical themes is Book's long account of the witnessing elements, extending from line 235 through line 248. This whole theme is itself a homiletic interpretation of part of the second chapter of Matthew, attached primarily to the feast of the Epiphany though sometimes to the Crucifixion. In the West, it is found in Augustine and in a famous pseudo-Augustinian sermon on the Creed, but it receives its definitive formulation in a homily by Gregory the Great on Matt. 2:1–12, delivered on the day of Epiphany:

> Indeed all the elements bore witness that their author had come. For (so that I may say something of them in human terms) the heavens acknowledged Him to be God, because straightway they sent a star. The sea acknowledged it, because it offered itself to be trodden upon by his footsteps. The earth acknowledged it, because when He died it trembled. The sun acknowledged it, because it hid the rays of its light. Rocks and walls acknowledged it, because at the time of His death they were cleft. Hell acknowledged it, because it yielded up dead those whom it held.

This passage is incorporated into the lections for Matins on the feast of the Epiphany; it is also repeated more or less closely in the Old English *Christ*-poem, and in a long series of medieval sermons and homilies on the Epiphany, including an English metrical homily of the fourteenth century.

In adapting this theme as a basic part of Book's speech, Langland is obviously utilizing both its inevitable correspondences to the Gospel account and its strong motif of literal, physical testimony, in order to establish Book's role as primarily the witness-bearing "letter" of the New Testament. Moreover, Book's extended opening reference to the familiar Epiphany-motif of the star of Bethlehem (ll. 231 ff.) and his extended closing reference to the wonders surrounding the Crucifixion (ll. 243 ff.) seem to throw particular emphasis on these two major traditional contexts of the witnessing elements theme—one standing near the beginning and the other at the end of Christ's earthly career. And these traditional contexts of the theme, in turn, further emphasize the role of Book's speech as the point of transition between Old Law and New: the Epiphany, despite its origins, traditionally celebrates the visit of the Magi, always interpreted as the first manifestation of Christ to the Gentiles, and often including a reproach to the Jews for their blindness to the promised Redeemer; the Crucifixion, as the completion of the Atonement, marks the final abolition of the Old Law and the beginning of the New.

A second major exegetical theme in the speech is based on Psalm 18:1–8, unanimously explained in medieval commentary as a prophecy of the life of Christ. In line 250, "*Gygas* the geaunt" is a clear reference to the giant of Psalm 18.6, "Exsultavit ut gigas ad currendam viam," who is identified with Christ by practically every commentator from Ambrose in the fourth century to Nicolas of Lyra in the fourteenth—a figure occasionally supported by manuscript illustration and particularly common in the Latin hymns and sequences. With this allusion as a basis, we may see a probable further connection between Book's opening account of the star of Bethlehem (ll. 231 ff.) and Psalm 18:1, "The heavens expound the glory of God," often explained by commentators as a prophecy of the star; and a similar connection between Book's closing remark about the conversion of the Jews to the New Law (ll. 256–257) and Psalm 18:8, "The law of the Lord is immaculate, converting souls," often explained as a prophecy of the New Law.

It is primarily through these two exegetical themes that Langland develops the Janus-like pattern already proposed for Book's speech. The significance of the literal present—that is, the change from Old Law to New—is emphasized by the theme of the witnessing elements, plus its traditional associations with the change from Old Law to New and from Jew to Gentile. The meaningful past—that is, the Old Law—is reflected by the allusions to Psalm 18, one of the most prominent Old Testament foreshadowings of Christianity. The future—that is, the time of the New Law proper—is directly foretold by the rest of Book's speech (ll. 252 ff.), with its further emphasis on the invalidating of the Old Law; a possible important allusion to Joachistic prophetic commentary in this final part of the speech is too doubtful and complex for discussion here. To the entire pattern, one might add the sharp division of Book's speech into a record of

miracles and a prophecy, dramatizing a common exegetical statement of the two basic means by which the Scriptures present
their testimony.

If this interpretation is generally sound, the speech of Book
emerges from its apparent chaos as one of the most originally
conceived, intellectually controlled and compact passages of allusion in *Piers Plowman* or elsewhere. Broader implications can
be found in this governing design, such as its probable relation
to the Book of Scripture and the Book of Nature. More to our
present point, however, the pattern is filled out by lesser exegetical details; as a single example, let us glance back to the sketch
of Book himself in the first two lines of the passage. Book's two
eyes seem to represent most immediately an antithesis to the
traditional blindness of the Jews and their Law—a common exegetical theme, actually found along with that of the witnessing
elements in the lections for Matins on Epiphany. Further likely
connotations drawn from Scriptural exegesis are the two Testaments themselves; the different senses in which Scripture is to
be understood; and particularly the relationship of the New
Testament to both past and future, following interpretations of
Apocalypse 4:6 like that of the ninth-century commentator Sma-
ragdus: "The four animals signify the four Gospels: they are
full of eyes in front because they preach concerning future judgment; they are full of eyes behind, because they give testimony
concerning the Old Testament. . . ." Book's boldness of speech
(l. 229) echoes a New Testament ideal familiar in the Acts and
the Pauline epistles. I read it as a particular allusion to Romans
10:20–21, concerning the boldness of Isaias in prophesying
the faith of the Gentiles by contrast with the incredulity of the
Jews—a passage unanimously interpreted as a statement of the
change in Laws and in the comparative importance of Jew and
Gentile, already outlined as the thematic center of Book's speech.

The exegetical tradition can also be fruitfully applied to some
of the difficult passages mentioning Piers himself. A good ex-

ample is the well-known allusion by Anima in the B text, in a passage referring to Charity:

> There-fore by coloure ne by clergye · knowe shaltow
>   hym neuere,
> Noyther thorw wordes ne werkes · but thorw wille one.
> And that knoweth no clerke · ne creature in erthe,
> But Piers the Plowman · *Petrus, id est, Christus.*
>
> (xv. 203–206)

Though modern scholars seem generally agreed that Piers here is to be identified primarily with St. Peter and the prelacy, the precise rationale of *Petrus, id est, Christus* has been left rather mysterious. One solution has been to refer, a little uncomfortably, to Konrad Burdach, who cites "an old, much ramified speculation"—undocumented—that the Apostle Peter is "a source of life for the community of human souls who seek God."[2] Whatever Burdach may have had in mind, I do not think we need go so far afield for an explanation. To begin with, the gloss "Petra, id est, Christus" is almost a refrain in biblical commentary—connected as it is not only with Moses' striking the rock in Ex. 17:6 and Paul's famous interpretation of it in I Cor. 10:4, but with a number of other familiar passages in which the rock signifies Christ. Langland's *Petrus, id est, Christus,* then, is really a metaphor—or, if we like, an allusive adaptation—using as its vehicle a recognizable cliché of biblical exegesis. *Petrus* (the Apostle and through him the prelacy) *stands for Christ* in the visible history of the Church Militant, just as *petra* (the rock) "stands for Christ" in the text of Scripture. The topical connection between *Petrus* and *petra* is of course found in Christ's words, "Thou art Peter, and upon this rock I will build my Church" (Matt. 16:18), consistently interpreted as the estab-

---

[2] *Der Dichter des Ackermann aus Böhmen und seine Zeit,* Vom Mittelalter zur Reformation, Band III, Heft 2 (Berlin, 1926–1932), pp. 311–312; cited by E. Talbot Donaldson, *Piers Plowman: The C-Text and Its Poet* (New Haven, 1949), p. 170 above.

lishment of the papacy. In other words, Langland is extending Christ's own pun on *Petrus* and *petra* to embrace also the great exegetical commonplace of Christ Himself as *petra,* an extension already familiar in commentaries on the verse.

But if this is so, what is the precise relevance of the figure to the theme of its immediate context, that is, to the surpassing need for charity, with particular reference to the clergy? The key seems clearly to lie in the interpretation of another of Peter's moments of prominence, at the end of the Gospel of John (21:15–17): "Simon son of John, lovest thou me more than these?" . . . "Yea, Lord, thou knowest that I love thee." . . . "Feed my lambs." And again: "Feed my sheep." The usual explanation makes Peter the exemplar both of a particularly fervent love for Christ, and of the special obligation for prelates to exercise the two great precepts of charity, love of God and love of neighbor. The fifteenth-century Denis the Carthusian explains that Christ questioned Peter

> so that He might teach that the prelate over others ought not only to love Christ, but ought also to love Him more fervently than others. . . . As though the Savior said: "In this it will appear that you love Me, if worthily you will feed my servants. . . . Because you love Me, you are fit to feed the flock of my people. . . ."[3]

In finally interpreting Anima's cryptic *Petrus, id est, Christus,* we should remember that it has grown out of Will's question about whether clerks who keep Holy Church know Charity. Seen in this context and in the light of the traditional commentaries I have cited, our passage answers, first, that neither clerks nor others can "know Charity" without the spontaneous, burning love for Christ manifested by Peter the Apostle, typified here in Piers Plowman; and secondly, that by means of such devotion one becomes Piers Plowman—here a figure of Christ through

---

[3] *Doctoris ecstatici D. Dionysii Cartusiani Opera Omnia* (Montreuil, 1901), XII, 616.

love, as Peter is a figure of Christ both through love and through his prelateship, and as the rock is a figure of Christ through its significance in Scripture.

My final example from *Piers Plowman* is the description of Christ's leechcraft, in the swift resumé of His life following the Allegory of the Tree. In the B text it is Piers who teaches Christ leechcraft—a difficult reference, which has been the despair of one of the keenest scholars to write on the poem in recent years.[4] In what sense can Piers, primarily a symbol of man, be said to teach Christ? Let us approach the passage by way of its clearer counterpart in the C text, which substitutes Liberum-Arbitrium for Piers:

> And in the wombe of that wenche · he was fourty wokes,
> And man by-cam of that mayde · to saue mankynde,
> Byg and abydynge · and bold in hus barn-hede,
> To hauen fouhten with the feende · ar ful tyme come.
> Ac *Liberum-Arbitrium* · leche-crafte hym tauhte,
> Til *plenitudo temporis* · hih tyme a-prochede,
> That suche a surgeyn setthen · yseye was ther neuere,
> Ne non so faithfol fysician · for, alle that hym bysouhte,
> He lechede hem of here langoure · lazars and blynde bothe;
>   *Ceci uident, claudi ambulant, leprosi mundantur:*
> And commune wymmen conuertede · and clansede hem of
>   synne.
>
>   (XIX. 134–143)

We may begin by observing that the central lines (136–141) are obviously an allegory, related to the larger allegory of the Christ-Knight, that they are part of a chronological though drastically condensed telling of the Gospel story, and that they occur between clear references to Christ's birth and to His public life. I believe that these lines allegorize, in highly compressed form, a series of events occupying a corresponding place in the Gospel of Luke, from near the end of Chapter 2 to about the middle

---

[4] Donaldson, 169 above.

of Chapter 4: the child Jesus in the temple, Christ's baptism, His fasting and temptation in the desert and His reading in the synagogue at Nazareth.

Lines 136–137 allegorize the verse introducing the story of Jesus in the temple (Luke 2:40): "And the child grew, and was made steadfast full of wisdom; and the grace of God was in Him." Line 136 seems to reflect this verse in detail—"byg" corresponding to "the child grew," defined in commentaries as a reference to physical growth; "abydynge" corresponding to "was made steadfast full of wisdom"; and "bold" corresponding to "the grace of God was in Him." Line 137 alludes to the frequent comment that Christ realized His full powers at the age of twelve, but waited until the *plenitudo temporis* of thirty to begin His public life.

Langland's association of Liberum-Arbitrium with the Holy Ghost has been clearly shown by Talbot Donaldson.[5] In Luke and its commentaries, the unifying theme of Christ's baptism, fasting and temptation, and reading in the synagogue is His guidance by the Holy Ghost, Who descends on Him at His baptism, fills Him and leads Him into the desert, and afterwards directs Him back into Galilee (Luke 3:22, 4:1, 14). Lines 138–140 seem to be a conflated allegory of this theme; their reference to it, however, is by way of the verses from Isaias which Christ reads in the synagogue (Luke 4:18–19), interpreted by commentators as an epitome of His baptism, fasting and temptation, and subsequent miracles:

> The Spirit of the Lord is upon Me, wherefore He hath anointed Me; He hath sent Me to preach the gospel to the poor, to heal the contrite of heart:
>
> To preach deliverance to the captives, and sight to the blind, to set at liberty them that are bruised, to preach the acceptable year of the Lord, and the day of reward.

Medieval commentary on these verses of Luke provides the images of the Holy Ghost as Christ's teacher, of Christ as physi-

[5] *Ibid.,* pp. 172–175 above.

cian and of the fullness of time. The great thirteenth-century commentator Hugh of St. Cher explains in part:

> *The Spirit of the Lord*. . . . In this [verse it is signified that Christ] is less than the Holy Ghost, insofar as He is man. . . . Likewise it is signified that He performed all the exhortations of the Holy Ghost. For He had upon Him the Holy Ghost as counselor and teacher. . . .
>
> *To heal the contrite of heart*. . . . [that is,] the Lord as the true physician heals [contrite sinners] with repentance. . . . For the words and commands of Christ are medicinal.
>
> *The acceptable year of the Lord*, that is, so that I might show the time of the fullness of grace to have come. . . .[6]

The expression *plenitudo temporis*—used in the New Testament only of the Nativity and the Last Judgment—is frequent in medieval commentary as a reference to the beginning of Christ's public life. After line 141 the allegorical theme of Christ's leech-craft blends into the literal account of His miracles, which in Luke (4:33 ff.) follows His reading in the synagogue.

Let us now turn back to the more difficult passage in the B text:

> And in the wombe of that wenche · was he fourty wokes,
> Tyl he wex a faunt thorw her flesshe · and of fiȝtyng
>   couthe,
> To haue y-fouȝte with the fende · ar ful tyme come.
> And Pieres the Plowman . parceyued plenere tyme,
> And lered hym lechecrafte · his lyf for to saue,
> That thowgh we were wounded with his enemye · to
>   warisshe hym-self;
> And did him assaye his surgerye · on hem that syke were,
> Til he was parfit practisoure · if any peril felle,
> And souȝte oute the syke · and synful bothe,
> And salued syke and synful · bothe blynde and crokede,
> And comune wommen conuerted · and to good torned;
>   *Non est sanis opus medicus, set infirmis, etc.*
>   (XVI. 100–110)

[6] *Opera Omnia in universum Vetus, & Novum Testamentum* (Venice, 1732), Vol. VI, fol. 155ʳ.

Much of what I have said about the passage in the C text will apply here also; the significant difference is in lines 103–106. One additional detail from the chapters in Luke is "to warisshe hymself," echoing Christ's words, "Physician, heal thyself" (Luke 4:23), a few verses after His reading in the synagogue. Commentary on this verse develops the popular theme of Christ as man's spiritual physician, often in the light of the medieval commonplace that what Christ preached He also performed. Usually it includes a reference to Christ's further remark (Luke 5:31) that the physician is needed not by the healthy but by the sick —a variant of which is quoted in the Latin tag following line 110. Medieval interpretation of this and other related biblical verses presents Christ as the unique physician who by His own wounds healed the sickness of mankind; as both healer, and warrior against the devil; and as the physician who first drinks the bitter medicine of temptation, hardship and suffering which He prescribes, lest the sick man should hesitate.

Now, within this context of allusion, what are we to make of Piers Plowman teaching Christ leechcraft? An acceptable interpretation of Piers, I take it, must bear some relation to the pertinent part of the Gospel narrative, must allow Piers to teach Christ without violating his own fundamental role in the poem as man and must credibly permit the substitution of Liberum-Arbitrium for Piers in the C text. Though the reference remains a difficult one, I believe these conditions are best met by a complex relationship between Piers and John the Baptist. John's prominence at Christ's baptism is obvious. His perceiving "plenere tyme" would allude generally to the *plenitudo temporis* of the beginning of Christ's public life, mentioned earlier; specifically, it would refer to the *plenitudo temporis* in which John himself began to preach—a familiar idea, developed by commentators from the list of rulers and high priests which in Luke (3:1–2) immediately precedes his preaching. John's relation to what is constant in the Piers-symbol would be through his traditional role as the last and greatest prophet, a representative of what Talbot Donaldson has called "that elevated portion of mankind which includes the patriarchs and prophets—Moses, Abraham, David, Adam and the others who prefigured Christ before the Incarnation just as St. Peter became Christ's vicar after the Ascension."[7] In terms of the surface Gospel narrative, John's teaching Christ leechcraft might be read as an allegorizing of his visible human role as precursor of Christ (much emphasized in the commentaries), living a similarly blameless life, preparing Christ's way by preaching a similar gospel, and at Christ's baptism serving as minister of the Holy Ghost. The more important allegorical significance of John's teaching Christ, however, would depend on the common spiritual interpretation of John as God's grace, here obviously suggesting the grace of the Holy Ghost by which Christ is taught after His baptism— and, incidentally, providing an understandable basis for the substitution of Liberum-Arbitrium (the Holy Ghost) in the C text. Hugh of St. Cher's comment on the later episode in which John sends his disciples to question Christ (Luke 7:19–22) establishes a meaningful connection between this spiritual interpretation of John and the theme of Christ's leechcraft:

> Mystically, John the Baptist is baptismal grace. . . . Note, moreover, what [Christ] says: "Report to John," that is, to the grace of God, to which the preacher ought to attribute whatever of good he performs or speaks. . . . In the following [verses], note what the preaching of Christ performs.[8]

The account of Christ's "preaching" which follows is really a spiritual interpretation of His leechcraft, based on the biblical verse (Luke 7:22) inserted near the end of our C text passage: *Ceci vident, claudi ambulant, leprosi mundantur.* Finally, to this whole proposed interpretation of Piers one should add that it would not necessarily rule out an interpretation of him in terms of Christ's own human psychology, if a convincing one can ever

---

[7] Donaldson, p. 172 above.
[8] *Opera Omnia,* Vol. VI, fol. 173ʳ.

be found, and that in any case, here as elsewhere in the poem, Piers as idealized mankind suggests Christ implicitly—a suggestion actually strengthened by the allusion to John, himself traditionally a figure of Christ. . . .

At the beginning of this paper I made basically two assertions. One was that the most convincing argument for the importance of exegetical interpretation lies in specific, documented examples of its importance. By these intervening examples, I have tried to show that the exegetical tradition is used with artistic intent by Langland and Chaucer, and that its controlled application to medieval literature constitues a valuable though difficult aid to literary interpretation.[9] To this statement I should add that so far as one can tell, work of this kind is still close to its beginning. Its canons, methods and major sources are still relatively undefined; some of what should be its basic apparatus is antiquated or nonexistent, and the great bulk of thirteenth-and fourteenth-century commentaries remain unprinted. My other beginning assertion was that exegetical imagery and allusion are employed by medieval writers with a poetic variety and subtlety much greater than is sometimes supposed. I hope that this claim too has found support, in the variety of meanings and emotional effects toward which we have seen exegetical images used— ranging from the sublimity of Book's apocalyptic time-vision to the civilized moral comedy of Chaucer.

[9] It may seem that by concentrating entirely on the existence of exegetical imagery in these few passages from the work of two fourteenth-century writers I have overlooked the larger and more important questions implied by the general title of this discussion. The importance of the exegetical tradition for medieval literature is, I am convinced, enormous in scope and varied in kind; but until Old and Middle English scholars possess a sizable area of enlightened agreement about its existence and significance in just such specific instances as these, I do not see how the broader aspects of its importance can be profitably debated.

14

PIERS PLOWMAN AS A FOURTEENTH-CENTURY APOCALYPSE*

Morton W. Bloomfield

I.

PROFESSOR C. VANN WOODWARD, the distinguished authority on American history, in a recent address, later printed, on the necessity of interpretations and analyses of new historical problems and issues by his fellow-historians, makes, toward the end of this interesting talk, the following point about our own times:

> The new age bears another and more ominous gift for the historian, one that has not been conspicuous in historical writings since the works of the Christian fathers. This gift is the element of the catastrophic. The Church fathers, with their apocalyptic historiography, understood the dramatic advantage possessed by the storyteller who can keep his audience sitting on the edge of eternity. The modern secular historian, after submitting to a long cycle of historicism, has at last had this dramatic advantage restored. The restoration, to be sure, arrived under scientific rather than apocalyptic auspices. But the dramatic potentials were scarcely diminished by placing in human hands at one and the same time the Promethean fire as well as the divine prerogative of putting an end to the whole drama of human history.[1]

* This paper is based on a lecture first given at the Modern Language Association convention in Philadelphia, December, 1960. Reprinted, by permission, from *The Centennial Review of Arts and Science,* v (1961), 281–295.

[1] "The Age of Reinterpretation," *AHR,* LXVI (1960–1961), 19.

Woodward is here stressing the advantages which our age offers for the writing of dramatic history. For the first time since the Middle Ages, historians as a whole can with justice be convinced of an appalling catastrophe hanging over the world and may use this threatening possibility to write with a fervor and sense of doom such as the Church Fathers possessed when writing of human history. Since the sixteenth century or even earlier, only a few historians could write their histories as if an end of human history could soon be expected.

This is a good point, and I hope modern historians may give heed to this advice from one of their number and inject more life and vitality into their work. Other professional scholars could also benefit by this advice. It seems to me, however, that there is another advantage, if such is the right word, to be gained from the history of our own time—a new ability to understand literary works and human beings of the past, obsessed or deeply concerned with the imminence of the end of human history by divine intervention. In short, we may now begin to understand anew the apocalyptic and eschatological element in the past.

There is evidence indeed that such is happening. Modern existentialistic theology is much concerned with the apocalyptic and eschatological. The apocalyptic interpretation or reinterpretation of Jesus' teachings and of early Christianity has by now almost become a commonplace. The discovery of the Dead Sea Scrolls has revealed the apocalyptic views of a Jewish sect, probably the Essenes, which flourished around the period of Jesus' life. Other Jewish apocalypses are also known. Christianity seems to have arisen out of a similar small Hebrew apocalyptic sect or at least found favor at first among those who believed that the end of the world was near and that a Messiah would come to prepare the elect for the Day of Judgment. This new knowledge explains much in the New Testament and earliest Christian writings.

As a result of all this, we can now reread certain apocalpytic writers of the past in a new light. All thinking men have been forced to consider the possible end of human existence on earth. In the past, since the Renaissance, this concern was always limited to the few. We can now better understand the implications of the Day of Judgment in the older Judeo-Christian tradition. The apocalyptic and catastrophic is not merely evidence of human aberration or eccentricity but a continuing and serious aspect of the human story. It is true that today it may be science and human nature rather than God which will destroy us all, but God may be working through science, and in any case the destruction of the world, if it comes, will be the same, whatever the cause.

It is true, of course, that apocalyptic thinkers were often eccentric and even mad, but we can at least see them as concerned with certain fundamental problems of humanity, no matter how wild their theorizings and beliefs may have been. The apocalyptic thinker is convinced that God's judgment hangs over the world and that it is his task to warn people because he can see correctly the signs of coming catastrophe, not always necessarily the end of the world.

In the Judeo-Christian tradition, the apocalyptic view of the world is enshrined in the dogma of the Resurrection and the Day of Judgment, but it also appears in other concepts and key notions such as those of the Kingdom of God, the Messiah, and Antichrist. The latter will lead the forces of evil and will be opposed by the Messiah or his representatives. In fact, all of history may be seen as a struggle between various Antichrists and various representatives of the elect and the chosen. The tradition, as we may even see in the New Testament, (e.g., 1 John 2:18 and 2 John 7), admitted the possibility of various Antichrists. In the latter part of the Middle Ages, this belief in a plurality of Antichrists was widely held, and, at the end of time there would be the greatest Antichrist of all. This period in history was especially rich in apocalyptic thinking of various sorts with paradoxical attitudes. We find in the fourteenth century a strong belief both in the imminent end of the world and in a great coming future after a time of troubles, a new age. In all this, some scholars have tried to find the medieval antecedents of the Renaissance.

As we pass from one age to another, there are persecutions of the righteous, widespread sin, and the advent of Antichrists; a time of troubles comes upon the world. But all for the ultimate purpose of renewal. The very sufferings of the age and of the Church were proofs of the coming new age or of a profound reformation.

II.

This apocalyptic current is not the only one in the later Middle Ages, but it is an important one. It is in its terms that I think we can best understand the work of the fourteenth-century William Langland who wrote a very long poem in three versions called *Piers Plowman* between 1363 and 1386, usually designated A, B and C. His apocalypticism, however, was centered around the ideas of order, moderation and temperance. It was through these virtues practiced by all groups in society, but above all by the friars, that he believed the crisis of his own time could be solved, so that a new age could dawn for humanity.

Piers Plowman is divided into two sections, the first called the *Visio* and the second the *Vita*. It relates the dreams of a rough, uncouth but yet self-conscious man named Will about the world around him, who seeks the meaning of the Christian life in this world. The *Visio* presents a picture of a corrupt society dominated by cupidity (personified as Lady Mede, that is Lady Reward) but which is attempting in a confused way to find the right way to God. Piers Plowman, a mysterious figure (who later in the poem turns out to be the human aspect of Christ), tries to help the world but fails. After this depressing picture, Will begins again in the *Vita* to search for an answer to his problems, in other words, for Christian perfection. The *Vita* is divided into three subsections, the life of Dogood, of Dobet(ter) and of Dobest. "Dogood" deals with Will's search for an authority within himself or in the world to answer his questions about Christian perfection and he is shunted from one authority to the other, but finally arrives at the answer that Dogood is to lead a life of humble poverty. In "Dobet," we are presented with the three Christian virtues of faith, hope and charity; this section culminates in a treatment of the scene of Christ liberating the saints of the Old Testament from Hell, an event usually known in the tradition as the Harrowing of Hell. Here Christ appears in His majesty. "Dobest" returns to the society of Langland's own time, with which the poem began. Here we see the forces of Antichrist rife, and all seems to be in a state of hopeless corruption. After various vivid descriptions, the poem ends on Conscience's setting out to find Piers Plowman again so that pride may be destroyed and the friars may have enough for their maintenance. Needless to say, as the above outline shows, this poem is difficult to interpret, and there have been various attempts to do so.

In recent years there has been a tendency to find in *Piers,* which is built around a quest by the hero Will, the journey of a mystic toward God, and perhaps in one sense this is true. But *Piers* is first of all socially oriented—that is, apocalyptic in its view of Christian perfection. History and society must come first as both the beginning and final sections of the poem show very clearly. The journey of the individual soul to God is perhaps also implied, but it is not central. It is Piers, not Will, who starting as a simple peasant becomes the human aspect of Christ. Piers, not Will, is deified. Will's quest is for the three "Do's"— Christian perfection—and he grows old in it, but he knows that Piers Plowman must be found by Conscience and returned to Holy Church, that is the society of Christians, before he can find his answer. He must, by a quest, cooperate with the grace which Piers represents and the Christ he stands for. But Piers is sought to save Holy Church, not primarily to save Will. And it is this which makes the poem basically an apocalyptic, not a mystical, poem. *Piers* is not fundamentally the story of the journey to God of the individual, and the three "Do's" of the *Vita* section are not fundamentally the purgative, illuminative and unitive ways of the mystic but belong to an older tradition, a monastic one originally, of the states of Christian perfection which involve fundamentally the Kingdom of God.

Moreover, the fundamental symbol of the poem, Piers, and its attendant agricultural imagery, together with other important classes of images in the poem like those of food and clothing, all reinforce the apocalyptic point. Any poem thus organized must at the very least in a Christian society have eschatological aims in mind. Both in the Old and New Testaments, agricultural, food and clothing imagery has a basic apocalyptic dimension.

Jesus' parables are full of these images. Jesus, interpreting his own parable of the tares, says: "He that soweth the good seed is the Son of Man; the field is the world; the good seed are the children of the kingdom; but the tares are the children of the wicked one; the enemy that sowed them is the devil; the harvest is the end of the world, and the reapers are the angels" (Matt. 13:37–39).

The harvest is paradise or salvation, and those who tend it lead man to his proper end. Christ is the supreme harvester or plowman, and all plowmen to some extent are symbols of his true followers—priests, religious or even laymen, who are creating or bringing in the harvest. The plow is the tool whereby He prepares the field of the world for His harvest of souls. "Dobest," the concluding section of the poem, begins with a description of Pentecost, and Pentecost is the feast of the Church, of the mission of the Holy Ghost, and also the feast of the end of time, of the Church Triumphant.

Throughout the poem, we also find particular apocalyptic passages. The prologue of the *Visio* with its picture of a corrupted society which holds promise of renewal sets the tone from the beginning. Evil has corrupted Christian society and the church militant; yet out of evil good may come, for God allows evil to flourish and the Church to suffer while He plans for its rebirth and regeneration. Conscience in her great speech before the king—who is also an apocalyptic figure—breaks out into an apocalyptic vision (B. III. 282 ff.). Langland's predilection for prophecies, usually of the most difficult kind for us, is further evidence of his apocalyptic frame of mind. Obscure prophecies are the stock-in-trade of all those who are convinced that history is soon about to undergo a profound change. They satisfy the love of the obscure and are a delight to those who look for self-justification and religious reform. To those convinced of their truth, they make sense out of the current miseries of history. They are also difficult to disprove and may be applied again and again *ad libitum,* not to say *ad nauseam.* Above all, they prove the superiority of redemptive to secular history. In a time of crisis, such as the later Middle Ages, they were very popular, especially with those concerned with the writing of history. These enigmatic prophecies are of the essence of the apocalyptic view of life.

Closely related to the prophetic frame of mind is the tendency to find eschatological signs in natural phenomena, especially those of weather and the sky. These are not wanting in *Piers,* but to Langland contemporary social phenomena were his main signs. The current social evils provide the main evidence that a new or reformed age is about to dawn. The evils of his time afford the best proof to Langland that, if God and His Church are realities, and to him there could be no doubt on these matters, good was to come out of evil. The persecution of the just and of the true church was a fundamental proof of their coming rehabilitation. Fundamentally, Langland, like all millenarians, was an optimist.

Omitting for lack of time the many other apocalyptic passages, or passages which have an apocalyptic dimension in the poem, I should like to point out that the culmination of the poem from Passus XVIII in "Dobet" to the end is openly apocalyptic. The Harrowing of Hell scene is a foreshadowing of the Last Judgment. Here Christ is seen in His majesty, not in His

345

suffering on the cross. The section beginning "Dobest," following on this scene, contains a long discussion on Christ the King. In the apocalyptic vision, it is the triumphant, ruling Christ who is to conquer. Then Langland goes on to picture the coming of Antichrist to whom he felt his own time and society had given allegiance.

Just as Satan and his minions were overcome in the Harrowing of Hell, so finally will Antichrist and all his hosts be subdued —when Conscience finds Piers Plowman and when the religious orders will be able to take over their fundamental task of transforming the world. The Antichrist scene which ends the poem on a realistic note is the antivision to the vision of the Harrowing of Hell—the present reality as opposed to God's reality. The concluding vision of "Dobet," however, foretells the true end to the Antichrist vision of "Dobest." The very presence of Antichrist is, to thinkers like Langland, actually evidence for the imminence of renewal and fundamentally a hopeful sign.

Piers Plowman is thus deeply immersed in the apocalyptic vision of the world and its history. The ideal Pope or spiritual leader is seen in Piers, who is a multidimensional symbol, and the savior-emperor or ideal king appears *in propria persona* in several of the more notable apocalyptic passages. These two figures of late medieval apocalypticism—the angelic pope and ideal king—are united in the figure of Christ in His majesty Who harrows Hell and Whose power and dignity are carefully described in "Dobest"—a section that concentrates on Jesus as Conqueror, King and Judge. Individual perfection becomes in the last analysis a problem of social perfection, and social perfection to a convinced Christian means the Kingdom of God.

Piers Plowman begins with a vision of society, a fair field full of folk, and ends with a similar vision but with the forces of Antichrist unleashed against the true church and the society of the elect, Unitas. In between we witness first the problems of society and of the proper distribution of earthly goods, the desire for salvation which is frustrated and finally the journey

346

of the self toward enlightenment in perfection which leads inevitably back to society. But the only answer is the help of God and His inscrutable will which ordains in this time of *Heilgeschichte* that sufferings be undergone, so that the just and the merciful may finally come into their own and a great social renewal may take place on the road to the Kingdom of God.

The greatest difficulty in seeing the basic apocalyptic quality in *Piers* is the strong and violent criticism of the friars which runs through the whole poem. This satire reaches its culmination at the very end of the poem when Conscience sets out to find Piers Plowman or Christ for two reasons—to destroy pride and to provide a minimum sustenance for the friars. The solution to the whole problem of the world for Langland turned to a great extent on the reform of the friars. How can we relate this violent attack on the friars and the conviction of the centrality of their role in the attainment of perfection with the apocalyptic frame of mind which informs the whole poem? If friars are merely one group in society among many, it is difficult to see why Langland should consider their reform the crucial problem for the solution of the problem of the world.

The answer to this question is complex. The greatest source of evil in his time, Langland thought, lay in the violation of their natural roles by all groups in society. Of these, the religious are the highest class in society, and their betrayal is the worst just because so much is demanded of them. The wickedness of the clergy is the classic case of all wickedness and the true symbol of the current debasement of society. Within the religious, the monks, or friars, represent the highest group. Monasticism is the quest *par excellence* for Christian perfection. Monasticism in its ideal form is the foreshadowing of the Kingdom of God. Monasticism is the eschatological element in history. These views are commonplaces of the monastic point of view. I believe that Langland was profoundly influenced by this point of view and that he felt the activities of the friars were the most blatant violation of the monastic ideal possible. In this, he was no doubt partly influenced by the quarrels between the monks and friars in his own time, but fundamentally he was sincerely concerned with the violation of trust involved.

Langland's attitude toward the friars was ambiguous. He honored them as types of monks, but he despised them for betraying their ideals. Of all classes of society, their betrayal was the worst just because they, of all groups, had the most to offer society as the exemplars of the Kingdom of God. They were most debased because they should be most elevated. Their debasement, Langland thought, was founded primarily on their view of the nature of poverty which they equated with mendicancy. The recognition of legitimate need on the part of the friars is the first step in the reform of the friars. If they abandon their erroneous concept of poverty and realize that the quest for perfection requires a minimum of food and clothing which can be obtained by legitimate labor, they can then give up their concern for wealth with the inevitable corruption which attends upon it and truly become, as their status on the highest level as religious demands, genuine seekers for perfection. They would then presumably set an example for all other estates and lead the way to a regeneration of society. If they could be reformed, then all society could be reformed. They are crucial to the salvation of Christendom. We may then, in some sense, all become monks, as Joachim of Flora, a medieval thinker of the twelfth century, had predicted.

III.

In discussing literature, it is not enough to be concerned with what it says; we must also be concerned with how it is said. The how must also be related to and reinforce the what. Literary form is what makes literature in the last analysis literature; otherwise, there is no fundamental difference between a series of notes or a loose discourse on a subject and literary endeavor. Form makes matter memorable; it lifts what is being said to the heights of art.

348

Now in dealing with older literature particularly, we must endeavor to find out what tradition the writer was working in. In the Middle Ages, the writer was considered a craftsman who knew his business and not merely someone inspired by his own psyche, although there were medieval theories of inspiration, especially connected with the role of the prophet. No doubt Langland and Dante worked under what we would call inspiration, but this did not mean that they could neglect the traditions of their craft.

Among the literary traditions available to these writers and others was the concept of genre. A literary work was thought to belong properly to a genre, an overall literary form, which controlled in general the aims and organization of the attempted work of art. There were other traditions too of style and figurative language, but we shall not concern ourselves with them here. If we can identify the genre or genres which dominated Langland's work, we may get valuable clues as to his intentions and understand better his artistic goals.

Let us now turn to the form of *Piers*. Is there such a genre as an apocalypse? Is *Piers* not only apocalyptic in content but also in form? Here we run into difficulties. What was the literary tradition in which Langland conceived his vast poem? I think part of the difficulty with the work lies in its confusion of genre. *Piers* is a combination of several genres, and in fact there is even a certain clash between them. The restlessness of Will's search for perfection is reflected in his author's uncertain sense of genre.

This is not the place to enter into a discussion of the importance of genre as one of the literary boundaries for the artist. Some have denied its validity in assessing and understanding art, but without committing myself on other periods, I think it is perfectly obvious that the medieval writer was very conscious of the kind of form in which he chose to present his artistic vision and that it is against the customary lines of this form that we can best understand his innovations and his uniqueness.

And with a certain form went certain expectations which the writer felt he must at least satisfy.

It is also true that genre analysis is not free of difficulties, great difficulties, especially of definition. What is one man's genre may be another man's theme or motif. Genres also overlap. I think, however, one must only accept as genres, literary forms defined as such before the time of the composition of the work being considered, for some forms are esoteric and others are so broad that they lose the distinguishing marks of a genre—a literary type which has a certain general organization and arouses certain definite expectations in its readers or listeners.

This problem of definition comes to the fore in connection with the quest around which *Piers Plowman* is mainly organized. The literary quest has been a most popular unifying principle in literature in all ages, but in the later Middle Ages it reached its zenith. But it seems to me that it is a theme or dominant image rather than a genre. If then *Piers Plowman* cannot be classified as a quest in regard to genre, what form is it cast in? One of the possible answers is that it is an apocalypse.

Is the apocalypse a literary genre? There are conflicting answers to this question. It is now recognized how indebted Jewish and Christian writings of the period just before, during and after the life of Jesus are to Greek literary forms and rhetoric. In particular, the influence of the genre called the aretalogy and of the eulogistic biography on the New Testament and early Christian writings such as the *Shepherd of Hermas* have been recognized.[2] The aretalogy is similar in many ways to some of the early apocalypses. Aretalogies were connected with Hellen-

---

[2] On the aretalogy, see R. Reitzenstein, *Wundererezählungen* (Leipzig, 1906), espec. pp. 7 ff; Moses Hadas, *Hellenistic Culture, Fusion and Diffusion* (New York, 1959), pp. 170 ff; and Georgius Manteuffel, *De opusculis graecis aegypto e papyris, ostracis lapidibusque collectis,* Travaux de la Société des Sciences et des Lettres de Varsovie, Classe 1 (1930) (Warsaw, 1930). On the pagan encomium and biography and their influence on saints' and martyrs' lives, see Herbert A. Musurillo, *The Acts of the Pagan Martyrs, Acta Alexandrinorum* (Oxford, 1954).

istic mystery religions and developed alongside the Greek novel. They are narrations of the theophany of a god among men with emphasis on his miracles.[3] No doubt the Semitic prophetic vision is another element in the apocalyptic form. The Books of Daniel and Second Esdras provided models here for *Revelation* and early Christian apocalypses. The characteristics of the early apocalypses include a vision form and direct revelations by God or angels. Yet I agree with Father Musurillo when he writes: "The form known as 'apocalypse' creates a problem, and perhaps no useful purpose is served in making the term a technical one applicable both to the Revelations of St. John and the so-called *Shepherd of Hermas*."[4]

The confusion implicit in the use of the term is seen in the fact that Klingner calls Boethius' *De consolatione,* the great philosophical work of late antiquity, an apocalypse like *Poimandres* and the *Shepherd of Hermas,* earlier works of an apocalyptic cast, while Northrop Frye sees it as a Menippean satire or anatomy.[5] It is clear that it can also be called a *consolatio,* that is a work written to console someone on a loss.[6] While there is

[3] I am indebted for this definition to Herbert Musurillo, "History and Symbol: A Study of Form in Early Christian Literature," *Theological Studies* XVIII (1957), 357–386.

[4] P. 365. CF., however, R. L. P. Milburn who writes that ". . . this type of imaginative novel-writing [stories about the Virgin] not seldom took the specialized form of apocalypse, perhaps the most influential of these compositions, though its fourth-century date makes it a fairly late one, being the *Apocalypse of Paul,*" *Early Christian Interpretations of History,* The Bampton Lectures of 1952 (London, 1954), p. 190.

[5] See Fritz Klingner, *De Boethii consolatione philosophiae,* Philologische Untersuchungen 27 (Berlin, 1921) pp. 112 ff. and N. Frye, *The Anatomy of Criticism* (Princeton, 1957), p. 312.

[6] On the *consolatio* as a literary genre, see Charles Favez, *La consolation latine chrétienne* (Paris, 1937); Michele Coccia, "Le 'consolatio, in Seneca," *Rivista di cultura classica e medievale* I (1959), 148–180; Sister Mary Edmond Fern, *The Latin Consolatio as a Literary Type,* Dissertation . . . of St. Louis University . . . Typewritten MS, 1931; Alfred Gercke, "De consolationibus," *Tirocinium Philologium,* Sodalium Regis Seminarii Bonnensis (Berlin, 1883), 28–70; Carolus Buresch, *Consolationum a graecis romanisque scriptarum, historia critica,* Leip-

no rule that a literary work must be written in one genre, and indeed deliberate mixing of genres is characteristic of many medieval literary works, it is true, I think, that one genre must be thought as somehow dominant in a work or the whole point of the genre as a controlling device is lost.

If the apocalypse is not a literary genre, it is true that it possesses certain characteristics, although not unique ones: it is cast in a vision form, it contains a revelation from on high, or at least a superior guide, and it is severely critical of contemporary history. In general it is oriented toward man's and mankind's final destiny and often contains prophecies under enigmatic figures. *Piers Plowman* possesses all of these elements with possibly the exception of a divine or angelic guide, although Lady Holy Church does briefly perform that function in Passus I of the *Visio.* Part of the problem of Will is actually to find an authority, and his quest is not only for perfection but for someone who can lead him to perfection, until finally he realizes that only Piers himself can.

There are differences too. The bitter and explicit satire of *Piers* is rarely to be found in the older apocalypses. Perhaps here we have some influence of the parodic medieval apocalypse such as the twelfth century Latin *Apocalypse* of *Golias* where Pythagorus serves as a guide to the dreamer and which is a violent attack on religious abuses.[7] This work was exceedingly popular in England and may have originally been written there.

Rather than set up a genre called the apocalypse which can only be very vaguely established, I prefer to think of *Piers* rather as an amalgam of the allegorical dream narrative as in certain

---

ziger Studien zur classischen Philologie IX (Leipzig, 1887), 3–170; Edouard Boyer, *Les Consolations chez les Grecs et les Romains,* Thèse . . . La Faculté de Théologie Protestante de Montauban . . . 1887 (Montauban, 1887); Constant Martha, "Les consolations dans l'antiquité," *Etudes morales sur l'antiquité,* 2nd ed. (Paris, 1905), 135–189.

[7] Ed. Karl Strecker, Texte zur Kulturgeschichte des Mittelalters 5 (Rome, 1928). I owe this suggestion to Professor John Conley.

French works; the vertical dialogue, *consolatio,* or debate[8] as in Boethius' *De consolatione;* and the encyclopedic (or Menippean) satire as in Nigel Wireker's *Speculum stultorum,* a twelfth-century poem about an ass who is looking for his lost tail and which is a satire on the church. These genres are not mutually exclusive, and genetically some are related. The *consolatio* in its classic medieval form is, for instance, also a dream vision. Even when this is admitted, however, it is still true that in the Middle Ages these forms were distinct in tradition, had a definite organization and were designed to satisfy certain expectations in an audience.

These three genres are all related in medieval times to the quest for perfection to which Langland was committed artistically and most certainly personally. In order to dramatize his complex theme, with its mixture of quest, debate and satire, Langland found himself, so to speak, in the midst of three literary genres which were well-established before his time; and from their conventions he attempted to weave together a unified work of art, a work which would reveal his basic perplexities, dramatize, and objectify them. He was perhaps attempting too much and this alliance was not always successful. And beyond all this hovers the apocalyptic urgency which must have been the driving force in his character.

The reform of the friars is to be the main task of his age, as Langland saw. Not scientists working in laboratories, not the proletariat, but monastic ideals as lived by monks and friars were to be his agent for the reform of the world, and their guidance would lead the world into the golden age awaiting it, hid in the womb of time. This was Langland's answer to his quest for perfection.

In spite of his propensity to ramble, to develop, to divagate, Langland is firm and single-minded in his essential point—in

[8] On the adjective *vertical* here see Stephen Gilman, *The Art of "La Celestina"* (Madison, 1956), pp. 159–160.

A, B and C and from beginning to end. The expansions and changes in the different versions do no more than add more material to build up the essence of what he has to say; they all reveal the hard struggle for Christian perfection. The basic answer, though, the answer Langland never doubted is set out in Passus I of the A text—moderation in self and society, victory over the betrayal of ideals especially by the clergy, the need for love and justice. In these essentials Langland never wavers. *Piers Plowman* is a monument to the struggles of a perplexed but hopeful, sensitive, fourteenth-century Englishman for a solution to the problems of his time and of all time in the attainment of Christian perfection which must, to his apocalyptic mind, be a social solution which would involve the setting up of the Kingdom of God on earth, very much as his master Jesus had Himself promised in the New Testament.

SELECTED BIBLIOGRAPHY

EDITIONS

Piers Plowman. Ed. Elizabeth Salter and Derek Pearsall. London, 1967.

Piers the Plowman: A Critical Edition of the A-Version. Ed. Thomas A. Knott and David C. Fowler, Baltimore, 1952.

The Vision of William Concerning Piers the Plowman in Three Parallel Texts together with Richard the Redeless by William Langland. Ed. W. W. Skeat. 2 Vols. Oxford, 1886.

Will's Visions of Piers Plowman and Do-Well. Ed. George Kane. London, 1960.

TRANSLATIONS

The Book Concerning Piers the Plowman. Trans. Donald and Rachel Atwater. Everyman's Library. New York, 1957.

Piers the Plowman. Trans. J. F. Goodridge. Penguin ed. Baltimore, 1959.

The Vision of Piers Plowman. Trans. Henry W. Wells. New York, 1945.

TEXT, DATE AND AUTHORSHIP

Bennett, J. A. W. "The Date of the A-Text of *Piers Plowman*," *PMLA*, LVIII (1943), 566–572.

————. "The Date of the B-Text of *Piers Plowman*," *MÆ*, XII (1943), 55–64.

————. "Lombards' Letters (*Piers Plowman, B, v, 251),*" *MLR* XL (1945), 309–310.

Blackman, Elsie. "Notes on the B-Text MMS. of *Piers Plowman*," *JEGP*, XVII (1918), 489–537.

Bloomfield, Morton W. "Was William Langland a Benedictine Monk? *MLQ*, IV (1943), 57–61.

Bradley, Henry. "The Authorship of *Piers the Plowman*," *MLR*, v (1909), 202–207.

———. "The Lost Leaf of *Piers the Plowman*," *Nation*, LXXXVIII (April 29, 1909).

———. "The Misplaced Leaf of *Piers the Plowman*," Athenaeum (April 21, 1906), 481.

———. "Some Cruces in *Piers Plowman*," *MLR*, v (1910), 340–342.

———. "Who was John But," *MLR*, VIII (1913), 88–89.

Bright, A. H. *New Light on Piers Plowman*. London, 1928.

Brown, Carleton. *"The Lost Leaf of Piers the Plowman,"* Nation, LXXXVII (March 25, 1909).

Cargill, Oscar. "The Date of the A-Text of Piers the Ploughman," *PMLA*, XLVII (1932), 354–362.

———. "The Langland Myth," *PMLA*, L (1935), 36–56.

Chambers, Raymond W. "Incoherencies in the A and B-Texts of *Piers Plowman* and Their Bearing on the Authorship," *London Mediaeval Studies,* I (1937), 27–39.

———. "The Original Form of the A-Text of *Piers Plowman*," *MLR*, VI (1910), 302–323.

———. "Robert or William Longland?" London Mediaeval Studies, I (1948 for 1939), 430–462.

———. "The Three Texts of *Piers Plowman* and Their Grammatical Forms," *MLR*, XIV (1918), 129–151.

Chambers, Raymond and Grattan, J. H. "The Authorship of *Piers Plowman*," *MLR*, v (1909), 1–32.

———. "The Text of *Piers Plowman*," *MLR*, IV (1908), 357–389.

———. "The Text of *Piers Plowman*," *MLR*, XXVI (1931), 1–51.

———. "The Text of *Piers Plowman*: Critical Methods," *MLR*, XI (1916), 257–275.

Coghill, Nevill. *Langland: Piers Plowman*. Writers and Their Work Series, 174. New York, 1964.

Coulton, G. G. "Piers Plowman, One or Five," *MLR*, VII (1911), 372–373.

Day, Mabel. "The Alliteration of the Versions of *Piers Plowman* in its Bearing on their Authorship," *MLR*, XVII (1922), 403–409.

———. "Duns Scotus and *Piers Plowman*," *RES*, III (1927), 333–334.

———. "The Revisions of *Piers Plowman*," *MLR*, XXIII (1928), 1–27.

Deakin, Mary. "The Alliteration of *Piers Plowman*," *MLR*, IV (1908), 478–483.

Dobson, Margaret. "An Examination of the Vocabulary of the A-Text of *Piers the Plowman*," Anglia, XXXIII (1910), 391–396.

Donaldson, Talbot. "MSS R & F in the B-Tradition of *Piers Plowman*," *Transactions of the Connecticut Academy of Arts and Sciences*, XXXIX (1955), 177–212.

_____. "The Texts of *Piers Plowman*: Scribes and Poets," *MP*, L (1952), 269–273.

Fowler, David C. "The Relationship of the Three Texts of *Piers the Plowman*," *MP*, L (1952), 5–22.

Gwynn, Aubrey. "The Date of the B-Text of *Piers Plowman*," *RES*, XIX (1943), 1–24.

Hall, Theophilus D. "Was Langland the author of the C-Text of *The Vision of Piers Plowman?*" *MLR*, IV (1908), 1–13.

Hulbert, J. R. "*Piers the Plowman* after Forty Years," *MP*, XLV (1947), 215–225.

Huppé, Bernard F. "The A Text of *Piers Plowman* and the Norman Wars," *PMLA*, LIV (1938), 37–65.

_____. "The Authorship of the A and B Texts of *Piers Plowman*," *Speculum*, XXII (1947), 578–620.

_____. "The Date of the B-Text of Piers Plowman," *SP*, XXXVIII (1941), 34–44.

Jusserand, J. J. "Piers Plowman, the Work of One or Five," *MP*, VI (1908), 271–329.

Kane, George. *Piers Plowman: The Evidence for Authorship.* London, 1965.

Knott, Thomas A. "The Authorship of *Piers the Plowman*," *MP*, XIV (1916), 531–558.

_____. "An Essay toward the Critical Text of the A-version of 'Piers the Plowman,' " *MP*, XII (1914), 23–62.

Manly, J. M. "The Authorship of *Piers the Plowman*," *MP*, VII (1909), 23–62.

_____. "The Authorship of *Piers the Plowman*," *MP*, XIV (1916), 315–316.

_____. "The Lost Leaf of *Piers the Plowman*," *MP*, III (1906), 359–366.

_____. "*Piers the Plowman* and Its Sequence," *CHEL*, Cambridge, Eng., 1908, II, 1–42.

Mensendieck, Otto. "The Authorship of *Piers Plowman*," *JEGP*, IX (1910), 404–420.

Mitchell, A. G. and Russell, G. H. "The Three Texts of 'Piers Plowman,' " *JEGP*, LII (1953), 445–456.

357

Moore, Samuel. "Studies in *Piers Plowman, I*," *MP*, XI (1913), 177–193.

————. "Studies in *Piers Plowman*, II," *MP*, XII (1914), 19–50.

Rickert, Edith. "John But, Messenger and Maker," *MP*, XI (1913), 107–116.

Ryan, William M. "Modern Idioms in *Piers Plowman*," *AS*, XXXIV (1959), 67–69.

Stewart, G. R. "The Meter of *Piers Plowman*," *PMLA*, XLII (1927), 113–128.

Stroud, T. A. "Manly's Marginal Notes on the *Piers Plowman* Controversy," *MLN*, LXIV (1949), 9–12.

Swieczkowski, Walerian. *Word Order Patterning in Middle English: A Quantitative Study Based on Piers Plowman and Middle English Sermons. Janua Linguarum*, NR 19. The Hague, 1962.

CRITICISM

Adam, Ray M. "The Use of the Vulgate in *Piers Plowman*," *SP*, XXIV (1927), 556–566.

Adams, John F. "*Piers Plowman* and the Three Ages of Man," *JEGP*, LXI (1962), 23–41.

Bloomfield, Morton W. "*Piers Plowman* and the Three Grades of Chastity," *Anglia*, LXXVI (1958), 227–253.

————. "*Piers Plowman* as a Fourteenth-Century Apocalypse," *CentR*, V (1961), 281–295.

————. *Piers Plowman as a Fourteenth-Century Apocalypse*. New Brunswick, N. J., 1962ᶜ.

————. "Present State of *Piers Plowman* Studies," *Speculum*, XIV (1939), 215–232.

Bowers, R. H. "*Piers Plowman* and the Literary Historians," *CE*, XXI (1959), 1–4.

Bright, A. H. "Langland and the Seven Deadly Sins," *MLR*, XXV (1930), 133–139.

Bruneder, Hans. *Personifikation und Symbol in William Langland's Piers Plowman*. Wien, 1963.

Burrow, John. "The Action of Langland's Second Vision," *EIC*, XV (1965), 247–268.

————. "The Audience of *Piers Plowman*," *Anglia*, LXXV (1957), 373–384.

Burton, Dorothy Jean. "The Compact with the Devil in the Middle English Vision of *Piers Plowman*, B. II," *California Folklore Quarterly*, V (1946), 179–184.

Carnegy, Francis A. "The Relations between the Social and Divine Order in William Langland's 'Vision of William concerning Piers the Plowman,'" *Sprache und Kultur der germanischen und romanischen Volker,* A, Anglistiche Reihe, XII (1934).

Cejp, Ladislav. *An Introduction to the Study of Langland's Piers Plowman: B Text.* Acta Universitatis Palackianae Olomucensis 9. Palackiko Universita V Olomousi, 1956.

Chadwick, D. *Social Life in the Days of Piers Plowman.* Cambridge, Eng., 1922.

Chambers, Raymond W. "Long Will, Dante and the Righteous Heathen," E&S, IX (1924), 50–69.

————. *Man's Unconquerable Mind.* London, 1939.

————. "Poets and Their Critics: Milton and Langland," *PBA,* XXVII (1941), 109–154.

Coghill, Nevill K. "The Character of Piers Plowman considered from the B-Text," *MÆ,* II (1933), 108–135.

————. "God's Wenches and the Light that Spoke: Some Notes on Langland's Kind of Poetry." *English and Medieval Studies,* XXII, ed. Norman Davis and C. L. Wrenn. Presented to J. R. R. Tolkien on the Occasion of his Seventieth Birthday. London, 1962, pp. 200–218.

————. "Langland and the Naked, the Naughty and the Dole," *RES,* VIII (1932), 303–309.

————. "The Pardon of Piers Plowman," *PBA,* XXX (1944), 303–357.

College, E., and W. O. Evans. *"Piers Plowman," Month,* XXXII (1964), 304–313.

Connolly, Terence L. *An Introduction to Chaucer and Langland: A Corrective of Long's History of English Literature.* New York, 1925.

Cornelius, Roberta D. *"Piers Plowman* and the *Roman de Fauvel," PMLA,* XLVII (1932), 363–367.

Donaldson, E. Talbot. "The Grammar of Book's Speech in *Piers Plowman." Studies in Language and Literature in Honour of Margaret Schlauch.* Warsaw, 1966, pp. 103–109.

————. *Piers Plowman: The C-Text and Its Poet.* New Haven, 1949.

————. *Piers Plowman: The C-Text and Its Poet.* With a New Preface by the Author. Hamden, Conn., 1966.

Donna, Sister Rose Bernard. *Despair and Hope: A Study in Langland and Augustine.* Washington, D. C., 1948.

Dunning, T. P. "Langland and the Salvation of the Heathen," *MÆ*, XII (1943), 45–54.

———. *Piers Plowman: An Interpretation of the A-Text*. London, 1937.

———. "The Structure of the B-Text of *Piers Plowman*," *RES*, N.S., VII (1956), 225–237.

Erzgräber, Willi. *William Langlands Piers Plowman (Eine Interpretation des C-Textes)*. Frankfurter Arbeiten aus dem Gebiete der Anglistik un der Amerika-Studien, Heft III. Heidelberg, 1957.

Fowler, David C. *Piers the Plowman: Literary Relations of the A and B Texts*. Seattle, 1961.

Frank, Robert Worth, Jr. "The Art of Reading Medieval Personification-Allegory," *ELH*, XX (1953), 237–250.

———. "The Conclusion of *Piers Plowman*," *JEGP*, XLIX (1950), 309–316.

———. "The Pardon Scene in *Piers Plowman*," *Speculum*, XXVI (1951), 317–331.

———. *Piers Plowman and the Scheme of Salvation: An Interpretation of Dowel, Dobet, and Dobest*. New Haven, 1957.

Gaffney, Wilbur. "The Christ-Knight in *Piers Plowman*," *PMLA*, XLVI (1931), 155–168.

Gerould, Gordon H. "The Structural Integrity of *Piers Plowman* B," *SP*, XLV (1948), 60–75

Hamilton, A. C. "Spenser and Langland," *SP*, LV (1958), 533–548.

Hanscom, Elizabeth Deering. "The Argument of the *Vision of Piers Plowman*," *PMLA*, IX (1894), 403–451.

Hoffman, Richard L. "The Burning of 'Boke' in *Piers Plowman*," *MLQ*, XXV (1964), 57–65.

Hort, Greta. *Piers Plowman and Contemporary Religious Thought*. London, n.d.

Howard, Donald R. *The Three Temptations of Man: Medieval Man in Search of the World*. Princeton, N. J., 1966.

Huppé, Bernard F. "*Petrus Id Est Christus*: Word Play in *Piers Plowman*, the B Text," *ELH*, XVII (1950), 163–190.

Hussey, S. S. "Langland, Hilton, and the Three Lives," *RES*, N.S., VII (1956), 132–150.

———. "Langland's Reading of Alliterative Poetry," *MLR*, LX (1965), 163–170.

Jack, A. S. "The Autobiographical Elements in *Piers the Plowman*," *JEGP*, III (1901), 393–415.

James, Stanley B. *Back to Langland*. London, 1935.

Jusserand, J. J. *Piers Plowman, A Contribution to the History of English Mysticism.* Revised and Enlarged by the Author. Trans. M. E. R. London, 1894.

Kane, George. *Middle English Literature: A Critical Study of the Romances, the Religious Lyrics, Piers Plowman.* London, 1951.

Kaske, R. E. "Ex vi transicionis and Its Passage in *Piers Plowman*," *JEGP*, LXII (1963), 32–60.

_____. "Gigas the Giant in *Piers Plowman*," *JEGP*, LVI (1957), 177–185.

_____. "Langland's Walnut-Simile," *JEGP*, LVIII (1959), 650–654.

_____. "The Speech of 'Book' in *Piers Plowman*," *Anglia*, LXXVII (1959), 117–144.

_____. "The Use of Simple Figures of Speech in *Piers Plowman* B: A Study in the Figurative Expression of Ideas and Opinions," *SP*, XLVIII (1951), 571–600.

Kean, P. M. "Langland on the Incarnation," *RES*, XVI (1965), 349–363.

_____. "Love, Law, and Lewte in *Piers Plowman*," *RES*, XV (1964), 241–261.

Kellogg, Alfred L. "Langland and Two Scriptural Texts," *Traditio*, XIV (1958), 385–398.

Kellogg, E. H. "Bishop Brunton and the Fable of the Rats," *PMLA*, L (1935), 57–67.

Kirk, R. "References to the Law in *Piers the Plowman*," *PMLA*, XLVIII (1933), 322–327.

Lattin, Linda L. "Some Aspects of Medieval Number Symbolism in Langland's *Piers Plowman*, A-text," *ESRS*, XIV (1965), 5–13.

Lawlor, J. J. "The Imaginative Unity of *Piers Plowman*," *RES*, N. S., VIII (1957), 113–126.

_____. *Piers Plowman: An Essay in Criticism.* New York, 1962.

_____. "*Piers Plowman*: The Pardon Reconsidered," *MLR*, XLV (1950), 449–458.

Longo, Joseph A. "*Piers Plowman* and the Tropological Matrix: Passus XI and XII," *Anglia*, LXXXII (1964), 291–308.

Maguire, Stella. "The Significance of Haukyn, *Activa Vita*, in *Piers Plowman*," *RES*, XXV (1949), 97–109.

Maisack, Helmut. *William Langland's Verhältnis zum Zisterziensischen Mönchtum: Eine Untersuchung der Vita im Piers Plowman.* Tübingen Inaugural Dissertation. Balingen, 1953.

Marcett, M. E. *Uhtred de Boldon, Friar William Jordan, and Piers Plowman.* New York, 1938.

Martin, Jay. "Wil as a Fool and Wanderer in *Piers Plowman,*" *TSLL,* III (1961–62), 535–548.

Meroney, Howard. "The Life and Death of Longe Wille," *ELH,* XVII (1950), 1–35.

Mitchell, A. G. *Lady Meed and the Art of Piers Plowman.* London, 1956.

Moe, Henry Allen. "The Vision of *Piers the Plowman* and the Law of Foundation." *PAPS,* CII (1958), 371–375.

Muscatine, Charles. "Locus of Action in Medieval Narrative," *RP,* XVII (1963), 115–122.

Owen, D. L. *Piers Plowman: A Comparison with Some Earlier and Contemporary French Allegories.* London, 1912.

Owst, G. R. "The *Angel* and the *Goliardeys* of Langland's Prologue," *MLR,* XX (1925), 270–279.

————.*Literature and Pulpit in Medieval England: A Neglected Chapter in the History of English Letters and of the English People.* Cambridge, Eng., 1933. Second Edition Revised, Oxford, 1961. Reprinted, New York, 1966.

Pepler, Conrad. "The Beginning of the Way," *Life of the Spirit,* I (1946-47), 101–105.

————. "Conversion in Langland," *Life of the Spirit,* I (1946–47), 136–141.

————. *The English Religious Heritage.* St. Louis, 1958.

————. "Langland's Way to Unity," *Life of the Spirit,* I (1946–47), 198–204.

————. "The Way Opens," *Life of the Spirit,* I (1946–47), 169–172.

Mroczkowski, Przemyslaw. "Piers and His Pardon: A Dynamic Analysis." *Studies in Language and Literature in Honour of Margaret Schlauch.* Warsaw, 1966, pp. 273–292.

Quirk, Randolph. "Langland's Use of *Kind Wit* and *Inwit,*" *JEGP,* LII (1953), 182–188.

Rauch, Rufus William. "Langland and Medieval Functionalism," *Annual Report of the American Historical Association,* III (1942), 39–56.

Reidy, John. "Peris the Ploughman, whiche a Pardoun he Hadde," *PMASAL,* L (1965), 535–544.

Robertson, D. W. "The Doctrine of Charity in Medieval Literary Gardens: a Topical Approach through Symbolism and Allegory," *Speculum,* XXVI (1951), 24–49.

Robertson, D. W., Jr. and Huppé, Bernard. *Piers Plowman and Scriptural Tradition. PSE* No. 31. Princeton, 1951.

Salter, Elizabeth. *Piers Plowman: An Introduction.* Cambridge, Mass., 1962.

Sen Gupta, Jasodhara. *"Piers Plowman," EIC,* XIII (1963), 201–202.

Smith, A. H. *Piers Plowman and the Pursuit of Poetry.* Inaugural Lecture University College London, 1950. London, 1951.

Smith, Ben H., Jr. *Traditional Imagery of Charity in Piers Plowman.* The Hague, 1966.

Spearing, A. C. *Criticism and Medieval Poetry.* New York, 1964.

_____. "The Development of a Theme in *Piers Plowman," RES,* XI (1960), 241–253.

_____. "Verbal Repetition in *Piers Plowman* B and C," *JEGP,* LXII (1963), 722–737.

Spitzer, Leo. "Note on the Poetic and the Empirical 'I' in Medieval Authors," *Traditio,* IV (1946), 414–422.

Stone, George W. "An Interpretation of the A-Text of *Piers Plowman, PMLA,* LIII (1938), 656–677.

Suddaby, Elizabeth. "The Poem *Piers Plowman," JEGP,* LIV (1955), 91–103.

Sullivan, Sister Carmeline. *The Latin Insertions and the Macaronic Verse in Piers Plowman.* Washington, D. C., 1932.

Traver, Hope. "The Four Daughters," *PMLA,* XL (1925), 44–92.

_____. *The Four Daughters of God: A Study of the Versions of this Allegory with especial reference to those in Latin, French, and English.* Philadelphia, 1907.

Traversi, Derek. "Langland's *Piers Plowman." A Guide to English Literature, I, The Age of Chaucer.* Baltimore, 1954.

Troyer, Howard William. "Who is *Piers Plowman?" PMLA,* XLVII (1932) 368–384.

Vasta, Edward. *The Spiritual Basis of Piers Plowman.* The Hague, 1965.

_____. "Truth, the Best Treasure, in *Piers Plowman," PQ,* XLIV (1965), 17–29.

Wells, Henry W. "The Construction of *Piers Plowman," PMLA,* XLIV (1929), 123–140.

_____. "The Philosophy of Piers Plowman," *PMLA,* LIII (1938), 339–349.

Woolf, Rosemary. "Some Non-Medieval Qualities of *Piers Plowman," EIC,* XII (1962), 111–125.

Yunck, John A. *The Lineage of Lady Meed: The Development of Mediaeval Venality Satire.* Notre Dame, 1963.

Zeeman, Elizabeth. "Piers Plowman and the Pilgrimage to Truth," *E&S*, N. S., xi (1958), 1–16.

NOTES

Ardeene, S.T.R.O.d.' " 'Me bi-fel a ferly, A Feyrie me þouhte' (P.Pl.A.Prol. 6)," *ES*, xlv (1964), Supp., 143–145.

Bennett, J. A. W. " 'Sum Rex, Sum Princeps,' Etc. (*Piers Plowman* B, Prologue 132–8)," *N&Q*, vii (1960), 364.

Cassidy, Frederic G. "The Merit of Malkyn," *MLN*, lxiii (1948), 52–53.

Coghill, Nevill K. "Two Notes on Piers Plowman," *MÆ*, iv (1935), 83–94.

Day, Mabel. *"Piers Plowman* and Poor Relief," *RES*, viii (1932), 445–446.

Fowler, David C. "The 'Forgotten' Pilgrimage in *Piers the Plowman*," *MLN*, lxvii (1952), 524–526.

Frank, Robert Worth, Jr. "The Number of Visions in *Piers Plowman*," *MLN*, lxvi (1951), 309–312.

Hall, G. D. G. "The Abbot of Abingdon and the Tenants of Winkfield," *MÆ*, xxviii (1959), 91–95.

Johnston, G. K. W. *"Piers Plowman* B-Text, Prologue, 78–79," *N&Q*, vi (1959), 243–244.

Jones, H. S. V. "Imaginatif in *Piers Plowman*," *JEGP*, xiii (1914), 583–588.

Kaske, R. E. "Langland and the *Paradisus Claustralis*," *MLN*, lxxii (1957), 481–483.

Kellogg, Alfred L. "Satan, Langland, and the North," *Speculum*, xxiv (1949), 413–414.

Jeremy, Sister Mary. " 'Leggis a-lery,' *Piers Plowman* A VII 114," *ELN*, i (1964), 250–251.

Oliphant, R. "Langland's 'Sire Piers of Pridie,' " *N&Q*, vii (1960), 167–168.

Quirk, Randolph. "Vis Imaginative," *JEGP*, liii (1954), 81–83.

Sanderlin, George. "The Character 'Liberum Arbitrium' in the C-Text of *Piers Plowman*," *MLN*, lvi (1941), 449–453.

Strang, Barbara M. H. *"Piers Plowman* B, Prologue 132–8," *N&Q* vii (1960), 436.

Walker, Marshall. "Piers Plowman's Pardon: A Note," *ESA*, viii (1965), 64–70.

Wilkes, Gerald L. "The Castle of Vnite in *Piers Plowman*," *MS*, xxvii (1965), 334–336.

INDEX